DATE DUE	

TRANSFORMING
MADNESS

OTHER BOOKS BY JAY NEUGEBOREN

TRANSFORMING
MADNESS

New Lives for People
Living with Mental Illness

JAY NEUGEBOREN

WILLIAM MORROW AND COMPANY, INC.
NEW YORK

Grateful acknowledgment is made for permission to reprint the following:

"Yehuda Ha-Levi," copyright © 1996 by Yehuda Amichai. Reprinted from *The Selected Poetry of Yehuda Amichai*, translated/edited by Chana Bloch and Stephen
Mitchell, with the permission of the Regents of the University of California.

"We Are the Psychiatric Diaspora," copyright © 1996 by Moe Armstrong.

Library of Congress Cataloging-in-Publication Data

Neugeboren, Jay.
  Transforming madness : new lives for people living with mental
illness / Jay Neugeboren.
    p.   cm.
  ISBN 0-688-15655-X
  1. Mentally ill—Rehabilitation.   2. Mental illness—Treatment.
3. Mentally ill—Rehabilitation—United States—Case studies.
4. Mental illness—Treatment—United States—Case studies.
I. Title.
RC439.5.N46   1999
616.89—dc21   98-50056
                                                             CIP

Printed in the United States of America

First Edition

2   3   4   5   6   7   8   9   10

BOOK DESIGN BY PAUL PERLOW

www.williammorrow.com

for Miriam and Seth

CONTENTS

ONE: It's Safe Here   1

TWO: The Psychiatric Diaspora   29

THREE: Travels with Moe   57

FOUR: Give Robert Back His Teeth!   89

FIVE: Expert Consensus Guidelines   111

SIX: Degrees of Discordancy   133

SEVEN: Respite   173

EIGHT: Moving Beyond Disability   205

NINE: Approaches to the Mind   243

TEN: Pathways to Recovery   285

EPILOGUE: Intimations of Possibility   327

ACKNOWLEDGMENTS   353

A NOTE ON SOURCES   359

INDEX   384

Grau, teurer Freund, ist alle Theorie
Und grün des Lebens goldner Baum.

Gray, dear friend, is all theory
And green the golden tree of life.

—MEPHISTOPHELES, TO A STUDENT,
IN JOHANN WOLFGANG VON GOETHE'S *FAUST, PART I*

ONE

It's Safe Here

*For the entire period of time between 21 October 1723 —
when the prior and nuncio agree to continue keeping Hu
shut up in Charenton as a charity patient — until 9 August
1725, a period of 658 days, only one single item of precise
information on John Hu is known. One of the staff at
Charenton gives him a warm blanket, of good quality, to
ward away the night cold. He tears the blanket to shreds.*

— Jonathan Spence,
The Question of Hu

On a bitter cold day in early March 1996, I drive down from
my home in Northampton, Massachusetts, to visit with my
brother, Robert, in his new home on Coney Island Avenue
in Brooklyn. This will be our last visit together for a while,
since, in a few weeks, I will be leaving the United States for
a four-month teaching position at the University of Freiburg,
in Germany. Robert's new home, Park Manor Adult Care Facility, a proprietary residence for some sixty to seventy adults
with physical and mental disabilities, is about a twenty-
minute walk from the four-room apartment on Martense

Street in which Robert and I grew up together in the years during and after World War II. Robert has been transferred to Park Manor from South Beach Psychiatric Center, a state mental hospital on Staten Island, where he has been confined to a locked ward for the past thirty-two months.

Eager as I am to spend time with Robert *outside* a mental hospital, during the drive down, and especially as I get closer to Brooklyn, I find myself becoming increasingly nervous — talking to myself, telling myself to slow down, to take it easy, to just relax. I find myself making an effort to bank the fires of my hopes and eagerness a bit, for not only do I want to be careful not to have my hopes become expectations Robert will feel as pressures, but I am aware that previous departures in my life — to Indiana, California, France, Massachusetts — have invariably been accompanied, in Robert's life, by psychotic episodes and breakdowns.

Robert experienced his first breakdown in 1962, two months before his nineteenth birthday, and he has spent most of the thirty-four years since then in and out of mental hospitals, day treatment centers, halfway houses, group homes, supervised residences, emergency wards, and welfare hotels. For the past half-dozen years I have been writing a book (*Imagining Robert*) in which I have tried to set down the story of his life — of our growing up together in Brooklyn, of his early breakdowns and hospitalizations, and of our relationship in the years since, years in which I have been his primary caretaker. Robert has collaborated with me on the book, recalling, in conversations and in writing, his life before and after his first breakdown, and, working together, we have chosen the family photos that appear at the start of each chapter, and that help chronicle our story.

Now, on a bright, icy day in early March, a month before Robert's fifty-third birthday, and for the first time in nearly three years, Robert has been released from his locked ward, and — a sweet convergence — on the day he is transferred from the hospital to his new home, I have mailed off the final draft of *Imagining Robert* to the publisher.

I bring things he has asked for: a camera, a deck of cards, marshmallows, some clothes—along with a copy of the book's title page, on which I have reproduced a photograph of the two of us. In the photo, taken in the summer of 1943, when I was five years old, I am sitting in a sunlit field, smiling down at Robert, who—born a few months before, on April 17—sits on my lap. I've kept the photo in an old oval silver frame on the night table beside my bed for years, and during the drive down to Brooklyn some of the peacefulness and happiness I have always found in the picture—some sense of a future that may yet be filled with easy, sunlit days—is with me again. "This is the most beautiful picture in the world," Robert says each time he sees the photo, and he has suggested we use it for the book's jacket.

Despite the sheer misery that has been the matter of so much of Robert's life, I am feeling once again, for him as well as for me, optimistic and expectant. It is as if Robert and I have *both* been set free this week—Robert from the locked ward where, most of the time these past two and a half years, he has been kept on isolation, often allowed out of his room for only one hour each day. And, the book completed, I am feeling that I have been set free too: from a story I first began trying to tell thirty-four years ago, shortly after Robert's first breakdown, and from the fear, through all the years since, that I might die without having done so.

Robert can now come and go in the world—visit friends, take trips, play lottery tickets, hang out at OTB parlors, eat in restaurants, find work, go to movies, concerts, plays, and museums, and wander the city—he can return, that is, to those things, old and new, that give him pleasure. And, the final draft of the book done, and my three children grown and out on their own (for the previous dozen years I have been a single parent to them), I can leave my home too, and return to my first love: the writing of stories and novels. The people, places, and things that have been roaming the caves of my mind while I tried to conjure up the world Robert and I *actually* experienced—these imagined and vaguely sensed characters, scenes, stories, and who-knows-what-else—can now be given their freedom too.

During the year preceding Robert's discharge from South Beach, I have been speaking with people in New York and Massachusetts about programs—for rehabilitation, housing, employment, education—that might be available for Robert once he is discharged, and I have been keeping Robert informed about what I have learned. What I have been discovering is that the world of individuals with mental illness is not at all what it was ten, twenty, and thirty years ago, when most people with conditions and histories similar to Robert's were condemned to lifetimes of hopelessness and institutionalization. It is not even what it was five or six years ago, when I began doing background research for *Imagining Robert.*

I have also been meeting people who share with Robert the fact of having a severe psychiatric condition, and a history of repeated and/or long-term hospitalizations, but who, unlike Robert, have recovered, and have made viable lives for themselves in our world. I have been meeting men and women who have been incarcerated for a dozen years and more in mental hospitals, who have had long-term psychiatric disorders, who have been given up on and abandoned by friends, families, and mental health professionals, yet who are out here with the rest of us, living lives like those most of us live: lives that include college educations, full-time jobs, friendships, marriages, divorces, children—lives marked and informed not by madness and the fear of madness, but by the ordinary joys, losses, and struggles that are the stuff of most lives.

While my discovery of several new and good programs for people with long-term psychiatric disorders does not make me believe Robert will suddenly, at fifty-three, recover into the kind of life he or I might have imagined possible for him twenty, thirty, or forty years ago—that some magical cure is imminent—I am convinced Robert can have a better life than the one that has been his.

When I visited Robert at South Beach a month before, he

had, for the first time in more than two years, been allowed out of the hospital on a pass. We had eaten lunch in a nearby restaurant, taken a long walk along a deserted beach, played lottery tickets, and passed the time talking and joking about things we usually talk about: reminiscing about the past— about friends, family, and times spent together—and making provisional plans for the future, when Robert would be out of the hospital again.

In the decade preceding his most recent hospitalization, he had done well—his hard times had become less frequent, his hospitalizations less lengthy. He had maintained himself for several years without any hospitalizations at all, and during these years he had spent his days working part time at various jobs in Staten Island Hospital, visiting friends and family in and around New York City and in upstate New York, vacationing in Atlantic City (both by himself and with me), and visiting me and my three children—his niece and nephews—in Massachusetts. At the time of his most recent hospitalization, in June 1993, he had been living with two housemates in a private home on Staten Island, without on-site supervision.

Now, three years later, emerging from the Brooklyn Battery Tunnel and driving along familiar streets, I find myself smiling at the prospect of being with Robert, and at the fact that he has made it back into our world. I drive along Ocean Parkway, where some of our cousins live, and then along a street that borders Prospect Park, a park where Robert and I spent many days together when we were boys. I turn into Coney Island Avenue, and the instant I spot Park Manor, I stop smiling. Damn, I think: We've been here before too, haven't we? I park in front of Robert's new home, a three-story building that looks substantial enough, but which, like the neighborhood, is run-down and dreary.

The sidewalks are littered with garbage and abandoned supermarket shopping carts, local storefronts and buildings are boarded up or shut down with metal grilles, and the thick security door to Park Manor is locked—but to protect the world from the mad, I wonder, or the mad from the world? I ring the bell several times before a man comes and asks who I am and why I am there. I give the man Robert's name, and he opens the door, then turns away.

I step into a large lounge area that reminds me of those dimly lit train stations and shelters where, in old World War Two movies, refugees gathered while awaiting resettlement. The lounge is filled mostly with empty brown plastic chairs, and the chairs, forty or fifty of them, are lined up in straight rows in front of a television set. Except for the chairs, the TV set, and a few long folding tables, the room is barren, the walls a murky dull yellow ("urine-colored," Robert later says). A dozen or so residents sit around the edges of the lounge, immobile, and they look neither mad, dangerous, nor sick: merely old, maimed, and lifeless. I am the only visitor this Friday afternoon, and it occurs to me that, at fifty-three years of age, Robert is going to bring down the average age of the population here considerably.

When Robert appears a few minutes later, he immediately begins offering me gifts—food, used clothing, coupons for cigarettes and magazine subscriptions—and introducing me to other residents. He tells each person we meet that I have written a book about him that is going to be published. He takes me upstairs and shows me his room (bare except for two beds and two dressers), the view from his window (of an alleyway), and introduces me to his roommate, Charles. Charles, a thin man about Robert's age, carries himself stiffly, and his responses—his lack of responses, really—suggest either heavy medication, and/or, my guess, neurological damage suffered early in life. The room, like the lounge, corridors, and staircase, is reasonably clean, and—like the people living here?—in a state of dull, advanced deterioration.

Robert, however, is full of energy, anything but dull and lifeless. He talks nonstop (without allowing me to finish sentences, or to answer questions he asks), shows me each item in his dresser and closet, tells me what I should bring on my next visit, asks me to take photos of him and Charles, asks about his niece and nephews, and where we are going to eat, and how much money he is going to make from our book. He asks about our mother, who lives in a nursing home in West Palm Beach, Florida (suffering from Alzheimer's disease, she no longer recognizes me, or her nurses), and if we should say *Kaddish* for her. He keeps removing his dentures from his mouth (all his own teeth are gone), then putting them back in—in and out, out and in—while he whispers secrets in my ear, moves from subject to subject without seeming transition, and howls with laughter at things I say or he says.

He is unfocused, restless, excited ("cycling up," as his doctors might say), and, when I don't agree with him or do exactly what he says, quick to anger. When we head downstairs and out into the street, for lunch, I glance back at Park Manor, and I think: My brother has gone through all he has gone through these past few years for *this*?

My brother has had to obey all the rules and regulations on his ward for an extended period of time, and he has had to deal with all that has been involved in effecting his transfer (and the transfer of prescriptions, social security payments, savings)—meetings, screenings, interviews, the filling out of forms—along with his anxieties and fears about living in New York City again—to be released to *this*—to earn the right to live in a bare room in a decaying building with several dozen disabled, forlorn, and forsaken strangers, and in a neighborhood where even the graffiti are without flair?

There must, I think, be other and better alternatives.

Although the staff at South Beach has declared that Park Manor is "the best and only" option for Robert, people I have spoken with in the weeks preceding Robert's release (including Marvin Newman, a junior high school friend of Robert's who has been a deputy commissioner in the New York City Department of Mental Health) have warned me about it ("A miserable place, " Marvin says, "—the bottom of the barrel"), and have offered to help get Robert into a better residence. But this will take time, and can be more easily arranged after Robert is discharged from South Beach. First get him out of the hospital, Marvin advises, and then we'll work on getting him into a better living situation.

Robert and I walk along Coney Island Avenue, Robert stopping in stores, introducing me to shopkeepers with whom he has made friends, and checking pay phones for change. By the time we arrive at a Greek restaurant he has chosen, a few blocks away, he is calmer, and we are, once more, relaxed with each other, happy to be together—to be talking, joking, and reminiscing the way we usually do—as if we might be any two brothers having lunch together on any ordinary day.

When, about midway through the meal, I tell him that I've sent off the final draft of the book, and when I show him the title page, he says nothing. He stares at the page for a few seconds, touches the photo of us briefly with his fingertips, then carefully folds the piece of paper several times, pressing down its edges with the palm of his hand. Just before he puts the page into the breast pocket of his shirt, he draws the paper to his lips and kisses it.

In the restaurant we take some photos, and during the walk back to Park Manor, despite an ice-cold wind that forces us to take shelter in doorways, Robert asks me to take more photos. As we get closer to Park Manor, however, he becomes impatient, irritable, demanding. When we arrive, though I tell him that I need to head north for home before rush hour, he keeps telling me that I *have* to come inside, that I *have* to visit his room again, that he *has* to show me things. When I say that I probably won't see him again before I leave for Europe, but that I will call and write, he does not respond, and no matter how many times I say good-bye, or begin to leave, he has more things to show me, more things to talk to me about. When I finally give him a farewell hug and kiss and start down the stairs, he becomes enraged—

eyes bulging, face red, neck muscles straining — and he starts screaming at me.

In front of Park Manor, we embrace again — he kisses me wetly but does not say good-bye — and after I get in the car and pull away from the curb, I look in the rearview mirror and see that he has stepped off the sidewalk and has begun following me. I slow down, and he turns away, wanders into the middle of the street. I hesitate, think of turning back, but see that, his beret pulled tight on his head, he has crossed the street and is heading in an opposite direction, and I think: He is not going to make it.

I make a call that evening, to the pay phone in the lounge, but nobody can find him. When I telephone the next day, a social worker informs me that Robert had come downstairs the night before with a belt buckled around his neck, as if to hang himself, had become loud and aggressive, and that — for at least the fiftieth time in his adult life — he has had to be hospitalized.

While I am in Germany I write and call Robert regularly (I also ask friends and family who know him to do the same; during my four months abroad, he receives one note and two calls from others), and before I leave, and while I am away, and after I return, I keep asking the same questions: Why was there nothing better than Park Manor available when Robert was ready to leave South Beach — and why, when people on the staff told me Park Manor was the only and best option available, did I encourage Robert to go along with them?

At the time, their explanation — that they had an arrangement with Park Manor whereby residents could be taken back to South Beach regularly by van for a day treatment program — seemed, for purposes of transition, to make sense. Clearly, having this arrangement made things easier for the staffs at both places. Clearly, too, it made things easier for me.

Although I rationalized my actions, and lack of actions, by saying that as soon as Robert was settled in at Park Manor, I would call on people to help him move into a better situation, now I have to wonder, and to second-guess myself, about not having explored other possibilities, about not having been more aggressive on Robert's behalf.

When in early August—my first week back in the States—I visit Robert at South Beach, my wonder turns quickly to sorrow, and to frustration. Robert is happy to see me—he is enormously affectionate, and somewhat less manic than he often is—but he looks terrible (pasty skin, half-closed eyes, stooped posture, shuffling gait, no teeth), and his demeanor (from medications?) unusually subdued and listless. His therapist, Mark Kaplan, sits with us for a few minutes, and when Robert goes to the bathroom, Mark whispers that Robert's "plateaus—his ups and downs"—seem to be coming in shorter and shorter cycles, and that, although they haven't told Robert this yet, the staff is considering trying ECT (electroconvulsive therapy) with him, that another patient on the ward recently completed a series of shock treatments, and "came out quite well."

I am astonished—appalled, really—that Mark is confiding this in me and keeping it from Robert, especially since, an ongoing issue, the staff rarely informs me about *anything* concerning Robert, and I remind Mark that Robert has had a lifelong fear of ECT. I say that it was my understanding that ECT was used only as a last resort for severely depressed patients, and that Robert has no history of severe depression.

Mark shrugs and says that in his opinion ECT has been "underused."

Robert returns, and announces that his problem with Mark is that Mark is both his social worker *and* his therapist.

Mark says that this is true.

"That's schizophrenic," Robert declares.

Robert and I laugh, but Mark does not, and when Mark says, in answer to a question from Robert about who he is—

"What I want to know is, what is my *identity*?" — that it seems to him that Robert is a Jew and a brother, Robert shakes his head sideways.

"They're not the same thing," he says.

I am heartened to see that Robert's sense of humor is alive and well, and when I call him that night, Robert tells me that, except for Mark's presence, he enjoyed our visit. "He ignored me and just kept asking you about your trip," Robert says. "He was very rude."

A week later, because routine lab work shows that Robert's liver enzymes are elevated, he is transferred to Bayley-Seton, a general hospital on Staten Island, where he stays for a week. After he returns to his locked ward, I call Mark, and Mark tells me that since Robert's tolerance for medications is getting lower and lower, the staff just doesn't know what to do for him anymore, and so they are still seriously considering ECT. When I ask about trying Clozaril, a new antipsychotic medication that has been remarkably successful in helping individuals like Robert who have long-term histories of mental illness, Mark says that since Robert won't agree to take the weekly blood tests that must accompany Clozaril (few patients *ever* immediately agree to these tests), this is "not an option." According to Mark, Robert is "abusing the phone," starting fights with other patients, and is also, the staff suspects, the patient responsible for stuffing sanitary napkins into the ward's toilets, although no one can figure out how he obtains them.

Robert is also angry with me, and sometimes screams at me and hangs up on me when I telephone ("It's smoking time and you took me away and why don't you adjust your life to my schedule, you goddamn fucking asshole!"). When, however, I call on the first night of Rosh Hashanah, the Jewish New Year, a half-year after Robert's brief stay at Park Manor, he is calm and talkative. We wish each other a Happy New Year — Robert asks that I and my children be inscribed in "The Book of Life" for good health, wealth, and happiness — and when I say, as gently as I can, that I hope, in the coming year, that *if* Robert wants to get out of the hospital, he will be able to, Robert says softly, "Oh no—I don't want to. I don't want to get out, Jay. I don't ever want to leave. This is my home."

I say nothing except "Oh," and a few seconds later, Robert speaks again.

"It's safe here," he explains.

During my time abroad, I have written several short stories, and have begun preliminary work on a new novel. I have also worked on an essay about the care and treatment of people who, like Robert, are judged to be "chronically mentally ill"—those whom the mental health system believes are beyond hope, and beyond recovery. I take up this essay again now, and decide to make use of what I think of as leftovers—material I cut out, or left out, of *Imagining Robert:* passages in which I put forth views on when, where, and why the mental health system was failing, and had failed, along with the ways in which it often gave the least and poorest care to those who were most in need of care.

I had not, in *Imagining Robert*, wanted to reduce Robert's life to an editorial about the mental health system and so, for the most part, I had put aside my analyses and recommendations in order, or so I hoped, to better serve the story of Robert's life, and of the miracle and mystery of that life. For though Robert's life is hardly enviable, it is, still, I wrote, a life at least as full and complex as any, and the wonder was not what had caused his repeated breakdowns and incarcerations, but what, given his life, had enabled him to survive—and to do more than survive: to retain his generosity, his warmth, his intelligence, his pride, his humor, his energy, and his sense of self. This, it seemed to me, remained, as ever, the true miracle and mystery.

Now, however, sad and frustrated that Robert is, once again, living most days on isolation (this is called, by the staff, "reduced stimulation")—and fearing for his future (except for the few days at Park Manor, he has been hospitalized steadily for more than three years now, the longest single hospitalization of his life), and feeling partly responsible for the relapse that has led him, for the first time in my memory, to move so swiftly from intense anger to intense hopelessness, I take up the essay again, both to relieve and to make use of my own anger.

At the same time, I find myself thinking about madness and of the ways, in life as in language, it is often synonymous with anger. For if love and guilt sometimes conspire to act as my muse, anger—being, that is, quite literally *mad*—is often, as now, the engine that seems to drive me and to keep me going. If only, I believe, I can make *sense* of things, of my rage and my outrage—if only I can, *in words,* explain and show and prove just how bad and unjust things are and exactly what we might do—*must* do—to make them better, all might yet be well. . . .

Why is it, though, I wonder, that I can at times transform my madness—my often wild, overwhelming, confusing, murderous feelings of rage, frustration, indignation, and helplessness—into a fuel that fires my prose and my life, while Robert, most times, cannot? Why is it that, similar to each other in so many ways, we have come to lead such different lives, lives in which I am sometimes able to do what Robert seems incapable of doing: to make my imagination and my anger work *for* me instead of against me?

A sane person, I recall our Hebrew school teacher, Dr. Baron, telling us when I was nine or ten years old, builds castles in the air, but a madman—and here was the difference, the answer to the riddle Dr. Baron posed for us—a madman *lives* in them. While Robert's flights of mind and feeling seem often to unmoor him from this world, the opposite is true for me: When the very stuff of my mind goes flying off, or burrowing down, into places that have never existed, and I live in them for a while—in these times and places that have never been—I often come to feel not only intensely exhilarated and clearheaded, but more solidly grounded in *this* world. It is as if the very ability to imagine lives I have never lived—to let memory and desire lead me where they will, and to see lives, lived or unlived, *as* stories—allows me, often, to get through: to find, to create, and to sustain a life that is, for the most part, both safe *and* surprising. Why is it, though, I wonder now, that Robert's thoughts, feelings, and memories, when they take flight, lead—as they do for so many others—to a grim life that is sometimes surprising, but rarely safe.

Four months after my return from Europe, on an early December evening, I attend ceremonies sponsored by Boston University's Center for Psychiatric Rehabilitation, at which ceremonies thirteen people, all with long-term histories of mental illness, graduate from a yearlong computer training program. A year before there were fourteen graduates of the program, eleven of whom went on to half- or full-time employment with organizations such as the Boston Symphony Orchestra, the U.S. Trust Bank, and the Lotus Development Corporation.

I sit in a wood-paneled amphitheater with about a hundred guests, and I listen to speeches—by faculty members, by university and state officials, by graduates of the program—and it is as if I am watching thirteen versions of Robert, all of whom, by their testimony, have had histories and lives very much like his, but none of whom are living in isolation on locked wards.

As the graduates accept their degrees, and at a reception afterward, they talk about their years in state institutions, about the abuse and neglect they have suffered, and about how often they had given up hope. They talk, too—something I will hear repeatedly in the months to come—of how doctors told them once upon a time that they would *never* get well and would have to be institutionalized forever. They talk of how doctors told them that if, by some chance, they were ever able to live outside hospitals, they would have to lead marginal lives—lives in which they should never even consider the possibility of holding down full-time jobs, or of having children, or of raising families, or of owning homes of their own.

During the previous ten months, these thirteen individuals—many of whom are married, have children, jobs, families, and homes of their own—have been attending classes at Boston University five days a week, five and a half hours a day, after which they have each served two-month internships. The director of the program, Larry Kohn—a six-foot one-inch, two-hundred-pound man in his late thirties who, with his broad shoulders, deep-set blue eyes, handlebar mustache, and rangy manner, looks as if he might have been a quarterback for a Big Ten football team, or, what he actually was for a few years, a lumberjack in the Northwest—opens the award ceremonies by informing us that ten of the thirteen members of this year's program have already been offered employment for the coming year.

This is good news, Larry says, but what he wants to emphasize tonight is not success, but struggle. He wants to emphasize what each of the thirteen graduates has gone through in order to complete the program, and not only with things any of us might struggle with—the difficulty of returning to school after having been away for a while, or of applying for a job after being out of work for an extended period of time—but with things most of us rarely if ever have to contend with: the mere getting out of bed in the morning and getting to the classroom—navigating a journey across a city via buses and trains when your head is logged down with psychotropic medications and you have a lifelong, paralyzing fear of crowds.

Larry talks about how hard it is for people who have for long stretches been both out of their minds and out of this world to go for interviews when *any* interview fills you with dread—with anxieties about revealing your medical history, with fears of being rejected and humiliated because of your history—*So, can you tell me about those missing years . . . and what if these mental problems recur while you're working for us . . . and oh, yes, one other thing: How often have you been violent . . . ?* — and with shame for being a person who possesses such a history.

Larry talks about the struggles these thirteen individuals have undergone in sticking with their studies when, in addition to problems that derive directly from the side effects of their medications (drowsiness, drooling, nausea, constipation, impotence, headaches, tremblings), and from their psychiatric condition (depression, mania, visual and auditory hallucinations), feelings of hopelessness, failure, and despair rise up on a daily and sometimes hourly basis — feelings that have pervaded large portions of their adult lives — and often threaten to wash them away.

Larry talks about the key element of any recovery process — *hope* — and when he does, I hear the word in a way I have never quite heard it before: as if it is something tangible — as physically real as a rock or a heart or a river or a car engine.

For the first time in memory I am reminded that hope — like love, like trust, and like faith — is not merely an abstract and most unscientific noun vaguely and loosely used most of the time, but can prove to be a genuine and quite solid element — a palpable force in a person's life and being. Clearly, for people in the room with me, hope has proved at least as significant — as life-*changing* — as any chemical or genetic marker, as any medication or molecular configuration.

What Larry says is elaborated on by others throughout the evening. Dan Fisher, a Harvard graduate who holds both M.D. and Ph.D. degrees, who was for five years a research neurochemist with the National Institute of Mental Health, and who is now medical director of Eastern Middlesex Human Services in Wakefield, Massachusetts, is the evening's keynote speaker. He talks about his own hospitalizations for schizophrenia, about his journey of recovery, and about how hope — having others believe in him — allowed him to believe in himself again.

In addition to his full-time responsibilities as medical director at the Eastern Middlesex Clinic (and to his life as the married father of two teenage children), Dan also serves as executive director of the National Empowerment Center in Lawrence, Massachusetts. Dan talks about the center, which is run by "consumer/survivors," people like himself who have survived and recovered from severe mental illness, and about the ways the center serves people who are still in, or are beginning, the process of recovery.

Discoveries in neurobiology during the last two decades help explain what, as on this night, we often sense from our lives: that our experiences not only affect us in passing ways—in our moods, feelings, and actions—but that these experiences actually, and all through our lives, physically change the structure of our brains, and the ways in which our brains function. The theory of neural plasticity, as set forth by writers such as Gerald Edelman, Leon Eisenberg, Edward Hundert, and Israel Rosenfield (as originally developed by David Hubel and Torsten Wiesel in studies that earned them the Nobel Prize in Medicine in 1981), has in recent years demonstrated not only why experiences such as love and loss, acting in and on the brain, can make us, for days or for years, happy or confused or sad, but how and why we know that any experience—*all* experience—can *transform* the ways in which the brain is constructed and functions.

Although the basic ground plan for the human brain (its map of neuronal pathways) is set for us genetically by being laid out in the genome, it turns out that the adult brain remains, from birth to death, capable of extensive functional reorganization. "The genome of a human being (the entire collection of an individual's genes)," Gerald Edelman informs us in *Bright Air, Brilliant Fire*, "is insufficient to specify explicitly the synaptic structure of the developing brain. Moreover, each organism's behavior is biologically individual and enormously diverse, whether or not that organism registers or reports subjective experience as human beings can."

"The number of cells being made, dying, and becoming incorporated is huge," Edelman writes, because "the entire situation is a dynamic one, depending on signals, genes, proteins, cell movement, division, and death, all interacting at many levels." The "main features of this drama," he adds, are "topobiological," or "place-dependent," so that "events occurring in one place require that previous events have occurred at other places," and that the processes of our minds, thus, become "inherently dynamic, plastic, or variable at the level of its fundamental unit, the cells."

"Even in genetically identical twins," he adds, "the exact same pattern of nerve cells is not found at the same place and time."

"The matter of shape," Edelman explains, "is critical."

> It means that *combinations* of genes act to give a heritable shape characteristic of that species. It also means that the mechanical events leading to the rearrangement and specialization of cells must be coordinated with the sequential expression of the genes. *This is the key requirement of topobiology*. It explains why genes specifying the shapes of proteins are not enough; individual *cells*, moving and dying in unpredictable ways, are the real driving forces. Making proteins or cell surfaces that latch on to each other, each specific for a given cell like a Lego toy, does not account for how genes specify shape. While the cells of an embryo of a species resemble each other *on the average*, the movement and death of a *particular* cell at any *particular* place is a statistical matter and that cell's actual position cannot be prespecified by the code in a gene.

Throughout our lives stimulus deprivation (as in the blocking of vision, or the blurring of sound) and enriched stimulation (as in the acquisition of language, or in postsurgical rehabilitation exercises) can lead either to anatomic and functional loss, or to increased neuronal density and reorganized neuronal functioning.

Although the *rate* of neuronal change slows down as we age (this is why it is easier to learn musical scales, or to acquire new languages when we are young), the precise details of our neuroanatomy are not fixed and determined by our genetic inheritance, but continue to come into being throughout our lives because of a kind of ongoing competition, especially during our early development, between our presynaptic axons for our postsynaptic neurons. The concepts of brain structure and function revealed to us by contemporary neuroscience, then, turn out to be in accord with what we know about the development of our behavior and of our identities, and about the nature of consciousness itself.

What we often sense to be true, that is—how each of us can suddenly feel like a different person: happier or sadder, older or younger, depressed or elated, grief-stricken or adventurous or miserable or terrified or timid or playful or bewildered; how we can often feel more or less like what we think of as our *selves* (as in, "I'm just not myself today," or "I'm feeling more like myself again"); and how we often believe we can trace our new feelings to particular events (falling in love, losing a parent or child, being humiliated or praised, mastering a sport or a musical instrument)—turns out to be *biochemically* true: Experience quite literally transforms us because it alters the synaptic connections and the very texture (neuronal density) of our brains. Our experiences, and our reactions (thoughts, feelings, choices) to our experiences (and our reactions to our reactions), thus, are constantly configuring and reconfiguring the very matter that determines how we feel, choose, think, and act.

Because we can, for the first time in recorded history, actually see what is going on in the living brain in ways previously hidden from us (through new technologies such as Magnetic Resonance Imaging [MRI], and CAT and PET scans), we have learned, for example, that sensory remapping of the brain in women who have had mastectomies begins as early as six days after surgery; that, because of their *in utero* auditory experience, four-day-old French infants will suck harder in order to hear French than Russian; and that Japanese adults, unlike Japanese infants, cannot hear a difference between the English letters "l" and "r," not because of neural atrophy but because language-specific phonemic categories have suppressed nonspecific auditory sensitivities.

And, as Oliver Sacks has informed us, "one of the most astonishing demonstrations of the plasticity of the nervous system, and the extent of its adaptability to a different sensory mode," can be observed in deaf people who learn and use sign. In deaf signers, Sacks writes, "the enhancement of evoked potentials [spreads] forward into the left temporal lobe, which is normally regarded as purely auditory in function. This is a very remarkable and, one suspects, fundamental finding, for it suggests that what are normally auditory areas are being *reallocated*, in deaf signers, for visual processing."

Biochemically, that is, the brain is continuously modifying its own responsiveness to incoming stimuli—to everything that, along with our genes, we inherit and experience: our small and large triumphs and tragedies, our schooling, our conversations, our work, our games, our interactions with family, friends, strangers, and the places in which we live. (The great fallacy of genetic determinism, R. C. Lewontin points out, is to suppose that the genes *make* the organism. "It is a basic principle of developmental biology," he explains, "that organisms undergo a continuous development from conception to death, a development that is the unique consequence of the interaction of the genes in their cells, the temporal sequence of environments through which the organisms pass, and random cellular processes that determine the life, death, and transformation of cells. As a result, even the fingerprints of identical twins are not identical.")

I sit in the amphitheater at Boston University's Sargent College of Allied Health Professions, then, and I watch and listen to individuals who have recovered from conditions of mind, feeling, and behavior that are generally considered chronic and incurable, and I look around and wonder: Where is Robert, and why isn't *he* here?

I close my eyes and see Robert lying on his bed, alone and

trembling, and I picture him reciting, as he often will when we are together, verses from poems he has written. I think of how much better his life was during periods when he had a long-term relationship with a therapist or social worker he had come to trust, and when he was able to visit regularly with friends and family—to give and take news and affection on an ongoing basis—and I find myself thinking, too, that poetic truth may yet turn out to be biological truth: that perhaps love and hope *are* chemicals whose effects can be as profound, wonderful, and abiding as the effects of medications.

Perhaps, I muse, since we are capable of influencing the nature of our minds throughout our lives, there is nothing romantic or sentimental in believing that love and hope *can* transform us. Since it turns out that we are not mere victims of the genetic hand life deals us at birth—that our choices all through life determine, in a most physical sense, *who we are*, why shouldn't it be possible for us to transform the very essence of our beings—what some would call our souls—and remake ourselves, redeem ourselves, and give ourselves new lives?

Although most of the thirteen graduates of the B.U. program, as I will learn when I talk with them later, are on psychiatric medications, they all tell me that without hope—without the belief in themselves given to them by their teachers, doctors, therapists, friends, and family members—they would *never* have recovered. Although a pill can ameliorate symptoms, they allow—and thank God that it can—it is hard to construct, or reconstruct, a life with a pill.

"I have sat on both sides of the prescription," Dan Fisher says at the start of his keynote address, and he talks about how being invited to the ceremonies this evening is a kind of homecoming for him. Dan is a wiry, silver-haired man in his mid-forties with an engaging smile, a delightful and self-mocking sense of humor, and a rambling manner. He wears a tan tweed jacket and a brilliant red silk tie, and he tells us that "recovery is about relationships"—about love, support, perseverance, comfort, encouragement, and friendship. Darkness, he says, comes to us again and again, as do fears, failures, and wipeouts. He knows because he has been there.

The obstacles to recovery are enormous, he continues, but the greatest obstacle of all is simply that most people think one can *not* recover. But people do recover. It is his belief, moreover—a message he carries everywhere—that "*everyone* has the capacity to recover from mental illness."

Most doctors, most of the time, however, feel helpless: They usually see patients with mental illness when the patients are in their most acute stages, they see them briefly— often in an emergency ward—they assume, or have been taught, that they can't be cured or changed, and so they medicate them or refer them elsewhere—to a community mental health center, or a case manager, or a social worker—and move on to the next patient.

Our job, therefore, Dan says, is to educate others about recovery. "You are pioneers in changing societal attitudes," he tells the thirteen graduates. But this is difficult work. "It took my own brother half a lifetime to understand my condition," Dan says. "My brother's a farmer—a good mechanic who loves working on machinery—and he never could figure me out until one day, when we were talking, the light suddenly came on in his eyes. 'Aha,' he said to me, 'I've got it now—you have to check your oil more often!' "

Although in his own psychiatric practice Dan usually treats individuals in conventional ways—with medications, therapy, and psychosocial rehabilitation—he believes that the wave of the future, in the care and treatment of people with mental illnesses, lies in peer support (people with mental illness, or in recovery from mental illness, helping one another), and in self-help. Given general societal attitudes toward madness, and the fears, inhibitions, and, perhaps most significant of all, the *isolation* in which most people with mental illness live—an isolation at least as devastating as the condition of madness itself—peer support and self-help are not only essential, he contends, but life-giving.

Several of the graduating students address the audience, and express their gratitude for the love and support they have received. A white-haired woman who has suffered from mental illness her entire adult life, and who looks and talks this evening as if she might be the dean of faculty at B.U.— assured, articulate, and radiant, she wears a tailored suit, a gorgeous purple-and-red wool shawl around her shoulders— says that her great fear, all year long, was simply that she wouldn't make it, that she would drop out, and fail yet again. She talks about how impatient and discouraged she often became, and how it was, most of all, the encouragement and dedication of her teacher, Lisa Bellafato, that got her through.

If not for this program, she and other graduates say, they would still be at home, hiding in back rooms and doing nothing—sleeping, smoking, watching TV—or they would have relapsed and would be back on a ward in a city or state hospital. But being in the program, they emphasize—thinking of themselves, and being able to identify themselves as students and not as mental patients—this simple shift has made all the difference.

Lisa Bellafato, a six-foot-tall black-haired woman in her early thirties, presents the graduation certificates. Lisa has been teacher to these thirteen students for the computer training course, and it is difficult at first to believe that this strikingly beautiful, elegantly dressed woman, her eyes burning with intensity, has spent most of her daylight hours during the past year working in a windowless room, teaching computer skills to thirteen people who might, with a bit less luck, be locked up on a hospital ward with my brother.

For a brief moment I feel as if I am watching one of those movies where a young teacher in an inner-city school is played by a Hollywood star, and in which movie the actress seems just that—a Hollywood star who has wandered into the wrong neighborhood, the wrong film, and the wrong story. But then Lisa speaks, and when she does, the directness of her words and the gentleness of her voice—and the fact of what she does for a living Monday to Friday, week after week, without cameras present — make it apparent that she is in the right place, and that she is a real element in a very real story.

Teaching this class, Lisa says, has taught her about what it takes to face fears and anxieties and still remain an active participant in life. She has marveled at the determination of her students to get to class even when the weight of the world felt heavy. She thanks the graduating class for showing her that the program has made a true difference in their lives, and she tells them that she thinks of them as friends who have greatly enriched her life.

When she awards certificates to each of the graduates, she speaks to and about each of them individually — about their struggles, their idiosyncrasies, their achievements. "Rose Miller," she tells us, "took the initiative to explore and experiment with different ways of solving problems, and she often discovered interesting shortcuts that she shared with the class. One of my greatest joys in teaching came when Rose told me that she now understood why I pushed her so hard."

About another student, Henry Cruz, she says, "Henry's determination and perseverance have been an inspiration to me and everyone else. Henry fought many fears just to make it to school every morning. He pushed through difficult times to focus on his work and learn new skills. No matter how difficult a day Henry was having, he always took the time to ask me and his classmates how we were doing. Henry is a compassionate and brave man with a true fighting spirit."

There is a lot of applause, laughter, and hugging, and some very moist eyes, and what surprises me is that even though I have been Robert's primary caretaker for more than three decades, most of what is happening in this amphitheater on this evening thirty-four years after Robert's first breakdown, and what has been happening for these thirteen individuals, is news to me.

Why are these thirteen people here, I ask myself, and why is Robert where he is, and what has made the difference? Why, through the years, were programs like this not available for Robert, and if they were, why didn't I know about them, and why didn't they work for him, and why have they worked for these people?

A few weeks before the award ceremonies, I had met with Bill Anthony, the director of the B.U. program. Bill Anthony, a tall, lanky, easygoing man whose manner, a combination of earnestness, gentleness, and humor that reminds me of the actor Jimmy Stewart had Stewart been running programs for people with disabilities (in addition to books and articles about mental illness, Bill is also the author of a delightful satirical book, *The Art of Napping*), founded the B.U. program in 1977, and he is generally credited with founding, in that same year, what has since become a worldwide movement in psychiatric and psychosocial rehabilitation.

Bill's premise, twenty years ago as now, has remained constant: that if you think of people with mental illnesses as having *disabilities*, instead of thinking of them as having *diseases*, all sorts of things become possible.

In an example he often uses, Bill talks about a person who has had his or her spinal cord severed, and who must spend the rest of life in a wheelchair. Although this individual will remain physically disabled for life, the individual can, with supports and rehabilitation, recover from the injury, as other people with handicaps do, and regain and create a full and meaningful life.

"The recovery vision," Bill has written, "transcends the arguments about whether severe mental illness is caused by physical and/or psychosocial factors. People with severe physical disabilities, such as spinal cord injury, can recover even though the spinal cord has not. Likewise, people with severe psychiatric disabilities can recover even though they still may experience symptom exacerbations."

Bill tells me that he believes the mental health movement

is about twenty years behind the physical disabilities movement. "And look at all the gains that movement has made for
handicapped people!" he exclaims. A generation ago, you
rarely saw a wheelchair in the street, yet now we take what
are truly revolutionary changes in services and attitudes for
granted—we have access to public events and in public transportation, support services in schools and factories, independent living units, a virtual absence of job discrimination, and
ramps, curb cuts, and special elevators everywhere.

Recovery, Bill has written, in a summary statement of his
beliefs, "means growing beyond the catastrophe of mental
illness and developing new meaning and purpose in one's
life. It means taking charge of one's life even if one cannot
take complete charge of one's symptoms." He also writes:

> Much of the chronicity that is thought to be a part of peo-
> ple's mental illness may be due to the way the mental
> health system and society treat people with severe mental
> illness. Contributing to people's chronicity are factors such
> as stigma, lowered social status, restrictions on choice and
> self-determination, the lack or partial lack of rehabilitation
> opportunities, and low staff expectations. Drastic system
> changes are needed if we wish to support people's recov-
> ery, rather than hinder people's recovery.

Although I am skeptical about Bill's central analogy—it
seems to me that the ignorant, fearful, and often hostile attitudes people have toward those who are different because
of their *mental* illnesses run much deeper, and have run
deeper across time and cultures, than the attitudes people
have toward those who have physical disabilities—I am impressed with the gains that are made once one stops thinking
of mental illness as an inborn, chronic, and incurable disease.

At the same time, I am also aware of the degree to which,
like my parents, I have spent much of my life thinking about
the possibility—and impossibility—of a *cure* for Robert, and

how I have, like others, assumed that Robert could not begin to lead anything like a normal life until what was designated as his illness was somehow *gone*.

The possibility that, whatever the origins of the condition we call madness, one can recover and reclaim responsibility for one's life without having to be fully cured, and that one can have a full life while still having symptoms (hearing voices, seeing things that are not there, going through periods of deep depression, withdrawal, or mania)—this, too, is news to me.

The cost of the B.U. program—which includes not only the ten-month computer training course and two-month internship, but a full range of services, including vocational, educational, and residential counseling, is $8,000, much of which is subsidized by scholarships and grants. Rob Salafia, a professional magician and former song-and-dance man who has had leads in local and national touring companies, works full time for the program developing job opportunities for the students, and counseling them during their time at Boston University, and after their graduation.

The cost of an excellent supervised residential program for individuals like those in the B.U. program—room and board, and a complete range of medical and psychosocial services—runs (in the Boston area) somewhere between $25,000 and $35,000 a year. The total annual cost, then, for a comprehensive program that provides skills (and hope) for an individual with severe and persistent mental illness, and in pleasant and humane settings, comes on average to around $35,000 to $40,000.

The cost of keeping my brother on a locked ward, without anything resembling psychological, vocational, or educational counseling—without anything that might offer the possibility for a fuller, more productive life—is, according to the New York State Office of Mental Health, $127,000 a year.

Perhaps, I think on the drive home from the B.U. award ceremonies, I have been so close to the particulars of Robert's life for so long that I was unable to see what was happening in the world *beyond* our lives. It is as if, especially during his years in state hospitals, Robert had been living in some Dantesque circle of hell where all hope had been abandoned—by him *and* his keepers—and as if, much of the time, like Robert and his keepers, I too had been blind to what was happening in the concentric circles spreading out around us, where men and women with histories and conditions similar to Robert's were finding ways out of the hell on earth that mental illness usually is.

When I return home from Boston, I put aside both my novel and the essay on the mental health system, and begin to imagine a new book, and nothing about this new book, except for the possibility that I might be able to write it, is imagined. I continue to search out programs that offer tangible assistance to people who have led lives like Robert's, and I talk with people who have recovered from mental illness and with people who are on the road to recovery. The more I look, the more I find. I meet individuals who have endured gruesome forms of neglect and abuse, both in and out of hospitals, who have led lives so horrific they make Robert's life seem almost blessed in comparison, and who have somehow managed to return to our world, into very full and very imperfect lives, to tell their tales.

What made the difference? And what, I begin to wonder, might make a difference for so many others who continue to languish in lives different in detail, but not in quality, from my brother's?

TWO

THE PSYCHIATRIC DIASPORA

Nothing is far and nothing is dear, if one desires. The world is little, human life is little. There is only one big thing—desire. And before it, when it is big, all is little.

—OLD WUNSCH TO THEA KRONBERG IN
WILLA CATHER'S *The Song of the Lark*

In 1993, the National Mental Health Advisory Council, in the largest and most exhaustive study of the prevalence of serious mental illness ever undertaken (*Epidemiologic Catchment Area Study of Prevalence Rates of Mental Disorders*, begun in 1980), determined that in any one year 2.8 percent of the adult population of the United States—or approximately 5.6 million adult Americans—suffer from severe and persistent mental illnesses, and that at least 1 million of these men and women are considered resistant to any and all treatment. Of these nearly 6 million people, the council estimated that 2.2 million adult men and women received no treatment at all.

There are, in addition, on any given day, at least a quarter of a million homeless people who have major psychiatric disorders, and at least 200,000 individuals with mental illness who are incarcerated in jails and prisons (put there, for the most part, for misdemeanors). A large percentage of these latter two groups also have coexisting alcohol and drug problems. According to the U.S. Comorbidity Survey, released in 1997, an estimated 10 million Americans have both mental health and substance abuse disorders, and an estimated 70 percent of the U.S. homeless population has a co-occurring disorder.

The National Institute of Mental Health estimates, further, that somewhere between 7 million and 9 million children and adolescents suffer from or are at serious risk for severe, long-term mental illness, while the Mental Health Advisory Council estimates that in any given six-month period, more than 2 million children and adolescents — 3.5 percent of those between the ages of nine and seventeen — will be found to suffer from a major mental illness.

Like my brother Robert, and like the thirteen graduates of the Boston University Training for the Future Program, each of these millions of individuals comes from and belongs to a family: to mothers, fathers, brothers, sisters, wives, husbands, grandparents, aunts, uncles, cousins, and children. If we leave aside all those adults who may, in any particular year, suffer from a diagnosable psychiatric disorder (according to the National Institute of Mental Health this will happen to 22.1 percent of the adult population), and concern ourselves only with the 5.6 million men and women who are afflicted *long term* with severe and persistent mental illnesses, and if we multiply 5.6 million by 2.1 (the figure the government uses for the average number of other adults in the average-size family), and if we then add these nearly 11.8 million family members to the 5.6 million, we see that, at the least, nearly 17 million Americans are directly affected, in their nuclear families alone, by serious and persistent forms of mental illness.

If one then adds to this figure the millions of sick children and children-at-risk, and the hundreds of thousands of homeless and imprisoned individuals with mental illness, along with friends, relatives, neighbors, classmates, co-workers, acquaintances, and mental health professionals who are involved, concerned, and affected—if, that is, we try to count all those whose lives touch and are touched by individuals with long-term mental illness (and do not even count those millions of individuals who suffer a single diagnosable psychiatric disorder in their lifetimes; the ECA estimates "lifetime prevalence rates of psychiatric disorders" to be between 28.8 and 38 percent)—the numbers only confirm what most of us already know: that individuals with serious mental illness are *everywhere*—among us, with us, all around us—and are a lot closer to home than we usually care to acknowledge.

The costs of mental illnesses are estimated by the government to be well over $200 billion (when costs attributable to alchohol and drug abuse are factored in, the total rises to more than $300 billion), with the indirect costs—loss of productivity, lost earnings due to premature death, law enforcement costs, etc.—comprising nearly three quarters of this amount. Because mental illnesses often strike at the beginning of one's productive work years, indirect costs are higher for mental illness than they are, say, for conditions such as cardiovascular disease, lung disease, Alzheimer's disease, or Parkinson's disease.

Ten days after the B.U. award ceremonies, I drive back to Boston to meet with Moe Armstrong, who is director of consumer and family affairs for the Vinfen Corporation, the largest nonprofit provider of mental health services in Massachusetts. Vinfen employs over 1,600 people, including more than 150 individuals who have or have had major mental illnesses (this latter figure is inexact since, even at Vinfen, many individuals with histories of mental illness choose to keep this part of their lives private), and it offers a variety of mental health programs for developmentally and emotionally disabled individuals, including inpatient psychiatric care; emergency psychiatric care; family support services; outpatient therapy; psychosocial rehabilitation programs, and supported employment and education programs that enable people with histories of psychiatric disorders to get and hold jobs and to attend school.

Vinfen also runs more than one hundred residences—residences for people with severe mental illness, residences for people in recovery from mental illness, residences for people who have been homeless, residences for people who have coexisting psychiatric and substance-abuse problems, and residences for single mothers with mental illness—and one of Moe's primary responsibilities is to work with the clients and staffs of these residences.

Like my brother, Moe has suffered from long-term mental illness, but unlike my brother—despite ongoing and recurring symptoms (hearing voices, seeing things that are not there, becoming suicidally depressed), despite occasional breakdowns, and despite being on psychiatric medications (Risperdal, the same medication Robert takes)—Moe enjoys a productive and rewarding life in our world. He has a full-time, well-paying job, and a comfortable five-room apartment in Cambridge he shares with a friend, Naomi, and her twenty-three-year-old daughter Sano, in what Moe describes as the best relationship he has ever had. He has many friends, along with an abundance of leisure-time pleasures—bicycling, boating, folk singing (he entertains in coffee houses), reading, and writing (poetry, cartoons, illustrated children's books, short stories). He has a bimonthly cable-TV show about mental health, and he serves as a member of the Cambridge Council for People with Disabilities, the State Rehabilitation Department's Advisory Council, and, in Washington, D.C., on the President's Commission on Employment for People with Disabilities.

LeRoy Spaniol, associate executive director of the B.U. Center for Psychiatric Rehabilitation, in charge of research and publications, had become friendly with Moe when Moe worked with the B.U. program, and when LeRoy and his wife had, for several years, owned an apartment in the same building in which Moe owned one. LeRoy has recommended I meet with Moe—that he would be an ideal guide to programs in and around Boston, and to the consumer movement—and has sketched in the basics of Moe's life for me.

Before Moe came to Boston to work for Vinfen, and before he owned his own apartment, and before his first breakdown, he had served as a medical corpsman with the U.S. Marine Corps, assigned to the elite 3rd Reconnaissance Battalion in Vietnam. Moe had trained reconnaissance forces and fought with them, had killed enemy soldiers and nearly been killed, and, for risking his life to rescue a wounded Marine from a streambed during a firefight near Da Nang, had been decorated for bravery.

After his breakdown in Vietnam, and after hospitalizations for schizophrenia in Vietnam and in Oakland, California, Moe had come to live a life that was, according to LeRoy, more exotic in the telling than in the living. Although Moe had grown up as a self-described all-American boy in a small Illinois town (Bushnell) — his childhood ambition: to become a career officer in the Marines — and although he had not used drugs before or during his time in Vietnam, after his discharge, partly in an attempt to self-medicate away his symptoms (hallucinations, depression, and alternating fits of rage and of weeping), Moe had begun drinking and doing drugs, and had become addicted to both.

After leaving the U.S. Naval Hospital in Oakland, and after working briefly for the U.S. Forestry Service in northern California, and after beating his head bloody against a truck window in a fit of manic frustration, Moe moved to the mountains above El Rito in northern New Mexico, where for three years he lived as a hermit in a tent, using his reconnaissance skills to survive as a "bush vet."

For most of the next twenty years, Moe's life was that of a homeless man, an alcoholic, and a drug addict on the streets of American, European, and Latin American cities. For a time in San Francisco, he was roommates with Neal Cassady (the prototype for Dean Moriarty in Jack Kerouac's *On the Road*). For four years Moe lived in Colombia, South America, where he nearly killed himself by burning out his stomach and intestines with an ingestion of the lye used to activate cocaine leaves. During these two decades, while continuing to experience auditory and visual hallucinations, suicidal fits of depression, and wild fits of rage (in San Francisco, he nearly beat a man to death), Moe married and divorced four times.

But before these years, and before his tour of duty in Vietnam, Moe had been an Eagle Scout, an Illinois state speech champion, and a highly recruited captain of his high school football team, holding the conference record for single tackles in a season (he made the Marine Corps football team, but left when he was selected for Special Operations). And following his years in the mountains of New Mexico, and his years of wandering across the United States, Europe, and Latin America, Moe settled in Santa Fe, where he got himself off both drugs and alcohol, and enrolled as a student at the College of Santa Fe. At the college, Moe worked for the Veterans Administration, recruiting and counseling veterans, and during an eight-year stretch he earned two bachelor's degrees (English literature, business administration), and two master's degrees — an M.B.A. and a Master of Arts degree in human resource development.

Driving around Boston and Cambridge — impatient to meet the man LeRoy has talked so much about — I lose my way, and by the time I figure out how to get to the coffee shop where Moe and I have arranged to meet, I am twenty-five minutes late. I park near Central Square, jog three blocks to the coffee shop, and arrive out of breath.

At a small table outside the shop's entrance, a very large man — six feet tall and weighing about three hundred pounds, with a round face and small, round, wire-rimmed glasses — a man dressed in a blue and white–striped polo shirt and corn-yellow overalls, a Boston Red Sox baseball cap perched on his head — stands up at once and puts out his hand.

"Jay?" he asks. I shake the man's hand. "Hi! I'm Moe Armstrong and I've been reading your book!" he exclaims. "Let me buy you a cup of coffee and we'll talk, all right?"

I apologize for being late, we get coffee and muffins, begin talking, and we don't stop for the next four hours. We talk in the coffee shop, at a sidewalk table where we stop for another cup of coffee and where Moe exchanges greetings and news with local people (mostly clients from Vinfen programs), on a walk with Moe and his dog, Lulu, to a nearby photocopy store, and on a walk with Moe and Lulu to Moe's home a few blocks away.

In the store, Moe opens his backpack and takes out some six hundred pages of material he has put together for me: newspaper, magazine, and journal articles by Moe and about Moe ("Supported Employment and the Integration of People with Psychiatric Disabilities in the Workplace," "Vietnam Veteran Finally Leaves the Hills—and the War—Behind"), and by and about Vinfen clients with whom he works ("Best of *The Vinfener Newsletter*, 1996"); documents from the Marine Corps, the Veterans Administration, and the *Congressional Record* concerning Moe's wartime heroism and hospitalizations; syllabi, notes, and handouts for courses he teaches ("EXTRA EXTRA EXTRA: Staff Doesn't Have to Burn Out"); autobiographical journals and tales (" 'madman in the madhouse,' by moe"); copies of letters he has sent to newspapers; and—the bulk of what he has brought—his own poems, articles, cartoons, drawings, and illustrated stories.

The illustrations, many in color, are marvelously detailed, and in their charm and playfulness, their quick lines and zaniness, they seem to me a delightful cross of drawings by James Thurber and Dr. Seuss, and I say so. Moe smiles, hands me one of his illustrated "K-Man" stories, "The story of K-Man and the Folks (7th Installment)."

K-Man, a cartoon character like Superman, wears tights, briefs, belt, boots, and cape, and has a large "K" blazoned on his chest.

"The 'K,' " Moe explains, "is for 'Krazy.' "

Like his maker, K-Man has a balding pate, an engaging smile, a round face, and round, wire-rimmed eyeglasses.

"The work of K-Man never ends," the story begins. "Neighbors know the truth. All the ills of society come from Krazy people. All Kriminals are Krazy. All murders are done by Krazy Folks. Get rid of people with a psychiatric condition and life gets better. . . ."

Moe tells me about how K-Man flies into neighborhoods, homes, and hospitals whenever people with mental illness are in trouble. I turn to page 2, and read: "Once Upon a Time, there were people who had a mental illness and they were forgotten and left to wander the streets of America . . . many citizens saw people with psychiatric conditions as the new danger. Enter K-Man!"

Moe talks about the time he got dressed up in a K-Man costume, complete with cape and a large letter "K" on his chest, for a convention of mental health professionals.

"I actually had it worked out for me to drop down through a skylight in the middle of things, onto the main floor, but LeRoy talked me out of it," Moe says. "I was just doing it for fun and to shake things up a little. The trouble with a lot of mental health workers and consumers is that we get too serious and forget to have a good time. I still think it was a good idea. If we don't have a sense of humor, we'll *really* be lost, know what I mean, Jay?"

I say that I do, and smile at the cover page of another of Moe's creations, five self-portraits (Moe as sultan, Moe as a member of the French Foreign Legion, Moe as Indian chief, Moe as Daniel Boone, Moe as Harlequin King) that surround the words on the title page:

GOOFY UNCLE
KRAZY ARTIST

KRAZY ARTIST
GOOFY UNCLE

GOOFY UNCLE
KRAZY ARTIST

GOOFY UNCLE
KRAZY ARTIST

KRAZY ARTIST
GOOFY UNCLE

GOOFY UNCLE
KRAZY ARTIST

Scribbles by
MOE ARMSTRONG
consumer at large
or a large consumer

Moe's spirit and imagination seem at least as large as his physical presence: He is enthusiastic, ebullient, expansive, and, despite his age—fifty-three—and all he has been through, amazingly boyish. His face is broad and innocent, and when he laughs—a deep-throated, rolling, infectious chuckle—I realize why he has seemed so familiar to me, and I make the connection: He is a dead ringer for one of my favorite childhood actors, Andy Devine, who played the comic sidekick to Hopalong Cassidy, Roy Rogers, and others in dozens of cowboy movies.

And I think, too: In his self-portraits, in his drawings, in his poetry, in his sense of humor, in his smile, in his generosity, his energy, his physical grace, his warmth, and his kindness—and in all those manic and depressed hours and days, in all those years of medications, mania, and misery— in everything that has been his life: those small and large moments and incidents that have come to comprise his particular store of innocence and experience, and that show themselves forth in his every word and gesture—he reminds me of Robert.

Although Moe is the same age as Robert, he weighs nearly twice as much, and—given his Midwest childhood, his Vietnam years, his marriages, divorces, and the rest—has had a life very different from Robert's; still, I find myself feeling that I have *known* this man my whole life long, and that, like my brother, he can understand me and Robert in ways few others can.

While we wait for Moe's material to be photocopied, his dog, Lulu, a brown and white mix of Jack Russell terrier and Chihuahua, sits patiently by Moe's feet.

"I really love Lulu," Moe says. "She senses my moods, stays close when she knows I'm starting to get into trouble. She's been a good friend, especially when I'm alone at night, because if I think I hear people moving around in the other rooms of my apartment, I start to get frightened, but if Lulu doesn't bark, I know the sounds and voices are only in my head, and then I feel better."

Moe shows me a flyer he has designed, to give to Vinfen human rights officers, and to Boston and Cambridge police, so that they will act in a more kindly way toward people with mental illnesses. "We tend to shoplift, and to annoy people, or to piss in the streets or in people's yards," Moe says. "But if they put us in jail, it costs the city more than five hundred dollars a night, and that's just a waste of taxpayer money. And it endangers us, too, because we're easy prey there for real criminals.

"We're really harmless and scared for the most part," Moe goes on. "The stuff about dangerous madmen is pure myth. The actual rate of violent crimes among consumers is slightly lower than the national average, and way below the percentages for people with criminal or substance-abuse histories. When you come with me to the residences and clubhouses, you'll see. As a group, especially given all the meds we take, we're about the most frightened, mild-mannered, unthreatening folks you'll ever meet.

"My idea, though, is this: that we should wear medical alert bracelets the way people with diabetes or epilepsy do. There's almost no stigma attached to med bracelets, and that way when a cop has to deal with us, he'll know who we are, and can get us back to our residences, or clinics, or to our case managers, and not be dragging us to court or jail. And think of this, too, Jay—it costs a thousand dollars a night to put us in an emergency psych ward, and we go back again and again, but they won't find a way to pay seventy-five or a hundred dollars for us to talk to somebody once a week or so, to help us stay out of emergency wards."

I notice that on the flyer, Moe has underlined the familiar

words of the Golden Rule (*"Do unto others as you would have them do unto you"*), and I say something about Hillel having written this nearly two thousand years ago, at about the time Christ lived. Moe shakes his head. "Well," he says, "it was a pretty hard sell back then, too."

Moe asks how Robert is doing, and if he is still writing poetry—Moe loved the poems by Robert that I included in *Imagining Robert*—and do I think Robert might like to read some of *his* poems? I say that Robert hasn't written any poems for a while, and yes, I think he'd enjoy receiving some of Moe's poems and stories, and I tell him that Robert hasn't been allowed out of his ward for nearly a year, and that entire years go by when he doesn't hear from anyone other than from me and my children.

Moe shakes his head again, says there are lots of things that would be helpful to Robert, but that constant isolation is surely not one of them. "I've known lots of Roberts," Moe says, and he proceeds to talk about another of his ideas: that hospitals and residences—any place where the Roberts of our world live—hire consumers to be companions to them.

"It could be somebody who's been or still is a mental patient, but who's in a little better shape than Robert—maybe a month or two ahead of him—and who understands him and what he's going through in a way most doctors and staff don't. The consumer could be paid minimum wage, giving *him* some meaningful work, and he could just be in the room with Robert, so Robert wouldn't feel so alone. That way, if Robert wanted to talk with someone, or do something, someone would be there. I mean, how much would it cost, for a few weeks, or a few months, or even longer, compared to the meds and the rest? But they won't pay people to talk with us, and it breaks my heart."

Moe says he has never been one to believe in miracles, but he does think that some of the new medications have worked small wonders for people he knows—Risperdal has been a lifesaver for him, the best medication he's ever been on; it doesn't sedate as much as other drugs do, and his head really stays clear now (Risperdal—generic name, risperidone—is a so-called atypical antipsychotic because it is less likely to cause some of the nasty side effects that accompany conventional antipsychotic medications)—but that medications are only the beginning of what works, or what can work, for people with psychiatric disabilities.

The consumer movement—people with psychiatric disabilities helping other people with psychiatric disabilities—is the other and the more important part of what works, and of what has to happen for things to truly change.

"We are a people with a legitimate condition that needs appropriate care," Moe states. "Easy to get tired. Easy to get hurt. Easy to get confused." He nods to himself, repeats the words as if he is reciting a prayer: "Easy to get tired. Easy to get hurt. Easy to get confused."

Moe adjusts the suspenders on his overalls. "A lot of us dress funny—and I don't know what it is about consumer males, but our pants are always falling down. Maybe we can get a federal grant to figure out why." He laughs. "Bill Murray makes a fortune playing me in movies, you know. And when I go to meetings of all these committees I'm on, the other people look like they work for the FBI. Even the head of one of the big state commissions, who's a friend, when I leave the room—he thinks I can't hear him—but I can still hear him saying to others, 'Why does he have to dress that way?' "

I tell Moe that those are the same words my mother was using about Robert nearly forty years ago. I talk about how distracted, unfocused, and volatile Robert has been lately, and about how, becoming angry and agitated, he keeps losing his privileges and being put on room restrictions.

"ABH and R-and-R," Moe says quickly, and when I say I don't understand, he translates the acronyms: "ABH stands for Anything But Hospital—that's what we say, since no matter what, it's better out here for most of us because in there it's always R-and-R: Rules and Regulations." He pauses. "BFSP," he adds. "Big Fucking Social Planners. They're everywhere, and they still run things, and they're trying to make Robert into someone he's not, see. They won't let Robert be Robert."

Moe takes my arm, his voice suddenly bright with enthusiasm. "But what I was thinking when I read your book," he says, "was that the thing to do for Robert would be to have him join a consumer vaudeville company. What do you think, Jay?"

Moe says there is already a consumer band called Tunefoolery that plays at day centers, clubhouses, and residences, and is starting to get gigs in regular Boston and Cambridge clubs. Moe quotes some of Robert's one-liners, from *Imagining Robert,* and when he does, I tell him that the previous week Robert was complaining about how awful and Pavlovian things were on his ward. Then Robert had paused, and asked if I knew what Pavlov once said.

No, I had said. What did Pavlov once say?

"Well," Robert answered. "What Pavlov once said was that if you give a dog a bone, the next thing you know he'll want the whole hand."

Moe laughs, says he thinks Robert would do really well as a stand-up consumer comedian. "He could go from residence to residence, entertaining consumers," Moe says. "I know at least forty residences where Robert could perform. We could build him his own set, and he could do song-and-dance routines, develop new routines, make friends, and get to know lots of people. I mean, what would it cost to design a program specifically for Robert?"

I say that I marvel at Robert's ability, given all the years, hospitals, and medications, to still have a sense of humor about his situation—to be ironic and funny about the very things that have been the source of his misery—and that this gives me hope, makes me believe there's still an enormous well of resiliency in him.

"Oh yes," Moe says. "I agree. I just think Robert's had a lot of bad luck, like most people with mental illness. I know hundreds of Roberts. I see them every day. And I know lots of Roberts who are out here now, with you and me, and doing better. But it takes a lot of work—a lot of one-on-one work—and a lot of dedication, and society doesn't want to pay for that."

Moe talks about people he has known who were on back wards of the worst state hospitals for years—men and women who were cruelly abused: beaten, raped, sodomized, drugged to the gills, and left to live in their own feces—but who have gotten out and have made new lives for themselves. He tells me about one man who was considered the craziest guy in the system out in New Mexico, locked away and on isolation the way Robert is. The doctors had declared him hopeless, but Moe met the man, negotiated with the hospital, and received permission to move in with him for a while.

"He weighed about three hundred and fifty pounds then, and had the med team terrorized—they were afraid he would pop somebody—but I just lay on the floor next to him. He was a broken man, and I opened my heart to him, and we wept together.

"That man has been out for a long time now, and has a job, and if you would see him passing by, you would never suspect the life he once had."

Moe talks more about Robert—about looking into possibilities for him in Boston, and through Vinfen, and then he is quiet for a few seconds. When he speaks again, he speaks more slowly, his words evenly spaced, as if rehearsed.

"I believe we are a people with a history," he says. "I believe we are a people with a history the same way other peoples are, and that we are a resource to the world, and because this is so—because our lives and our brains work differently from those of so-called normal people, we can enlighten others about the human mind and the human condition.

"I believe that we consumers who are learning to deal with our condition are pioneers, Jay. Sometimes I don't have a lot of optimism about what's going to happen for us in *my* lifetime, but I believe that the work we are doing now is going to help the next generation to change."

Moe also says that he is not one of those advocates who believes that the best thing that can happen to people with mental illness is to be mainstreamed — medicated, educated, rehabilitated, and given special consideration so they can be like everybody else. Most of the time, mainstreaming is just the state's way to save on services, he believes, and he talks about a passage in *Imagining Robert* where I write, concerning a group of Robert's friends at South Beach Hospital, that there seems to be something strangely and unnaturally *child-like* about them.

"You were right about us, and most people don't see this, or want to admit it," Moe says. "But there's no shame in having a psychiatric condition or caring for another person who has one.

"Take away shame, and anything's possible," Moe states. "So I go out into the world and I say, 'This is who I am — and I am not like you, and to try to make me like you is not only unethical, but it is foolish. It won't work.'

"What we have to do," Moe insists, "is to see each consumer — and I *hate* that word, but we don't have anything better yet — to see each of us as an individual. I believe that for most of us, having a psychiatric disorder is going to require low-cost lifetime maintenance, the way diabetes and other chronic conditions do. These are conditions that are not going to go away and we need to start out by assuming they'll need to be managed with all their ups and downs for our entire lives. And that's why we have to individualize the program and treatment for each individual.

"There is no such thing as *a* schizophrenic or *a* manic-depressive or *a* borderline," Moe says. "We're each different, and our problems each need different solutions. Otherwise, it's like trying to put square pegs into round holes."

Moe stops. "And what if I'm a hexagon?" he asks. "A lot of us are hexagons, you know."

Before I leave Cambridge, we go to Moe's house, where I meet Naomi and Sano. Naomi, who has three daughters from an early marriage — Sano, at twenty-three, is her youngest — is director of a Vinfen residence in which twenty people with psychiatric disabilities live in their own apartments. Naomi was a street person—homeless—by the age of fourteen, and, like Moe, was addicted to hard drugs. For many years she was hospitalized for schizophrenia; when she was thirty-six years old, she returned to college, and earned a B.S. in psychology. She tells me she has begun reading my book, but that she is going slowly because it is very painful, reminding her of her own hospitalizations, and of friends who, like Robert, never made it back out into the world.

When I say something to her about Moe telling me he has begun losing weight, she rolls her eyes. "I think he's hallucinating again," she says.

Naomi and I talk about her work at the Vinfen residence—Moe says I will be amazed at the people there, many of whom have been hospitalized for at least as long as Robert has, and who are now living on their own—and I tell her about some of what Moe and I have been talking about. She smiles. "Moe is very attached to his opinions," she says.

Moe shows me Naomi's bedroom, which, neatly and warmly furnished, looks like a guest room in a New England bed-and-breakfast, and he tells me that Naomi likes "low stimulation," but that he needs to be able to get things when he wants them.

We go into Moe's room, and it is bursting with books, papers, computers, phones, a fax machine, stuffed animals, comic books, sports equipment and memorabilia, model cars and planes and trucks. The walls are papered with drawings, letters, photos, and newspaper clippings. A cloth patch—the insignia of the 3rd Reconnaissance Battalion, a skull and crossbones at its center above the battalion's motto (*Swift, Silent, Deadly*)—is pinned to the doorjamb, below medals and ribbons. Moe's bed, a mattress covered with a patchwork quilt, is on the floor, and he steps across it to get to more of his drawings, including one he wants me to give to Robert.

"I like being surrounded by everything," Moe says. "It makes me feel good to be able to touch things, to have information literally at my fingertips." He lifts two toy tractors from a shelf. "I wanted to be a farmer, so I have tractors too, but just a few of them."

The drawing Moe picks for Robert is of a large orange, brown, and purple donut, drawn in crayon, surrounded by a prose poem, the words in neatly penciled script: "DO NUT my DO NUT," it begins, and ends: "I walked home romantic remembering other times and other places I had stayed up eating Do Nuts."

When I ask Moe if he has any sense of what it was, other than his Vietnam experience, that brought on his condition, he says that when he was growing up, he always heard voices—"A kind of rustling sound, like the wind, or like people whispering"—but that he couldn't make out the words. He saw things, too: a cat crossing the room, say, when there was no cat in the house, or roaches crawling on the floor when there were none. He says that most consumers he knows can recall exactly what happened the first time they broke—that it's probably like reliving a car accident would be for other people, the way everything is slower and clearer.

He talks about his breakdown in Vietnam, about how he was a medic there and told his commanding officer that he thought he could save the lives of some Viet cong prisoners who had surrendered, but that his commanding officer told him they were "just gooks," and to let them die.

"By this time I'd been in combat for over a year," Moe says, "when I should have only been in combat for six months and located out. We were special soldiers, like the Green Berets, and people kind of left us alone. We would just live on the beach for a while, and then we would go on these long-range patrols and stay out in the bush for two or three months at a time.

"It's funny to think about it, but what we were trained for mostly was to *not* crack up under any kind of condition, whether it was mountain climbing or prisoner-of-war school. We were trained to have incredible mental fortitude, and to be mavericks. I once spent four days and nights without food and water there, with a half-dozen other guys I was on patrol with. We were caught in an ambush and retreated to this mountaintop, and had no food or water—our lips and tongues were cracked and bleeding and the Vietcong were all around us, and we thought we were goners. We survived by licking the dew off leaves in the morning."

Moe laughs, pats his stomach. "I haven't stopped eating since!" he exclaims, and begins showing me how he stashes boxes and cans of food everywhere, and always has wherever he has lived. "I went to scuba school in Okinawa," he says, "and I learned Vietnamese there—I was the only one in my unit who could speak it—and I'd been in the Marine Corps for three years before I broke, doing all this recon work, with rubber boats, and jumping off submarines.

"But when I broke, after the prisoners died, I just started crying and I couldn't stop. I kept breaking down and I had this weird vertigo where I kept getting dizzy, and I had anxiety off the scale, and it was like my life was a nightmare of restlessness and agitation, and I kept taking showers, you know— eight or ten or twelve a day—it was the only way I could figure to cool out. And I kept hearing this rushing sound in my head, like the wind whispering to me, *all* the time.

"And I scared people because I was so out of control. The time I recall most of all was just before they decided to evacuate me. I came in from patrol, and I was packed with a grenade launcher, six grenades, and a submachine gun, and I just kept crying and saying things—crazy things—and the guys in my unit were around a campfire, and I noticed them get up one by one, very slowly, and leave. I could have done anything—taken my own life, or killed all of them. I was really destroyed. I was trembling and shaking, and I just couldn't stop crying. I cried for days and days because I couldn't save lives, all the way to the hospital in Da Nang, and then to Oakland, where they put me on a lot of medications, Thorazine and other stuff."

When I ask him how much he thinks his condition in the years since came from his Vietnam experience, and how much was in him—how much, in the usual way of putting it, was nature and how much resulted from nurture—Moe says that he thinks some people have a genetic predisposition to a psychiatric condition the way he has, that there is definitely a biochemical basis for it.

If he hadn't gone to Vietnam, does he think something else would have set off whatever genetic predisposition he had for a psychiatric condition?

"It's hard to say," Moe answers. "Hard to say. I don't know. I don't really know. Sometimes I think I might have had a better chance if I hadn't gone through all that in the Marine Corps. But it's hard to say."

We talk about research that is beginning to show that what is now called "post-traumatic stress disorder" (PTSD)—what used to be called "shell shock" or "battle exhaustion"—actually changes the structure and functioning of the brain, and how laboratory studies have shown that these traumatic experiences produce lasting alterations in the endocrine, autonomic, and central nervous systems.

We talk about articles and books we've read, especially those by Bessell A. van der Kolk, that are persuasive concerning the ways in which PTSD can result in permanent neuronal changes that have decidedly negative and long-term effects on learning, habituation, and stimulus discrimination, and that these effects, which are *not* inborn, can be shown to derive from specific ways traumatic experiences act on the cerebral cortex and the limbic system.

Studies of men and women who have suffered traumatic war experiences, or sexual abuse, seem to confirm that these people are out of touch with their feelings because the parts of the central nervous system necessary for being *in touch* with one's feelings have been significantly altered and impaired. Thus, for example, people with PTSD, when compared to matched controls, have decreased hippocampal volumes and increased serotonin levels, which may help account for their increased impulsivity and aggression, their ongoing dissociation, and their inability to interpret new, threatening experiences realistically. In victims of severe trauma, it seems, what often presents itself as uncontrollable, dangerous, and inexplicable hostility, and a puzzling, long-lasting inability to learn from or evaluate experience — or to integrate one's memories into an ongoing life the way most of us do — appears to have a psychobiological basis that derives from the traumatic experience itself.

And if negative experiences can act upon us in such ways, I speculate, why shouldn't positive experiences be able to act upon us in different and opposite ways, not merely to reverse negative effects, but to *enhance* our lives? Although it is hard to imagine joyful experiences that are the equivalent in intensity and effect of severe trauma, we do know that intense religious experiences, for example, or intensely happy experiences (falling in love, bearing a child) can radically transform our feelings, and our sense of who we are.

Perhaps, I suggest, the positive equivalent for trauma is not joy or ecstasy — or great good luck — but the sustained retraining of feelings. In my own life, the many years of work I put in in an analytic therapy, not only learning new ways to cope, but slowly retraining feelings that had seemed impervious to change or even to modification, enabled me to alter essential elements of my behavior so that new ways of feeling and being gradually became natural for me, and I became, to my surprise, a quite different and much happier person than I had been.

During these years, I tell Moe, I used to feel, going to and from my therapist's office, very much the way I feel most mornings when I approach my desk to work on a story or novel — apprehensive, eager, expectant — unsure of what is going to happen yet happy, mostly, for the chance to get on with the work itself: discovering, making, and remaking myself — my life, my stories — out of memories, desires, imaginings, and emotions that often seem as terrifying, wonderful, and confusing as they are new. Best of all, I say — this was especially true once the initial work in therapy was done; once, that is, I had dealt with the violent impulses and suicidal feelings that had first brought me there — was the sense, throughout the working through, that I never really knew, as in any good story, what was going to happen next.

"I think most psychiatric conditions are about twenty percent biological and about eighty percent life," Moe says. "I still hear things and see things, but I've learned to cope and to live with them. Medications help, though I think the doctors usually prescribe them way too high."

Moe tells me that he is on 2 milligrams of Risperdal a day; the doctors originally started him on 3 milligrams—and he talks about other medications and of dosages, much lower than those usually prescribed, that can be used to maintain most consumers.

I offer an analogy I have sometimes used—that medications for psychiatric disorders can be compared to bandages for badly sprained ankles: Bandages can stabilize our ankles and allow us to walk, run, and get on with our lives. But once the ankle is stabilized, more important questions arise: Where do you want to go, and how will you get there, and when you get there—whatever "there" may be—what will you do, and what will you *want* to do? And what about the fear that once you start moving, the bandage may not hold? What about the fear that the ankle is not merely sprained, but diseased, and that the source of the disease will infect the rest of your body—and your soul—and that the condition is fatal and beyond help? What about the fear of having disability, pain, helplessness, and terror return, again and again?

Once, that is, one's head is cleared of confusion, delusion, depression, mania, or hallucinations, what does one do *then*? Robert might feel fine on some new medication, but if one evening he *does* suddenly feel clearheaded and healthy, and gets a good night's sleep, what does he do the next morning? What does he do about a place to live, and about getting meals regularly, and about managing his finances, and about a job and school and friends and health care and dental care—about an ongoing life that has been, for years, nonexistent for him?

And if, say, Robert, or somebody with a history like Robert's, wants to look for work or for a new place to live, what does he tell prospective employers or prospective housemates—or friends—about his hospitalizations, his medications, his breakdowns, the missing days and months and years of his life?

"Everybody's so worried about dependency on the system," Moe says, "but what I'm worried about is that there's too many people being left without care. I see more people who are being left without care than I see people who have a dependency on the system." He shrugs. "From what I've seen, I think people always go for the least dependency possible—if they're able to go there.

"And what's wrong with caring? I think we have to sit down and ask—what's actually wrong with caring for somebody for their entire life? I mean, we're talking about sending people to Mars and we can't even care for each other while we're here on this planet.

"For example, there should be courses for staff members on how to eat with us," Moe suggests. "Simple things like that can make a difference for people like Robert. It shouldn't be *them* and *us* all the time. That way, which is the way it is most places, we always think of our differences as being something *wrong* with us, so that we wind up believing what others believe: that we're freaks and moral failures somehow—outcasts who should remain outcasts."

Moe talks about Vinfen being ahead of the national curve in making the hiring of consumers a priority, and he talks about how much more economical it can be for the society at large to actually involve consumers—to ask them what they want and need, and to work with them.

"You can avoid a lot of mistakes if you simply talk with people," Moe says. "You can increase levels of understanding, and—for starters—find out what triggers their breaks by asking them what *they* think helps, and what they *know* sets them off. That way you can avoid a lot of things that bring on breakdowns and lengthy hospitalizations."

Moe talks about the difference it can make in the workplace for mental health professionals to work side by side with consumers. And yet all across America, most state departments of mental health, most managed care companies, most mental hospitals, and most community mental health centers do not employ consumers. This, Moe says, is insanity.

"I mean, can you imagine a women's rights organization that employed only men—or a black rights organization that employed no blacks?"

He tells me that at the Dimock Community Health Center in Boston, where he teaches courses for students who will be working in hospitals, residences, and day treatment centers, Moe is the only teacher who ever brings consumers to class with him.

Moe gives me a copy of an eleven-page handout he has prepared for his class:

THE MAD AMONG US
A HISTORY OF THE CARE OF AMERICA'S MENTALLY ILL

by Gerald N. Grob

A Condensed Version

by Moe Armstrong

I have read Gerald Grob's book, and Moe and I talk for a while about it and about the history of mental hospitals in America. For all the shortcomings and horrors of state mental hospitals, Grob reminds us that in these hospitals, *comprehensive* care and treatment (food, shelter, medication, therapy, rehabilitation) were provided for residents in a single setting, and that substantial numbers of individuals did improve and recover. Once the hospitals began discharging people to the streets and the community, however—the process usually known as deinstitutionalization, which began in the mid-sixties—the previously unbreakable ties between care and treatment were systematically and cruelly severed.

Individuals like Moe and my brother were often sent into communities that were not prepared for them, and that they were not prepared for. Millions of people with severe, long-term psychiatric disorders, temporarily stabilized by being sedated on antipsychotic drugs such as Thorazine, Haldol, and lithium, were released into the world without plans, pre-

scriptions, or destinations, so that the fragmented nature of
the care and treatment that ensued, if there was *any* care and
treatment—the almost total lack of planning, along with the
assumption based upon the untested theory that life in the
community would somehow be better for these individuals
than life in the hospital—made what was called community
mental health not only a misnomer, but a national tragedy.

In addition, the money did not follow the patients; the
largest part of state and federal funding for mental illness
remained tied to state hospitals when the largest percentage
of those needing services for mental illness were no longer
living in these hospitals. (For example, in the 1950s, New
York State had eighteen state hospitals for 93,000 patients;
in 1990, it maintained twenty-two state hospitals for 12,000
patients, yet was still spending more than two thirds of its
mental-health budget on these hospitals, even though the
vast majority of people with mental illnesses were living—or
trying to live—in the community.)

People can talk all they want about new ideas and new
medications, Moe says, but in the long run nothing except
dedicated people working individually with consumers, and
committed to working with them for as long as it takes, is
going to do the job. There are no easy answers, no quick
fixes, no single programs or pills that are going to work for
all people. But once you understand this—once you give up
the illusion of *cure*—all kinds of amazing things can happen.

And we can learn a lot from studying the past, Moe says,
as he has from reading Grob's books. "Society has never
done especially well in caring for those it considered mad,"
Moe remarks, and he scoffs at New Age romantic tales about
madmen in other cultures being revered as shamans, vision-
aries, holy fools, and the like.

Here and there, we know, some societies, in some times
and places, have tolerated the mad more than they have in
other times and places. And here and there, as in our own
country, when we have treated them as fellow human beings,
and not as pariahs, we have done a little bit better.

State "lunatic" asylums in the middle of the nineteenth century, for example, their funding and programs inspired by the work of Dorothea Dix, Horace Mann, Charles Sumner, and others, were created on the assumption that intervention could make a difference, and that people could get well, and, even without modern medications and technology, a lot of them did—probably as high a percentage as in the large state (and small private) institutions in the first part of the twentieth century—and this was because, Moe believes, people *cared*, and they cared within a setting whose scale was human.

"Kindness," Moe says, "makes a difference."

Early-nineteenth-century asylums in the United States were usually limited to 250 patients, each of whom had his or her own private room. One of the first such hospitals—where Gerald Grob began his research—was opened in 1833 in Worcester, Massachusetts, less than an hour equidistant from Moe and me. Such asylums were run by directors who had full authority over inmates and staff, who regarded patients as their children, and who ate with them and lived with them, treating them according to principles of what was then called "moral treatment"—principles initially espoused by Philippe Pinel, in France, in the late eighteenth century, when he liberated patients from their dungeons and chains.

Pinel and others believed that the major cause for madness lay not in madness itself but in the barbarous forms of treatment inflicted on the mad. They believed that all individuals, no matter how insane, had the potential for health and redemption. Patients were regarded as dangerous or childlike objects who could be manipulated through their passions, and by the doctor's force of character—nurtured with kindness, firmness, and coercion; or tricked and lied to—and whose evil ideas and dissolute habits could be replaced by good ideas and good habits.

In 1851, and again in 1853, the Association of Medical Superintendents of American Institutions for the Insane adopted resolutions recommending that the maximum populations of its hospitals not exceed 250, with a maximum of

200 the preferred figure. Overly large hospitals were deemed incompatible with moral treatment.

Until well into this century, Moe notes, virtually the only work that psychiatrists ever did was with individuals suffering from severe mental illness. A psychiatrist was defined as a doctor who worked with madmen, and in the medical profession he was as highly regarded as a surgeon or an internist. On the eve of World War Two, more than two thirds of all American psychiatrists were still working in state mental hospitals. It was only when psychiatrists began treating the rest of us—the so-called walking wounded—outside of mental-institutions, Moe points out, that their status, both in thedical profession and with the general public, began to decline.

He shows me one of his own poems, inspired in part by Gerald Grob's book:

WE ARE THE PSYCHIATRIC DIASPORA
A History

Never,
thought of
as a people

Diaspora,
left to wander
unknown,
misunderstood

Our condition
told to us,

Rather
than,
understand
who we are

The
human condition
and our condition

Understanding
one from the other

People didn't
ask questions

We were
social problem

When
personal
social
breakdowns
are part of
all civilizations

Then
recovery for us,
can someday
be recovery,
for others

People in
recovery,
might also be
part of new,
human service
system process

Getting others
across
to recovery.

What happened
to us
can happen to you

Can happen
to others

We have been
around for
centuries

We are a people,
people with a
psychiatric condition.

We have a legitimate condition,
which needs appropriate care.

When I leave, to head back to Northampton, Moe walks me downstairs, gives me a hug, tells me to say hi to Robert when I see him. "I hope I can meet him some day," he says.

I thank Moe for spending time with me, we talk about my returning to Boston so I can visit some of Vinfen's programs, and I say something, too, about the good work Moe is doing with consumers. Moe shrugs away my praise.

"Caring for a person with mental illness is an honor," he says.

Moe stands next to my car, and as I pull away from the curb, he waves to me and, smiling broadly, he calls out, in words I recognize as the same words he has used to say good-bye when we have talked by phone: "See ya later, Jay!"

THREE

TRAVELS WITH MOE

The soft hairs on the back of his neck
are the roots of his eyes.

His curly hair is
the sequel to his dreams.

His forehead: a sail; his arms: cars
to carry the soul inside his body to Jerusalem.

But in the white fist of his brain
he holds the black seeds of his happy childhood.

When he reaches the beloved, bone-dry land—
he will sow.

> —YEHUDA AMICHAI,
> "Yehuda Ha-Levi"

Like civil rights workers I knew in the sixties, Moe has chosen to try to help others make their way out of the grim conditions that inform and define their lives in ways comparable to conditions that once informed and defined his, and as we go around Boston together, visiting programs and residences, it occurs to me that he has experienced not only the miseries and ravages of mental illness, but many of the worldly irritations that usually come with it: stigma, discrimination, and humiliation.

This comes home to me when, in the city in which I live, Northampton, Massachusetts, there are front-page stories in the local newspaper because a group of townspeople is demanding that the city stop a local human service organization, ServiceNet, from renovating a deterioriating building under a $600,000 Department of Housing and Urban Development (HUD) grant so that the building can be made into six one-bedroom apartments for people with psychiatric disabilities.

"News that the grant will be used to buy and renovate the house for use by mentally ill people has inflamed some neighbors," the *Daily Hampshire Gazette* reports.

> Neighbors are so angry they are organizing a property tax strike, according to Maria Tymoczko, city councilor for Ward 3. . . . They say their neighorhood is over-burdened with programs designed to help people with a variety of problems. . . . "People are really riled up about this. I've never seen the neighbors so upset since the 1977 rock concert," Tymoczko said.

"My neighborhood and ward feels betrayed by the city," Maria Tymoczko says at a city council meeting. Social programs, says another woman from Ward 3, must not be allowed "to come in and basically rape a neighborhood."

"It's simply not something we want to have in our neighborhood," declares another resident, a man who has consulted a lawyer about putting his taxes in escrow until he is assured the apartments will not be built.

Residents of Ward 3 form a committee (3-For-All), raise funds, hire a lawyer, file a complaint in Superior Court against the Zoning Board of Appeals, meet with their U.S. congressional representative's staff, and publish a newsletter (GREETINGS TO OUR FRIENDS AND NEIGHBORS IN WARD 3

FROM 3-FOR-ALL). A short while after this, a representative of HUD contacts ServiceNet to inform them that HUD is "having second thoughts" about the suitability of the building for use as a group residence.

"The 'case' against group homes and other community programs often includes a discussion of decreases in property values and increases in crime rates," Susan Stubbs, CEO of ServiceNet, tells the city council. "Several studies have examined the relationship between the opening of group homes and subsequent property values and crime rates. No change in either has been found to exist. However, if we were [really] interested in reducing violent crime rates, we should restrict the number of unmarried males under the age of 25 who are allowed to live in that community. We should be talking about the concentration of that group — not about mentally ill people who, as a group, have little or no correlation with violent crimes."

Stubbs goes on to make some basic points: about the ways in which the Fair Housing Amendments Act of 1988 protects people with physical and mental handicaps, as well as handicapped people in group homes, from discrimination in housing; and about the fact that the law states that only the people themselves have the right to determine who knows about their handicaps.

"To be completely honest," Stubbs says, "we have learned from our own experience, and from a growing body of research, that the less communications, community meetings, coffees, etc. that happen before a group home opens, the greater the acceptance and comfort level of the neighbors later. Simply put, people's fears are quickly put to rest when they find that homeless people and people with mental disabilities are just people."

Northampton is a thriving New England college town of thirty thousand, home to Smith College and located in the Connecticut River Valley, a few miles from four other colleges: Amherst, Hampshire, Mount Holyoke, and the University of Massachusetts. I consider writing a letter to the local newspaper, protesting the concentration of professors in my section of town, and the ways in which their presence diminishes the quality of my life, but decide that my antic impulse would diminish the seriousness, and sadness, of what is happening.

The resistance of communities to having people with mental illness move into their neighborhoods is hardly news. Virtually every attempt in the United States to set up a halfway house, supervised residence, supported apartment program, or group home for people with mental disabilities has met with protest and resistance, and the resistance has often been mean-spirited, vindictive, and successful.

In *9 Highland Road*, an account of the attempt in 1987 to open a group home for a dozen individuals with mental illness in Glen Cove, New York, Michael Winerip points out that in the early 1980s not a single group home for people with mental illness existed in all of suburban Long Island. In 1975, according to Winerip, there were only 209 group homes for people with mental illness in the entire country. By the late 1980s, however, there were more than 700 in New York State alone, and as only one indication of community hostility to these homes, Winerip notes that during the late eighties and early nineties, six group homes on Long Island were firebombed.

Susan Stubbs is aware that some areas of towns and cities frequently house more social programs than others, and that, from the point of view of people and businesses in these areas — especially when it is the state that places the programs there, as it did between the years 1978 and 1992 during the closing down of Northampton State Hospital and the discharge of its more than two thousand patients to the nursing homes and streets of Northampton and neighboring towns — such placement of programs can seem unfair.

"It is a fact," she says, "that both poor people and handicapped people often cluster in the downtown areas of our small cities and towns across the country, where housing is affordable and public transportation is accessible."

She, and many of her clientele, might wish that other neighborhoods of Northampton were as affordable and accessible as Ward 3, but they are not, and therefore she suggests that the town "stop our conversation about concentration and saturation, and that we cease the exercise of counting and charting where stigmatized people live" and "shift our conversation from exclusion to inclusion.

"Think of how mortified you would feel if someone in our community was counting and charting where gay people or African Americans or AIDS patients were living," she says. (Northampton has a large gay and lesbian community; in 1995, in an article titled "A Town Like No Other," *Newsweek* named Northampton "Lesbianville, USA.") "Would we be talking about saturation? Would we be saying 'My ward has too many gay people; your ward doesn't have enough [so] let's have a moratorium on allowing gays to move into Ward 3?' "

I follow the arguments and comments, and they often sound almost identical to those I heard thirty years ago when middle-class whites were resisting the movement of black Americans into their neighborhoods. I remember hearing whites say "they had nothing against blacks," of course, but "why didn't they live somewhere else—with their own kind?" I also remember hearing whites say they were all for civil rights, but weren't blacks "going too far?" I remember hearing whites claim they objected to blacks moving into their neighborhoods for "practical" reasons only: because the presence of blacks in their communities would lower property values, or hurt business, or endanger their children.

When it came to enacting and enforcing laws that would allow blacks to vote, live, work, and go to school where they wanted, the usual argument for denying them equal rights, especially loud during the presidential campaign of 1964, from the Barry Goldwater camp and its followers, was that one couldn't and shouldn't "legislate morality," or "go against human nature."

"First," Goldwater was fond of saying, in defense of retaining laws designed to preserve segregation, "we must change the hearts of men."

First we must change the hearts of men? Good luck! I think. But, as I said then, and as I find myself saying again when I hear people in my town talk about not wanting *them* living near *us*, I agree. You probably can't change human nature, and we probably shouldn't try to legislate morality. Which is precisely why we must have and enforce laws that protect minorities, especially those who are most vulnerable, since the majority protects itself by virtue of being the majority. People will doubtless continue, as they have for millennia, to mistrust, fear, stigmatize, castigate, humiliate, abuse, imprison, ostracize, exile, demean, and kill those who are different simply because they are different, whether that difference shows itself in skin color, in accent, in ethnicity, in religious practice, or in behavior.

Doubtless, too, they will continue to hold to, and to purvey, erroneous and harmful stereotypes of people unlike themselves, as they do toward individuals with psychiatric disorders. According to all epidemiological studies, however, it turns out that the vast majority of people with mental illness, including those with the most severe disorders, are neither dangerous nor violent. Whether studies look at assaults within hospitals, posthospitalization arrests, or self-reports of aggressive acts, most come up with the same results: Violent or dangerous behavior occurs in only about 10 to 12 percent or less of those diagnosed as having a mental illness, or about the same percentage as exists in the general population.

Following the July 1998 killing of two Capitol police officers in Washington, D.C., and responding to appeals by E. Fuller Torrey and others for greater use of involuntary commitment and involuntary (forced) medication of those people with mental illnesses determined (but by whom?) to be likely to be violent, Dr. Charles Lidz, a professor at the University of Massachusetts Medical School, in a letter to *The New York Times*, noted that "several recent studies have shown that among people with mental illness, people with schizophrenia are the least likely to be violent."

Moreover, a July 28, 1998, front-page *New York Times* article reported that according to a MacArthur Foundation study, "the only major empirical effort made to assess whether or not people with mental illness are more likely to be violent than the rest of the population found that they were not."

"Schizophrenia," Dr. Lidz concluded, "is a terrible disease that afflicts several million Americans. Occasionally it contributes to a tragedy like the one last week in the Capitol. But it would be a greater tragedy if we allowed this incident to tar all the people who suffer from this disease with the brush of violence."

Given that epidemiological studies demonstrate that at least one out of every four Americans will experience a diagnosable psychiatric disorder in the course of a lifetime, and given the emotional, social, and economic stresses that permeate the lives of people with mental illness, the fact that nine out of ten individuals with severe mental illness are neither violent, dangerous, nor criminal, seems remarkable.

Nonetheless, consider this: A seventeen-year exhaustive study of television content revealed the fact that 72 percent of characters labeled "mentally ill" in prime-time dramas were portayed as violent, and that 22 percent of those labeled "mentally ill" killed someone. Even women characters, much less likely to be violent than men in prime-time TV, were found to be violent 60 percent of the time if labeled "mentally ill," and to be killers 17 percent of the time, thus (as one researcher noted) making mental illness "the only label in the world of television that renders women as violent as men."

I recall working in New York City in the sixties for a fair housing organization. After a black man of roughly my age and situation was refused a rental, I would apply to rent the same apartment, and would usually be offered it. I would then work with the fair housing organization, not to take the landlord to court but to pressure him to open his building to people of color who wanted and could afford to live there.

If, in the supposedly most liberal and enlightened city in our nation, middle- and upper-class people of means were being discriminated against in such ways, what else did one need to know about how deep the streams of racism ran? And if, in a thriving, progressive, New England college town, citizens are willing to take extreme actions to stop a half-dozen individuals with histories of mental illness from living in a state-of-the-art, newly renovated, carefully supervised residence (a building known as a haven for prostitutes and drug dealers), what else did one need to know about how deep the streams of fear, prejudice, and hostility toward people like Moe and my brother ran?

Or, in an even more dramatic example, consider: If the Utah state mental hospital still, after twenty-five years, sponsors a Halloween celebration each year by creating a haunted house at the state mental hospital in which the residents are featured as star attractions, what else do we need to know about how deep and profoundly ignorant general attitudes toward people with mental illness are? (When NAMI protested this Halloween "celebration," in 1997, a spokeswoman for the governor's office said that "concerns were raised that deserve serious review and state officials will be asked to investigate.")

"I was fifteen years old when I hooked up with the mental health system," Rose Tompkins tells me when we meet in Boston in early January 1997. "And I'm forty-six years old now—that's thirty years in and out of the system—and today is a really big day for me because I'm being accepted into a master's degree program so I can become a rehabilitation counselor."

Rose is a very pretty and very heavy black woman, with a round, open face, an engaging smile, and large, penetrating, light brown eyes. She wears a bright red sweater, purple stretch pants, new white New Balance sneakers, large silver hoop earrings, and a blue turquoise pendant necklace; her hair is set in a short Afro, and despite her weight—just over three hundred pounds—she carries herself in such a way that though my initial guess at her height is correct—five feet three—my estimate of her weight turns out to be nearly a hundred pounds too low.

Rose was born in Birmingham, Alabama, the next oldest of seven children (she has five brothers, one sister), and moved to the Boston area when she was six. She attended public schools in Alabama and Boston, and graduated with a B.A. from Tufts University. Rose has been diagnosed as having unipolar (major) depression, and MPD (multiple personality disorder); she has been hospitalized more than sixty times for mental illness, is on several psychiatric medications, and sees a therapist once a week.

"For someone like me, having a life is an on-again off-again proposition," Rose tells me. "A lot of people think it's magic when someone like me gets well, but I can't rely on the magic to rescue me. What *works?* Having people in your life who know that when things get bad for you, it's just a pit stop. All my life I used to think there'd be some 'Aha!' moment, when everything would be clear, and that after that all would be well.

"But what I've been finding out is that there is no 'Aha!' moment, and that life is a process, not an event. People like to think they know what's wrong with me—doctors, that they know more about me than I do—but *I'm* the real expert on me.

"Now, my sister, she watched *60 Minutes* one time and she thought she found out why I get depressed. She told me it's because I have a biochemical condition in my brain which only a chemical can correct. So I said to her that maybe I have an imbalance in my head because I was hit over the head so many times!

"I was beaten up, sexually abused, and mistreated so many times I came to think the real beginning of saving my own life was when I refused to *go* back home. My father would abuse me, and then give me money." She stops, is quiet for a few seconds. "Maybe that's why I let Larry Kohn handle my money for me still," she says. And then: "I got pregnant by him—my father—when I was thirteen. I didn't even know what it was going on inside me, and I slept for two weeks and almost died. The problem is, how do you tell the truth about a person you love who has done wicked things to you and you still love him?

"I also had a ruptured appendix, and nearly died from that. I learned to be hypervigilant in my family, and then I took that attitude out into the world. And I had all my 'alters' too, to protect me. I consider them a gift from God. Believing in God had another side to it too, though, because for years and years it kept me from being angry at anyone but myself.

"When I get sick, and I'm in the hospital, my mother won't visit me. 'If you had a *real* sickness, we'd visit you,' she says. But I think people are afraid of that old mind-body split because all of us, we *all* have these demons, only what I think madness is, is they act out more in *some* of us.

"I have different pictures in my head of things that happened to me, like snapshots. But what made the difference? The difference was people. That's what kept me going. There was this minister and his wife, the parents in a halfway house called The Canterbury House, and they made the big difference in my early years. I didn't like them at first—I was about fourteen—because they had southern accents, so I thought they were prejudiced. But no matter what I did, they kept being nice to me, and they said two important things. Mr. Woodson, he said, 'Just get your ducks in a row, and don't foul yourself up,' and Mrs. Woodson taught me to follow the road that would make my dreams come true. You have to have your dreams, she taught me, because even though you can't see them out here, they're what keep you going.

"They had a house on Cape Cod, and they would take me there with them on weekends, and sometimes, after the halfway house, if I got upset or if I just needed to leave where I was—if I was at school, or whatever—they had an open-door policy with me, and took me in as if I was their child.

"It was quite an experience, to have somebody really *care* about you. This was happening when I had been in Boston State Hospital for two years, and I refused to go home because my father was still there. The danger from him didn't stop until I went to the hospital, but that was the last time I felt danger of that kind.

"I don't really know how early it all started. I have this picture in my mind, though, this one time I was doing dishes and my father came in. He locked the back door and a glass slipped out of my hand and I was so terrified of him that when I saw the glass dispersing everywhere I thought all these other selves were coming out of it, onto the floor—they were my 'alters,' you see, and that was my way of protecting myself, of asking for help. I don't know if I had multiple personality before then, but that was the first time that, in my consciousness now, I can remember them being there to help me."

Rose smiles. "Except for the tea parties," she says. "I used to always have these tea parties, and everybody at the tea parties was my 'alters'—Sandra, and Grace, and Sarah, and the Girl in the Gray Overcoat—she's *very* intellectual—and The Boy—that's what I call him, The Boy—and Sheila, and Peaches, about six or seven of us, and somebody I call *Me*, with a capital 'M,' and we were getting the rules together as to how to live in this world.

"Now I used to be very ashamed of Sarah—she's quite mature and sexual, and she's a real handful, she is, and I hope she never comes out again. She's the one that used to . . ." Rose stops, shakes her head sideways. "I don't know. I can't go into details because she's just *outrageous,* but do you know how I got to know them?"

Rose and I are having lunch in an Italian luncheonette on Commonwealth Avenue in Boston. The luncheonette is next to a police station, and most of the people eating at the tables and booths are policemen and detectives. Rose tells me about her different "alters," and how she got to know them by working with a doctor who asked her if she wanted to get acquainted with them. (Later, Larry Kohn will tell me he was skeptical about Rose's alters and MPD until he saw them in action: saw them come out, heard them begin speaking from her in totally different voices, saw Rose acting—*being*—these different human beings. It was an amazing, and a convincing experience, he says.)

Rose names many of the hospitals she was in, and tells me about things that happened in each of them, and she also talks about some of the doctors she had, and the one who helped her get to know her other selves.

"I met him when I was about nineteen, and I saw him for a dozen years or so, and we sort of grew up together, and he—that's Doctor Browning—was one of those yuppie types, I guess, but he just had the kindest look on his face the first time I met him. I was frightened because my last therapist before him had sexualized everything, and then had left me—just one day said, 'I'm leaving in three weeks, and moving away,' and that was that—and I wanted to show Dr. Browning I could be friendly, so I took out a piece of Juicy Fruit gum and asked him, 'Would you like a piece of Juicy Fruit gum?' and he said, 'Yes, that's my favorite kind of gum. Thank you,' and after that we were friends for life.

"I've been lucky that way. People have really given to me. Dr. Browning, he's a Quaker, and he didn't accept a penny when I wasn't working. He regulates his therapy so that fifteen percent of the people who get therapy from him get it for free, or for reduced fees, because he believes that's his obligation—that he makes enough money with rich people that he can leave some room. I fell in love with Dr. Browning and I told him so and he said, 'Oh Rose, you can fantasize about me all you want, but that's it.' "

Rose laughs. " 'Thank you, thank you,' I said, because I had the experience of one therapist who kept coming on to me, and I thought of taking a complaint out against him, but suppose he just did that with me and not with anybody else?

And he did do it with me, sure, and do you know that I'm scared of him to this day? Because he told me nobody would ever believe me. And he said this: 'When women get what they want, then they cry rape!' And this was after I trusted him and told him about a guy who had raped me, with a knife to my throat and the only way I could get out was by agreeing to be his wife, and then, using my head, telling him my clothes were dirty and I needed to go out for a while so I could get some clean clothes. But he—the therapist, I mean—he didn't believe me. My gaining all the weight I have, I see now, was a way of stuffing down reality. But now that I have strength again, I can let the reality come out. I've lost thirty-eight pounds the last few months, and I'm seeing a nutritionist regularly."

Rose shrugs, apologizes for not giving me a clear timeline about her life. Then she laughs.

"You know, about these different 'alters' of mine, even *I* still have a hard time believing that they're true. I just know that they've saved my life, and every time I've denied them, it only makes matters worse. My doctor says I need to recognize them, and what they did, but not to have them in my life the same way, only it's hard, because you *miss* them."

Rose talks about the first time she saw Sandra. She believes this happened when she was a little girl, and then, again—the next time—when she was in her late teens.

"I saw her in the mirror when I was staying at the Y because I didn't have a place to live," Rose says. "She came out in the mirror and 'Yaaaaggghhhh!' I was screaming, and I was totally panicked and freaked out, and I called the hospital and told them I was in a desperate situation, that I had seen this woman's face in the mirror and she was coming from the inside out and I couldn't stop her and I was afraid that she'd be the only one here. I only wanted one voice, one person, and she was in *my* voice, and they told me to get a cab and come over. I told them I didn't have cab money and they told me to call the police. But I was afraid of the police. They used to come and take my father away—for being

drunk, or cutting my mother's clothes off with a straight ra-
zor—all kinds of things like that."

Rose talks about the pain of her condition being intensified
by the pain of not being believed; and she talks about the
worst hospital she was ever in.

"They used to really hurt people there," she says, and she
tells me about how she was beaten up, her foot and ankle
broken, and of how she was kept on seclusion, without any
human contact, for entire days. When she tells me this, I
recall a friend of mine, a psychiatric nurse, telling me that
when she worked as a supervisor in a Boston city hospital
she would never allow female patients to be kept on seclusion
overnight because of what was done to them by some of the
male attendants.

"You know, there's a certain pain that comes with being
on the other side of the keys when you're locked in. Not only
are you scared you're going to get the hell knocked out of
you, but people don't think you have the ability to tell the
truth about your status. *They* have to find out what's wrong
with *you*—instead of listening to what you tell them.

"But I got out eventually. I was stubborn—I was always
stubborn, you know. I knew what I wanted even when I was
a girl sitting in my house at One Thirteen Brunswick Street
in Roxbury with my mother, and I could look out the window
and see all the people hanging out at the corner, and I said,
'Please, dear God, don't make this happen to me.' I knew
right from the start, when I could put the pictures in my head
into words, that I was meant to be in college.

"In my last year of high school I was with my academic
adviser and she was talking to me, like 'Well, maybe, Rose,
you should try business school'—which was less than what I
was, so I said, 'Why do I get A's here and I can't go to college?' and she said, 'You can try to go to college but you'll
be very disappointed when you see you can't work up to the
standards of what other people are doing.' Then I got so mad
because I wanted to say to them: 'What the hell do you all

think you've been doing with me for all these years if you don't think I can go to college?' But I knew I could go to college, and I did — I put my tail to the fire, and I graduated and got through, even when I was commuting back and forth from hospitals.

"But do you know what captures you in the system?" Rose asks. "The fear of not being able to make it out in the world. Sometimes I tell my therapist — I look out the window of her office, and I say, 'You know, I'm really scared about going out there. What if I go out there and get this degree and then I get a job and then I can't pass the test?'

"I have MPD. I know I *have* it — I just don't *like* it. People get skeptical about having different selves, but it's real as stone, believe me. I know it's a defense against my past, and against implosion because of this damned fear that you'll be reduced to nothing, absolutely nothing. It's a terror like none other, and you'll do anything to avoid it.

"One of the cruelest things for a person is loneliness. That's why things changed when I was studying in the B.U. program and was hospitalized, and Larry Kohn came and visited me after work a few evenings — and I thought: He really cares about *me*. He's really visiting *me*, and nobody's making him do it. He must believe in *me* then, doesn't he? That made more difference than all the pills. It fired my will to keep going.

"You know what people in the streets need? They need warm companionship and a loving attitude. I've talked with them, and all they want is a little closeness and respect, like they're human beings. I want to see people working as outreach workers to people, to understand how to greet a person who's hostile because he's scared of you, and maybe hallucinating, and maybe you offer them a cup of coffee. But you go back and you go back and you go back. You want to know what I think? I think all these programs, they try for a little while but when the going gets too hard, they close up their doors and take off, most of them.

"Which is why I want to get my master's and work on recovery issues, especially with black women. I want to teach professionals, so they won't be so formula oriented. I want to teach what it feels like to be on the other end of the keys because I know the pain of being on both sides. I'd like to see more black voices having a say in what happens to people with mental illness, and more training of basic staff."

I repeat something Rose has said earlier about having, in her words, a double whammy: having to fight both prejudice *and* stigma—about having a mental illness *and* being black.

"And I'm *fat!*" Rose exclaims, and then she leans back and laughs and laughs, and, though startled at first, in an instant I find myself laughing with her. "Oh, I'm a woman of substance," Rose says, and grins. "And I talk a lot too."

When I meet with graduates of the Boston University Training for the Future Program, or with ex-patients living on their own, or in residences and programs Moe supervises, and when I ask what they think made the difference, the answer is invariably the answer Rose has given me. What made the difference, they each tell me, was a relationship— meeting a particular individual at a particular time: someone who believed in them, and who promised to work with them and stand by them for the long run, no matter what, and through all the ups and downs of their lives. What made the difference, they all say, was having someone believe in them so that they learned to believe in themselves enough to begin to do the work that was bringing them back to this world.

"I guess my worst times were these two years at Westboro State Hospital," Gaston Cloutier tells me. Gaston and I are having lunch at a McDonald's in Quincy, Massachusetts, a five-minute drive from the Quincy Mental Health Center, where Gaston works full time for CAUSE, an organization that assists individuals with psychiatric disorders who want to go to college or to return to college. With great pride, Gaston tells me that CAUSE has a client list of over two hundred and a waiting list of an additional two hundred, and that the dropout rate for its clients at local colleges is below the general average at these schools, while their grade point average is higher.

Gaston wears a salt-and-pepper wool cap, a shirt and tie, and a red pullover sweater. He is forty-seven years old and looks a few years younger. A religious medallion on a silver chain—a pewter dove representing the Holy Spirit—hangs around his neck, and though his eyes are puffy, his face and voice are animated. He laughs easily and often.

"I was being physically worked over by the staff [at Westboro]," Gaston says, "and I was placed in four-point restraints many times, stripped of all my clothing, and forced to spend hour upon hour in a seclusion room that stunk horribly of urine. When the toilets clogged because patients liked to throw full rolls of toilet paper into them, patients kept using them anyway, and they used clean towels—the one thing the hospital had a million of—to wipe themselves. The result was clogged toilets running over with feces and urine, and sinks filled with vomit.

"The worst places, though, were the so-called showers. There were three shower stalls, and they were covered during my entire two-year stay with layers of slime and ugly black bacteria. The benches were infested with cockroaches too. The greatest inhumanity, though, was that several male patients chose not to use the toilets, but to defecate in the showers. One time, when there were feces in all three shower stalls, I reported it to a staff person, and he said that if I didn't like it, I should clean it up myself. In my two years there, I don't recall, even once, seeing a janitor."

Gaston Cloutier was president of his senior class at Ashland (Massachusetts) High School, where he was also co-captain of the cross-country track team, a National Honor student, captain of the debating team, and founder and president of the Ashland Teen Center. His high school girlfriend, voted Best-Looking Girl in their class, was a fashion model for Jordan Marsh. In addition to running track, Gaston played on the basketball team for two years, composed and performed songs at the Youth Fellowship Coffeehouse, produced, directed, wrote, and starred in the senior class variety show, was selected to the Ashland High School Key Club, and went on to become lieutenant governor of Division 3 in the New England District of Key Clubs, after which he ran for and was elected to the position of Key Club International Trustee. In his senior year, he was accepted to Cornell University on a full scholarship as a Cornell National Scholar.

But the following year he had his first major breakdown and was hospitalized, and for the next sixteen years he was in and out of mental hospitals, diagnosed with both unipolar and bipolar disorders, or as having a schizoaffective disorder.

"I was on a manic high from January 1974 to January 1975," he says. "I flunked out of college before the end of my first year, experimented with drugs like LSD, amphetamines, and barbiturates, got a young woman pregnant, joined the Navy, went AWOL after three weeks in boot camp, hitchhiked to Montreal and lived there under four different aliases, was brought back to the States by my mother when I was in a state of starvation, and finally ended up on the Navy psych ward.

"It was on this ward that I entered a more serious depression, and I was honorably discharged for medical reasons and sent home. That was in January of 1975. I was utterly destroyed, and spent nine months without speaking to *anybody*. I slept all day, hardly ate, and, if not for my mother's presence, I would have killed myself.

"Then, just as inexplicably, I skyrocketed out of my depression into mania for the next few years, and they were disasters. I got into lots of fights with men in bars—and I lost *all* the fights. I got involved with dozens of women—four at once one time. I lived on the streets, homeless, playing guitar to earn a few bucks. I never held a job for more than three months. And I stole cars. I'd drive one until it ran out of gas, then get out and hitchhike somewhere else. I hitch-hiked clear across the country, and back, sometimes hopping freights, and in Florida I got caught in a stolen car and I spent six weeks in jail. Hitchhiking and riding freights may sound glamorous and romantic—the way it did when I read *On the Road*—but it wasn't so, believe me. I was really just frightened, destitute, and hungry all the time.

"Then, in 1979, I got totally depressed again, and I was sent to Westboro State Hospital, where I did piecework in a sheltered workshop, but this got me depressed even more, so I walked out one day—escaped onto Route Nine and tried to kill myself by diving in front of a tractor-trailer truck. Thank God I jumped too early and the truck swerved around me. I still hear the horn sometimes, blaring away."

After returning home, and entering an outpatient clinic, Gaston came under the care of Dr. Jonathan Cole, of McLean Hospital, who diagnosed him as manic-depressive and medicated him with lithium. Gaston did well for a year, and then went into another manic state, stopped taking his medications, caused a major disturbance during Catholic mass in a local church, and was hospitalized again, this time for two years, at Westboro State.

"One time at Westboro," Gaston says, "I took a huge white sheet, and painted on it in big purple letters—GOD—and I put my head through the sheet and walked around blessing everybody. I also went by the alias of Leonardo de Woo, and made lots of long-distance calls, collect, using his name. Leonardo was for Da Vinci, and Woo was from a Steely Dan song. And I tried to put together an outdoor concert for five hundred thousand people, to take place at Westboro.

"I wrote to Governor Michael Dukakis, and I kept trying to get in touch with Jean-Luc Godard. I called it the 'Concert on the Roof' instead of 'Fiddler on the Roof,' and I envisioned all these musicians on the roof of Westboro State Hospital looking out at the surrounding pastures and meadows, à la Woodstock, and at this enormous audience. I spent a lot of time on the hospital pay phone trying to get information for Godard's number in Paris.

"I used to remember this teacher in high school — a friend's mother — she would always say to me, 'Strive for mediocrity, Gaston!' " Gaston laughs. "There's something to that," he says.

Gaston shows me wedding and vacation pictures of him and his wife, Christine Duffie. He met Christine, who had been a nun for five years, when they were living in a group home and were both in recovery from breakdowns and hospitalizations. He fills me in on some basics about the years between Westboro and the present: how he was in and out of McLean Hospital several times; how he enrolled in Framingham State College in 1986, but dropped out three times and had four hospitalizations during the next three years that included electroshock treatments (ECT) for his depression; how he rediscovered his religious faith after twenty years and became a religious candidate in order to become a Brother in the Augustinian Order in the seminary at Assumption College, in Worcester; and how he sucessfully completed courses in the B.U. Career Education Program.

In the fall of 1990, he enrolled at the Massachusetts Bay Community College in Wellesley, Massachusetts, and was stabilized on a new medication: Clozaril. He attended school for six consecutive semesters, and in the spring of 1993 received an associate's degree in liberal arts, with high honors. Then he transferred back to Framingham State College and in August 1994, he received a B.A. Two months after this he accepted the position as academic counselor at CAUSE, and a year later he and Christine were married.

"At one point — about a dozen years ago — I found myself curled up in a ball in a state hospital seclusion room. Not just at one point — this happened many times, really, and I was alone, really alone: just me and a plastic-covered mattress that reeked of urine. I had no faith in God. I had no faith in humanity. I had no faith in psychiatry or medication. I had no faith in myself. Most people classifed me as a 'lifer'—somebody who would stay in the hospital his entire life, and I thought I was a lifer myself. I had lost all hope.

"When I come home from work at night to our apartment now, my wife has dinner waiting for me. We sleep in one room, and the other room is a study-prayer room where Christine and I hope to keep our child, if God sends us one. For five hours each Saturday I work with three retarded clients I've been working with for ten years, but my main job, forty hours a week, is with CAUSE. I love my work there— I can make a difference—but what I'd really like to do eventually is to go back to school and get a master's so that I can do pastoral counseling. But how did I get from point A to point B?"

Gaston talks about his religious faith; he talks about his alcoholic father, and how he has worked through many of his feelings and fears in therapy; he talks about Clozaril, and the difference that medication has made in preventing relapse; and he talks about how understanding his boss, Elsa Ekblaw, at CAUSE, has been in giving him flexible hours. Gaston comes to work at noon and stays until eight in the evening, which also allows him to see clients who have jobs and classes during the day.

"It's wonderful," he says, "when just these small adjustments can make such a big difference for your life. The Clozaril makes me so groggy in the mornings—so damned sleepy—that I'm not much use to anyone. But ever since I started taking it, in 1989—that's eight years now—I haven't had to be hospitalized. I've had a few close calls, but no major relapse. What the Clozaril does, I think, is it attacks the physical aspect of my condition. But I believe that mental illness also has a large spiritual aspect."

Gaston tells me that reading about Robert has reminded him of the pain he's been through, and of how blessed he feels that the pain has stopped. He asks if Robert has been on Clozaril, and when I say no, he urges me to have him try it. Lithium, he says, controlled his mania for a while, but Clozaril made a true *difference.*

"I didn't really begin to improve until I went to these healing services, though. That's the spiritual aspect. The minister said something to me that I heard—he said that you never make it until you make it with God. So I got down on my knees and did a heartfelt Our Father for the first time in twenty years, and the Holy Spirit came into me. That was 1986, when I still had a ways to go, but I realized what a loss it had been, trying to make it without God.

"I fell in love with an older woman at that time, and then I met this other girl—I'm no Don Juan, but I've had a lot of girlfriends in my life—and she had an M.B.A., and was a painter, and a concert and jazz pianist. We met at McLean, and both her parents were suicides. She was very well-to-do, and the first time I held her after we made love, she said to me, 'Now tell me something, Gaston—how am I going to support you, me, and a nanny at the same time?'

"I still go to healing services. What we do is called resting-in-the-Spirit, and two men hold me, and they sprinkle holy water on my face, and one of them places a hand on my shoulder, and I just fade back until I faint." Gaston closes his eyes, leans back in his chair so that it tilts. "And when I regain consciousness I'm on the floor. Now I'm a very *rational* person most of the time, and I don't know what happens to me, neurologically or any other way. I'm really at a loss to describe it medically, but I know it increases faith—that whatever resting-in-the-Spirit is, it's something awfully powerful.

"There have been a lot of small and large miracles in my life, you see, but the one that affected me most dramatically was my getting involved in the B.U. program. This happened when I was about to be discharged from Westboro and a woman from the Alliance for the Mentally Ill who was visiting her daughter asked if I had any plans. I said no, and she told me about a program starting up at B.U., and I enrolled, and for the first time since high school, I was a real student again. I was not manic. I was not depressed. I was not homeless. I was not an ex-mental patient. I was a *student*. What this did for my self-esteem was immeasurable.

"No matter what has gone on in my life since, and all through breakdowns and hospitalizations, I was given the constant support of my instructor, counselor, and friend, Larry Kohn. He stood by me all the way. I shudder to think of what might have happened to me if he hadn't.

"In a gesture I would never have dreamed possible, he gave me his home phone number and encouraged me to use it any time. *Any time!* I was amazed. We took to playing basketball together, going for walks, visiting each other's homes, and going out to dinner together. Larry was the first person to make me feel like a *person* instead of a *patient*.

"He helped me get my job, and helped me to keep it, and when I was hospitalized, he helped me get good treatment, and he visited me." Gaston pauses. "He was the older brother I never had," he says. "There's a lot of terror in psychiatric illness, you see, and it makes all the difference in the world to have someone there with you in the darkness."

Several weeks later, when Larry talks with me about Gaston, and about being at Gaston and Christine's wedding, and what a joyous day it was, he says, "I couldn't have been more proud if he was my own brother."

Larry Kohn recites his favorite quote for me—the ideal he lives by (from G. Gurdjieff)—that "our responsibility here on Earth is to lighten the common sorrow of our Father." He says that he thinks of the work he and others do with people who have psychiatric disorders as being like drops of water on stone—you never know which drop is going to make a difference, the differences usually seem imperceptible, and they may take five or ten years sometimes until you see them.

"There are no shortcuts," Larry says. "There's nothing to do but to walk the walk and talk the talk: to work individually with each person day by day and drop by drop and step by step."

I say that I have often used a metaphor like that of water dripping on stone, but in a somewhat different way—that I often think that we all have the equivalent of fault lines inside us, and we never really know which drop of water will make us break—what, from within or from without, will cause that fault line to open up. We don't really know very much, do we? I say, about where the emotional and neurological fault lines in us come from, or what creates them, or what sets them to trembling, or what might *keep* them from opening up and causing damage and misery.

Like Gaston, Larry is a religious man, and like Gaston, he is also a very worldly guy: He loves sports, dotes on his family (he has four children, the oldest of whom is eight), and, having been something of a wanderer in his early years, he feels surprised, and blessed, to have settled down and to actually have a family of his own. The first time we meet he tells me he had been reading *Imagining Robert* one evening, and had forgotten that his two sons, then five and seven, were upstairs, camping out inside a tent Larry had set up for them. When Larry realized it was past their bedtime and went upstairs, he found that his sons had fallen asleep, the younger son's head on the older brother's lap. "They looked so sweet and peaceful," Larry said, "and I just stared at them for a while, and then what I'd been reading about you and Robert came back to me in a rush, about how you were boys together once just like my sons, and then I lost it completely."

When I am in Boston I take to meeting with Larry in his office, and swimming laps with him at noon in the B.U. pool. We talk regularly, by phone and e-mail, about Moe, Gaston, Rose, and others, and about our work, but more frequently our conversations are like the conversations I have with my childhood friends from Brooklyn: We talk about basketball, baseball, and football; we reminisce about games we saw and games we played, and about women we've known. Along with material about psychosocial rehabilitation, Larry sends me long e-mail messages analyzing and comparing players and coaches, past and present.

I talk with Larry about Robert, and what might be done to better my brother's situation, and he, along with Moe, LeRoy Spaniol, and others, advise against a transfer for Robert to Massachusetts, either to the Boston area or to western Massachusetts, for many reasons: The unstable political and economic situation in Massachusetts and in the Department of Mental Health; the state policies that urge swift discharge for patients like Robert, in addition to Robert's probable need for long-term institutional care; the increased dependency Robert would have on me, along with my possible move, now that my children have left home; the fact that Robert is fifty-three years old, and has never lived anywhere but in New York City.

In my mind, as I drive the turnpike between Northampton and Boston, I hear Larry and Gaston telling me of their affection for each other, and I also hear, again, something LeRoy Spaniol has emphasized several times — that, in his opinion, the key to recovery has to do with *responsibility*. If individuals believe their condition is caused solely or mainly by chemicals, they are thereby *relieved* of responsibility, he explains, for this means that their mental illness — and a large portion of their identity — is a disease, and if it's a disease, then other people don't have to change *their* attitudes. You're the one who has to change, and what you have to change is *who you are* — and the only way to do that, according to this model, is to take your meds. Thus, you are not an active agent in your own healing process. And if you're not an active agent, your chances for improvement and recovery are greatly diminished.

I also hear Moe warning me about the visits LeRoy and Larry have set up for me with individuals, and that Tony Zipple, vice president of Vinfen, has set up for me at various Vinfen programs.

"It could be like those towns and factories and schools in

China, with all these young Chinese children smiling and waving flags," Moe says. "So watch out, Jay!"

I visit several residences in Boston, including one—Vinfen's newest—on Beacon Street in Brookline. The residence, in the heart of an upper-middle-class neighborhood, houses thirteen men and women in a four-story turn-of-the-century brownstone mansion. The exterior looks like that of the neighboring brownstones, well preserved, stately—and the interior is equally handsome: The oak staircase, doors, banisters, and wainscoting have been refinished, and they gleam; the dining room table is set, with a tablecloth and place settings for thirteen, as if for a diplomatic dinner; and the rooms themselves, some with fireplaces, have been lovingly renovated, the woodwork stripped and varnished.

There is no social worker or case manager on the premises—each of the thirteen residents has a room of his or her own—and part of the monthly rent that each resident pays, between $300 and $400, goes toward the salary of a cook who prepares a meal each evening for the residents. I talk with several of them. A few have been in state hospitals for upwards of a dozen years, but now have part- and full-time jobs—as a clerk in a supermarket, as a computer programmer, as a sales clerk in a record store—and they are all delighted by their new residence, by the neighborhood, by the convenience of living near stores and public transportation, by the friendships they are making. When they talk with me, they refer to their residence as home.

"I've been out for over four years now," one man tells me, "and being given the opportunity to live here seems a real break and I don't want to mess it up. But if I do, and have to be hospitalized, I know I won't lose my room. That's the really good thing—that it's mine for as long as I want, that if things keep going well for me, I can live here forever. Which is a good thing, given my family. I'm Jewish, you know, and all the stuff about close-knit Jewish families, and how loving they are, et cetera—well, see what happens if *you* get an illness like mine! See how loving they are then! So I know what I have to do to survive, and not to depend on them. But my job and my music—my friends here, and people like Moe and Tony—I know I can count on *them*."

Moe and I talk about the fact that in the past, residences like this—and several others we visit in middle- and upper-middle-class neighborhoods, in Jamaica Plain, and in Brighton/Allston—didn't exist for people when they left mental hospitals. In the sixties, in fact, when Creedmoor Hospital, in Queens, had a population of more than six thousand, there was not a single halfway house in all of Queens or Long Island to which the hospital could refer the patients it discharged.

Moe says that setting up these residences has not been easy, and that in each case Vinfen has had to fight local citizens and zoning boards, and often go to court. He doesn't know why, but his experience, which research studies confirm, says that it's so: the wealthier the neighborhood, the greater the resistance.

In Brookline I spend a few days at Webster House with Moe. Webster House is a clubhouse-model day center that uses a modified version of the Fountain House (New York) program to help individuals with mental illness return to the work force. There are over 350 such clubhouse programs around the world, and an international organization that trains, supports, and certifies staff and programs worldwide. The programs are highly successful, not only in helping tens of thousands of people get and keep jobs (mostly entry-level, along with some that require advanced degrees and special skills) and stay out of hospitals, but by also offering comprehensive residential, educational, and social services, in helping them to reclaim lost lives.

At Fuller Mental Health Center in Boston, I visit a crisis stabilization unit (CSU) whose aim is to enable people with histories of repeated psychiatric breakdowns avoid lengthy hospitalizations. The average length of stay for individuals brought to the CSU is 2.7 days, and the approach is intense and comprehensive: A team of medical doctors, social workers, and rehabilitation specialists begins preparing a plan for the client even before the client arrives — as soon as the case manager, or the mobile emergency team, telephones — and an essential part of the plan, from the onset of the crisis, is to prepare for the client's *discharge*. From the time the first call arrives, the CSU team begins working on a discharge plan that will pay attention to medications, therapy, housing, family situation, and finances, and includes an outreach component: for example, having case managers seek out the client to make sure he or she keeps appointments and takes medications instead of waiting for the client to check in with the case manager.

In my travels with Moe, I meet night watchmen, convenience store clerks, janitors, plumbers, electricians, teachers, social workers, physicians, all of whom were hospitalized for mental illness for varying lengths of time, and all of whom are now out in the world with the rest of us. Within a few weeks of the publication of *Imagining Robert*, three friends in the Amherst-Northampton area — a well-known professor and writer, the owner of a successful rare-book business, and one of my most gifted graduate-student advisees — tell me, in confidence, that they had been hospitalized for extended periods of time for mental illness, one of them in the same psychiatric ward of Elmhurst Hospital in which Robert was first hospitalized thirty-five years ago.

I talk with psychiatrists who have worked with men and women labeled hopeless — individuals who have languished in back wards for years — and with medications and psychotherapy have had successes: have seen their patients improve, recover, and return to our world, where they lead distinctly uncrippled lives. I talk with psychoanalysts who have worked, long-term and, in these last years of this century, most unfashionably, three, four, or five hours a week for five, six, seven, or more years, and who provide well-documented case studies of successes that are not only moving, but convincing.

And when I talk with these physicians, and with some of

the individuals with whom they have worked, I am impressed all over again by the quiet heroism such lives—and alliances—represent. Freedom, I think, truly is, as the civil rights song tells us, a constant struggle. It is not an end, or a given.

Hearing and witnessing stories of individuals who, through hard work, have regained and made new lives from lives they and others had declared lost—beyond hope and beyond redemption—reminds me of what, through discouraging times, I sometimes forget: that the human spirit is often amazingly and mysteriously resilient, and that most of what we come to value in life are those accomplishments, whether in music, athletics, science, parenting, writing, or friendship, that take sustained and steady work, involve goodly measures of conflict and struggle, and are, over long periods of time, hard earned.

Driving along the Massachusetts Turnpike one evening, from Boston to Northampton, and hearing voices in my head, as I often do—Rose, Moe, Gaston, Larry, and others—I suddenly hear Robert's voice too.

Hey—what about me? I hear him ask. *Why can't anyone help me—and I mean* **you,** *big brother!—the way all these other people you're visiting are being helped?*

I think of something Rose said in passing, about whether I thought we would ever have a pill for persistence that could give people the *will* to want to get well—and I think, too, of what Moe and others have been saying, by way of warning: that although stories of individual recovery, or of the dedication of family members and therapists to afflicted individuals may be moving and inspiring, these are only anecdotes, and therefore repesent *merely* personal solutions.

"It's all about systems," Moe says. "I'm just one person, so what we have to do is to come up with ways of helping people that make people like me replaceable and interchangeable. What we need are systems that can go on with or without me, and that make me irrelevant."

I have lunch with Kristin Bumiller, a professor of political science at Amherst College, the single parent of an eight-year-old boy diagnosed with Asperger's syndrome, a so-called high-functioning form of autism (people with Asperger's syndrome are usually exceptionally gifted and intelligent, and can talk of their experiences as well as their feelings, whereas those with classical autism usually cannot). After I tell Kristin about what some of the people I've been meeting have been telling me — how what made the difference in their lives was a particular individual at a particular time being there for them — she reiterates what Moe has said.

The dedication and love that enable some individuals to survive, and to thrive, are admirable, of course, but they don't address essential issues because, as in sentimental Hollywood movies, they reduce large social, political, and economic problems to *personal* solutions: to stories that celebrate the ways in which the individual hearts of individual men and women are changed, thereby suggesting that answers to our most serious and most refractory problems lie in having heroes and heroines (K-Men?) work heartwarming miracles in the lives of individuals less fortunate than they are. This, Kristin says, reduces things public to things private, thereby freeing all who are not directly affected, or who believe they are not affected, or who don't want to be affected or involved, from responsibility, while at the same time — something anyone who has ever been caregiver to a loved one suffering from a chronic illness knows — isolating both the caregiver and the afflicted family member from sources of ongoing aid and sustenance.

And if it is true, as it seems to be, that loving, caring, and dedicated individuals can and do make crucial differences in the lives of those suffering from mental illness, then one also has to ask the logical next question: How do we replicate loving, dedicated, caring, and heroic human beings?

What we need to think about, Kristin Bumiller suggests, is this: What are the conditions — the systems, the programs, the contexts — that encourage and maximize the *possibility* that dedicated, talented, and well-trained individuals will *want* to work with people like her son and my brother? What are the programs that can be replicated and will have better outcomes — greater successes — than what we have had until now?

Clearly, from the evidence of Robert's life, we know what does *not* work and has not worked for large numbers of people with mental illness. The failures, individual and systemic, are all around us. But when we find what works — what treatments and programs make real and positive differences — how can we get the word out to others? How can we see that the good programs drive out the bad, and that they are encouraged, financed, and implemented?

She's right, you know. I mean, I know you love me, Jay, but what I want to know is this, I hear Robert say, his voice rising. *How the hell am I ever going to get out of here and have a life again?!*

I recall how pleased Robert had been, a few weeks before, to receive Moe's poems and drawings, and I hear Moe telling me that he would love to meet Robert sometime, and suddenly I am imagining Moe and me in commando uniforms, and it is past midnight and we are scaling the chain-link fence that surrounds Robert's hospital, making our way across shadowless grounds and into Robert's room. We whisper to him to get dressed, to move swiftly and silently, that we are here to take him with us, and to set him free.

A few days after I return from Boston, I find that this imagined scene is still with me, of two middle-aged men — a large and overweight Green Beret, and a short, gray-haired novelist — going on a rescue mission together to save my brother. On impulse, I telephone Moe and ask him if he thinks he might be willing to drive down to New York with me sometime, to visit Robert.

"You bet!" he says. "When can we leave?"

FOUR

GIVE ROBERT BACK HIS TEETH!

*When suffering knocks at your door and you say there is
no seat left for him, he tells you not to worry because he
has brought his own stool.*

— CHINUA ACHEBE,
Arrow of God

Three days before Moe and I drive down from Boston to New
York to visit with Robert, I telephone Robert's therapist,
Mark Kaplan, to let him know I'll be coming, and that I'd
like to bring a friend with me. I tell him that the friend —
Moe — has been corresponding with Robert, and that Robert
is enthusiastic about our visit.

Mark asks why I didn't inform him earlier about my visit.
This is the second time in a row I have not informed him
that I was coming to visit Robert, he says. He tells me Robert
thought I was coming to visit him yesterday — Monday — and
that he became very agitated and confused when I didn't
show up.

I explain that before I visited two weeks ago, I did telephone and, since Mark was away, I left a message with Ben

Katz, the other therapist on the ward, and that Ben assured me he would give the message to Mark. I remind Mark that I never call until a day or two before a visit because I don't ever want to tell Robert I'm coming, and then, because something unexpected might occur, have to cancel. I listen to Mark talk about how much trouble I make for Robert and the staff by my visits and telephone calls, yet all the while he is speaking I find myself remembering how good the visit with Robert two weeks ago was: how pleased we were to see each other, and how happy I was to be able to give Robert the first copy I had received from the publisher, a few days earlier, of *Imagining Robert*.

Robert had set the book on his bed—"I can't look at it yet," he said. "I need some time, all right?"—and we had talked about other things for several minutes. Then he had reached over and picked up the book, smiled, said something about how much he liked the photo of us on the front cover (me at eight, Robert at three), and started reading, verbatim, data from the copyright page. He turned to the title page next, saw the inscription I'd written to him, and the photograph of us—the frontispiece—that now faced the title page. It was the photo I had originally copied onto the cover page of the manuscript—of me at five years old, Robert at three months old—that Robert had called the most beautiful picture in the world.

Now, neither of us speaking, Robert sat on the bed staring at the photo: the two of us sitting in a peaceful, sunlit meadow, Robert cradled in my arms. Then, his eyes filled with tears, he had reached down and had begun caressing the photograph with his hand, very gently, as if the picture itself were an infant. He had looked up at me, and swallowed.

"This is something no one can ever take away from us, Jay," he said.

I remember Robert's head on my shoulder, afterward, while he wept softly and told me that it was all right, that he was really very happy even though he was crying, and I think of saying to Mark that perhaps Robert thought I was coming yesterday because he *wished* I were coming earlier rather than later in the week. I think of saying that clearly it would be much easier for Mark and the staff if family members not only never called or visited, but didn't *exist*. I think of saying lots of things, but the only thing I do say is that since there seem to be no objections to our visit, I will call again to give Mark the probable time of our arrival. We'll need to check on the weather, I say (when I'd visited Robert two weeks before, the temperature, with wind-chill, had been thirty below zero), since that might affect our plans.

Robert has told me that after our last visit he gave Mark the book jacket *of Imagining Robert* to hold for safekeeping (he had asked me to take the book itself home with me, for the same reason). Mark does not mention the book.

When I telephone the next day, the first thing Mark says is that Moe and I cannot meet with Robert in his room. "It sets a bad precedent for the ward," Mark says, and "goes against general policy." Although Robert and I have been meeting in his room for years, I say nothing. Then Mark adds that we will have to limit our visit to one hour because Robert is not doing well, and Mark talks, again, at length, about how before and after my visits, Robert becomes agitated.

And I think to myself: Well, maybe Robert becomes agitated — excited, eager, nervous, happy, confused, whatever — because he is still *alive*. I think of what the ward is generally like — most patients gazing dully at the TV, sleeping in chairs, or wandering around aimlessly, and I want to ask: When Robert is not agitated, before and after my visits, what's he like?

Bored, I hear Robert reply. *And very lonely.*

I say something about how well our visit went last time — that Robert had seemed quite calm, coherent, and affectionate, and Mark interrupts with a question.

"Are you going to give me a copy of your book?" he asks.

His question takes me by surprise, and, to buy some time,

I repeat the question, then say that it hadn't occurred to me to give him a copy since I only receive a few copies of the book free, and have to pay for the rest.

"Well," Mark says. "Do you think it would help us in our treatment of Robert if we read the book?"

"I suppose so," I say. "I mean, you'd know him better, and the better you know him, the better his treatment might be—"

"Well, then," Mark interrupts. "Don't you think you *should* give us a copy of your book?"

I experience a surge of adrenaline—feel unsure of how to respond, or if I should respond at all. I have had confrontations like this with Mark before, and what I am feeling most of all is what, I know from talking with others, most family members feel in such situations: the fear of retaliation. How will they take out their resentment of us on our loved one?

So I take a deep breath and say a few things I hope will reduce the tension, and will help me to calm down (I see that my hand, holding the phone, is trembling), about having given copies of the book only to Robert and to my children, and I add something I think will be inoffensive: Aren't Mark and other staff members curious about what's in the book?

"What I'm curious about," Mark says, "is why you won't give us a copy."

More than five thousand advance copies of the book have, in fact, been distributed during the previous few months to reviewers, bookstores, and mental health professionals; a few sections of the book have appeared in print, and the book itself has been available in stores for several weeks. During the past year, my greatest worry concerning the book has been about what is happening now: the hospital's response to the book, and how this might affect its care and treatment of Robert.

I say something about the tens of thousands of dollars the hospital spends for Robert's care, and how the cost of the book is only about $20, but before I can say anything else, Mark interrupts to say that the money for Robert's care comes from the state, but that the money for the book would have to come out of his pocket.

When he says this, I realize I have been more defensive—and talkative—than I need to be. I take a deep breath, say I will see what I can do about getting him a copy of the book, and that I am looking forward to seeing him when I visit Robert. And I tell myself that even though nobody at the hospital seems to have seen or read a copy of the book yet, most staff and administrators there are probably more nervous and scared than they are hostile. A few minutes after I hang up, I autograph a book to the staff of Robert's ward and put it, and a brief note of thanks, into the mail.

When, on the drive down to New York, I tell Moe about my conversation with Mark, he laughs but says he is not surprised.

"They're just trying to push your buttons," he says. "It's always a power trip with people like that." He shakes his head, boggled by the way grown-ups—including some, like Mark, who have doctorates or medical degrees—can act sometimes, and how much harm they can do. I say that I believe Mark really cares about Robert, that I don't think he and others intend harm, and that for me the truly sad thing about Mark and some mental health professionals I've known is that they're simply not very good at what they do. Moe disagrees.

"Some of the birds I've seen working in these places do lots of harm, Jay," he says. "From where I sit and from what I see, and with the power they have over others, they seem pretty evil to me."

Moe has brought a large shopping bag with him, packed with food ("That's what I learned from the Marines," he says. "Never to go anywhere without food"), and during the five-hour drive we eat, trade stories, and talk about all kinds of things: about Moe's childhood, his combat years, and his life since (I learn that when he was a child his mother used to lock him and his sister in their basement and tell them that the Soviet Union was coming to interrogate them); about when he had been lead singer with a rock band that toured Europe and one of his wives named him "Moco Loco" and left him when he refused to do hard drugs with her (*"Every-body* wants to get high with a crazy man," Moe explains); about his sister's life, marked by repeated mental break-downs and hospitalizations, and his parents' inability to ac-cept or understand either of them ("My father still thinks I'm going to be a pro football player, but the truth is, for all my troubles and hard times, I'm a much better person now than when I was an Eagle Scout or a Marine"); about Naomi and Sano and the life he has made with them; and mostly about his thoughts concerning current trends in therapy ("It's a crock that families are *never* to blame," Moe says. "Of course they are sometimes"), and about what might make a differ-ence for individuals like himself and Robert.

"I'm a crafty dude," Moe says, "but it's a gulag out there for most of us, and most of us, like most people anywhere, are not especially crafty, which is why I'm not fond of the idea of integrating us with everybody else. I'm too weird, if you want the truth, and I need to be with others who un-derstand me instinctively, who've been where I've been, and are off-center the way I am."

I tell Moe that my heart was pounding for a good twenty minutes after my talk with Mark, and that I wonder how other people manage when they feel hostage to a situation in which someone they love is locked up the way Robert is, and staff members give them a hard time. I'm very persistent, and I've become pretty good at knowing when to be assertive, and when to back off. But how do families that have to struggle against multiple demands and conditions merely to stay alive cope? How do they cope if, in addition to having a family member go mad, they're poor, hungry, and unemployed, or if they're working at full-time, low-paying, demanding jobs, or at a bunch of part-time jobs, or if they have major health problems of their own? How do they cope when, in the midst of already burdened lives they suddenly have to deal with the terrors and heartbreak that come with having a family member incarcerated in a state mental hospital, and then find themselves having to deal with and depend upon people like Mark?

"They give up," Moe says. "It's as simple as that. They just give up. I've been in hundreds of hospitals like South Beach, all over the country, and I see it again and again. Lots of the people in these places *never* have a visitor."

When we arrive (as it turns out, we are the only visitors on Robert's ward this afternoon) Moe introduces himself to Mark by telling him he is director of consumer and family affairs for Vinfen. Mark says that the consumer movement has already reached South Beach, and that Robert's ward, like all others at South Beach, has a "consumer representative" who attends meetings and represents patients on the ward to the staff of the hospital.

Mark tells us that Robert is not doing well, that we can only have one hour with him, and that Mark will go and get him. Mark leaves, and Moe looks around, points quickly to uncollected refuse on the floors, to overflowing ashtrays in the courtyard, to patients sleeping across couches, to a staff member yelling at a patient.

"This place is terrible," he says. "This is not a place that cares about consumers."

Robert and Moe take to each other like old friends: Moe has brought Robert a carton of Benson & Hedges cigarettes, ("Cigarettes can buy a lot of freedom on a psychiatric ward," Moe says). Robert thanks him, shows us pictures from magazines, of clothing and cigarettes, that he has saved for us. He shows Moe books he has been reading, from a bookshelf in the lounge — mostly old copies of *Reader's Digest Condensed Books* from the sixties — and where, in the books, he has put pieces of paper with his secret place marks. He also shows Moe that the bookshelf itself is removable. ("So much for security," Moe remarks. "Anybody who wants can pull it out and whack someone.")

To my surprise — given what Mark has told us about him —

not only does Robert seem to be in excellent shape, but for the first time in several months he has no shakes: His hands and feet are steady, and his talk and laughter are easy and natural. He explains to Moe that he has no teeth because Mark took them away a few months ago, saying he was afraid Robert would break them, and that Mark won't give them back.

I have brought food for Robert, but cannot leave any of it with him because, since my last visit, the padlocked refrigerator, which was there for patients to keep their snacks in — unlocked twice a day at "refrigerator time" — has been taken away. I inquire about this. "We had to get rid of it because it created chaos," one of the aides tells me.

Robert thanks Moe for the drawing of the donut, tells more jokes, talks about Camp Winsoki, the summer camp he and I went to, sings snatches of old camp songs, and gets into a conversation with Moe about joining a consumer band like Tunefoolery and becoming an entertainer again. Robert is excited about the idea, and Moe promises to send him a good songbook with old standards and show tunes.

After a while, Robert says he'd like to spend some time just with me, and suggests that Moe walk down the corridor and look around. Robert asks me about his niece and nephews, and about the book, and if there are any reviews yet, and about our mother, and about other friends and relatives, and he talks about things he wants to do when he gets out of South Beach, and about how terrible Park Manor is.

I smile and tell him we've had an unexpected book dividend: Because of *Imagining Robert*, people at several hospitals and residential programs have written and called, and have offered to work with Robert — to see if their programs can be useful to him. But there's no rush, I say. There's no pressure to do anything now or to make any decisions; as always, the choices and decisions, about what to do and where to go and when, are Robert's.

"That's good, that's good," Robert says. "That's good, Jay."

A few minutes before our hour is up, Mark returns. Moe and I tell Robert we expect to come back the next day, and that we will probably bring Lori Grinker—a professional photographer who visited Robert with me a month before, and who is working on a photo-essay about Robert—with us. Mark had come into Robert's room the previous month while Lori was taking photos of us, and he says it will be all right if she visits again.

"He's better than I thought, and the place is worse" is the first thing Moe says when we leave.

Do you think he can make it on the outside? I ask.

"Easy," Moe says. "All he needs are some people to work with him and believe in him while he makes his reentry. The problem here is that they're doing nothing to prepare him for life in the community."

Moe's greatest concern, he says while we walk toward the parking lot, is for Robert's safety and well-being.

"Robert's an old-time patient," Moe says. "And he's easy prey for street people like those I saw on his ward, and my big fear is that the longer he stays here, the greater the chance that they're going to exploit him and abuse him."

The population in most state hospitals has changed radically in recent years, Moe says. There are fewer old-style mental patients like Robert in them, and a much higher percentage of individuals who have what is commonly called "dual diagnosis," a major mental illness accompanied by a history of serious substance abuse. In 1996, according to SAMHSA (the Substance Abuse and Mental Health Services Administration of the U.S. Department of Health and Human Services), 27 percent of people with serious and persistent mental illnesses had a coexisting substance abuse disorder.

One of the most prevalent and erroneous myths about deinstitutionalization, Moe continues, is that the people discharged from state hospitals have become the homeless people with mental illnesses who wander the streets of America. In fact, the population of drug-using individuals with mental illnesses who have become street people, and who move in and out of mental hospitals and shelters, is a largely new one, not at all the same population that lived on most of the wards and in most of the residences Robert has known during the four decades in which he has been a mental patient.

The movement, begun in the sixties, to get as many people with mental illness out of state hospitals and into the community as possible, and reinforced increasingly, and often for economic reasons, by state mental health departments and by managed care companies (hospitalization being the most *expensive* form of treatment), along with laws that have made the major (and often only) criterion for psychiatric hospitalization the narrowly legalistic standard of "dangerous to self or others," has had a predictable result: Those who are hospitalized in psychiatric institutions are all too frequently those who, no matter their emotional or mental states, have been deemed "dangerous" by the criminal justice system.

Individuals like Robert whose psychiatric problems make it difficult or impossible for them to cope on the outside for long periods of time—and who, along with elderly individuals suffering from dementias and senility (in 1962, the year Robert was first hospitalized, 153,309, or 29.7 percent, of resident patients in state mental hospitals were sixty-five years of age or older), used to make up the bulk of the population of state mental hospitals—have become a minority.

Robert is also, as I am learning and as Moe confirms, in a minority of individuals with mental illness who may still require long-term inpatient care. ("He is," says one doctor, after reviewing Robert's thirty-plus years of institutionalization and treatment, "an iatrogenic nightmare.")

Moe now tells me something he didn't tell me on the ward—that while he was walking along the corridor, two men in suits, carrying charts, came toward him. One of them, from Moe's description, was Nick Farini, the team leader (chief administrator) for Robert's ward. Nick had nudged his colleague, pointed to a patient who was standing nearby. "And *that*," he said, not realizing, or caring, that Moe could hear him, "is our consumer representative! Ha ha."

"Ha ha is right," Moe says, and, after imitating Nick's laugh, he slaps me on the shoulder, puts an arm around me. "Oh, we're going to do these guys a big favor, Jay. Did you know that?" he asks. "We're going to be good guys. We're going to get Robert out of here."

When Moe, Lori, and I drive up to South Beach the next afternoon and stop at the security checkpoint, the guard comes out of his booth, leans down, looks in at Moe, and asks, "Is this a dropoff?"

Moe laughs. I tell the guard that this is not a dropoff, that the three of us are here to visit my brother. The guard waves us past while Moe continues to laugh.

"Maybe he meant me," Lori offers, from the backseat.

"Oh no," Moe says, still laughing. "He meant the fat guy in the front seat with the weird hat!"

Although the idea of Moe being a "dropoff" becomes a running joke with us, he finds the incident revealing. The tone of an institution is set at the top, and it permeates all levels of a system. What if Moe *had* been a patient, and we had been bringing him back after he'd been out on a pass from the hospital for an afternoon or a weekend?

"If he doesn't think twice about calling me things like that, it's because nobody has ever bothered to teach him *not* to. Because nobody cares. It's like what I noticed yesterday about your visit," Moe says. "Here you've come from two hundred miles away to visit your brother—you're a family member—yet nobody on the staff even seemed to notice. Nobody bothered to welcome you, or to sit down with you and talk with you, or to sit with you and Robert, or with you and me and Robert. In a good place, visits from family members are encouraged and welcomed."

Robert is delighted to see Moe and Lori, and, ever the ham, to have his picture taken with me and with Moe. A few

minutes after Lori begins taking photos, though, we are surrounded by administrators. Mark, Nick Farini, a staff nurse,
Dr. Agha Shah, the head of services for the hospital, and a
security officer stand around our table—we are sitting in the
snack area—and lecture us concerning hospital rules while
demanding that Lori turn over her camera to them. (This is
the first time I have met the head of services, and the first
time Nick has ever come onto the ward to talk with me.)

Lori explains that she has not taken pictures of anyone but
Robert, and I say that the administrator Mark told me to
speak with assured me that as long as Robert agreed to have
his picture taken and we didn't photograph anyone else, it
would be all right. I say that Mark had been in Robert's room
with me and Lori when she last visited, and that she had
taken pictures of Robert while Mark was there. Mark now
says this never happened.

Lori explains who she is, where her work has appeared, and
that she is familiar with institutional rules governing privacy.
She refuses to give them her camera unless they will assure
her in writing that they will take full responsibility for its
value. And all the while staff members are interrogating me
and Lori, Robert, sitting next to us at the same table, ignores
what is going on around him—he never even looks up—and
carries on an animated conversation with Moe as if they might
be sitting across from each other in a Cambridge coffee shop.

When we leave, Robert gives Moe and Lori hugs and
kisses. He also presents Moe with a self-portrait, asks Lori to
send him copies of the three photos she took, and tells us
he loved our visit and hopes we all come back soon.

On the drive back to Manhattan to drop Lori off before
Moe and I head for Boston, Lori tells us she had been pho-
tographing people in a prison the week before, and that, were
she forced to choose between being locked up in the prison
or on Robert's ward, she would choose the prison. She also
remarks on Robert's warmth, his intelligence, his sense of
humor, his sweetness—how he seems to have so much more
energy than anyone else on the ward.

"Robert's great strength," Moe says, "is that he won't buckle to them — to all their rules and regulations — and they don't like that."

Given the confrontation about the photos, we wonder whether it's worth the trouble for Lori to come back. What Moe says he found most interesting, however, was not the fuss made about the photographs, but something else. Did we hear what one of the patients said to the staff about Robert?

This patient, dressed, indoors, as if for a snowstorm — in coat, earmuffs, and mittens — had gone to the nurse's station and had pleaded with the nurses, and then with Mark, on Robert's behalf. I tell Moe that one of the reasons Robert was on room restrictions, and had lost all privileges, was that he had gotten into a fight with this man a few days before.

"What he said was this, Jay," Moe says and, quoting the man verbatim, he talks slowly: " 'I'm sorry I fought with Robert, but I'm just as much to blame as he is. Maybe I provoked him. But how is he going to *live*? You're taking away his smoking and you've locked him in his room all day and won't let him out. He can't talk to anyone, and if you keep doing this to him, you're going to turn him into a woman!' "

I tell Moe that I heard the patient talking with Mark, and with the aides, and that shortly before we left, I saw him go up to Robert and tell him he was sorry he broke his glasses. Then he had come over to me and introduced himself because he had something important he wanted to tell me: He had had a dream in which Robert was being turned into a pregnant woman without arms, and in the dream he kept trying to wake Robert up before the dream became real. The man had shrugged, and had begun walking away.

"It could happen here," he said to me as he left. He looked back, over his shoulder, and smiled. "A lot of crazy things happen here," he added.

I tell Moe about the people I've been talking with who have offered to help, and to see that Robert has his choice of residences and programs whenever he is ready to leave South Beach, and Moe says that what he thinks we should do is round up hundreds of consumers—all of Robert's friends and admirers—and that we should gather outside the chain-link fence and picket the hospital, demanding Robert's release. "We could all carry signs"—Moe describes an arc in the air with his hand—"FREE ROBERT NEUGEBOREN, or better yet"—his voice rises: "GIVE ROBERT BACK HIS TEETH!"

Moe shakes his head. He cannot believe Robert is only allowed out of his room for one hour a day, and that he does not have a discharge planner or a real social worker. What Robert needs most of all is simply people who will let him be Robert. Moe nods to himself, talks about getting Robert into a better situation, and then, his voice wistful, he repeats what he has just said, but as a question, and more softly: "Why can't they just let Robert be Robert?"

A month later I visit Robert again, and again, despite Mark's warnings about how poorly Robert is doing, and how agitated my visits and calls make him, Robert and I have an easy time together, our visit lasting an hour and a half this time. (A week earlier, Mark claimed that after my call the day before, Robert had set off the ward's fire alarm; I replied that I didn't call Robert the day before because I was on a book tour, in airplanes and airports all day long. Mark then said that from now on, to avoid trouble, I should call Robert only on the staff phone. Two hours later, when I called Robert on the staff phone, Mark answered and told me to call back on the patients' pay phone. I did, and got a busy signal.)

Robert and I talk about lots of things—about the possibility of his going to the Bronx Psychiatric Center, which is a teaching hospital for the Albert Einstein Medical School, and where I have gone a few weeks before, on a visit to their "open" ward (patients on this ward can come and go as they please, though they cannot leave the hospital grounds; and they run a coffee shop where they earn hourly wages and share profits); about his niece and nephews and their doings; about Lori and Moe (Moe has written an eight-page story entitled "Visiting Robert" that he sends to each of us); and, especially, about the letters and calls Robert has been receiving from old friends who, since the book's publication, have written or called me, eager to be in touch with Robert and asking that I forward their messages. When I tell Robert that people keep wanting to know what his reaction to the book is, and if there is anything they can do to help, he smiles. "Tell them to write!" Robert says. "Tell them to send letters!"

For the first time in many months, our entire visit passes without Robert becoming at all angry or irritated with me, or with any of the patients coming by and begging for some of the food I've brought. When I ask if Mark is working on the ward today, Robert says yes, yes, and that we should hurry and visit him before I leave.

So we knock on Mark's door, and then sit in his office — it is tiny, with barely enough room for the three of us — and, as usual, Mark offers little. When, after a few longish periods of silence, Mark asks if Robert has any "issues" he wants to discuss, Robert says no, no, but adds, in a loud voice, "*Except that my brother wants to put me in the Bronx Psychiatric Center!*" I say this isn't so, but that it is true I have been speaking with people at Bronx Psychiatric Center, and that it might be possible for Robert to transfer there if things can be worked out and if Robert wants to go.

Mark then asks Robert to step outside his office, stating that he wants to talk with me privately. He has never done this before, and I tell him that I came down from Massachusetts in the morning, and have to head to Penn Station soon to catch a train home.

As soon as Robert leaves, Mark asks me if I have legal guardianship or custody of Robert. I say no, and Mark says that my book certainly gives the impression that I am his guardian. Mark then says he has a question for me: Why haven't I moved Robert to another hospital?

I say that, as I just explained, I'm not Robert's guardian —

that I don't have that power and have never wanted it; that I don't ever want to take this freedom away from him—but, as Robert indicated when he mentioned the Bronx Psychiatric Center, and as I've previously informed Mark, I have been making inquiries and talking with people about other possibilities.

Mark asks again why I have not assumed legal power over Robert in all these years, after which he informs me that he has read about half my book.

"It's very critical of us," he states. "And since you don't have much good to say about us, or about the treatment your brother has received here, don't you think it's irresponsible of you not to move him elsewhere?"

To my surprise, I don't feel the least surge of adrenaline. "Look," I say. "You're bringing up some very large questions, and opening up a discussion we can't really have in a few minutes, especially with Robert waiting for me outside your door."

But Mark persists and asks again why, if Robert's treatment has been so awful, I haven't moved him elsewhere. "You've been working on this book for years, and you've been traveling around the country talking about it," he says. "Haven't people been asking you why you haven't moved your brother, or do they just ask you marshmallow questions?"

I say that, in fact, nobody has asked me about moving Robert, and that, as he knows, for the ten years preceding Robert's last breakdown, he had been doing well, had been living outside hospitals more than he had been living inside, and that his hospitalizations themselves had been relatively brief. There seemed no reason to seek out new places for him. Now, I say, although I have been making inquiries, I don't want to be hasty—that I don't want to suggest a transfer until I have an alternative that promises a real possibility of making things better.

Mark scoffs at the notion that Robert might be ready to live outside a hospital. "My professional opinion is that on a scale of one to ten, where ten means he is ready to leave, Robert is at one. In fact, if he keeps attacking people the way he did this week"—he has told me earlier that Robert scratched one patient and tried to choke another; I have told him that Robert informed me of the incidents—"we'll have no choice but to use ECT. Lithium doesn't work because he can't tolerate it, and the other drugs are not working either."

What about trying olanzapine? I ask.

Mark shrugs, says he doesn't know what olanzapine (Zyprexa) is, that he has never heard of it, and doesn't even know if the hospital has it. He is not a medical doctor, he states, but he has decided to recommend a course of electroshock—ECT—for Robert.

I remind Mark that when I returned from Europe a half-year ago, and he suggested the possibility of using ECT, Robert was very much against it—terrified, in fact—and that I was not in favor of it either.

"Well, we just don't know what alternatives we have. But we would be happy to help you transfer your brother somewhere else," he offers. "What about California? Or Florida? Or Massachusetts? Or how about having him move in with you?"

I say that I have made inquiries in Massachusetts, and the people I have spoken with there have not encouraged me about a transfer.

"Oh come on," Mark says. "Why not? It should be easy, and we'd be happy to facilitate things for you."

When he mentions, again, how critical my book is of South Beach, I state, very simply—a sentence I've been practicing for weeks—that I'm sorry he feels the way he does, and that I tried to be fair, and to tell the story as truly as I could, and from my point of view—but I say nothing else, except that I will consider what he has been telling me about a transfer, and about ECT.

I stand, say that I really do need to hurry in order to catch a ferry and a train.

"Well, we think the responsible thing for you to do is to place your brother elsewhere," Mark says as I open the door.

Robert is not waiting for me outside Mark's office, but I find him alone in his room. He thanks me for visiting, asks me to call when I get home, and walks me to the front door. We hug and kiss, an aide unlocks the door, and I leave.

When I arrive home that night there is a message on my answering machine asking me to please call Dr. Alvin Pam at home. Alvin Pam is principal psychologist at Bronx Psychiatric Center, a clinical professor at Albert Einstein Medical School, and the director of Bronx Psychiatric Center's open ward. It was at his invitation a few weeks before that I spent a day at the Bronx hospital, and attended the weekly TC (therapeutic community) meeting on the open ward. Having read my book, Al wanted me to see some of the ways in which a state hospital could do good work with individuals who have histories similar to Robert's.

Although many of the patients on the open ward had been hospitalized for at least as many years as Robert, and though most of the patients had had histories at least as grim as his (some of them, incarcerated for homicide and arson, knew they might have to live out their lives on this ward), and though the physical conditions at the hospital were standard institutional—long dreary corridors, high barred windows— the atmosphere seemed infinitely more pleasant than the atmosphere at South Beach.

At the meeting, more than forty patients had sat around a large day room, along with all the ward's doctors and staff, and had conducted an hourlong session that could have been a model for a meeting in the graduate student dormitory of a university. All the patients arrived on their own, and on time. They voiced opinions and complaints, observed rules of decorum (raising their hands, waiting to be recognized), responded warmly and feelingly—and most of the time realistically—to what other patients said, and to what staff members said.

They applauded at the announcement that two members of the ward were graduating—leaving the hospital—and several patients spoke up and told the graduates how much they loved them, how much their friendship with them had meant, and how they wished them the best of luck in their new lives.

The graduates themselves—until one identified herself, I had assumed she was a staff doctor—talked of their gratitude to staff and friends, and of how long and difficult the road to recovery had been. The meeting was run by an elected president, notes were taken by an elected secretary, and when patients voiced complaints—about food service, staff attitudes, the behavior of other patients—the staff took notes. After the meeting, I sat in with the staff, many of them young interns and residents, while they reviewed, one by one, not only each complaint and request, but their own observations about individual patients, their thoughts concerning individual treatment plans, and possible modifications of these treatment plans.

What amazed me most of all was what should have been taken for granted: that they considered their clients and the needs of their clients with great care and seriousness. They took delight in any signs of improvement; they did not condescend to or laugh at anyone; and they saw each person on the ward as a separate, unique, and distinctly nonidealized human being capable of improvement.

Afterward, when I met with Al Pam, I remarked that, clichéd and banal as the words might be, it really did make a difference if people with mental illness were treated with *dignity* and with *respect,* and that, alas, as we knew too well, this was all too often not the case.

I said that I had also begun, if tentatively, to notice something else: that in those programs that were more successful than others in enabling individuals to recover, there was something else present that was, if less tangible than the element of hope, and less apparent than the effects of treating individuals with respect and dignity, more central to the process of recovery. In the programs that worked—whether at Bronx Psychiatric Center, at B.U., at Fountain House, at CAUSE, or elsewhere—the simple working assumption, from which all care and treatment flowed, was that the major, ongoing task was to see that individuals with mental illness could and should take as much responsibility as possible for their own lives, and their recovery.

And I thought, too—smiling at its obviousness—that this was not so different from what most parents knew about raising children: that the essence of the job was to gradually enable your children to be able to make it on their own, without you. You never took away your love and assistance, and your children could always come back home when they wanted or needed to—for good times and for bad—but the name of the game, as I had often said to my children—*my* responsibility—was doing whatever was necessary, long-term and short-term, to enable them to become responsible for their own lives, and to others for all those large and small matters that kept the workaday world going.

A healthy *in*dependence, I recalled my own therapist emphasizing once, comes from a healthy *de*pendence, and sometimes if we have not experienced a healthy dependence—if we have lived a large portion of our lives without being able to count on others—we need to go back developmentally, as it were, and by depending upon people who are truly dependable, to learn to trust others, and to trust ourselves. People like Robert and the residents of Bronx Psychiatric Center were no longer children, of course, but given their lives and histories, if they were ever to free themselves from conditions that had made them excessively dependent—on hospitals, drugs, medications, case managers, self-destructive behaviors, etc.—they might need, temporarily, and for varying lengths of time, to learn to rely on individuals who could nurture in them the potential for recovery and independence.

Now, when I call Al Pam at home late on a Friday night after my return from South Beach, and tell him again how pleased I was to have visited his ward, he tells me that he has good news: He has received approval from the director of Bronx Psychiatric Center for Robert's transfer there, and he itemizes the five major benefits that might accompany a transfer: (1) Bronx Psychiatric Center is a teaching hospital, and so Robert would be working with young, enthusiastic, bright, and dedicated interns and residents; (2) Robert would be receiving psychotherapy at least once a week; (3) there would be a welcoming attitude toward family members and family involvement; (4) Robert would graduate, as soon as it seemed appropriate, from Ward 15—a locked ward, where he would have to start out—to the open ward; and (5) the hospital was closer to my home, making it easier for me to visit Robert more often, and to confer regularly with staff.

Al says that as long as Robert and I realize there are no miracles promised, the director and staff would like to work with him, and to show the good work their hospital can accomplish. Al then lays out the logistics: the letters I need to write; what we need to do about having Robert come to the Bronx for a preliminary visit; the visit the medical director and Robert's prospective therapist want to make to South Beach; the problems that will have to be overcome concerning admission of a patient who does not live in Bronx Psychiatric Center's designated catchment area, etc.

The next day I telephone Robert, and give him the news. He is delighted, and asks when he can make the visit to the Bronx. I tell him more about the hospital—warn him that physically it is an old-style mental hospital like Creedmoor and doesn't look nearly as pleasant as South Beach, and that Dr. Pam says that the food isn't as good either (the state gives the hospital approximately $4 a day per patient for meals)— and I tell him, again, that in the end the decision is his, but that I think a transfer to Bronx Psychiatric Center is a possibility he should seriously consider, that I think there might be some real gains to be had from a move there.

FIVE

EXPERT CONSENSUS GUIDELINES

The enemy of pluralism is monism — the ancient belief that there is a single harmony of truths into which everything, if it is genuine, in the end must fit. The consequence of this belief . . . is that those who know should command those who do not. Those who know the answers to some of the great problems of mankind must be obeyed, for they alone know how society should be organized, how individual lives should be lived, how culture should be developed. This is the old Platonic belief in the philosopher-kings, who were entitled to give orders to others. There have always been thinkers who hold that if only scientists, or scientifically trained persons, could be put in charge of things, the world would be vastly improved. To this I have to say that no better excuse, or even reason, has ever been propounded for unlimited despotism on the part of an elite which robs the majority of its essential liberties.

— ISAIAH BERLIN,
"Pluralism"

In 1955, when our nation's population numbered 170 million, nearly 600,000 Americans with mental illness were living primarily the way Robert and the majority of individuals designated as mentally ill had been living for the past two hundred years: in state institutions like South Beach and Bronx Psychiatric Center. In 1999, when our population has passed 270 million, fewer than 60,000 individuals live in those institutions. (Over the course of a year, however, more than 200,000 men and women will, for shorter or longer periods of time, pass through and reside in state mental hospitals.)

Still, despite this enormous migration from asylum to community, and despite all the talk about normalizing lives for people like Robert and enabling them to live in communities with the rest of us, millions of individuals with serious mental illness often remain, like the poor, largely invisible. Now, as ever, out of mind usually means out of sight. Although state mental hospitals no longer provide most long- and short-term housing for people with serious mental illnesses, those community programs that have replaced them tend to perpetuate the isolation in which people like Robert have traditionally lived.

Set apart in day treatment programs, group homes, supervised residences, residential treatment centers, drop-in centers, peer support centers, respite programs, SROs (single room occupancies), and private clinics; or abandoned to state mental hospitals, private sanitariums, or to the streets, parks, train stations, subway tunnels, bus stations, shelters, and rooming houses of our cities and towns, individuals like my brother often lead lives marked not only by recurrent illness, but by poverty, shame, stigmatization, discrimination, abandonment, and loneliness.

In 1991, NAMI (the National Alliance for the Mentally Ill), in conjunction with Survey Research Associates, interviewed a national sample of 552 individuals diagnosed with major mental illnesses in order to find out, simply, what was most important to them. Seventy-six percent of the people interviewed had been given a diagnosis of schizophrenia, and 88 percent were taking antipsychotic medications.

Survey Research Associates used a structured interview to obtain information about what the perceived needs of these individuals were in fifteen areas relating to what they termed "elements of daily living," including medications, doctor's appointments, housing, finance, employment, and personal relationships.

What the interviewers discovered was that few of those interviewed wanted more help with their "illness" — with keeping doctor's appointments (10 percent), or with taking medications (5 percent). What they cared about most (19 percent to 39 percent) was keeping busy; not being bored or lonely; finding or getting along with a boyfriend or girlfriend, husband or wife; making and getting along with friends; getting and keeping a job; finding and maintaining decent housing; and managing their finances.

The highest levels of need were in the areas of what the interviewers called "role restoration" — the restoration of "role functioning as it relates to work, satisfactory social and intimate relationships, and involvement in meaningful activities."

What the survey discovered was what I, too, was discovering: that people with serious mental illnesses only wanted what most of us want — that what they cared about above all, to use the words of the NAMI report, were "enhanced opportunities for friendship, intimacy, meaningful employment, and constructive activity."

And yet the lives of people who suffer from mental illness are shaped, defined, and ruled most of the time not by what they have in common with the rest of us — the desire, in this life, for good and constant measures of work, play, love, and companionship — but by the stigma, secrecy, and shame that accompany the fact of having or having had a mental illness.

Writing about the Progress Foundation in San Francisco, Steven Fields, who helped develop and administer, over several decades, a program of treatment facilities designed to prevent or minimize institutional care for people with acute mental illnesses, reports that "the single most frequently cited reason that patients identify as a factor in their psychiatric crisis is 'loneliness.' Whatever biochemical or social origin of the phenomenon of mental illness that we are attempting to treat, one thing has not changed in 2 decades: we are treating alienation and loneliness."

What I was also discovering was that it was only recently that many of those with the power to do good—doctors, social workers, administrators, legislators, and researchers— had begun to ask the people they were treating what they felt, and what they thought, and what they wanted.

In the fall of 1997, for example, when I am in Denver to give a talk for the Colorado Mental Health Association, I meet Dr. Robert Freedman, professor of psychiatry and pharmacology at the University of Colorado Medical School, and director of the Schizophrenia Research Center at the Denver Veterans Administration Medical Center. Dr. Freedman is in charge of a research project that is exploring the beneficial uses of nicotine (and of nicotine substitutes) in the amelioration of some of the nastier side effects of psychotropic medications. Speaking at a morning panel discussion, Dr. Freedman makes a simple and obvious point.

"All these years," he says, "we thought their smoking was just a bad habit, and not a biological clue to their illness. All these years we never did what we should have done first of all: We never asked our patients why they smoked so much."

That we did not, he continues, should be a cautionary lesson to those in his profession who continue to take an autocratic or narrowly biomedical view of their patients, and who believe that *we* always know what is best for *them*. If we don't speak with and work with those we have for too long referred to *as* "them," we will continue to fail them because, among other things, we will cut ourselves off from our primary source of knowledge, and of hope.

On the basis of interviews and laboratory studies, Dr.

Freedman's research team has concluded that one of the major reasons so many people with serious mental illnesses, especially schizophrenia, are chain-smokers is that smoking temporarily relieves several of the worst side effects of antipsychotic medications while also countering the effects of what researchers hypothesize is a genetic defect responsible for one of the salient traits of schizophrenia: the inability to filter out stimuli—especially sights and sounds—commonly results in sensory and information overload and an inability that generally leads to fear, confusion, delusions, and panic.

Somewhere between 74 percent and 92 percent of individuals with schizophrenia, and 35 percent to 54 percent of all other mental patients are heavy smokers, Dr. Freedman informs us, compared to the 30 percent to 35 percent of the general (adult) population who are smokers. For Robert, as for most patients on his wards, the five-minute breaks given every few hours for cigarettes are the high points of his days. Although Robert and I talk nearly every day, and he looks forward to my calls and our talks, if I call near the time when he is being allowed out to smoke, he will usually yell at me: "Why are you calling *now*, Jay? Don't you *know* it's smoking time? Why do you always do this!" and hang up on me.

The fact that *all* patients report feeling wonderful after smoking—that they have extended moments of clarity in which the sensory overload, along with the general grogginess that comes from the sedating effects of their medications, is diminished—led researchers to link a gene that appears responsible for the inability to filter incoming stimuli to a brain receptor in the hippocampus that can be stimulated by nicotine. What Dr. Freedman's research team discovered was that, when they smoke, individuals diagnosed with schizophrenia receive enough nicotine to switch on this receptor temporarily (thereby compensating for a presumed "deficit"), thereby gaining relief from incoming (and overwhelming) sensory data most of us learn to screen out and/or ignore: ambulance and police sirens at night; the humming of a refrigerator or an air conditioner; the sound of rain on the roof; the music, TV show, or voices coming from a neighbor's apartment.

In their literature, lobbying, and public presentations, organizations like NAMI, NDMDA (the National Depressive and Manic-Depressive Association), the Mental Health Association, and others that provide services for and/or advocate on behalf of people with mental illness often compare and equate severe mental illness with the flu, cancer, diabetes, or heart disease, conditions that would seem to have more obvious biochemical origins, and more predictable and manageable courses. (Significantly, they do not compare it to multiple sclerosis, the neurological condition that, especially in its chronicity, in its lability, and in the unpredictability of its course most resembles mental illness.)

For many reasons, among them the desire to reduce stigma and to alleviate feelings of guilt, along with practical reasons having to do with obtaining Medicaid payments, insurance reimbursements, and funding for research and for organizations that advocate for individuals with mental illness (NAMI has more than 185,000 dues-paying members, and over 1,200 chapters; the NDMDA has 275 chapters), these organizations regularly refer to mental illness as "an illness like any other," and to mental illnesses as "brain disorders" or "brain diseases."

"Don't let the words 'mental illness' scare you," the NDMDA's organizational brochure states. "You, or your loved ones, aren't crazy. You simply don't function as well as you did because you are ill. It's not 'all in your head.' You suffer from a real illness, just as real as the flu or heart disease."

But the corollary of believing that mental illness is primarily or exclusively a brain disorder with specific biochemical and/or genetic causes is the belief that since the condition is chemically and/or genetically caused, it can be chemically cured (with medications) or genetically fixed.

Although many organizations, including the National Institute for Mental Health, may refer to the need for, and the beneficial effects of, psychotherapy or psychosocial rehabilitation, the first line of treatment recommended for mental illness in most guidelines and brochures is *always* medication. (For example, NAMI's *60 Signposts for Siblings and Adult Children* states: "It is absurd to believe you may correct a physical illness such as diabetes, the schizophrenias, or manic-depression with talk, although addressing social complications may be helpful.")

But many research projects—including exhaustive meta-analyses that have tabulated hundreds of studies comparing the outcomes for patients who have been treated solely with drugs, with drugs and with psychotherapy, and solely with psychotherapy—demonstrate that various kinds of psychotherapy are often at least if not more effective than medications in treating different forms of mental illness—for example, as a first-line choice of treatment for depression.

In addition, many studies point persuasively to evidence demonstrating that psychotherapy is not necessarily more costly than medications; that its beneficial effects are often longer lasting; that it results in fewer relapses; that it has fewer complications and side effects; that it enables individuals to avoid dependency and addiction; that it carries with it benefits for other conditions and problems; and that it has the added benefit of enabling the individuals in treatment to have significant responsibility for their own recovery.

In a lengthy meta-analysis concerning anxiety disorders, researchers at the University of Nevada School of Medicine and Veterans Affairs Medical Center conclude: "Patients who attributed their improvement to medications during treatment did worse at post-taper than those who felt that improvement was due to their own personal efforts."

And again, concerning the treatment of unipolar (major) depression, researchers at the University of Nevada School of Medicine report the ways in which a "meta-analysis of 56 controlled outcome studies considered the relative effectiveness of drug therapy and psychotherapy for treating unipolar depression in adults," and how the evidence suggested that "in comparison with a control group, psychotherapy had a significantly larger impact than drug therapy."

Despite evidence from such studies, even our government often endorses a largely biomedical model of mental illness. In guidelines for the treatment of depression, for example, as set forth in National Institute of Mental Health brochures, the government recommends that primary care physicians (in the United States, psychiatrists write only 31 percent of prescriptions for all antidepressant medications) not refer a client to a mental health specialist until at least two trials of antidepressant medications have been attempted, and have failed.

And yet, those who choose psychotherapy instead of or in addition to medication are highly satisfied with the results. A 1994 *Consumer Reports* survey of approximately seven thousand individuals concerning their experience with psychotherapy resulted in the single most overwhelmingly favorable endorsement of a product or service in the magazine's history. According to those who had sought psychotherapy and experienced it, the findings demonstrated that psychotherapy usually "worked" for the respondents (87 percent); that long-term therapy produced more improvement than short-term therapy; that there was no difference between psychotherapy alone and psychotherapy-plus-medication; that active shoppers and active clients did better in treatment than passive recipients; and that those whose choice of therapist or duration of care was limited by insurance coverage did significantly worse.

While I am not surprised that mental health professionals disagree strongly with one another, I am startled, occasionally, by the virulence with which they attack each other. "The worst thing that has ever happened to mental health in America," one psychiatrist tells me, "is NAMI," while the director of NAMI's Research Institute claims that due to the efforts of former mental patients who advocate against involuntary hospitalization, "at least a half-million persons who were severely psychiatrically ill are now prematurely deceased."

Although the debate between advocates of medication and of psychotherapy (generally between psychiatrists and psychologists) is often, as it has been historically, intense and hostile (and absurd), with each side claiming that the other's claims are self-serving, erroneously based, and, even, worthless or malign, what seems clear from a review of programs, treatment modalities, and outcome studies is that the issues are, at the least, debatable.

When it comes to mental illness, an enormous number of informed and reliable studies call into question both the efficacy of various forms of psychotherapy and psychosocial rehabilitation, and the presumed superiority of the biomedical model and of antipsychotic medications. In the latter model, for example, the ineffectiveness of medications is often construed, not as a failure of the medications, but as proof of a patient's chronicity and hopelessness. Similarly, some psychotherapists will claim that therapy has been ineffective because prescription drugs have medicated away a client's will to work things through.

Whether or not and to what degree mental illnesses are primarily or exclusively biologically based, or primarily or exclusively experientially based, and to what degree more or less purely psychopharmacological or more or less purely psychological treatments should be the primary form of treatment, doctors, therapists, and researchers would surely seem to have more in common than some often care to acknowledge.

Whether writers, advocates, and researchers cite—or attack—the *Consumer Reports* studies; or the reports of the American Psychological Association that do (or do not) prove the effectiveness of psychotherapy; or the twin studies that do (or do not) demonstrate the heritability of schizophrenia and manic depressive disease; or the outcome studies that do (or do not) demonstrate that one mode of treatment is more effective than another—what seems clear is the following:

When one visits mental health centers and treatment programs, attends conferences, or reads a sampling of the vast literature on mental illness, not only are there genuine bases for honest disagreements, but, more significantly, when it comes to understanding madness—the whys, wherefores, and ways in which human beings come to think, feel, behave, and suffer so that we call them mad, or that they call themselves mad—we still know very little. (Cf. the seventeenth-century playwright Nathaniel Lee, protesting against his consignment to Bethlem (Bedlam): "They called me mad, and I called them mad, and damn them, they outvoted me.")

Psychiatrists, psychologists, researchers, policymakers, and organizations are unanimous concerning the fact that we do not yet know what *causes* these conditions; nor have we as yet discovered any biological diagnostic markers for them, as we have for other neuropsychiatric diseases such as Huntington's disease, Canavan's disease, Tay-Sachs disease, and Charcot-Marie-Tooth (CMT) disease. Most mental health professionals and researchers also agree that there is no such thing as, and probably never will be, a true, much less simple or long-lasting, *cure* for these conditions.

For the majority of us, then, the essential question and task remain: What can we do that will help us understand, alleviate, and prevent the worst effects of mental illness, and what can we do to help those who suffer from mental illness regain their lives in such a way that the condition, like others, becomes merely another part of their history and their ongoing lives? And how might we best work together in our common enterprise: in the search for the best ways to be of assistance to individuals afflicted with conditions that are, commonly, catastrophic?

Treatment guidelines issued by the government, mental health organizations, state mental health agencies, managed care companies, professional medical groups, medical journals, and medical schools now routinely do what they did not do a few years ago — they all *mention* the fact that psychotherapy and psychosocial rehabilitation (and, sometimes, self-help recovery groups and peer support groups) may prove helpful in the treatment of mental illness. Invariably, though, and encouraged by drug companies and managed care companies — often motivated, that is, in a free-market economy, by the desire to increase profits — the primary and nearly exclusive emphasis in these guidelines is on medication.

The *Journal of Clinical Psychiatry* — in its brochure devoted to "The Treatment of Schizophrenia," from its *Expert Consensus Guideline Series*, which guidelines, in addition to a consensus of recommendations from eighty-seven "experienced clinicians," make use of other "expert consensus" guidelines (put out by the American Psychiatric Association and the Schizophrenia Patient Outcomes Research Team, which are, in turn, sponsored by the Agency for Health Care Policy and Research, the National Institute of Mental Health, the University of Maryland Medical School, and the Rand Corporation) — devotes less than a quarter-page of a fifty-eight-page document to psychosocial rehabilitation, and does not mention self-help groups, peer support centers, or any other programs having to do with recovery, empowerment, or the consumer movement.

"These guidelines employ the latest technology on consensus surveys to encapsulate the opinions and practice of experienced clinicians," the authors of the guidelines state. Although the guidelines are "based on a wide survey of the best expert opinion," the authors do add "a few quiet cautions" in their introductory remarks:

A century after Kraepelin, psychiatry remains a descriptive science. We still treat syndromes rather than diseases. The syndromes reflect heterogeneous pathological conditions that have common behavioral constellations. Hence patients vary in their responses, and practitioners should not feel constrained within arbitrary boundaries of treatment. . . .

The other caveat is that practice does not always make perfect. Even when noted academics and expert clinicians achieve consensus, they may or may not be right. . . . What's more, in conditions such as bipolar disorder and schizophrenia, where the primary treatments are medications, industry is a looming presence. Pharmaceutical companies devote enormous sums to academic departments and individual faculty members who consult, conduct research, and teach under the auspices of the company. These then are the experts who create consensus guidelines. While few of us sell our opinions to the highest bidder, fewer still are immune from financial influence.

Despite such words about both the heterogeneity of the condition and the use of medications, in these guidelines as in others, the presenting condition of a patient is invariably regarded as a singular, recognizable, and homogeneously diagnosable entity (schizophrenia, unipolar depression, or bipolar depression), from which treatment, by medication and often by medication alone, follows. (For an "Acute Psychotic Episode," for example, we are told that "experts recommend high potency conventional antipsychotics or risperidone as first line treatments. When positive symptoms predominate in the first episode, a high potency conventional antipsychotic is the treatment of choice and risperidone is a first line alternative," and that "the approach to selecting an initial medication does not differ very much between first episode and multiple episode patients.")

This way of understanding mental illness prevails despite the fact that, as one researcher, echoing a large body of informed opinion (as well as the guidelines themselves), puts it, "The likelihood that researchers are studying different illnesses without being able to specify these differences must be recognized as the superordinate problem. It is not a subproblem that can be ignored. It is the major obstacle to scientific progress."

The *Journal of Clinical Psychiatry Guidelines,* like other consensus guidelines, has useful things to say about what to do when individuals are in crisis and is sometimes refreshingly modest in its recommendations. ("One thing that the history of medicine teaches us," the guidelines state, "is that expert opinion at any given time can be very wrong.")

Still, they have virtually nothing to say about what will be required *long-term* for individuals who have repeated episodes of any of the major mental illnesses, and, equally important, how what may be required long-term will be provided and paid for.

The guidelines may refer to psychotherapy and psychosocial rehabilitation—to cognitive behavioral therapy, to the B.U. Psychiatric Rehabilitation Program, or to ACT (Assertive Community Treatment) programs as examples of potentially beneficial options—but they do not indicate how such labor-intensive programs will be funded, or brought into existence.

For those individuals with mental illness who are fortunate enough to have health insurance, managed care companies commonly discourage hospitalization, other than brief stays for acute crises. And for those individuals who have no health insurance, who live in rural communities, in inner-city projects, or are homeless, access to anything resembling psychotherapy or psychosocial rehabilitation remains, in most instances, nonexistent.

Because funding for mental health programs and human service organizations is generally dependent upon state and local budgets, which are often dependent upon the vagaries that lead to and follow from elections; and because human service organizations, like managed care companies, come and go and change administrators, policies, and affiliations regularly, depending upon state and local elections and budgets, corporate decisions and mergers, and local and state contracts that are usually short-term (two to five years) and are based upon bids that reflect the perceived vagaries of funding sources (as well as the political deals and favoritism that may accompany and influence these funding sources); and because even when programs with proven efficacy in preventing hospitalization and reducing relapses, such as those based on the Fountain House clubhouse model, or ACT programs, are available, they are usually underfunded and understaffed (since direct-line service workers—those aides, attendants, and counselors with whom people with mental illness will interact daily—are paid, nationally, an average of less than $18,000 a year and are generally without sufficient skills, training, or motivation to assist people with psychiatric conditions); and because, due to the low pay and the often grueling work, frequent turnover of even moderately competent staff is a commonplace in the world of mental health (administrators tell me that keeping a direct-line service worker on staff for even a single year—given that they are competing, in pay, with fast-food chains—is a goal rarely reached); and because the inconstancy of staff makes many community programs unattractive to individuals whose lives are already overly laden, internally and externally, with inconstancy and the dismal consequences of inconstancy; and because individuals and families coping with mental illness often don't have the vaguest idea of how and where to seek and get and keep help for themselves; and, finally, because primary-care physicians and psychiatrists, schooled to think mainly in terms of medications, may, like family members, be equally ignorant concerning the advisability and availability of anything but medications (which are more readily paid for by insurance companies, state agencies, and managed care companies than other forms of assistance), it is difficult to understand how clinicians are to make use of even those minimal recommendations concerning psychotherapy and psychosocial rehabilitation that exist in these expert consensus guidelines and that might prove helpful for the long-term needs of their clients.

The guidelines "do not replace clinical judgment," the *American Journal of Psychiatry* guidelines state, with an awareness, absent a generation ago, of how various and complex individual situations may be, and of how flexible practitioners need to be.

"We describe groups of patients and make suggestions intended to apply to the average patient in each group," the guidelines state, and add, in bold-face type: **"However, patients will differ greatly in their treatment preferences and capacities, in their history of response to previous treatments, their family history of treatment response, and their tolerance for different side effects. Therefore, the experts' first line recommendations may not be appropriate in all circumstances."**

The authors of the PORT (Patient Outcomes Research Team) *Recommendations*, which are "evidence-based" and "focus on those treatments for which there is substantial evidence of efficacy," are aware of their psychopharmacological bias. "There are many more recommendations about pharmacotherapies than about psychosocial treatments," they write. "This does not mean that psychosocial treatments are less important than medications, but reflects the fact that we know much less about which psychosocial treatments are helpful. Future research may shed light on these other aspects of care that are often viewed by practitioners, consumers, and families as vitally important, but for which we lack adequate scientific evidence for efficacy and effectiveness at the present time."

"Treatment may be unsuccessful for a variety of reasons," the American Psychiatric Association's schizophrenia guidelines state in a brief paragraph near the end of their sixty-three-page brochure. "Some patients may be unresponsive or only partially responsive to available treatments (i.e., treatment resistant); this is the case for 30% to 60% of schizophrenia patients. Up to 50% of patients experience serious side effects, and others are noncompliant with treatment."

Compounding the fact that the best we have may not, as

in this view, work for from "30% to 60% of schizophrenia patients," and that half of this population experience serious side effects, is that even when we think we know what services and treatment will work best, we may not be able to deliver them to more than half of those who might benefit most from them.

This depressing news, substantiating what family members know from experience — and what individuals with mental illness whose family members have abandoned them surely know — gained additional confirmation in 1997 when a PORT study survey undertaken to determine "conformance of current patterns of usual care for persons with schizophrenia" found that "the rates at which patients' treatment conformed to the recommendations were modest at best, generally below 50 percent."

Not unexpectedly, the PORT study also discovered that conformance rates "were higher for pharmacological than for psychosocial treatments and in rural areas than in urban areas." The conclusion: "The findings indicate that current usual treatment practices likely fall substantially short of what would be recommended based on the best evidence on treatment efficacy."

Commenting on this PORT study, NAMI declared that "the results are nothing short of an outrage." NAMI itemized the specific outrages (only half of those suffering from serious side effects of medications receive appropriate treatment; only 29 percent of people with schizophrenia receive appropriate medications; African Americans are more than twice as likely as Caucasians to be overmedicated with antipsychotic medications; as few as 2 percent of individuals with schizophrenia receive the benefits of ACT programs, etc.), and added, "The virtual absence of education and support for both the consumer and the family all but thwart any real chance for recovery."

What the various guidelines offer is often useful, especially for first-time acute crises, where medications are generally most effective, not only for the crisis itself, but if initiated early enough, in helping prevent future relapses. However, the authors of these guidelines continue to view the situation from a particular and often narrowly medical perspective. They seem to think largely in terms of fixing what is wrong, and not in terms of enhancing what is healthy and life-giving (they do not, as with other illnesses, make initial soundings for health, but instead search for deficits and symptoms as if these elements, which commonly express themselves not in quantifiable terms, as in blood tests and X rays, but in behavior, are isolated from the rest of an individual's mind, body, identity, history, and biology). Thus, the guidelines end by having little to say about what is needed in the lives that follow from initial psychiatric crises: in the opportunities, for example, to use crisis as a way of beginning the long and difficult process of recovery, and/or in trying to understand what, aside from or in addition to medications, might prove helpful in the process of recovery, and of how what might prove helpful can be implemented.

For individuals who have had large portions of life stolen from them by mental illness and by everything that ordinarily accompanies mental illness, the reconstructing of a damaged life, and the retrieving of lost hopes and feelings, remains the most difficult and refractory of tasks. Still, the work necessary to reconstruct such lives can also be the most rewarding and inspiring of experiences.

This comes home to me in the early spring of 1998, when, while reviewing these expert consensus guidelines, I visit the Odyssey Behavioral Health Care Residence in New York City. This residential program, which serves sixty individuals with severe and persistent mental illness, all of whom have a co-existing substance abuse problem, and most of whom have criminal records, has its home in a handsome new building at the corner of 121st Street and Second Avenue in Harlem.

I spend a morning visiting with residents, and seeing how they live and work. Their rooms are more spacious, and more neatly kept, than most dormitory rooms at the university where I teach, or at any of the universities my three children have attended. Most of the rooms — the classrooms, exercise rooms, and meeting rooms on the fifth and sixth floors especially, which look out in all directions on the city — are wonderfully bright with daylight. The residents I talk with take great pride in their home and, by accepting increasing levels of responsibility (all residents work to maintain and enhance the building, performing housekeeping, kitchen, and security duties), are making steady and often remarkable progress.

I talk with men and women who have been hospitalized dozens of times, who have been addicts for years, and who have experienced all the despair and confusion that come with depression, schizophrenia, and other major mental illnesses. That virtually all of them have grown up in poor households and communities, and have been both victims and perpetrators of violence, has clearly exacerbated their problems. And yet, through a well-conceived program and a competent and dedicated staff — and through their own efforts — they are making gains that seem amazing, even to them.

Some elements of the program, grounded in behavior-modification principles derived from a therapeutic community model some forty years old — a program in which clients move from level to level, earning privileges as they take on responsibilities — give me some pause. Like many twelve-step programs, it is based, largely, on a structured set of rules and regulations that controls virtually every part of a client's life and every stage of a client's recovery: If and when the client can receive mail, or make or receive calls, or have visitors, or wear a wristwatch or jewelry, or use makeup, or grow a beard.

Many individuals with coexisting conditions of mental illness and substance abuse reject programs like this, and refuse to put up with such a restricted life, preferring to risk the dangers and problems of street life rather than give up their freedoms — including the freedom to be who they want to be, even if this means living miserably and dying young. For those who choose to become members of the Odyssey community, however, the program works, and works remarkably well.

Arnold Unterbach, vice president of mental health services, shows me around the Odyssey facility, which is, he says, conceived of as "a step down from hospitalization," and he also gives me tables of statistics concerning the first twenty-five graduates of the program. For a parallel cohort of individuals with similar diagnoses and histories at a state mental hospital (Rockland Psychiatric Center), the average length of stay during a two-year period was 405 days, 354 of which were spent in the state hospital system. In comparison to this group, *none* of the twenty-five Odyssey graduates were rehospitalized in a state hospital facility during an equivalent period of time, and only six needed to be rehospitalized at all, and then for one-week periods only.

Even more heartening, four of the twenty-five graduates have been accepted to college, seven have received their GED certificates (general equivalency degrees are the equivalent of high school diplomas); fourteen were accepted into job-training programs; another six completed parenting-skills training courses; six who had previously lost visitation rights to their children were granted visitation rights; and another two were granted full custody of their children.

Arnold and I leave the residence and walk across the street to a family center set up and administered by Odyssey—both buildings were opened in June 1994—and visit with people in this facility. We talk about how and why the Odyssey programs succeed where others fail, and we talk about our brothers: about Robert, and about Arnold's brother, Kenneth, who was born four years before Robert, who suffered from mental illness for many years, and who died, a suicide, in 1988.

Arnold and I enter a crowded health center, and walk through a waiting room, full mostly of parents and small children. The center seems much like any modern HMO, except that almost all the clients are black or Latino. We look in on some examining rooms, meet and talk with several staff members, and then Arnold opens a door, and steps aside. I take a few steps into a silent, semidarkened room the size of a small gymnasium, look around, and grab on to Arnold's arm to steady myself.

I take a deep breath, close my eyes, open them again, and, in the silence, I let my gaze move across the room to where along the far walls I see a series of perhaps a dozen cribs, end to end, and where, in a half-dozen or so of the cribs, infants and toddlers are sleeping.

This is the nursery, Arnold whispers, and we have arrived a few minutes after lunch, during naptime. Arnold and I move into the room, several aides and parents wave greetings, and Arnold whispers that there are sixty mothers living in this building with their children. All the mothers are single parents who have substance-abuse problems (I later learn that there are a few fathers who live here too). Most of the single parents also have psychiatric conditions, but the conditions are not serious enough to warrant their moving into Odyssey's (locked) sister building across the street.

We walk through the nursery and I marvel at the peacefulness of the scene, and the clear and apparent pleasure the mothers, teachers, and aides take in living and working here, and also at the generous way in which the facility has been furnished: lovely new wooden cribs, brightly painted walls and murals, huge windows that look out on a large play yard, and, in the room and in the play yard, games, toys, climbing towers, tricycles, and other equipment that would make any parent or child smile with delight and expectation.

Arnold leads me through this room and into another room filled with two-, three-, and four-year-old children, some eating, some playing — alone or with one another — and some, as in the nursery, asleep in cribs and on mats. This is the day care center, Arnold tells me.

I stand and stare for a while — and imagine what none of these children can possibly be imagining: what their lives might be like if this room did not exist for them — and then

Arnold touches my arm, says we should go upstairs to see where the mothers and children live.

The second-floor rooms, like those in the residential treatment center, are spacious and clean, decorated with photos and posters (each set of two rooms has its own lounge area), and filled with worldly items—hair dryers, diapers, magazines, books, stereos, blocks, Legos, board games, clothing, mobiles, toiletries, cosmetics, stuffed animals—that might fill any American home in which young children were living.

This is what it's all about, isn't it? I say to Arnold, and add what seems equally obvious: that if this building and program did not exist, these sixty children would be growing up in crack houses, shelters, and abandoned tenements, and that living here during the first few years of their lives gives them a fighting chance they might not otherwise have. Arnold nods in agreement. Later, I will ask Arnold what will happen to these children when they reach the ages of, say, eleven, twelve, or thirteen. We don't know yet, Arnold says. Are there any programs for them and for their mothers that follow from this progam? No, Arnold answers. Not yet.

But now, watching these infants and toddlers with their mothers, I think: If this program and building were not here, these children would be moving from one place to another with their mothers (even if the mothers and children were able to stay together), subject to all the violence, filth, disease, fear, and ordinary madness that are the daily matter of such lives, and whose issue is usually devastating and lifelong. They would be living without large and small comforts, and without anything we ordinarily think of as love or hope.

Because of this program and this place, the children—like the adults in the Odyssey Residential Treatment Center across the street—will be spared the worst medical and psychological afflictions that come with drugs and with poverty. It seems clear that these children, and their mothers and fathers, like the adults living across the street, now have a chance they might otherwise never have had.

But what is also clear, I remind myself a few hours later when I walk through Harlem to the 125th Street subway station, and think of the trip I will be taking the next day on the same subway line (the number 6 Lexington Avenue local) to visit Robert—now living at Bronx Psychiatric Center (after six months of negotiations and bureaucratic red tape, he has been granted permission to transfer there)—is the fact that too often in this life, as with Arnold's brother Kenneth, no matter the best will, the best programs, the best treatment, and the most devoted families, sometimes things don't work.

SIX

DEGREES OF DISCORDANCY

"Let's split," Coffin Ed said. "Jazz talks too much to me."
"It ain't so much what it says," Grave Digger agreed. "It's what you can't do about it."

— CHESTER HIMES,
Cotton Comes to Harlem

The total cost for the Odyssey Family Center program for single parents and their children is about $17,000 per year per client. The total cost of a comprehensive program for the men and women who live in the Odyssey House Behavioral Health Care Residence, including housing, food, clothing, and medical care, a full array of psychological, vocational, educational, and rehabilitation services, and individual psychotherapy several times a week for many of its clients (and including an average of about $6,000 a year per client received from Medicaid), is approximately $38,000.

The cost to the city of New York for "three hots and a cot," Arnold Unterbach tells me — for a bed and three meals a day in one of its shelters — is approximately $24,000, and this figure does *not* include any services beyond bed and board, or any costs borne by Medicaid and other agencies for medications, medical supplies, emergency medical care, etc.

While cost-effectiveness is hardly the primary reason to champion programs such as this, it seems a most happy fact to find, as with the B.U. program, that programs that work, and pay off in incalculable long-term and long-lasting *human* dividends, often make sense economically too, in both the long *and* the short run. What seems more significant, though, when I consider these programs in relation to the cost of care and treatment for somebody like my brother ($127,000 a year), and in relation to what I find in the consensus guidelines, is what, in both instances—in the old state hospital systems, as in the new expert consensus guidelines—is missing.

Given the fact that individuals who experience a single sustained psychiatric crisis are likely to experience repeated crises and breakdowns throughout their lives, and to experience them progressively, what impresses most when I review the expert consensus guidelines is not so much what is there, but what is *not* there.

The guidelines repeatedly allude to the fact that data and outcome studies for the efficacy of psychotherapy or psychosocial rehabilitation "have not been studied adequately." But as Dr. Michael Hogan, director of the Ohio Department of Mental Health, points out in his response to the PORT recommendations, the search for verifiable data and "doable" studies "can obscure other sources of knowledge and inspiration."

It is, he suggests, much easier to quantify "symptom reduction" than, say, "an increase of hope," or the long-term effects of either, and easier to quantify "shorter hospitalizations" than "a fuller sense of well-being." Vague as the concepts of hope and well-being may seem to a physician, a researcher, or a managed care company, they are quite real to a person recovering from mental illness. Individuals who have recovered from mental illness repeatedly insist that hope itself—the belief that one can recover and that one's own efforts toward this recovery make a crucial difference—becomes a tangible source of genuine change.

Given the complexity of schizophrenia, and "the distinct possibility that schizophrenia is a spectrum of disorders," Hogan writes, "the search for treatments that are specific to this condition is likely unwise. Given the heterogeneity of schizophrenia, developments in other fields should be *better* considered and integrated into practice and treatment research. But current research emphasizes narrow advances."

Dr. William A. Hargreaves of the University of California Medical School in San Francisco, in his response to the PORT Survey, points out that the

> relative emphasis of the PORT Treatment Recommendations is itself revealing. Of the 30 treatment recommendations, 21 address pharmacotherapy or electroconvulsive therapy. To what extent is this research emphasis a balanced response to current knowledge about schizophrenia treatment? How much of this emphasis on somatic treatment is because it is easier and cheaper to study somatic interventions than psychological ones? How much is due to the large research investment that private firms must make in order to market profitable pharmaceutical products? I wonder whether a more vigorous investment in research on psychological treatments and on the delivery of services might improve the quality of life of persons who suffer from schizophrenia.

And in our times, when the treatment most individuals are likely to receive for mental illness is dictated by recommendations such as those in the expert consensus guidelines, most of the research that informs these recommendations is being funded by private drug companies.

While drug companies spend more than $15 *billion* a year in research on new medications, and at least an additional $10 billion a year in promoting medications, the entire budget for the National Institute of Mental Health—including its research budget—is $750 *million*. SAMHSA (Substance Abuse and Mental Health Services Administration) has a budget of slightly more than $2 billion, yet allocates only $58 million of this budget for research. The National Alliance for Research on Schizophrenia and Depression (NARSAD), the leading private, noncommercial organization conducting research on mental illness—a foundation made up of the five major mental health organizations in the United States—disbursed a sum total of $55 million to researchers in its first eleven *years* of existence (1986–1997), and a considerable portion even of this money came from drug companies.

At the same time, the average cost to a drug company of bringing a *single* new psychiatric medication to market is $230 million (Eli Lilly estimates its pretax cost per new medication at $500 million), or about four times the amount of the entire annual research budget for SAMHSA, and more than four times NARSAD's total research budget during its first eleven years. In a growing market for psychiatric drugs, where global sales of antidepressants alone passed $6 billion in 1998, research and development of psychiatric medications is now second only to cancer in the amount of money invested in it by drug companies.

Still, the needs of human beings and their families for help that will be responsive to their long- and short-term situations, especially when these situations are highly individual, may not always be congruent with the needs of corporations to be responsive to their stockholders, and to the ways in which such needs determine medical and research priorities.

Drug companies consistently enjoy the highest profit margins of *any* American industry. From 1980 to 1990, while general inflation rose 58 percent and health costs rose 117 percent, the cost of drugs rose 152 percent. During this same decade, the average profits for the ten largest pharmaceutical firms was 15.5 percent, whereas the average for all other companies in the *Fortune* 500 was 4.6 percent. Drug companies continue to pour money into research and development of new psychiatric drugs(16 cents out of every prescription dollar), and into the marketing and advertising of these drugs (22 cents out of every prescription dollar).

And the marketing and advertising, at $10 billion a year, when monitored by independent parties — whether *The Wall Street Journal, Consumer Reports,* the U.S. Congress, the Public Citizen Health Research Group, or the Federal Drug Administration (FDA) — often turn out to be so misleading, and the drug industry so remiss at self-policing, that Congress and the FDA frequently intervene and legislate against the more outrageously corrupt practices: for example, the gifts to doctors and health care administrators of luxurious vacations and other perks, or the false claims made to doctors and to the general public about unproven effects of medications.

According to a 1992 study prepared for the inspector general's office of the U.S. Department of Health and Human Services, 60 percent of drug ads in medical journals were "poor or unacceptable," while in a 1996 review of the reliability of direct-to-consumer ads, *Consumer Reports* came up with a comparable figure, finding that only 40 percent of these ads were honest about the efficacy, benefits, and risks of the medications being promoted.

In one of the more egregious attempts to encourage people to use antidepressants, Eli Lilly, the maker of Prozac, used National Depression Awareness Day to educate high school students about its product. Claiming that it was sponsoring an educational forum, representatives of Eli Lilly handed out Prozac pens and notepads to high school students, and had them fill out and self-grade questionnaires that inquired if, for example, they ever thought of death, or ever felt inadequate, unsure, and moody. "How soon will I start feeling better?" asked a Prozac brochure given to students after they had completed the questionnaire.

"It was kind of hypocritical," one ninth grader said, "when you think about all the other 'Just Say No' to drug talks that we hear." Given that Prozac had not been approved by the FDA for children or youth, and given what any parent knows about the mood and behavior swings, and the suggestibility, of teenagers ("Some kids claim they are depressed just to get attention," one student remarked. "They are proud to be on Prozac"), small wonder that a reporter covering the event for *The Washington Post* began her article by saying that what had happened reminded her of Aldous Huxley's vision in *Brave New World*.

Physicians and HMOs, under constant pressure from managed care companies to save time and money, and ordinary citizens, under pressure to lead anxiety-free lives (OVER 10 MILLION AMERICANS LEAD TROUBLED LIVES DUE TO PERSISTENT ANXIETY. ARE YOU ONE OF THEM? reads the headline in a Bristol-Myers Squibb advertisement for BuSpar), are urged and encouraged by drug companies to believe that pills will solve most problems, and will do so quickly. "[But] how can a society that says you must be stressed and happy forbid chemical efforts to resolve tensions?" Harvard sociologist David Riesman asks, and goes on to wonder whether antidepressants and other such drugs would be as popular in other cultures, where there might not be the same pressure to be "busy, stressed, *and* happy."

In addition to underwriting events such as National Depression Awareness Day (50 percent of whose budget is paid for by drug companies) and donating millions of tax-deductible dollars to mental health organizations such as NAMI, NDMDA, and NARSAD, drug companies also court doctors and health care administrators with dinners, trinkets, weekend getaways, free medical supplies, subsidized seminars, and, less visibly but more significantly, with office visits. Several studies have demonstrated that a majority of physicians base most of their information about drugs not on research studies, but on drug company advertisements; given the assiduity with which drug companies pursue doctors, this is not surprising.

There is one drug company sales representative for every twelve prescribing doctors in America. The typical American physician sees two to three sales representatives each week, and drug companies spend nearly $15,000 a year in marketing and promotion for each of America's approximately 550,000 physicians. Drug companies also sponsor meetings that provide doctors with the Continuing Medical Education (CME) credits necessary for retaining their medical licenses (more than half of all CME credits are sponsored by drug companies), but so loosely administered is this process that in 1996, simply by filling out a form given to me by one of my students, which had been given to her by her psychiatrist, and mailing it in, I was able to receive an official certificate from the Annenberg Center for Health Sciences of Rancho Mirage, California, attesting to the fact that I had received one (AMA-Category 1, 1.00 Hours Approved) Continuing Medical Education credit.

Then, too, in their direct-to-consumer promotional efforts—in magazines, in mailings, and in our doctors' waiting rooms—drug companies disseminate an abundance of optimistic messages about mental illness, as in the following, from page 1 of "New Hope for Depression and Other Mental Illnesses," an eight-page glossy brochure produced by America's Pharmaceutical Research Companies (which in 1993 changed its name from the more accurate Pharmaceutical Manufacturers Association) given away with millions of issues of the September 2, 1996, edition of *Time* magazine:

MENTAL ILLNESSES ARE AS TREATABLE AS PHYSICAL ILLNESSES

Mental illnesses such as panic disorder, depression and schizophrenia affect approximately 40 million Americans each year.

These illnesses strike individuals from all walks of life, regardless of age, race, income or education. They can affect the person's ability to think clearly, act appropriately and relate to others—and reduce the chances for a happy, productive, "normal" life.

What many people fail to realize, however, is that mental illnesses are medical illnesses just like diabetes, high blood pressure or heart disease. And like physical illnesses, most mental disorders can be treated effectively.

And below this, in a half-page box, and alongside the photo of a happy, pretty, smiling young woman, they offer us this tale:

ONE WOMAN'S STORY

Laura Waskey, 29, had her first episode of depression in high school. A guidance counselor recognized that Laura's behavior problems were more than just a teenage phase and suggested that Laura see a psychiatrist. She did, but only for a short while, and without medicines. It wasn't until 10 years later, after joining the Navy, that Laura was put on antidepressant medication. "The medicine changed my life," says Laura. "I've never felt better." Her symptoms of sleeping all day, no appetite and lack of interest in things have disappeared. "It's so comforting to know that I don't have to live miserably anymore," Laura says with a smile.

Whatever drug companies and mental health organizations may say about mental illness being "an illness like any other," however, the truth is that few people with or without a mental illness think of it as being similar to diabetes, cancer, high blood pressure, heart disease, or the flu.

Although mental illness may have many things in common with these illnesses—that, like diabetes, it usually requires careful monitoring and lifetime management; or that medications may, as with heart disease and the flu, regulate and/or alleviate many of its symptoms—its *differences* from other illnesses are what invariably matter most, not only to those individuals who suffer from it, but to the families and friends who love these individuals, who live with them, and who care for them across their lifetimes.

I have known people for years—friends, colleagues, neighbors—before they told me that they too had brothers, sisters, sons, or daughters who suffered from mental illness and had been institutionalized. My own father did not tell any of his eight brothers and sisters about Robert's breakdowns for the first seven years following Robert's initial hospitalization. "Why should anyone else have to know?" he said. "When people ask about Robert, what I say to them is that he'll probably be going back to college soon, and that he's still trying to find himself, and that's all."

Although friends might have known about Robert for decades—had met him and spent time with him—when they finally revealed to me that they too had family members who suffered from mental illness, they would frequently do so in the secretive way in which people used to whisper to one another about someone who had cancer.

Even at meetings and fund-raising dinners sponsored by chapters of the Alliance for the Mentally Ill or the Mental Health Association, most people who come up to me after I give a talk will wait until we are alone before they will confide, softly and hesitantly, and looking around first to make sure nobody can overhear, that they too have a brother or sister, son or daughter who suffers from mental illness.

I have friends, colleagues, and acquaintances (including mental health professionals) who continue to hide the fact of their own past history of mental illness, or that they take psychotropic medications, or that they have family members with serious mental illness, not only from close friends and from colleagues with whom they work every day, but—if, for example, the family member is a brother or sister—from their own children.

I talk with a forty-year-old M.D., Lynne Douglas, a radiation oncologist in Seattle, Washington, the married mother of two young children, who tells me that although she had repeated hospitalizations for mental illness during her twenties, and lost years of her life to her struggles with mania and depression, she still keeps this part of her history secret. When an article about Lynne, with accompanying photo, appears in a newsletter ("Welcome to Lynne M. Douglas, MD, who will direct radiation oncology at the new Seattle Central Campus. She joins Cancer Care from the Washington State Health Sciences Center, where she had been program director and interim director of the Radiation Therapy Division"), she sends me a copy, with a Post-it attached below her smiling photo, arrows pointing to it, and this note: "If they only knew . . ."

"For me, being public about my mental illness has always seemed like the natural thing to do," says Robert O. Borstin, senior advisor to the treasury secretary of the United States — a man who has suffered from manic depression most of his adult life, and that rare public figure who has never been ashamed or embarrassed about his psychiatric condition. "I was lucky: I had the best treatment in the best private hospitals; a family that supported me emotionally and financially; friends who never turned away; employers whose only questions were about what they could do to make my life easier; and enough experience in the media to know how little they know."

I am friends with a couple whose twenty-year-old daughter, Sarah, who graduated a few years ago from high school, where she made excellent grades, now stays in her room most of the time, either watching movies or sleeping. Her behavior is, by conventional standards, bizarre and troubling: She confronts telephone callers and strangers with uncontrollable rage; she is alarmingly withdrawn, has no friends, and no seeming desire or ability to make friends; she has irrational and paranoid fears; and she has attempted suicide three times. When she does venture out into the world on her own, she often becomes lost and acts in ways that result in her being picked up by the police and taken to local emergency wards. Sarah has been diagnosed as having schizophrenia, she is on antipsychotic medications, and she has, in her young life, seen and been seen by dozens of psychiatrists (and emergency room medical doctors), none of whom she trusts; when she finally found a psychiatrist she liked and began to confide in him, he moved away (and on short notice), after which Sarah again attempted suicide.

Sarah is not disturbed enough to require hospitalization, nor is she well enough to work or to attend school, either full time or part time. Each time she tries work or school, she "fails," in her own eyes, and in the eyes of others, by having a breakdown. Her parents have searched out day treatment programs, mental health centers, and special programs, but whenever Sarah visits one, and for different reasons each time, though usually because she finds them boring or smoke filled (for example, day centers where people older and more disturbed than she is hang around smoking and watching TV) — Sarah returns home vowing never to visit one of these places again.

Sarah's parents have not been away by themselves for even a weekend during the past four years. They take turns staying home with their daughter; they consult me and others about possible programs, residences, doctors, and medications; they spend countless hours researching possibilities and visiting new programs; and, most of all, they worry about Sarah's severe mood swings (from wild tantrums to sullen and depressed withdrawal), her tendency to violence, and her inability to relate to others. They worry, too, about how long they can continue to take turns tending to her without becoming so exhausted, physically and emotionally, that they become useless, and less than useless, not only to Sarah, but to themselves and to each other.

They are, in effect, hostage to a situation whose presence in their lives they can barely comprehend, and despite being successful middle-class Americans living in a lovely private home in a moderate-sized, middle- and upper-middle-class American city, and despite using all the means at their disposal, not only can they find no solution to their problem, but they are afraid of letting anybody other than their closest friends know the truth of their situation. Although the mother, in her job as director of a public relations firm, has had occasion to work with mental health organizations, she has yet to tell any of her colleagues that her own daughter suffers from mental illness.

When I talk with my friends, and visit with them, and watch them growing old before their time, I think: Here is the late-twentieth-century American version of Gregor Samsa's family. What *does* a family do when its child has a condition others regard as supremely repellent, and one for which, most of the time, there is no solution—neither medical, nor human—and whose course, as with Robert's condition, is unpredictable, sad, and exhausting in the extreme?

And if a family with means and education that should enable them to obtain the best of care for their daughter is so overwhelmed and lost—can find no solution or even, as of this writing, no respite for themselves, and feel, also, such an enormous weight of shame and secrecy—what of those millions of families without the means and wherewithal available to Sarah's family?

When it comes to psychiatric disabilities, lives that are already difficult in the extreme are made excruciating most of the time not only by the unpredictable and tragic course of these conditions, but by the lack of and difficulty in obtaining decent care and treatment.

Although outcome figures for the treatment of mental illness are at least as good, and in many cases better, than they are for illnesses such as heart disease, diabetes, and hypertension, managed care firms have instituted limits, caps, and deductibles for mental illnesses that are patently discriminatory. While in the general health sector there has been a shift to greater outpatient care, when it comes to mental illness, both inpatient *and* outpatient care have been cut back. From 1988 to 1997, for example, the number of plans with limits on outpatient behavioral health visits increased 48 percent (from 26 percent), while, from 1990 to 1997, the number of plans that imposed limits on inpatient psychiatric care increased from 63 percent to 86 percent. And while total health care expenditures by managed care companies fell by 7 percent between the years 1988 and 1997, expenditures for mental health services during the same period fell by 54 percent.

If you are "diagnosed with clinical depression," Kelly Williams, president of the Greater Tampa Bay Mental Health Association, says, "and have to make five or six different calls to five or six different people and get five or six different answering machines — that right there is a deterrent to your accessing that system. If you didn't already have a diagnosis for depression or anxiety, you surely would after having made repeated attempts to access your mental health benefits."

Responding to the medical director of the local managed care firm, who justified cutting back long-term benefits by referring to therapy as "rent a friend," Williams makes the obvious point: "If that comment were made about a person with long-term care needs such as Alzheimer's, cancer, and diabetes, that would be unacceptable. Therein lies this huge amount of stigma, the huge gap in the way people view mental illness versus physical illness. Can you imagine if he said, 'Those people who are going into chemotherapy are stretching it out for years'?"

When it comes to psychiatric disabilities, lives made difficult in the extreme are constantly made more excruciating by the omnipresence of "this huge amount of stigma": by the ways in which stigma influences and informs the policies, budgets, and organizations that provide care and treatment; by the ongoing ignorance, prejudice, and hostility of others — individually, collectively, and institutionally; by the insidious ways in which this ignorance, prejudice, and hostility affects those afflicted (as in Ward 3 of my own city), and — worst of all perhaps — by the way these attitudes are often internalized by those affected, thus intensifying already terrible and terrifying feelings of helplessness, despair, and shame.

Old stereotypes of and attitudes toward madness, and old habits of care, of treatment, and of thought, die hard; and though lives like those of Dan Fisher, Moe Armstrong, Rose Tompkins, Gaston Cloutier, and Lynne Douglas may be exemplary, they are hardly representative.

For in this world, having a mental illness—being mad and having a history of being mad—often means believing of yourself what others believe about you: that you are less than fully human, and less worthy—have fewer rights, and fewer possibilities—than the rest of us, and that others have the right to mock you.

"ESPNEWS is the perfect cure for the maniacal, sports-obsessed addict who can't wait to find out the very latest sports news," reads the text at the top of a full-page ad in the *ESPN College Basketball Issue* for 1996–97. The only other sentence on the page, at the bottom, is this: "I believe the other cure is Thorazine."

In *The Frontiers of Medicine*, a fall 1996 special issue of *Time* magazine, the feature article about mental illness, "Targeting the Brain," reads as if it has been written by the same people who wrote the American Pharmaceutical Research Companies' *Health Guide* on mental illness. The special issue appears, in fact, in the same month, September 1996, that the *Health Guide* is given away with millions of copies of *Time*.

In the article, *Time*'s writers announce that "the 3-lb. organ that rules the body is finally giving up its secrets," that most mental illnesses, including schizophrenia, panic disorder, post-traumatic stress disorder, and obsessive compulsive disorder, "turn out to be caused by specific chemical imbalances," and that "the good news is that many if not most of these brain afflictions can now be remedied by increasingly precise psychoactive drugs."

"The Oedipus complex," *Time* declares, "has been reduced to a matter of molecules," and in such a brave new world, "the superstar of the hour" is the "family" of antidepressant drugs such as Prozac, "Eli Lilly's $2.1 billion-a-year baby."

By describing mental illness in pseudoscientific terms, and by regarding it as a disease like any other and, as such, remediable by miraculous new scientific discoveries, such prose may seem to to be creating tolerance, compassion, and hope for individuals and families afflicted by mental illness. But it seems more likely that, by pandering to dreams of quick fixes and miracle cures, articles such as this help sustain those very illusions that enable us to deny reality and so hold to false beliefs and attitudes. (See also E. Fuller Torrey, director of NAMI's Research Institute, in a February 1998 *New York Times Magazine* article about him, stating his belief that we will have "a cure" for schizophrenia "in the next 5 to 10 years.")

But what if the myriad forms of mental illness can *not* be reduced to molecules and chemical imbalances that can be remedied by increasingly precise psychoactive drugs, and if we do not find a "cure" for mental illness within the next five to ten years? If mental illness is not amenable to cures and treatments in the ways other illnesses are, how can we *not* continue to believe what we have previously and perennially believed about it?

Despite such articles then, and sometimes because of them, and because of all the other hype and literature put out by drug companies, the popular media, and, at times, mental health organizations, most people, in my experience, including and sometimes especially those who suffer from mental illness, continue to believe what they have always believed: that those designated as mad are dangerous and to be feared; that they are more like children than adults; that they will never get well ("once-a-schizophrenic-always-a-schizophrenic"); that they must remain permanently dependent upon others to make major decisions for them and to manage the essentials of their lives; that their wishes and words can be ignored because they are without sense or meaning; that they should not be allowed to take risks, and must be protected from failures, large and small; that they are disabled people, rather than people with disabilities; that they are fatally flawed due to an inherited condition that in other times might have marked them as being possessed by demons or the devil; and that, if no longer regarded as innately evil and/or alien to things human, they are, at the least and in effect, damaged goods: permanently in need of patronizing and infantilizing care, which care invariably deprives them of basic rights, and of access to the ordinary matter of life.

"In other times and places," the mother of a ten-year-old boy diagnosed as having a developmental and neurological disability tells me, "my son would probably not have been allowed to live. I suppose I'm grateful—of course I am—but do you know what's hardest of all? It's seeing the way the other children at school treat him. They don't *like* him, and they don't like him because he's different, and yet the truth is that his difference from them is really very, very slight. It breaks my heart."

In other times and places, as we know from books that have chronicled the history of the mad, the mad have not only been caged, imprisoned, tortured, murdered, castrated, sterilized, used as beasts of burden and as subjects for medical experimentation, but, more traditionally, they have been abandoned, held up to public ridicule, and exiled from the families and communities into which they were born.

"Where in the global burden of disease should sorrow rank?" asks the World Health Organization in the opening sentence of its 1995 *Report* on disease, and it goes on to summarize the global situation, and to do so without any least measure of optimism: "Mental ill-health is at the bottom of the medical pecking order," the *Report* states, and provides statistics to indicate the scale of the problem: "Some 500 million people are believed to suffer from neurotic, stress-related and somatoform disorders (psychological problems which present themselves as physical complaints). A further 200 million suffer from mood disorders, such as chronic and manic depression. Mental retardation affects some 83 million people, epilepsy 30 million, dementia 22 million and schizophrenia 16 million.

"Only the most severe cases, such as schizophrenia or

manic depression," the *Report* states, "receive what minimal care there is, even in developed countries."

And even in this last decade of our century (the "Decade of the Brain," so-named by our president and our Congress), in this most enlightened of times and nations, when we are publicly and repeatedly entreated to believe that mental illnesses do not reflect moral failures and are no different, and just as treatable and curable, as physical illnesses, old habits of thought abound. When *The New York Times* runs a front-page story about the millions of Americans taking Prozac, all of those interviewed praise Prozac to the skies, and claim that it has changed and/or saved their lives. Still, the *Times* notes, "the stigma associated with a psychiatric condition like depression, and with using drugs to combat it, remains great: everyone interviewed declined to allow their name to be published, although they were eager to talk about how the drug had helped them."

This is so despite the fact that Prozac is, as the *Times* points out, "legal and regarded as relatively harmless," and despite the fact that the use of antidepressants, especially among the middle class, is widespread. Dr. Peter Kramer, author of *Listening to Prozac*, maintains that "no one in the middle class is further than three (or is it two?) degrees of separation from Prozac," and statistics bear him out: In any given year, 11 percent of Americans will be taking psychotropic medications, and of the approximately sixteen million Americans who visit doctors each year because they are feeling depressed, a full 70 percent will wind up on antidepressants. "If Prozac ever goes over-the-counter," my local pharmacist says to me, "I go out of business."

When I visit with a group of upper-middle-class families — doctors, lawyers, professors, executives, therapists — in an elegant private home in Cambridge, Massachusetts, at a meeting of the local chapter of the Alliance for the Mentally Ill, what the family members talk about above all is how lonely and isolating it is to care for a family member who has a history of mental illness.

"When I had a minor woman's problem last year, and was in the hospital for a day, I received lots of visits, tons of cards and flowers and calls," a middle-aged woman says while we are all eating supper together. "Everybody cared. But when my son was hospitalized again recently—he's been living with us, and getting along pretty well, going back to school and the rest—nothing: no visits, no cards, no calls, no flowers."

When I talk with mental health workers, they tell me that often their employers—state departments of mental health, local human services providers, or charitable organizations—encourage them to go out and try to educate the public about mental illness (ask them to join, for example, in NAMI's five-year "Campaign to End Discrimination"), but that they feel such work is a waste of their time and energy.

"I'd rather use my time and skills to work with people who *have* mental illnesses, and try to free *them* from all the self-blame and stigma they live with," David Hilton, director of consumer affairs for the state of New Hampshire's Department of Mental Health, says. "This seems a more real task, and one where I have a fair chance of succeeding, and of making a difference."

Moe Armstrong says much the same thing. "Oh, they're always trying to get me to speak at schools and Rotary clubs and to police groups and stuff, and sometimes I say yes, Jay, and it helps, I suppose—education always helps—but my most important work is still with consumers. I can make a *real* difference there. At least I think I can. But change the way *most* people think about us? Good luck!"

When Moe, David Hilton, and others speak like this, I am reminded of similar statements civil rights leaders were making in the sixties, when many of them turned their efforts away from trying to change the attitudes and actions of the larger American society—from petitioning it for equality and justice, in the courts and in the streets—and began instead working to empower black people, especially black children, so that they might take rightful pride in themselves, their history, and their achievements, no matter the ignorant and cruel attitudes of others toward them.

I recall how sensible this shift in attitude — and politics — seemed, when, during the sixties, I taught for brief periods of time in Harlem, in the Williamsburg section of Brooklyn, and on New York City's Upper West Side. How much easier a job it was for me to be in a city school helping to educate young black and Latino students so that their lives might be changed for the better than it would have been to try to educate (and change) middle-class white Americans about *their* attitudes, and about what it would take to have anything like a truly integrated and just society.

As with housing — whether in New York City in the sixties or Northampton, Massachusetts, in the nineties — or with employment, or with education, or with any of the other essentials of life, why, I wonder, should people who are discriminated against because of the pigmentation of their skin, or their mental disability, have to wait for, and beg for, what should already be theirs, and what should be basic rights for any human being? And why, then as now, should the burden of proof, and of change, be forever laid upon the backs and minds of those people who have already been victimized, disabled, and dispossessed by laws, discrimination, and oppression not of their making?

I recall, in the sixties, reading James Baldwin's early autobiographical essays about growing up in Harlem, where he writes of the everyday experience of watching black people try to lighten their skin and straighten their hair — where he writes about witnessing the racism of the majority culture make its way through skin, and down into the very souls of black people, so that they came to believe, along with those who hated, oppressed, belittled, and murdered them, that it was so, that it was a curse — an indelible mark of inferiority and hopelessness — to be born with pigmented skin and kinky hair.

And so, even while I continue to put myself to school concerning ways in which *we* try to help *them* — and often do so effectively and humanely—and even while I try not to ignore or devalue real differences that can take place in the lives of people with mental illness through programs such as Odyssey House, or NAMI's antistigma campaign, or new and improved medications, or legislation that grants to mental illness insurance parity with other illnesses, or efforts to get managed care companies to be more responsive and responsible concerning benefits for mental illness—I find myself more curious and moved by those programs in which people who have experienced the worst ravages of mental illness are trying, and succeeding, in helping themselves, for it is through these programs, I sense, that new hope for real and lasting change may lie. It is through these programs that individuals can not only recover, but move *beyond* disability into lives where their condition becomes irrelevant to the primary and workaday ways in which they identify themselves and are identified by others.

I begin to believe this can happen because I see it happening: I see individuals who have been at least as severely emotionally disabled as my brother begin to turn their energies from the tasks of recovery to the tasks of ordinary life. I see individuals creating new lives and new possibilities for themselves even while they bring their old memories, fears, struggles, and symptoms into these new lives with them. And in these new lives I also see them finding those unexpected and unpredictable moments, feelings, and experiences that are the essence—and richness—of *any* complicated, ongoing life.

On May 19, 1997, not long before Robert moves a dozen miles north, from Staten Island to the Bronx, I drive a hundred miles north from Northampton, to West Lebanon, New Hampshire, to spend a day at West Central Services, Inc., one of New Hampshire's ten private, not-for-profit mental health centers.

West Central Services, located five miles from Hanover

(home of Dartmouth College, and of the Dartmouth-Hitchcock Hospital and Medical Center), has a catchment area of 950 square miles, and provides a population of seventy to eighty thousand residents with a full range of mental health services, including personal and family counseling and education, emergency and crisis intervention, treatment for substance abuse, vocational rehabilitation, peer support programs, and residential programs. In cooperation with the Dartmouth-New Hampshire Psychiatric Research Center, West Central Services also collaborates in research and development of new treatment programs.

West Central Services is housed in a beautifully restored nineteenth-century mill building that overlooks the Mascoma River, and that dates from the time of the Civil War. Its offices are spacious, full of brightly colored tapestries and wall hangings, and furnished with handsome new furniture and equipment. The people who work here, for the most part, are young, bright, and enthusiastic, and they act, talk, and dress very much like young professionals I meet when I am in New York City.

I recall the dingy day care centers, offices, and residences Robert and I have known through most of the last four decades, and the weary, phlegmatic, ill-dressed social workers Robert has often been assigned to, and I wonder if coming to a place like this would allow Robert to feel that he truly mattered to others — or if the graciousness of such surroundings would seem a reproach that might cause him to despair, again, about the distance between what his life is and what it might have been.

"We are small and homegrown," Phil Wyzik, the director of community support services, tells me a short while after we meet. "We are proud of our innovations, our results, and our consumers, and most of all we are proud of our outcomes."

Phil is a wiry, scholarly-appearing man in his early forties who dresses and looks as if he might be the dean of the

School of Engineering at a university. He is direct, thoughtful, and intelligent, and when he warms to his subject—his pride in West Central's achievements—enthusiastic.

He talks with me about West Central's basic philosophy, and its governing assumption: that individuals like Robert have "the right to a real life in the community," and that West Central's job is to do anything and everything to make this possible. When it comes to managing medications and problems of noncompliance, for example, Phil says that West Central finds it makes sense to visit clients in their homes and neighborhoods because that's where their shopping centers, pharmacists, and medicine cabinets are. In this way, the skills that clients acquire are acquired not in institutions, but in the real world.

"We will even employ twenty-four-hour round-the-clock staff to keep a person in this world, somehow and in some way—or have one of our outreach nurses visit and stay with a client, rather than make them come into our offices."

If Robert were living in New Hampshire, Phil says matter-of-factly, he would not now be in a hospital. In fact, he informs me, New Hampshire no longer has a state mental hospital. It maintains a 140-bed unit in Concord, but this is for emergencies only. It also maintains some places for elderly citizens who cannot care for themselves, and a few homes for other individuals who absolutely cannot cope.

The scale of things in New Hampshire and at West Central, we both agree, helps.

"One can make large changes if one is small enough," Phil says, and he notes that all ten of New Hampshire's regional mental health centers could fit into one of New York City's catchment areas. "If I come up with an idea—an innovative idea for a new program, or a modification of one of our programs—I don't have to go through an immense amount of paperwork to put it into effect. A phone call does the job. I call Concord—that's where the DMH is—and we talk, and if my idea seems reasonable, and sometimes if it doesn't, I get the go-ahead."

Because of its emphasis on helping individuals like Robert make and maintain lives in the community, West Central is "all outreach oriented," and it uses a team model much like the ACT (Assertive Community Treatment) model developed in the late seventies by Leonard I. Stein and Mary Ann Test in Madison, Wisconsin. At the time Dr. Stein was a professor in the Department of Psychiatry at the University of Wisconsin Medical School and the medical director of the Dane County Mental Health Center, and Dr. Test was a professor at the University of Wisconsin's School of Social Work.

Despite the fact that many outcome studies reported on the ACT teams' successes, particularly in reducing hospitalizations and stabilizing housing, until very recently (when it was endorsed by NAMI), the model was infrequently replicated outside Wisconsin and its neighboring state of Michigan. The basic elements of the ACT model include a multidisciplinary team, ordinarily consisting of a psychiatrist, a nurse, and at least two case managers — and it is the team *working as a team* (not an individual doctor or case manager), with varying numbers of other professionals (psychologists, social workers, psychopharmacologists, vocational and educational support specialists), as situations dictate, that takes responsibility for each individual client.

When first developed and employed two decades ago, ACT teams were, for state-sponsored care of people with severe mental illness, unique in that they provided *comprehensive* services on a twenty-four-hours-a-day, seven-days-a-week basis. Their programs were developed as a direct reaction to the disarray in which services were being provided at that time, if at all, to individuals like my brother when they were discharged from state mental hospitals.

In those days, even when community mental health resources existed, they were generally underfunded and fragmented. Clients would have to go to one place for medications, to another for therapy, to another for general medical care, to another for day care programs, to another for help with financial management, to another for housing services, etc. In such circumstances, where there was little if any communication or cooperation among local, private, and state human-service providers, and where there were few community mental health resources, there was also virtually no outreach, and little follow-up by mental health professionals of the kind West Central now routinely provides.

Clients and their families, lacking the ability or the means to organize the essentials of their lives—food, clothing, housing, medical care, and work—often despaired and dropped out of whatever systems of assistance existed, or were recycled repeatedly through emergency wards, jails, and mental hospitals. To cite one telling statistic, fewer than 50 percent of patients discharged from state mental hospitals ever showed up for even a first scheduled outpatient visit at the office of the doctor or clinic to which the hospital referred them, if and when a referral was made.

In a 1998 retrospective review of models of community care for severe mental illness, the *Schizophrenia Bulletin* reports:

> The basic tenets of the ACT model include (1) low patient to staff ratios (e.g., 10:1, rather than 30:1 or higher); (2) most services provided in the community (e.g., patients' homes, restaurants), rather than in offices; (3) caseloads shared across clinicians, rather than individual caseloads; (4) 24-hour coverage; (5) most services provided directly by the ACT team and not brokered out; and (6) time-unlimited service.
>
> The low patient to staff ratio, the emphasis placed on treatment in patients' natural environment, and the preference for providing direct services rather than referring patients elsewhere reflect the ACT model's priority on providing practical supports in daily living, such as shopping, laundry, and transportation.

The ACT principles were often, as at West Central, adapted to meet the unique needs of specific patient populations, geographical settings, and state or local agencies. By providing comprehensive care on a round-the-clock, year-round basis, what the ACT programs attempted to do, above all, was to address the major problems resulting from deinstitutionalization—the fragmentation and inconstancy of care.

At West Central, Phil Wyzik and other staff members use the basic ACT principles while focusing on employment: on helping clients find and keep jobs, and on using vocational support services and peer support centers to enable individuals to get and keep these jobs and, through them, begin to recover from their illnesses and thereby to regain and to make lives for themselves in their communities.

The West Central staff, unlike the early ACT teams, which functioned for time-limited periods (one to three years most often), takes a long-range view of recovery, and of what will be needed long-range to effect recovery. This leads the staff to think and act "in terms of small increments," Phil explains, and of having "one success build upon another."

Phil has worked at Fountain House in New York, at day care centers in New York and New Hampshire, and he has also, for a half-dozen years, run dual diagnosis groups at West Central. What he has found is that the skills clients acquired in day care centers or clubhouses did not often carry over into their lives when they moved out into the world beyond day care centers. What worked, in his experience, was breaking patterns of dependency.

For all the good that the Fountain House clubhouse model provides, Phil says, it can also foster dependency in the way Alcoholics Anonymous groups do—a sense that one cannot and never will be able to make it on one's own. To break such patterns and enable clients to take increasing responsibility for their own lives, West Central has found that providing skills in natural environments works best for almost everybody.

Training people for jobs in sheltered settings, and then sending them out to perform the same jobs in the world, for example, didn't work nearly as well as placing people in jobs first—securing employment for them, and then training them on the job while at the same time providing supports and coping skills, whether these had to do with personal hygiene, with dress, with getting to work on time, or with resolving conflicts with fellow workers.

When a client first comes to West Central Services, the client draws up a detailed master treatment plan in collaboration with a case manager, a plan that focuses not so much on deficits as on "client preferences and strengths," on three-month and one-year goals, and on tasks and aspects of daily living (financial skills, self-care skills, home management, relations to family and community, and components such as "hopefulness," "survival skills," and "instrumental skills"). The client and case manager review and, if necessary, modify the plan on weekly and monthly bases.

Anticipating the possibility of future crises, the client also draws up emergency plans, and because the client has helped draw up his or her own treatment plan, the client does not become a mere "victim of the system," Phil points out, but remains, instead, "a responsible partner in the important decisions that affect his or her life."

At weekly meetings of dual diagnosis teams, this approach—of giving clients as much responsibility for their own lives as possible—prevails. The two staff members who run the dual diagnosis groups go over the case of each individual in treatment and try as much as possible to help the client work toward discrete, concrete objectives. They try to bring families into their groups when this seems wise, and their ultimate goal is to turn as many programs as possible over to the clients themselves.

Bud Ross, who is one of two staff members running the group, says that he sees his job as working to make himself *irrelevant* to the process of recovery, except in the early stages, which can last for one to two years, as a coordinator.

At one point during a session, Julie Sarzynski, a middle-aged woman who runs the team with Bud Ross, turns to Bud, laughs, and asks: "Can you remember when I was incapable of making a decision about *anything*?"

Julie is stylishly dressed, articulate and, when she laughs, radiant. She has been hospitalized frequently for depression and substance abuse ("My worst memory somehow—the real bottom—was when they took away my dental floss," she says. "Of all the horrors I've known, why that?"), and she now works part time for West Central, helping to run dual diagnosis groups, and providing case management and peer support.

Bud and Julie point out that a major reason they can work toward making themselves irrelevant, and the groups and individuals self-sustaining, is because they are "encouraged to take risks."

"We know we have the backing—resources and money—to try things," Bud says, "and to try things that value risk and adventure over safety."

"When we start getting too conservative," Julie adds, "Dave Hilton, our boss, is always there to jangle our chains!"

Like Phil, Julie and Bud spend much of their time helping clients find and keep jobs in the community. More than all the talk in the world, it's being out there with other people, in real jobs, they believe, that cuts into tokenism, stigma, and stereotyping.

"For persons who have been hospitalized and brutalized and out of it for years," Bud says, "simply being able to think of themselves as something other than mental cases—loons or nuts or schizos—and to have others not think of them this way—can make all the difference."

After lunch, I drive out to CRREL, the Cold Regions Research and Engineering Laboratory, a U.S. Army Corps of Engineers facility in Hanover that employs more than six hundred workers, including seventeen from West Central Services. CRREL is the major U.S. government facility for the study of what happens to people and things at below-freezing temperatures, and for the development of solutions to problems that arise in the world's cold regions. CRREL's engineers, scientists, and technicians deal primarily with snow, ice, and frozen ground, and with the effects of these conditions on construction, transportation, and military operations. CRREL also does research on the influences of low temperatures on biological systems and human physiology.

CRREL maintains approximately 285,000 square feet of structures on 31 acres. These structures include computer centers, machine shops, remote-sensing analysis centers, experimental sludge-freezing facilities, saline ice-testing facilities, deep refrigerated wells, chemistry and electron microscope laboratories, and some of the largest refrigerated-hydraulics and refrigerated-soils laboratories in the world.

Four years ago, West Central bid for and won the contract to provide all of CRREL's custodial services. At CRREL, I meet some of the West Central workers, all of whom have histories of severe mental illness. They earn the state minimum wage—$7.88 an hour—and though some of them work at higher-skilled jobs than others (one works a regular forty-hour week as a general handyman), they have decided, jointly, that they should all receive the same hourly wage. This is so, in part—according to Lisa Mueller, a West Central therapist who works with West Central's clients at CRREL—because to keep the jobs, workers must take and pass government tests, and because test anxiety for most workers is generally off the spectrum.

Some of the workers work four-hour shifts, and some come in at unorthodox times—very early, or midday, or late night, depending upon their medications, sleeping patterns, and family responsibilities. Lisa herself is at CRREL two hours each day to oversee things and mediate problems, and "simply to be there," she says, "and to talk with people, for whatever small or large needs arise."

When West Central first won the contract four years ago, they organized introductory educational meetings for CRREL workers, but fewer than fifty people attended, Lisa informs me, and though the other government employees at CRREL have come to accept the West Central employees—

the building supervisor tells me they are "better than government workers because," in his opinion, "they are more highly motivated"—the West Central workers tend to go their own ways, and not to interact much with other CRREL employees.

West Central has also, within the past year, bid for and won the contract for CRREL's mailroom, and this contract has provided five additional full-time jobs for West Central clients. The work includes the usual tasks that come with any mailroom in a large organization, and also includes responsibility for international mailings and insurance, money exchanges, the dissemination of CRREL's many publications, and the assembling of special scientific, military, and government mailing lists.

While I talk with these workers (one, a young woman who is also physically disabled, tells me that because of the confidence she has gained from working full time in the mailroom, she has enrolled in college courses for the fall), I think again, as I did when visiting Gaston at the CAUSE offices in Quincy, of how large a difference in people's lives a small amount of flexibility, tolerance, and opportunity can make. I think of how wonderful it is to be with people who might otherwise be warehoused in some dull hospital or day center, but who are, instead, here: taking real pride in real work in this place we refer to as the real world.

I think, too, of something Jeffrey Geller, professor of psychiatry and director of public sector psychiatry at the University of Massachusetts Medical School (one of only a handful of medical schools in the country with a program that places a priority on public service for mental health), said to me. It is Jeff's belief that what often makes a crucial difference in outcomes—in rates and degrees of recovery and remission—has to do not so much with programs, medications, policies, and therapies, but with something more basic: what he refers to as "the degree of discordancy."

"If you attend your tenth or twentieth high school reunion, and you were class valedictorian once upon a time, and you've had breakdowns and have been hospitalized and the rest in the years since, and now you work as a custodian or a night watchman, then there's a good chance you're going to feel pretty bad about yourself," Jeff explains.

"It often seems to me that a lot of how lives turn out, and which people do or do not make it back in our world, and with what degree of fulfillment and happiness," he continues, "has to do with *expectations*—expectations of self, of family, of community, and of society—and with how far expectations are from reality. So that if you go back to a high school reunion and most of your old buddies are now janitors, or night watchmen, or run filling stations—and if half of them, say, have had broken marriages, and drinking problems, or both—which is pretty likely these days—then if you've been hanging out in a clubhouse for a few months or years, or working as a janitor or dishwasher, and living alone, you're not going to feel so bad about yourself."

What happens in New York City, in Boston, and in Northampton—Jeff has worked in all three places—is not typical of what is happening in the rest of America, Jeff contends.

"What happens in Lowell, or Worcester, or a small town in New Hampshire is more typical," he says, "and in my experience, the people who do better are those who fell the least because they started lower."

Later that afternoon, back in West Lebanon after my visit to CRREL, I visit a peer support center housed on the first floor of a renovated two-story family dwelling near the city's center, and talk with its executive director, Shery Mead.

Shery, a single parent of three children (ages nine, twelve, and fifteen), runs *two* peer support centers, the Next Step Center, in West Lebanon, and the Stepping Stone Center, about twenty miles away, in Claremont. Before becoming executive director of these two centers, Shery worked for ten years as a high school music teacher at Roberts Union Academy, a private preparatory school in Sheppard, New Hampshire, the town where Shery lives with her three children. Before she taught at Roberts Union, Shery did two years of postgraduate work at the Berklee School of Music in Boston. Shery also, for a period of about ten years, earned a living as lead guitarist for numerous musical groups (jazz, folk, blues, rock-and-roll, country-western). In 1995, after she received her master's degree in social work, she came to work as executive director of the two peer support centers.

Shery, who is in her mid-forties, has large blue eyes, a small, straight, upturned nose, and bewitchingly thick black eyebrows. These, along with her short jet-black hair (which used to hang down past her waist, she tells me later) and her irrepressible enthusiasm ("There's nothing laid back about Shery!" one center member declares when Shery introduces him to me), give her an appearance that in other times might have been called tomboyish.

She is five feet seven inches tall, and moves with the easy, graceful gait and focused determination of an athlete who is not afraid to do whatever it takes to get where she wants to go—and to *win*. She regularly jogs anywhere between three and fifteen miles a day, skis (cross-country) all winter long, has biked across Canada, competed in triathlons, and has been willing to try just about any activity—ice climbing, rock climbing, mountain climbing, hang gliding—that promises adventure and exhilaration for body *and* soul.

Like Phil and Bud, she prefers risk to safety, both for herself and—when she finds it appropriate and timely—for her clients. "Why isn't there more *adventure* therapy?" she will often ask, in groups and in one-on-one conferences. "Let's talk more about adventure—about putting more *life* into our lives—and less about what might go wrong, okay?"

Shery was a philosophy and religion major at the University of Vermont, and she still reads broadly and voraciously—from books on philosophy, religion, neurobiology, psychopharmacology, and women's history, to nineteenth- and twentieth-century novels about which she talks lovingly, as of dear friends. She herself has authored and coauthored essays for professional journals, and when, as I will see in the months to come, she runs groups at peer support centers, or speaks before large audiences (she regularly gives Grand Rounds presentations at hospitals and medical schools, and workshops at mental health centers), she fairly reeks of intelligence: Her references are wide ranging, her comments and answers to questions succinct, well-informed, and specific, and her anecdotes—many drawn from her own life—relevant and touching. Her sense of humor is ever-present, often self-deprecating and enchantingly childlike. "I guess it's time for The Shery Mead Show!" she will sometimes announce as she gathers people for the start of a training session.

At the same time, because of her own history and struggles, she is never glib. She is also, as one after another member of her peer support centers tell me, "a *really* good listener." Given her accomplishments as musician, teacher, parent, author, administrator, therapist, athlete, and public speaker, and given the admiring ways in which everyone at West Central has spoken about her ("You can't leave town without meeting Shery," Phil advises. "She's extraordinary—the best we have, really. Sometimes, when I'm most optimistic, I think Shery *is* the future"), and given her direct, self-confident, and warm manner, I am, in fact, somewhat surprised when I learn from her, a short while into our conversation, that she herself has had a long history of mental illness and hospitalizations. I am even more surprised, during our visits and talks in the months to come, to learn just how terrifying this history has been, and of the painful ways in which, despite the outer successes of her life, her inner struggles and terrors persist.

Shery had her first major breakdown at the age of seventeen, when she was a senior in high school. Then, and in the fifteen to twenty hospitalizations that have followed, she was given massive doses of drugs ("tons of Thorazine") and was also, without her consent, subjected to repeated courses of electroconvulsive therapy. There were times she was so heavily medicated that she could not physically rise from her bed, or get words to flow from her mouth, or walk without help.

And there were times, between hospitalizations, when she would find herself waking in towns and cities without knowing how she had come to be there, or, most frightening of all, who she was. While she was completing her master's degree she lived at home with her children during the week (commuting 110 miles each way to school, three days a week, for three years), "and then," she tells me, when she had coverage for her children on weekends, "I took back roads and snuck away—I was so ashamed and embarrassed—to the mental hospitals I was living in."

Shery was advised by her clinicians to give up her three children, to sell her house (a house she designed and built, with help from a local carpenter, during and after her divorce), to quit her job and go on SSI and take a menial, mininum-stress job, and not to even *think* about completing her degree or of *ever* returning to graduate school.

While Shery and I trade stories, anecdotes, and views—about our children, Robert, recovery paradigms, and Shery's history of mental illness—she also tells me about a crisis respite program she has been developing. The respite program, for which training sessions are to begin midsummer, will provide an alternative to hospitalization that will offer up to seven days of respite care for people in crisis. The respite center will be able to accommodate two people at a time in separate guest rooms at the Stepping Stone Peer Support Center, and—this is what thrills Shery—it will be completely designed and run by patients and ex-patients who are members of the peer support centers, who have themselves been hospitalized for mental illness, and who are in various stages of remission and recovery.

I tell Shery about Moe's idea of paying consumers simply to be companions to patients in hospitals, and we talk for a while about this, after which I mention that I've just come from CRREL. I talk about my fascination with the work CRREL does—with simulated ice-jam breakups, blast-damaged pavements, and various engineering inventions (some for the Alaska pipeline)—and about how moved I was to see West

Central clients working at regular jobs, and, mostly, of how proud the staff at West Central, the administrators at CRREL, and the clients themselves are about what they've accomplished.

To my surprise, Shery nearly flies out of her chair in frustration.

"But they're still *janitors!*" she exclaims.

She sits back, shakes her head, starts to apologize — says something about never knowing how to keep her mouth shut — and I find myself both astonished, and delighted, by her reaction.

Yes, I say, smiling. *But they're still janitors.* Tell me more.

Shery shrugs. "Is that really the best we can do?" she asks, and she sighs and begins talking about her belief: that the individuals who now populate clubhouses and peer support centers will not exist in twenty years; that the peer support centers and clubhouses themselves will wither away. She tells me how she wants to work toward creating something that's *different from* and *more than* most drop-in centers, day treatment centers, and group homes, where, generally, people sit around with other consumers and do nothing, or smoke all day, or watch TV. She talks about how she believes that the relationships and knowledge people gain at peer support centers should and can serve as bridges to the worlds beyond those centers, and, more important, to the worlds within these individuals that, sadly, have been shut down for years, but that she believes — and *knows*, from her work with them — are still very much intact and alive.

She says she believes true recovery begins not with diagnosis, but with a shift in one's identity and sense of self. She laughs, recites the mantra from *The Little Engine That Could* — "I think I can I think I can I think I can" — and talks about how people with histories of mental illness and institutionalization often, in her words, get *stuck*, and stop believing they can improve and recover because the only way they can conceive of themselves is as passive recipients of services. Thus, they come to carry within themselves internalized labeling that corresponds to the external labeling the world has put on them. This passivity, she says, which the literature, in Martin Seligman's phrase, calls "learned helplessness," is at least as lethal as the disease.

She often thinks anger, frustration, and indignation—rage and real madness! she exclaims—instead of being regarded as symptoms that have to be controlled, can, as in her own life, serve as the beginnings of real *change*. Why can't therapists see crises as opportunities, and rage and anger as behaviors that hold within them real strengths and tremendously useful energy? she asks. Why is their first move always to shut us down and control us?

Shery talks about how she sees it happen again and again: Those people who can walk across the bridges, from the world of the mad to the world the rest of us live in, are able to do so because they have come to a point in their lives where they begin to say: *I hate my meds, and I hate the drop-in center, and I hate living in isolation, and I hate my life, and I hate being on SSI, and I hate being dependent.*

She sees no reason why anyone should ever be content just to take his or her meds, or just take whatever menial job is offered. Why should a diagnosis be a life sentence? She talks about programs being developed at the National Empowerment Center (NEC) that are based on the belief that recovery and empowerment are not privileges of a few exceptional leaders, but are possible for *every* person diagnosed with mental illness. She asks if I know about the NEC, and the work being done there.

I tell her I've met both Dan Fisher and Pat Deegan, have visited the NEC offices in Lawrence, and that I've been impressed not only with their results and with the intelligence and humanity of their approach, but—contrary to what people assume, and to what I assumed before I went there—with the fact that they are not ideologues: that they are open to anything and everything—medical, pharmacological, psychological, or spiritual—that works and makes a difference, in helping people move toward better lives. I tell her that they seemed infinitely more open-minded than those who, from a narrow biomedical perspective, often attack them.

Shery then says she is writing an essay in which she has been trying to set down some of her thoughts (its working title: "Moving Beyond Disability"), but that she doesn't know if any of it makes sense. If she sends it to me, would I read it and give her my thoughts? She knows she is not a good writer, she says. She's too impatient, uses too much jargon, and hates editing, though she does reams of it. Shery also invites me to return to New Hampshire in two months, for the start of the series of respite-center training sessions.

She apologizes for talking so much (even while, in the midst of talking with me, she's been attending to people coming into her office, interrupting with questions, problems, and news), and says it's just that she has "a bazillion ideas" about what needs to be done, and that it's just so exciting to think that some of it, like the respite center, might actually *get* done.

Then she laughs easily, and says that of course she thinks it's *wonderful* that West Central has gotten the contracts for custodial services and the mailroom at CRREL. She hopes I understand that.

She shrugs. "I'm for whatever works," she adds. "Really. I'm not against CRREL or janitors or menial jobs, if that's where we have to start. I'm not against meds, and I'm not even against hospitals for some of us some of the time and for a few of us all of the time. But I do think we can do better. Don't you think we can do better?"

Yes, I say. And I find myself smiling in amazement, both then and on the two-hour drive home, at Shery's extraordinary optimism, exuberance, and—most of all—hard-edged and hard-earned realism. (At a statewide mental health conference a few months later, when a man introduces himself to Shery, telling her he runs a residence for violent men—convicted criminals, rapists, and pedophiles—and that he's beside himself with problems, and that people said she was the one person who would be able to tell him what to do,

Shery smiles and, the first time the man pauses, asks, "What about prisons?"")

"I love my work," Shery will say to me a few weeks after we meet, "and I love seeing how far some of the people at the centers have come—you wouldn't believe what some of them were like a year or two ago!—but I really do yearn to talk about things that are not defined solely by our disabilities and by my job—to talk with people who are *not* consumers, and to talk with people who have other interests, and—I hope you won't think I'm a snob, or elitist, or anything— with people who have more academic interests than most of the people I interact with every day at the centers. I really do yearn to talk about things that have *nothing* to do with respite, or the consumer movement, or mental health. You wouldn't believe."

On the drive home, I think, too, about Kay Jamison, a woman about Shery's age, whose memoir, *An Unquiet Mind*, tells of her struggles with manic depression, and of the ways in which, while achieving large successes as a writer and doctor, she continued to do battle with her depressions and her manic sprees. I find myself musing, again, on what happens in people like Shery Mead and Kay Jamison that enables them to take the energies that flow from their mania, their rages, and their sorrows—from the deepest wounds and darkness of their lives—and join them so productively and generously to their passions.

If we could take some of the things that *do* work at West Central, and at CRREL, and at Shery's peer support centers, and replicate them elsewhere, wouldn't it, I hear myself asking Shery, be like taking trees and flowers from someone else's garden and learning to make them grow in our own?

On the drive home, I continue to carry on a dialogue in my head with Shery. We talk about the gains that might ensue if large mental health systems were decentralized and the scale of things were smaller and more manageable; about the benefits that do ensue when we stop thinking in terms of short-term cures, and begin thinking instead in terms of long-term care; about the benefits that ensue when we stop thinking in terms of trying to medicate deficits, and think instead of reconstructing lives; about what happens when we are eager not just to correct or fix what is malfunctioning or "defective" in a person, but pay attention instead to that person's assets, and work to enhance those qualities that are life-giving and can be turned toward good use.

Shery reminds me of the wonderful things that can and do happen when we look for opportunities to value risk over safety, and employ commonsense principles of vocational support like flex-time, and implement outreach programs that are comprehensive, and when we work on the assumption that a diagnosis is not a life sentence, and that most people are capable of regaining full lives in the community. I hear us talking about what happens when we do all these things while also acknowledging our responsibility to go further: to do *whatever* seems necessary—in terms of planning, medical care, therapy, supports, funding, and follow-up—to encourage people to take as much responsibility for their lives as possible, even as we help them regain and create these new lives.

On this early spring evening in May, it doesn't seem difficult to recognize and name what works, and what might work, whether it's the principles of the ACT program, or the principles on which West Central bases its policies when it sends nurses to clients' homes, or has Lisa on-site at CRREL for two hours a day, or places people in jobs first and then trains and supports them, or takes calculated risks and invests money and time in peer support centers, community education, or a consumer-run respite program. Nor is it difficult to imagine other mental health organizations learning from and implementing many of the principles and programs that work at West Central.

But how—is this the rub?—do we locate, encourage, and replicate individuals like Shery Mead, Phil Wyzik, and Bud Ross? In my conversation with Kristin Bumiller a few months before, when I told her about the difference people like Moe

Armstrong, Dan Fisher, and Larry Kohn were making in people's lives, I remember her pointing out that the stories and accomplishments of these people, while moving and inspiring, represented, still, personal solutions to what remained large social and political problems.

While we can't, obviously, replicate any individual, exceptional *or* ordinary, and while we can't, most of the time, even inspire those qualities — desire, will, dedication, and passion — that exceptional individuals bring to us, any more than we can teach people to be more intelligent, or more talented, or more loving, we can still, Shery and I agree, do some things, and we can do them well.

What we can sometimes do, as at West Central, is to create contexts that make it possible — and sometimes probable — for exceptional human beings to develop their ideas, to put them into motion, to sustain them, and to see them through. What we can do is to provide settings and programs (and funds!) that bring out the best in them, so that chances increase that they can do the same for others. What we can do is to make structural changes in the organization and delivery of services — as West Central does at CRREL, and as Shery intends to do at her respite center — that are based on attitudes and beliefs that are themselves based upon the working assumption that people with severe mental illness can take responsibility for their own lives, can become increasingly autonomous, can rejoin the larger communities beyond the world of mental illness, and can, like the rest of us, regain and make for themselves very full if imperfect lives.

And, as at West Central — or Fountain House, or the B.U. program, or Vinfen, or Odyssey House — we can do this in ways that ensure that the programs will work, and continue to thrive even when people like Shery are not running them.

"I've been getting requests and calls from all over about our respite program — and we haven't even opened yet!" Shery had said to me at one point during our conversation. She had laughed, and now, heading south on Interstate 91, somewhere near the Vermont-Massachusetts border, remembering Shery's laugh, it occurs to me that the people I've met who have had histories of severe mental illness and who have survived to tell the tale have each been blessed with a large, wonderful, and idiosyncratic sense of humor. Is there, I wonder, a genetic marker for a sense of humor? Is there a cure for humorlessness, or pills to correct the *absence* of a sense of humor, an absence that usually seems to coexist with a distinct lack of generosity?

"It's nuts, and I have to keep writing and calling to say we haven't even *started* our training program yet," Shery had said. "But once we get going, and if things work the way I hope they will, then these other places should be able to learn from us, and to adapt what we're doing to their needs. And the program has to be able to run without me, because I'll tell you one thing—if it has to depend solely or mainly on Shery Mead, then forget it. Then even if it succeeds, it fails."

SEVEN

RESPITE

If there is no struggle, there is no progress. Those who profess to favor freedom and yet deprecate agitation are men who want crops without plowing up the land. They want rain without thunder and lightning. They want the ocean without the roar of its many waters. The struggle may be a moral one, or it may be a physical one, or it may be both moral and physical, but it must be a struggle.

—FREDERICK DOUGLASS,
"The Significance of Emancipation in the West Indies,"
address delivered at Canandaigua, New York, 1857

When, two months after my visit to West Lebanon, I return to New Hampshire for an all-day training session at the Stepping Stone Peer Support Center, in Claremont, early-morning clouds hang on the highway like fog. Corn is up everywhere, and as the fog lifts, the landscape, in varying shades of dusty greens, yellows, and browns, seems especially peaceful and muted. The highway is nearly deserted so that, alone in my car, I feel the way I often do when I take the ferry from Manhattan to Staten Island to visit Robert—I'm happy to be alone, and happy to be without responsibility for anyone but myself, and happy to be between here and there, and happy to be enjoying — the word seems wonderfully apt — a bit of *respite* from the ordinary stuff of life.

I follow Shery's directions, leaving Interstate 91 near Bellows Falls, crossing over the Connecticut River, from Vermont to New Hampshire, and paying a thirty-five-cent toll on the far side of a narrow bridge in the town of Charleston, where, on this Friday morning, citizens are in costume for a reenactment of a battle that took place here more than two hundred years ago during the French and Indian Wars.

I wind my way along country roads and arrive in Claremont before nine A.M. The Stepping Stone Peer Support Center is located just south of the town's center on a wide street lined with dentists', lawyers', and real estate offices, and across the street from Claremont's high school.

Stepping Stone rents an eight-room apartment on the first floor of a rambling three-story building that was once a private home. The center's office and other rooms are tastefully decorated — clean, curtained, carpeted, pleasantly furnished — and, especially in the kitchen and dining area, very lived in: The counters and dining room table are covered with plates, bowls, and food, the refrigerator and cupboards full, backpacks and books lying about, notes and announcements pinned up here and there.

On the wall near the meeting room — a large modern room with floor-to-ceiling windows that look down upon the high school football stadium and athletic fields — is a sign:

PEER SUPPORT MEETING RULES

1. NO CRITICISM
2. GIVE SUPPORT & NOT ADVICE
3. CONFIDENTIALITY
4. NO MAKING FUN
5. NO JUDGING
6. WAIT YOUR TURN TO TALK

7. RESPECT FOR OTHERS

8. PEER SUPPORT IS SERIOUS

A dozen or so people have arrived, and they are eating bagels and doughnuts, drinking juice and coffee, laughing and talking, and most of the talk is not about things having to do with the respite center, or with the usual matter of conversation in day treatment centers and clubhouses: medications, side effects, money, cigarettes, and what patients and ex-patients refer to as "war stories," the trading of tales about one's worst interactions with mental hospitals, doctors, bureaucracies, shelters, and police.

Instead, people are talking about summer vacation plans, and about setting up tennis matches. They are lamenting the ways air pollution is diminishing the views from Mount Washington, and they are talking about the ironies of politically correct environmentalists selling cars and technology to China. People are dressed casually, in light and colorful summer clothing, and by the time we are ready to begin the session, there are eighteen people present, all of whom intend to train for positions as crisis respite workers, and all of whom have themselves had extensive histories of mental illness and psychiatric hospitalizations.

Although a few individuals seem, by the evidence of their mannerisms — studied gestures, heavy-lidded eyes — to be either very sleepy or mildly medicated, I feel as if I might be attending some ordinary gathering of local teachers, doctors, clerks, farmers, or merchants on any Friday morning in a small New England town.

Shery introduces me to Dave Hilton, director of consumer affairs for the New Hampshire Department of Mental Health. Dave is sturdily built, has a neatly trimmed reddish-brown beard, and deep-set eyes. Dave asks me how Robert is doing, and I tell him that Robert will be transferred to Bronx Psychiatric Center within the month, that he visited there with me a few weeks ago, that he seems happy about the transfer, and that the staff at Bronx Psychiatric Center seems eager to work with him.

Dave tells Shery how impressed he is by the turnout, but Shery rolls her eyes and says that everybody's going to say they're only here because she *made* them come, and she talks about having gone out jogging first thing in the morning, before her children were awake.

"I'm just so goddamned compulsive," she says, laughing. "If I don't get exercise—if I miss a single day—I really fear that I'm gonna *die!*"

We gather in the meeting room, where Shery hands out inch-thick training manuals that contain information about the respite center: house rules, interview guidelines, relevant case studies, reprints of essays. Shery opens the meeting by asking each of the people in the room to talk a little bit about themselves and why they have chosen to do crisis respite work.

Dave Hilton, sitting next to Shery, speaks first, says that this has been a dream of his for a lot of years and that he is "joyfully proud" to be here. Julie Sarzynski, who hopes to add a dozen or more hours of respite work to her schedule at West Central, speaks next. She says she wants to help create places that are "more human" than the places she's had to go to when things became difficult for her.

As we go around the room, most people say they are here because they "want to make a difference," and because they "want to give back" what's been given to them. Some people say very little, and others are surprisingly forthcoming about their histories and about how confused, lost, addicted, ill, and plain crazy they have been.

A man who has spent most of his adult life plagued by unbearable nightmares and auditory hallucinations (in and out of mental hospitals in New York and New Hampshire for more than thirty years) says that being a part of Stepping Stone has changed his life. He talks about his voices. "I think of them as cobwebs," he tells us, "and what I am doing is clearing them out, for better things to take their place."

"I am a severely depressed person, and I suffer from sleep deprivation, suicidal impulses, and many suicide attempts," a white-haired woman says. "I was trained and worked as a registered nurse, but I am dependent on medications and know I will need to be taken care of, one way or the other, for the rest of my life. For most of the last thirty years I never left my apartment. But by coming here I am out of the box I was in. I was chronically mentally ill and permanently disabled, you see. I don't feel that way now." She grins broadly, revealing the fact that her four front teeth are missing. "I took a job last week."

Everyone applauds.

"Six years ago when I was in bad shape and totally whacked out," Shery says when her turn comes, "there was no hospital program to meet my needs."

Shery then explains the ways in which she thinks a respite center will fill a large need, and also the ways in which it will begin to create "a knowledge base." At present, she says, a gap exists in resources, between community care—peer support, therapy, mental health centers, clubhouses—and hospitalization. When a client's needs go beyond community resources, the client's only option is usually hospitalization, and hospitalization brings with it situations that not only severely limit one's choices, but creates memories and fears that are connected to previous crises, and to institutionalization.

"When people are able to help in somebody else's process," Shery says, "feelings of self-confidence and value replace need and pathology." If respite had been available in 1996, West Central's 153 admissions to New Hampshire hospitals could have been reduced to well under 100. By having people "who have been there themselves" as guides, a movement toward mutuality develops and with it a stronger desire to take responsibility for one's own "wellness," and to share the knowledge gained through this experience with others. As people acquire the opportunity to stay connected with peers, even while moving through their crises, Shery adds, the need for external intervention and emergency hospital admissions diminishes. New choices are generated, old roles become less automatic, and the long-term effects "can result in decreased use of high-end services and in greater reliance on self and community."

The average cost of state hospitalization, Shery informs us, is approximately $500 a day, while private hospitals can run as high as $1,500 a day. When both guest rooms in the center are in use, the cost of respite to the state, including that of the required sixty hours of training for each respite worker, will be $128 a day. In addition, respite should decrease the number of times an individual will need to seek crisis intervention, thereby cutting costs even further.

More significant, though, will be the human savings derived from the lack of severe disruption to an individual's life, and the normalization that being in a homelike setting, and being free to come and go from this setting, will bring.

At this meeting and throughout the day, the language Shery and others use to describe what they are doing—the talk about "wellness," about building "authentic relations," about "learning attending skills," about being "proactive," or "mutually supportive," or "in or out of one's box"—sometimes makes me wince. I urge myself to ignore the language, though, and to look at the reality: Eighteen individuals with histories like Robert's have gathered here in order to create something new—and the very act of believing they can be useful and make a difference in the lives of others seems, already, to be making differences in their own lives.

Now, in practice interviews later in the day, and in questions and answers about ways to handle problems ("What do I do if a guest threatens me?" "What do I do if a guest locks himself in the bathroom and threatens suicide?" "What do I do if a guest is hallucinating really badly and won't take his meds?"), Shery repeatedly emphasizes mutuality by saying that what you have to do is to keep saying to yourself: "This has to work for both of us."

Dr. Kim Mueser, a professor in the departments of Psychiatry and Community and Family Medicine at Dartmouth Medical School, with whom Shery is collaborating on several projects, has written about the origin and rationale for the kind of thinking that underlies both peer support and consumer-run respite:

> Consumers frequently express their dissatisfaction with the hierarchical nature of traditional helping relationships in which professionals assume the role of omniscient "expert" and consumers are expected to take the submissive role of compliant "patient." Consumers who fail to take on their assigned roles are viewed as "non-compliant," their normal responses are pathologized, and coercive methods are often used to force them into treatment, leading to a clash of values and fear or anger over mental health treatment. As a result, many consumers experience traditional services as dehumanizing and lacking the reciprocity necessary to help them achieve their goals. Peer support has been directed at empowering consumers to take charge of their own treatment.

"Related to the objection of consumers to the hierarchical and formal nature of relationships with mental health professionals," Mueser adds, "is the hypothesis that the person who helps benefits as much (or more than) the person helped (known as the 'helper's principle')."

The "Mission Statement" for the Stepping Stone Peer Support Center, designed to empower patients and ex-patients in the ways Mueser describes, and in language not so different from his, begins as follows:

> The Stepping Stone Drop-In Center is a consumer run, consumer driven non-profit organization that is committed to a non-hierarchical, supportive, educational and safe environment for people with emotional/mental challenges. All decisions, rules, policy and direction are created by the community and responsibility for all aspects of the center is shared equally by all members.
>
> By offering groups and events that emphasize shared leadership, skill development, team activities and holistic

models of health, we empower ourselves to achieve our highest life goals and to consequently help decrease stigma and oppression by educating the larger community.

Just as Shery makes clear in the Peer Support Manual what peer support centers are *not* ("Peer support is not about 'joining a club for the mentally ill.' It is not a competition of stories or symptoms or about being rescued or infantilized. Neither is it in competition with other service providers. . . ."), so she is, in directing the training session, clear about what the respite center is not: It is not a hospital, clinic, or shelter, and respite workers are not doctors, therapists, nurses, or clinicians. "We do not," Shery emphasizes, "do treatment here."

Shery talks about situations in which the center will not hesitate to call in the police ("Anytime someone is asked to leave Crisis Respite and they refuse to leave, they will be warned . . . [but] if the staff person on duty feels that an act of violence is in progress and that a verbal warning might increase the likelihood of injury, they may decide to call the police without warning"). She talks about medications (guests will be responsible for their own medications, which will be kept in a locked cabinet in the guest's room), about evacuation plans, about housekeeping rules, and about the fact that a respite worker's primary responsibility is to *attend* to the guest. She also says she will not hesitate to call in "the jargon police" if and when her language deteriorates beyond the pale of human tolerance.

"We cannot be all things to all people," she says. But, inviting suggestions, she begins to list some of the things that the respite center *can* do, and that attending to a guest might entail: active listening, sharing common experiences, taking walks, shopping or cooking or eating meals together, helping to deal with friends, family, or employers, etc.

Guests, Shery suggests, should be encouraged to use their respite time as "an opportunity to grow, as opposed to simply containing or moving backwards to a baseline." They should be challenged to look at their automatic "default" positions, and through "the development of nonjudgmental long-term relationships, explore new ways of responding, or, at least, of minimizing old negative patterns." Respite will be based on the assumption that "even people who are experiencing acute crisis know best what they need and that one can move in and out of roles even when things are most difficult."

In order to use the respite center, a guest must be a recipient of state mental health services, or at risk for becoming a recipient of such services, and—the major prerequisite—a guest must, when *not* in crisis, come to the center and have at least one substantive interview with a respite worker, during which interview the guest "will produce a crisis plan that may ultimately be used to prevent crises."

The crisis plan is central to respite, its rationale simple and sensible: to have people who think they may need respite in the future come to the center when they are doing well so that they can become familiar with the center and its rules, and so that they can draw up their own crisis plans. In drawing up these plans, they will anticipate what their needs might be, and how those needs might best be met if and when life again becomes difficult.

We have a lengthy discussion about what might go into the interviews and about the drawing-up of crisis plans. Much of the talk, with lots of laughter and self-mocking commentary about past hospitalizations and possible respite scenarios ("What do I do if *I'm* a guest and my voices start insisting that I strip off all my clothes . . . ?"), concerns what has *not* worked during previous crises. Again and again, for example, people say that if any emergency room or hospital employee—or respite worker—ever (again) asks, "*Do-you-feel-safe?*" or "*Are-you-taking-your-meds?*" they may go totally ballistic.

Instead of the kinds of questions asked by people working, for example, in hospital emergency rooms, the group comes up with dozens of suggested interview questions they believe will prove useful: "When you are in crisis, are you likely to tell the truth or to lie?" or "When you are bouncing off the walls is it best to leave you alone, or to put an arm around you?" or "When you had breakdowns before, what helped—and what hurt? . . ."

We have to think ahead, everybody agrees, because once a crisis is upon us, we don't think well at all, and we usually become at least as difficult for others as we are for ourselves. As the discussion proceeds, the benefits of drawing up such crisis plans become more apparent, and while Shery writes them down on a large blackboard, the group begins enumerating them: They put the individual in charge of how not to get sick again, and about what to do if he or she does; they reduce the terror that accompanies the fear of the unknown; they assume that people want to take responsibility for their own crises, and for their own lives.

Real life, Shery suggests, is not about safety. It is about building authentic relationships that require risk, adventure, patience, constancy, and commitment. The respite center will exist as an attempt to normalize crises because—well, Shery declares, simply because *everybody* has crises. Crises are a part of life for all people—and so is respite: That's why people take long drives, or go to the Cape or to the Bahamas for a weekend, or—we all laugh—go jogging at five A.M.

People talk about being careful not to impose their views on others—a practice members of Stepping Stone laughingly refer to as "Nazi peer support"—since this is the very thing that creates feelings of powerlessness.

Yes, Shery says, and we want to be "exquisitely careful" about not imposing our views on others because what we are doing here is all about choice.

When, further into the summer, Shery draws up interview guidelines, they will include questions that further specify what respite will and will not do: For example, "In what sort of situations would you see yourself using crisis respite and what should be known about these times? What do you think the differences might be between hospitalization and respite?

What is your understanding of the role of the staff at the crisis respite center?"

These staff guidelines will come to include questions aimed specifically at developing individualized and detailed crisis plans: "What does a really great day look like for you? What do you keep hidden from people when you are in a crisis? Are there people, places, or things that have been helpful in past crises? . . ."

The individual crisis plan itself, in addition to containing suggestions about strategies and activities designed to ease the guest through the crisis and back into the world, will also address basics concerning medications, physical health, dietary needs, psychiatric history, emergencies, and follow-up: e.g., "In the past, have your medications been increased when you enter crisis? Who are the people you would like us to call in case of an emergency? Can you ensure that you have a supply of medication before coming to respite? Would you be willing to participate in our program evaluation?"

After lunch, and before we pair off to work on interviews, Dave Hilton volunteers to take part in a practice interview with Shery, with Dave playing the part of a potential guest who has come to find out about the respite center. He sits across from Shery, leans forward, turns his baseball cap around so that it is on backward, and suddenly transforms himself from an athletic-looking, clear-thinking, level-headed administrator into a restless, disoriented man who starts out dissociating in a very quiet manner, but soon takes flight with a wild nonstop monologue about loving to get high, but knowing that when he gets high he winds up losing his job, and his girlfriend, and his apartment — it happens again and again — but that the meds the doctors prescribe for him make him feel crappy, and the day treatment centers they send him to are really weird, with buckets of weird, spaced-out people sitting around like deadbeats, and when everyone tells him that what he has to do each time he gets out of a hospital is to *just-take-his-meds-and-go-to-therapy*, he says okay to them, but then he feels so damned bored and shut down that he gets high again because—you know why?—*because it feels so goddamned great to be high and he loves getting high!*—so that he doesn't see why he should take his meds at all, since no matter what program or doctor he deals with, he always winds up wanting to get high again, and when he's high he can go five or six days without sleep, and then he guesses he acts pretty weird because his father will call the cops on him—and guess what?—that's the part he *really* likes because it pisses his father off so much. "The thing of it is," he says to Shery, "I don't understand why people just won't let me be."

I sit there like everyone else in the room, awestruck by Dave's performance. Then, quietly and firmly, and improvising as she goes along, Shery asks Dave if he knows what peer support is, and if he's ever felt or done certain things when he's been sick, and she mentions, almost in passing, that she's been high too, and has been hospitalized on psych wards a lot of times.

Really? Dave asks.

They continue to talk, but now Shery has his attention. She asks him some of the questions we've been collecting, encouraging him to talk about what a really good day is like for him—one when he's not high *and* not hospitalized—and gradually she has him interested in finding out how she was able to work through long-term problems with professional help, sometimes without medications, and she is getting him to consider coming back to the center to work on drawing up a plan for himself, one he can put into use to avoid hospitalization the next time he falls off the edge of the world.

"I really didn't know what was wrong with me—what was *different*," Shery tells me. "I mean, I remember that in high school and even in junior high, I'd go through these periods where everything just *changed*. That's the only way I can put it. I didn't feel I even knew the people around me—who they were—and I'd start to shake uncontrollably and to stutter and say things that apparently didn't make any sense, and I'd end up in places where I didn't know how I'd gotten there.

"What happened finally was that I ended up at this teacher's house a couple of times, and her husband was a psychiatric resident, so she got me hooked into therapy, but my parents were pretty oblivious to the whole thing, and therapy proved pretty worthless too. I'd just go stone quiet. I don't really know *what* I did there—I have no memory of being in therapy at all, in truth, and for my parents, with the attitudes toward mental illness that prevailed back then, and in a college community, it was like—'If you're like that, you're not our child.' And—'We don't talk about that stuff.' So it was very hush-hush, which made me feel incredibly secretive and ashamed.

"Then I went away to a boarding school called The Mountain School my senior year, and my life started getting even weirder. I'd stay up all the time, and would go on all-night walks where I had this absolute belief that I could fly. So I'd spend hours running down hillsides or jumping out of trees, and I had some kind of mind-over-matter belief, I guess, and I was reading all these Hermann Hesse books and other stuff like that, but finally at Christmas I was home and I guess I lost a lot of time—it's the only way I can put it—I mean, it's as if I literally *lost time*—and I started having these shaking attacks and my mother started in shaking me and screaming at me. 'You will stop this now!' she kept screaming, and she was furious and eventually took me to the hospital, and that was when they kept me there for three months and gave me lots of electroshock and tons of Thorazine.

"They did brain scans too, and I remember the big thing back then was that they tested everybody for epilepsy. After one of the scans, where they put wires all over your head, the only thing I remember is I came back and I asked the psychiatrist, 'What'd you see?' because I was really interested in knowing what my brain looked like—what was going on inside it—and he said, 'It's the strangest thing but it's just dead blank.' I thought he was being serious.

"So I remember that, but not much else. I still get nightmares about having wires and straps all over my body. And the electroshock was pretty awful too. The weirdest thing, though, was that no one ever came to see me. I mean nobody."

It is two weeks after the first training session, and Shery and Lynn Haas—a member of Stepping Stone's board of directors, superintendent of schools in the Claremont district, and a mother who has a son in his twenties diagnosed as having schizophrenia—have driven down to Northampton to spend a day with me. They have come to talk about the crisis respite program and ways to set up outcome studies for it. They also want to spend some time with Jeff Fortuna, the director of Windhorse Associates, a Northampton-based program that provides comprehensive treatment for emotionally disturbed people in *home* environments.

Shery is sitting on the floor of my third-floor office, directly below a framed picture of my elementary school graduation class (Class of June 1951, JHS 246, 8-1). She shakes her head sideways at times, as if astonished to discover that the person known as Shery Mead has actually gone through the experiences she is now describing.

"And the reason I sometimes laugh when people talk about their fear of suicidal thoughts," she says, "is because there hasn't been a day in my life since I was probably a year old when I haven't been suicidal. This is what I go through every day, Jay, and I have to keep saying, okay, here it is again, and blah blah blah—and all the rest of it. It's just part of my everyday thought process. And I think I've already told you how I almost died several times from hurting myself—from self-destructive behaviors that I understand now were largely a result of my extensive trauma history.

"This was after I was in grad school, and I was leading a pretty fragmented life, and I was in therapy with a wonderful therapist—a psychiatrist I still see—and you think you have things pretty well sorted out until it all sort of blows apart again. Which it did. There were times when, by all rights, I should have been involuntarily committed. But my psychiatrist went out on a limb for me—a big limb. She thought I could make it, and she believed in me. That made all the difference.

"But I was really self-destructive, and then I wouldn't remember what happened, or why the hell I was bleeding at the neck—like: 'You know, *it's news to me!*'—and I'm sure it was terrifying for her, but she stuck by me, and it was a period then—the really bad times, when my ex fought for custody, and I thought I'd lose my own kids—when I was in and out of hospitals all the time. I'd do these weekend things where my kids were gone with him and I'd go into the hospital and try to do some intensive work and pull it together. I went through months of not sleeping—through like three *years* of not sleeping more than two hours a night.

"So I was in school and with my kids during the week, and thinking about big stuff like human rights and justice and feminist theory—and then I was hospitalized every weekend just about, and nobody knew, and I sort of came out for my classes and my kids, and I said nothing else to anyone.

"What's most painful about all that now is that there were many years where I was totally not present for my kids. I wasn't a bad parent—I know that. I was good enough, and I didn't abuse them, but I was so lost in my internal processes and so totally overwhelmed that I just wasn't there. And it's painful because now I can see the contrast—like I took them out to dinner last night and I felt very present to them and it was like, 'Where *were* you, Shery? Why were you so damned self-absorbed?' "

Shery and I talk for a while about being single parents, and laugh about the ordinary and ingenious ways our teenage children have sometimes found to drive us crazy.

"But I think I've discovered the bridge to finding the soft spot of adolescence," she says. "I've been teaching my daughter Ashley hot licks to old heavy-metal tunes, and showing her how to read guitar music. She's great—picks stuff up really fast, and at least for this quick moment in life I get to fit into her definition of 'cool.' "

Shery talks about growing up in Hanover, the middle child of three daughters, in a community dominated by Dartmouth College. Her father ran a small advertising business, while her mother did volunteer work in the schools but was mostly a homemaker. Shery remembers feeling that you were "either Dartmouth, or Hospital, or you were Nobody." Mostly, she remembers very little of her childhood—of her life before high school: before the shakings, stutterings, and hospitalizations.

After high school, she took a year off, played lots of guitar, and then entered the University of Vermont, where she began playing guitar professionally. She dealt with most of her problems during these years, she says, by putting all her energy into playing, singing, and composing. "Oh I wrote tons and tons and tons of songs!" she says. "And music became pretty much my focus—even though *I* didn't."

She moved to Boston after graduation, and was able to get full-time work as a guitarist, and though she knew she was good, she began to believe that she just didn't have the skills to be the kind of musician she yearned to be. She married a bass player from one of the bands she played lead guitar for, and they had three children within five years. The marriage went pretty bad right from the start, however ("So long as we were doing music, we were okay," Shery says. "But when we stopped, oh boy!"), and all through these years she continued to struggle with the kinds of internal chaos that had led to her hospitalization in high school.

"I guess the reason I even had kids was because at some level I felt so at sea in this world that I needed to have an authentic connection with *somebody*, and that I knew I'd always had good relationships with kids. So I sort of jumped into having kids without even thinking about the consequences, and then when I went to grad school, it all became really chaotic again, and that was when they—clinicians, and even my family—tried to get me to give up custody of my children, and my house."

Shery pauses, after which she speaks more slowly.

"But then one time—this is what I was coming to—I was in the hospital in Hanover, and in terrible shape, and my therapist then, Layne—she's my clinical supervisor now for my job at Stepping Stone, because I swore I'd never work without a supervisor in this job—she came up to me, and she said—I'll never forget it—'You know, Shery, it's really all up to you. You do have choices. You can either become a social worker, or you can be a mental patient for the rest of your life. I'll be back in an hour, and you can give me your decision then.' "

Shery closes her eyes, shakes her head. "That's what she said, and that was the turning point." Shery laughs. *"So I became a social worker!"* she exclaims.

I tell Shery that the late Elvin Semrad, a professor of psychiatry at Harvard Medical School who was for many years the director of residency training at the Massachusetts Mental Health Center, and who is revered by all the psychiatrists I know who trained under him, used to say much the same thing to the patients there, especially to those who were most deteriorated: " 'You know,' he would say to them, 'it's really up to you—what you do with your life.' To his residents, he would say, 'Keep the patient responsible,' and he would counsel his residents to say to their patients: '*You* were there; you did it. What did you do and what did you think while you were living your life?' You help a patient take responsibility by making him responsible for everything he says."

"Oh yes," Shery agrees. "I needed a kick in the ass, and Layne gave it to me.

"Because you know, you have a choice, no matter how bad it gets, and you either choose to stay in that other world and bitch and moan about it and stay stuck, or you choose to get a life. I know I'm kind of nasty about this stuff, but I think we all know on some level that there's *always* a choice. I know I have my limits too—that when I travel and lose sleep, for example, I can get crazy again, and things get dangerous for me. Nobody had ever really taken care of me, and when Layne said I had an hour to decide, I was scared—terrified, and still pretty out of it—but I guess what I think is you reach a point where you have to make a leap of faith, and recovery for a long period of time was a leap of faith for me, and I think that's what Layne was telling me.

"I knew I went out of control, and lost memory of things, but what I was told by Layne and others was, 'Okay—tough luck, Shery, but you're still responsible for your behaviors,' and I guess I believe that's true for everybody, and the more I teach that it's so, the more it comes true for me. I mean, every day I get stuck in my own victimhood, but I work my way out of it. Compulsiveness can sometimes be a friend, right?"

Shery, Lynn, and I have lunch with Jeff Fortuna in a Chinese restaurant next to the professional building where Windhorse has its offices. I have known Jeff for several years, have spent time in one of the residences he has set up, have met some of his clients and staff members, and know firsthand of the effective and loving care Windhorse's staff provides for its clients.

In our discussions concerning the respite center, Shery and I have talked about other organizations and other small-scale programs, here and abroad, that, like Windhorse, have successfully provided *in-home* care for people with acute psychiatric problems, and that might provide models for crisis respite: Crossing Place in Washington, D.C.; the Venture program in Vancouver, Canada; the Soteria projects in San Jose, California, and Berne, Switzerland; Burch House in Bethlehem, New Hampshire, and others.

At lunch Lynn and Shery ask Jeff questions about how his residences are set up, and ask him to tell them whatever, from his experience, he thinks might prove useful so that they can, at the least, avoid the most obvious mistakes.

Jeff suggests, first of all, that in setting up guest rooms they pay special attention to the details of the domestic environment—to mirrors, colors, paint—whether the paint is flat or shiny, for example, because people in crisis are very suggestible and impressionable. He suggests that people in crisis prefer flat to shiny, soft and soothing earth colors to colors that are bright or intense, and that mirrors be avoided. He recommends setting houseplants around, and that for the first six months they use only one bedroom at a time, until they see how that works, and that they take more risks as they learn. They need to be sensitive to the community and to their neighbors, especially early on, since an incident in the first or second month—a guest acting out, for example— can prove more fatal to the project than the same incident at the end of the first or second year. If possible, they should try to take in a quieter person as a guest the first time, and— he laughs, remembering his own errors—he recommends that they not ever put two hypomanic people together! And no visitors, he says. No people coming to see how this thing works.

We walk over to Windhorse's offices after lunch, and I am impressed again with how professional and welcoming they are. The Windhorse program—there are six of them worldwide—is based, in part, on principles that Edward Podvoll, a psychiatrist, set down in a book called *The Seduction of Madness*, especially principles relating to what Podvoll calls "islands of clarity," those "moments of natural recovery" that occur "all the time within the experience of psychosis," and that can not only be "recognized and acknowledged," but need to be protected. By "perceiving and nurturing these islands of clarity," full recovery from psychosis can be accomplished, Podvoll asserts, "without aggressive or physically intrusive methods of treatment."

Windhorse's principles also have a goodly amount of Eastern (Buddhist) philosophy attached to them, and these philosophical attitudes and beliefs coexist, happily, as in Jeff Fortuna, with a most practical sense of how to care for individuals in the here and now.

Although all team leaders at Windhorse, for example, are required to practice some form of ongoing contemplative exercise "as a way," Jeff says, "of taking responsibility for their own experience," the Windhorse program employs fully trained and certified psychiatrists, psychologists, nurses, and social workers. Each Windhorse client receives regular psychotherapy, including cognitive behavioral therapy, geared toward finding practical solutions to worldly problems of functioning, twice a week.

Individuals who have been in the program, including one recent client who is now a student at Harvard, are unanimous in agreeing that it is "the personal attention" and "the emphasis on community participation" that differentiates Windhorse from other mental health programs they have been through. By living in their own apartments, with roommates—much as my brother did when he was living in a private home on Staten Island (sponsored by Beacon of Hope and Catholic Charities U.S.A.), in what was the best living situation he has had during the past thirty years—they learn to deal with the nitty-gritty of daily life, such as budgeting their money, buying food, and learning to get along with others.

Windhorse conceives of itself as striving to maintain "active collaboration between professional, client and family members," and sees "the combined task of client and housemate" as being the establishment of "simple, predictable daily routine activities of 'sane' living."

> This involves attending to basic needs for regular cycles of exercise and rest, proper food intake, order and cleanliness in the home, with focus upon simple activities such as shopping, walking, reading, and having a conversation. . . . Each client has regular daily contact with members of the treatment team (which includes a team leader, team ther-

apist, housemate, and nurse) in one of several settings. These settings include: weekly meetings of the team members and client, household meetings with client and housemate, several sessions a week of basic attendance, individual psychotherapy, nursing consultation (to consider general health, exercise, nutrition), and regular meetings with the psychiatrist to review medication. In addition, the entire community has monthly meetings for clients and staff together as well as social events and seasonal celebrations. This pattern of meetings and events provides an added dimension to the relationships formed in the treatment settings. In this way the program begins to resemble the full and diverse schedule of a balanced life, with its attendant responsibilities and rewards.

When I say something about my impressions of the Windhorse residence I visited with Jeff—a three-room apartment in which a young man in his late twenties lived, on a quiet side street in town, next door, as it happened, to my rabbi's house—and of how peaceful and lovingly cared for it seemed in its domestic detail, I do so because Shery and Lynn have been admiring similar qualities in the design and atmosphere of the office.

The space in which Jeff practices psychotherapy with his clients is spare yet inviting: a small, rectangular area rug composed of green and beige squares, two upholstered armchairs, a handsome wooden table between the chairs, a vase of flowers on the table. When I remark on the sweet orderliness of things in the room, Jeff smiles and says that it is his belief that "a certain discipline and formality allows for openness and freedom in communication."

The basic premise requiring all clients to do two hours a week of intensive psychotherapy with a trained therapist (Jeff has a master's degree in psychotherapy), Jeff says, derives from the belief that "human intimacy can be a signficant catalyst for recovery from psychosis."

Jeff then talks about the principles that guide the Windhorse program: the belief that psychosis is "a major disruption in the balance of the body-mind environment that dislocates a person from the functional reference points of ordinary life"; the belief that "significant recovery is a real possibility for anyone with psychosis," and that it can occur "naturally when catalyzed by authentic therapeutic friendships in a homelike setting."

Therapists, Jeff explains, are informed "by the essential Windhorse premise that recovery from psychosis is a difficult process requiring great courage and persistence on the part of the client and that motivation for this is kindled by an attitude that balances expectation of change with respect and acceptance."

"Grouping severely disturbed people in one place of treatment may risk the health of patients *and* staff," Jeff suggests. "An ill person is more likely to become healthier if he or she is in the company of other healthy people in a sane environment."

What strikes me now, as I listen to Jeff, and what has struck me during the past few years, as I have watched Windhorse clients move from severe psychosis and withdrawal into more active lives within the Northampton community, is simply that when it comes to programs that seek to help people with lengthy histories of psychosis recover and return to our world, no matter the philosophical, medical, or therapeutic bases for the programs, a good measure of ordinary human kindness—of extensive labor-intensive care performed by skilled people committed to caring for the individual for as long as it takes on any given day, or for as long as it takes for any number of years—is itself the worldly expression, and issue, of love and of hope that often makes recovery possible.

Jeff's teams of full- and part-time social workers, aides, psychologists, psychiatrists, nutritionists, and nurses (Jeff's wife, Molly, who works at Windhorse part time, is a psychiatric nurse and has a master's degree in psychotherapy) will devote whatever means and personnel are necessary for any given client at any given time—for example, three or four people working with the client around the clock in the home environment during a crisis, or one part-time person visiting the client on a regular basis when the client has progressed to a point of greater health and self-reliance. Windhorse is a private nonprofit organization but, to Jeff's relief, it has become increasingly successful at obtaining third-party reimbursements from local HMOs and the state DMH. "When all traditional methods of treatment fail," Jeff says, "they will turn to us now."

Windhorse also works hard at finding employment in the community for its clients, and providing its clients, as needed, with on-site support in the job situation. Windhorse sponsors its own small business—Four Guys and a Big Truck—and for $40 an hour, staff and clients will perform most varieties of yard work and hauling. "When you're working," one staff member, Eric Chapin, who oversees the work crews, says, "you're both giving and taking." And the physical work of raking leaves or moving furniture also helps people coming off medications to become more "grounded" in their bodies. "Work is a great healer," Eric says. "It's amazing to watch how the body starts firing again."

Two weeks later, on the day before I drive up to Claremont for the final day of respite training, I drive down to the Bronx, to be with Robert during his first day at the Bronx Psychiatric Center.

I had visited the center with Robert two months before, on a broiling hot day the first week of July, and Robert had started out this visit parrying with and testing virtually every person we met. When he got out of the car that had driven him from South Beach, for example, and I introduced him to Al Pam, and when, a few minutes later, Al remarked casually about the flowers Robert had stuck through the air vents of his baseball cap, Robert had, without missing a beat, replied: "Why are you obsessing so much about my flowers?"

When Robert attended the weekly meeting on the open

ward, he spoke out loudly without being called on, asking if he would have to take his pills if he came here, and immediately answering his own question by declaring that he would *never* take his pills because, he declared, "I was born a Christian Scientist but I have become a Jew and a Baptist!" (Though his remark may have seemed nonsensical to others, I knew the probable reference points — my girlfriend during my senior year of college was a Christian Scientist; my first wife was born a Baptist and became a Jew — and so could begin to make some sense of it.)

At this point one of the four dozen or so members of Ward 12 had raised his hand and, with a lilting Hispanic accent, had spoken to Robert: "If you don't take your pills, my friend, nobody gonna *help* you. . . ." When Robert shouted back that he didn't *want* to take pills anymore, another patient turned to him and waved his hand in a gesture of farewell. "Then good-bye!" the patient called softly.

Robert demanded coffee. When it was given to him hot, he wanted it cold; when it was given to him cold, he wanted it hot — and had taken off his eyeglasses and washed them in the coffee. During the meeting he walked back and forth across the room to get water from a water cooler, sprinkling pepper and other condiments into the water, then mixing this with his coffee, after which he returned to the cooler to create new concoctions.

When I whispered to him to try to stop — to try to *cool* it — he sat down next to me, and for most of the rest of the afternoon, he had been friendly, relaxed, warm, funny, and very open about how fearful and nervous it was making him to think of leaving South Beach — a hospital that, through all his ups and downs and ins and outs, and despite them, had been his primary home for more than two decades.

Sally Mills, the psychology intern assigned to be Robert's therapist on Ward 15, met with me for a while. The staff and hospital, she said, were very committed to working with Robert — to trying to show that they could, in fact, do good work with patients who had chronic histories of mental illness. They also wanted Robert to understand that he was not going to be treated as "a star mental patient."

Sally also warned me that the hospital itself, under pressure from managed care–style budget-cutting practices, was becoming more and more like a prison. The clientele were, increasingly, individuals with criminal records and histories of substance abuse, and the facilities (the hospital, which rises prisonlike from fields that adjoin the Hutchinson Parkway, opened, complete with surgical suites for the performance of lobotomies, in 1963) left much to be desired. Except for cigarette breaks, she noted, patients stayed on locked wards *all* the time, and even for those with 'honor passes' that gave them the right to roam the hospital's corridors, there was only one small, fenced-in piece of outdoor space— of earth, concrete, and air—for the hospital's eight hundred patients. Although Ward 12, the hospital's only 'open' ward, served its patients well—heroically, really (according to Sally, wards 12 and 15 were the only decent wards in the hospital)—at four o'clock each day it became a closed ward. Security, Sally said, was becoming tighter and tighter.

Ten days before the actual transfer to Bronx Psychiatric Center, and six weeks after Robert's visit there, I had driven down to Staten Island with a friend from the Northampton area, Larry Hott, a documentary filmmaker. Larry's father had been a psychiatrist at Gracie Square, one of the New York City hospitals where Robert had stayed and where Larry had worked as an aide during his college years. Robert, whose behavior and condition, by all accounts—including that of the South Beach staff—had improved miraculously in the weeks following his Bronx visit, had, for the first time in seventeen months, been granted a pass to leave the hospital so that he could have lunch with me and Larry.

We ate at Rio Bravo, a Mexican restaurant situated in a large shopping plaza on Hylan Boulevard, a half-mile or so from the Beacon of Hope home where Robert had been living a few years ago. Larry brought a small camcorder with him, and before, during, and after lunch, he videotaped me and Robert. Robert was relaxed, conversational, animated. He gave me a gift he had been saving—a dollar bill with the letter "J" on its face. He recited, from memory, some of his poems; he told old jokes ("Why does Imogene Coca take a bath alone?" he asked, and then answered: "Because Sid Sees-Her!"); he drew Matisse-like self-portraits; he talked about himself and his past without embarrassment, and he talked, too, about the possibilities he still felt were there for him in the years to come.

"Wilhelm Reich, you know, believed that there are three essentials to life—work, play, and love," he said to Larry at one point. "And I agree with him. *Work—Play—Love.* But did you know that the government got after him and banned his orgone boxes from being shipped interstate?"

After we returned to South Beach, Larry videotaped the two of us again. A few minutes later, as Larry and I were about to drive away, our car was surrounded by six people, including Nick Farini, the team leader of Robert's ward, and four uniformed guards. Nick demanded that Larry turn over his film and camera to him, and he reprimanded me severely for violating hospital rules concerning picture taking. I replied that, as he knew, I had spoken with a hospital administrator, and had been assured that as long as Robert agreed to have photos taken and we did not photograph anyone else, patients or staff, there was no problem. In fact, I reminded Nick, Robert's therapist, Mark Kaplan, had been in Robert's room with us a month or two before, when another friend had been visiting Robert with me and had taken pictures.

In addition, I said, Robert had been at South Beach on and off for twenty-three years, this would be our last visit here together, Robert had said he would like to have some souvenirs—some memories—of South Beach, and he had *asked* me to bring a camera.

When Larry refused to take the videotape out of his camera, Nick confiscated the camera and ordered us to go with him to the security office, where an administrator, Nick, and a security officer, looking into the camcorder, reviewed the videotape Larry had taken that day. Sitting on a wooden bench outside the security office, Larry remarked that he felt very much like a child waiting outside an assistant principal's office.

About twenty minutes later, the administrator came out with the camera and videotape, and confirmed what I had said earlier: that since we had not photographed anyone else, and since Robert had agreed to be photographed, there was no problem. She gave Larry back his camera, and we were on our way.

When I telephoned Robert from Northampton that night, he thanked me for the day out, told me how much he liked Larry, how much he was looking forward to going to the Bronx, and then added, softly, "But I was sad to have to go back to my locked ward."

Now, less than two weeks later, on August 21, 1997, Robert and I sit in the triage room at Bronx Psychiatric Center, while Robert waits for the interviews, exams, and paperwork necessary for admission to his new home. When the psychiatrist assigned to conduct the interview arrives and asks Robert if he wants me to come in with him or to wait, Robert says he wants me there.

The doctor looks through the large stack of paper that has come with Robert—easily, in two volumes, more than a foot high—asks Robert basic questions about his history and health, and other questions (including those from a standard Mini-Mental State Exam) designed to gauge cognitive, neurological, and psychological levels. The doctor seems surprised, and says so, to find that a man who is so intelligent, witty, and direct—who seems "so together"—has had such a long history of institutionalization.

When he asks Robert about Clozaril, and whether he would be willing to take it, Robert seems to have anticipated the question, for he answers immediately and with great force—"*Yes!*"—and then adds: "And I'll take the blood tests too."

Robert also says that he wants new teeth. His old dentures—taken away from him nearly a year ago and lost, we assume, somewhere at South Beach—have not been sent with him.

"He's really maintained his spirits, and his individuality, hasn't he?" the psychiatrist says when Robert leaves, briefly, to go to the bathroom. The doctor remarks on the soundness of Robert's memory, and on his energy levels. "It's amazing, really—and very encouraging."

Because of bureaucratic delays, Robert and I wind up spending more than four hours in triage, yet Robert, often so restless he is unable to sit *anywhere* for more than five or ten consecutive minutes, remains calm the entire time. He kibitzes with the office workers doing the paperwork, talks with people who come and go, asks questions about friends and family, and watches TV (reruns of *The Cosby Show*, and an afternoon talk show, *Women Who Are Slaves*, featuring women who are vociferous about the joys of being servile to men). When one of the two men doing the paperwork leaves the room, he touches Robert on the shoulder, asks him what he drinks, and, as if it the most natural thing in the world, brings back two cans of soda for Robert, and waves away Robert's money and thank-yous.

Late in the afternoon, this man and I pick up Robert's bags, and the three of us ascend in an elevator to the fifth floor, and to Ward 15, Robert's new home. As Robert walks down a long corridor, from the locked steel door to the nurse's station, we pass patients, some who seem quite lively and alert, others who appear as sad, disabled, and sedated as patients on Robert's ward at South Beach. Robert takes a deep breath, lifts his head, and as he passes each patient, he veers slightly to the right or left, to get closer, whispering each time, "*New man . . . ! New man . . . !*"

The nurses show Robert to his room—he will have a room of his own here; it is clean, with a single large window that lets in lots of light—and then show him the dayroom, which is not as new and modern as the dayroom at South Beach, but where, by happy contrast, there is no nurse's station at its center, and no patients lying around sleeping. Robert also meets his social worker, Alan Epstein, who has been waiting for Robert's arrival and has stayed past his regular hours; Alan, it turns out, used to work at South Beach, where he and Robert knew each other. In silence, I help Robert unpack. When Robert looks at me, his expression melancholy, it is as if his eyes are saying, *Well, here I am again, I guess, in another ward, and how many years have gone by, Jay?*

Before I leave, I make a list of things Robert wants me to bring the next time I visit, and then—it is time for supper—we embrace, I wish him luck, and tell him I'll see him soon.

When I arrive home in Northampton three hours later, I telephone Robert and he tells me how much he misses me, and how nice the staff is—"They're really kind, Jay. They're so *kind* to me!" And then: "You pulled some strings to get me here, didn't you?"

I say that the transfer, from one catchment area to another, did take some doing, and that our book can probably get some of the credit. (Al Pam has told me it happens "once in a million times," and that if not for *Imagining Robert* it would not have happened.)

"Then good, Big Neugie. That's good. That's very good."

Both Robert and I, like my sons Aaron and Eli—and like my father and his brothers before us—grew up being called "Neugie" by our friends, and "Big Neugie" has become Robert's preferred way of referring to me lately (he has asked me to call him "Little Neugie")—a sweet and affectionate revision of his old, and often angry way of referring to me as his big brother, as in "That's Jay, he's my *big* brother, and he thinks he knows everything and that his shit doesn't stink"—and we talk for a while more. I tell him I hope to come back soon and spend more time with him.

"Then good night, Big Neugie," he says.

"Good night, Little Neugie," I reply.

Early the next morning I head for Claremont and, thinking of the day ahead, and of being with Shery, Dave, Julie, and the others—people who have recovered from mental illness and have gone on to make careers for themselves in the world of mental health, I recall my mother's wish, voiced often, that Robert be kept in a mental hospital on a permanent basis and be given some kind of job there.

Recalling those years, it occurs to me that the people who will be at the training session today—individuals who have themselves been frequently institutionalized and who are now going to be paid to work with people who have histories like Robert's—though not being kept in mental hospitals, are nonetheless choosing, for the most part, to spend large parts of their lives in places that have become the community equivalents of the old state hospitals: worlds that keep them among their own kind and isolated from the larger society, and that doubtless give to them some of what my mother believed permanent residence in a mental hospital would give Robert: friendship, safety, comfort, security.

I think, too, of my talks with Shery, and of her desire, as she has put it in the draft of the essay she sent me, to "take the next step in defining recovery as a process and product by which people move beyond disability" so that they may "in fact, no longer consider themselves disabled, impaired, or dysfunctional," and so that their symptoms at "some point in recovery may be no more significant to us than someone else's occasional stress headaches or mildly stiff joints."

"The prevailing vision," she writes, "is that people with 'severe and persistent mental illness' will never recover, but rather may experience an increase in coping skills, develop abilities to work in supported employment, if only in menial jobs, and maintain their own apartments with support. People who move beyond that lifestyle are often considered exceptions to the rule."

In "less tactful language," Shery continues, "we make assumptions about people being either 'high'- or 'low'-

functioning,' " and this results in "the high-functioning individuals often being seen as having little in common with their counterparts." What Shery believes, though, and with a passion equal to her energy and her intelligence, is that "people who experience psychiatric symptoms can move beyond defining themselves as disabled, and can experience recovery so as to lead lives where personal challenges are no longer so significant that they are thought of as 'symptoms,' and where those of us who have experienced these symptoms consider ourselves as everyone does: unique individuals with a full capacity to work toward our dreams and goals."

While I drive north, thinking about Robert in his new home and of imaginary guests for whom the respite center, and not a locked psychiatric ward, will soon be home, I also find myself thinking of people I have been meeting who have suffered from mental illness but who, once they recovered, did *not* choose to stay in the world of mental health and make careers there. Instead, moving beyond recovery and beyond disability, they have slipped quietly back into our world and live and work beside us like any of our other colleagues, friends, and neighbors.

EIGHT

MOVING BEYOND DISABILITY

TABLE 1.

CONCEPTION, REALIZATION, AND TIME LAG FOR TEN INNOVATIONS

INNOVATION	YEAR OF FIRST CONCEPTION	YEAR OF FIRST REALIZATION	DURATION IN YEARS
Heart Pacemaker	1928	1960	32
Input-Output Economic Analysis	1936	1964	28
Hybrid Corn	1908	1933	25
Electrophotography	1937	1959	22
Magnetic Ferrites	1933	1955	22
Green Revolution: Wheat	1950	1966	16
Organophosphorus Insecticides	1934	1947	13
Oral Contraceptive	1951	1960	9
Videotape Recorder	1950	1956	6
AVERAGE DURATION			19.2

—GLASER, ABELSON, AND GARRISON,
Putting Knowledge to Use

On September 7, 1997—two weeks after Robert's transfer to the Bronx—I drive to Nashua, New Hampshire, for a Partners for Change Conference on Recovery, entitled "Moving Beyond Disability." The conference is held at the Nashua Marriott, and is cosponsored by the Alliance for the Mentally Ill of New Hampshire, the New Hampshire Department of Health and Human Services, the New Hampshire Division of Behavioral Health Services, and the New Hampshire Mental Health Consumer Council.

More than four hundred mental health professionals attend this annual daylong conference of talks, panels, and workshops, and—a first for the sponsoring organizations—several hundred more are turned away for lack of space. As I wait in line for registration, talking with Shery and with Dave Hilton (who will give the welcoming remarks), and with people they introduce me to, I look around and I think: I could just as well be attending a regional conference of business or public relations executives, and not a conference of social workers, therapists, mental patients, and ex-patients. What amazes Shery and Dave, and what they comment on repeatedly, is that they could not have conceived of organizing a conference like this even two or three years ago.

For, as becomes clear during the course of the day—starting with the opening plenary session (at which Dr. Paul Carling, the keynote speaker, informs us that the conference was largely inspired and organized by Shery), and continuing through lunch, at coffee breaks, and in workshops (a dozen are offered)—nobody is questioning basic assumptions and views concerning mental illness that were considered radical and heretical only a few years ago:

- that, for people with severe mental illness and histories of severe mental illness, rehabilitation and recovery are possible;
- that people with severe mental illness—with supports, and, increasingly, without them—can marry and raise children, can successfully hold down part- and full-time jobs, and can live in communities with the rest of us;
- that people with severe mental illness can attend colleges and graduate schools and succeed there;

- that, when it comes to thinking about and designing programs for people with severe mental illness, "wraparound" services such as the ACT programs are imperative, and new ideas and risk taking are welcome and encouraged;
- that people with mental illness and in recovery from mental illness—"consumers"—*must* be consulted about what they want and about what they know, and in all decisions affecting their lives;
- that people with mental illness and in recovery from mental illness must not be infantilized and condescended to, but can and should be encouraged to take increasing responsibility for their own lives;
- that the fight against discrimination and stigmatization is a good fight and has only just begun;
- that being a mental health professional is good and honorable work that one can take pride in; and
- that not only have we moved in recent years, as Dave Hilton states in his remarks, along the spectrum from deinstitutionalization and community mental health to recovery, but that we are beginning to believe what we have been telling ourselves and have started telling the rest of the world: that recovery from mental illness is possible for *everyone,* and that, knowing this, we can now not only begin to move beyond disability, but beyond recovery, too.

Although some of the talk at the conference is a bit more upbeat than seems realistic and, especially when it merges with positivistic talk I associate with the so-called human potential movement, too vague to seem credible ("Adventure-Based Therapies, by design, [will] allow individuals to have direct experience in moving beyond perceived limitations and into a more complete sense of themselves and their true potential"), most of the presentations are refreshingly optimistic while being solidly grounded in direct clinical experience, carefully designed and informed research, and well-conceived outcome studies ("This presentation will review the two dominant theories of mental illness, i.e., psychodynamic theory of social and environmental stress and the bio-genetic model of brain disease").

The conference makes it clear, too, that not only has it become possible for individuals with serious mental illness to change so that they can move beyond disability and recovery, but that it's even possible for entire state systems of mental health to change and to recover their true mission: helping individuals afflicted with serious psychiatric problems to move beyond survival and into full and productive lives.

Two weeks after this conference, I fly to Denver to give a talk for the Mental Health Association of Colorado (this is the conference at which Dr. Robert Freedman talks about research on the relation of mental illness to nicotine), and once again, at workshops, and especially at a gala fund-raising dinner attended by more than five hundred people, at which more than $120,000 is raised, the organizers of the conference tell me they could not have conceived of an event like this taking place in Denver until recent years, and that this good news is all around us in the presence of the people in attendance — most of Denver's major "movers and shakers" in business, politics, and society. This is especially heartening, they say, since virtually all the people at the conference, including those who sit at expensive corporate tables, have family members with serious mental illness or have themselves experienced serious mental illness. Only a few years ago, the president of the Mental Health Association confides, few of them would have been willing to go public about the presence of this fact in their lives.

A short while before I give my talk, and while walking around the hotel plaza outside the banquet room, looking at the materials in the information fair and browsing through a large display of books on mental illness and allied subjects, the woman in charge of this display introduces herself, and tells me she has been reading *Imagining Robert*.

The woman's name is Paula Kline, she is in her late forties, and she works in the conference department of Denver's The

Tattered Cover, one of the largest independent bookstores in the country, organizing, servicing, and running book fairs at conventions. A few minutes into our conversation, Paula tells me she has just finished reading the section of my book that tells of Robert's time on an insulin-coma ward at Creedmoor, and that she found the section fascinating because, she says — and she does so as easily as if she were telling me that she once had treatments of ultrasound for a sore shoulder — "I had lots of insulin shock treatments too."

"You're kidding," I say and, remembering just how god-awful these treatments were — treatments that by inducing insulin comas in patients brought them to states of unconsciousness that were about as near to death as anyone comes in this life — and looking into the face of a woman who seems as sane, bright-eyed, and capable as any of the doctors, lawyers, business executives, and others all around us in the plaza — I am stunned. "You're kidding," I repeat. "You *really* had insulin shock treatments?"

"Oh, yes," Paula says, smiling. "And it was pretty much as you describe it in your book. I mean, it was *horrible*. I was a young woman then, but I had *dozens* of insulin coma treatments. Lots of Thorazine too."

We talk for a few more minutes, after which Paula excuses herself to attend to other customers. Then she asks me how Robert is doing, and if I am working on a new book, and while we talk I realize I am in a kind of recovery myself — in recovery from the shock of finding someone close to my brother's age who has been through some of the worst he has been through, yet is out here in the world, seemingly unembarrassed about a history most people hide, and seemingly as unaffected by this part of her life as other people might be about a minor car accident or unhappy relationship they'd once been in.

"Look, would you be willing to talk with me more about this?" I ask. "If I call, or write — would you be willing to talk with me?"

"Oh sure," Paula says. "Actually, I'd love to. Being here,

and looking around at the people attending this conference, it makes me realize that it would be really *helpful* for me to talk about this finally, or to write it down. For my children too. It's something I've been wanting to do for years really."

When I telephone Paula a week later, she fills me in on some basic facts of her life. She is a single parent to four children, three boys and a girl, ages twenty-five, twenty-three, twenty, and eighteen, and she talks about what they do and don't know about her past history of mental illness. She and I trade single-parent anecdotes for a while—the equivalent of consumers' "war stories"?—and we agree that, against popular notions, we found our children's teenage years to have been much *easier* for us than their earlier years; for there was less hands-on parenting to do, and more *mutuality*—more give-and-take, more of the kind of talking, reasoning, and understanding one expects and gets from adult friends—and that when we treated our children as people capable of being responsible, they usually responded by *being* responsible.

Paula talks about her work at The Tattered Cover, and how much she loves it—how it allows her to get out into the world more, to travel, to meet interesting people. Before she took the job at the bookstore, she taught aerobic dance classes to adults for six years, and before that—when her children were younger, and before her divorce—she worked as a volunteer in her children's schools, held various board positions with the school's Parents and Teachers Organization, and became its president. She worked in AIDS education for her school district for three years, and when her children were teenagers she returned to college, part time, attending the University of Colorado, and is now twenty credits shy of her degree.

Paula tells me that her mother, who lives in Kalamazoo, Michigan, is dying of a brain tumor, and that she'll be going to Michigan soon. "I may not be able to write to you in the next few months, while I help my mom go through the end of her journey," she says.

On this next trip to Michigan, she adds, she will stop in Chicago, the city where she was hospitalized and received insulin shock treatments two decades ago, and she expects to spend some time there with one of her closest lifelong friends, Carl D'Agostino, a well-known Chicago jazz musician.

Paula tells me she has enjoyed writing down some of her story since our meeting in Denver—she will send me a few pages before she heads to Michigan—and offers the information that her friend Carl has asked that, when she is with him and his friends or fellow musicians, she never allude to, or let anyone know, where and how the two of them first met.

"He was a patient on the psych ward with me at Chicago Wesley Memorial Hospital," Paula says.

A half hour or so after I get off the phone, it rings again, and it is another Carl this time—Carl Pickus, a former student of mine at the University of Massachusetts. Carl and I have been collaborating on an original screenplay he began working on in a fiction workshop I taught nearly a decade ago. Since that time, Carl has become a producer of MTV videos and TV commercials, traveling around the country and the world to create videos for major corporations (Absolut, Reebok, Banana Republic), and of well-known musicians and musical groups (Phish, Pearl Jam, B.B. King, Jane's Addiction, Hootie and the Blowfish).

Carl moans, and laughs, about the unreal hours he has been working on recent shoots—fourteen- and fifteen-hour days for eight or ten days in a row. "I've really been in the nostril," he says, and then says that he thinks it is "truly insane" for people to be entrusting him—"me—Carl Pickus!"—with budgets of more than a million dollars.

He is glad to have the work, and the money, but mostly he is happy that he doesn't have a gig for a while so that he can concentrate on our script. We reminisce about his years at UMass, about people who were in workshops with him and with whom I've stayed in touch, and Carl tells me, as he does almost every time we talk, how important it was for him to have *finished* the script. He talks of the time, less than thirty seconds after he had set down the last word, and seven years after he had, in my class, first started the script, that he telephoned me with this news, saying again that he considers this accomplishment to have been the high point of his life.

He asks about my children, I ask about his family and his personal life, and we arrange to get together on my next trip to New York, to talk about revisions, and about possible agents.

I get off the phone, and I think: *Carl too.* Carl, too, was hospitalized for mental illness though not long-term, and has, like Paula, returned, productively and creatively, to our world. In his late teens, Carl spent several months at The Retreat, a private psychiatric facility in Brattleboro, Vermont (like Shery, he has discomforting memories of shuffling through downtown Brattleboro with other patients, all of them heavily medicated, and being stared at by the locals). He also spent three years as an outpatient at McLean Hospital, a private psychiatric facility outside Boston, in Belmont, Massachusetts, where, during these three years, he attended the Arlington School, on the hospital's grounds, a school whose student body was made up largely of inpatients.

I think of Dori Fagerson, a forty-year-old woman who lives on my street in Northampton. I see her regularly on walks, at local readings and book signings, and in the synagogue— she is a social worker who is also a published writer with whom I correspondenced nearly twenty years ago when she was hospitalized for mental illness.

I think of Lynne Douglas, who has been writing me from Seattle, Washington, about her breakdowns and hospitalizations, and of how she recovered, completed her M.D. and her residencies, and is now director of radiation oncology at a medical center and the married mother of two children.

I think of other people I have met—Gaston Cloutier, Rose

Tompkins, Pat Deegan, Dan Fisher, Dave Hilton—who, like Shery Mead and Moe Armstrong, have had histories of madness and hospitalization and have become leaders in the world of mental health. I think of famous people of the past (Leonardo Da Vinci, William Blake, Robert Schumann, Virginia Woolf), and of the present (Patty Duke, Jimmy Piersall, Robert Lowell, William Styron, Dick Cavett) who have been afflicted with mental illness, and have spoken and/or written of their experiences.

And then I think of those individuals who are neither leaders in the world of mental health nor well known in other professions: I think of Ed Roy, a fifty-year-old married man (and father) who is a night-shift counselor in a residential facility for the elderly, and who was hospitalized dozens of times, beginning at the age of fifteen, and who recently enrolled in a graduate program and is working toward a master's degree in psychology—and of how Ed took himself off Social Security disability income (SSDI) several years ago with the full knowledge of how difficult it might be to regain his coverage if he ever had another breakdown.

I think of Richard Hayes, a middle-aged man with a long-term history of mental illness, who works full time as a night janitor in a local community college and who, too, has taken himself off SSDI voluntarily.

I think of Kate Fontaine, a woman of thirty-four who has been hospitalized more than thirty times, including eighteen stays at Worcester State Hospital and who, like Richard and Ed, has voluntarily taken herself off SSDI. After working at several full-time jobs (as mailroom coordinator at the Worcester Art Museum and as credit manager and purchasing agent for two large industrial food suppliers) and maintaining herself in apartments by herself, Kate now lives with her father, a credit manager at a Chevrolet dealership. She works full time as a production assistant in food service—her happiest job—at Memorial Hospital in Worcester, and delights in telling me about her relationship with her sister and her sister's children, and how she and her sister love to play Bingo, and to go to gambling casinos together on weekends.

I think of Louise Carr, a forty-year-old African-American woman born and raised in New York City, who has been hospitalized for psychiatric problems numerous times, beginning at the age of twelve. Louise has been in and out of jail more times than she has been hospitalized, and has spent a good portion of her life as a homeless drug addict. She is now certified by the state of New York as a security guard, and lives in her own three-room apartment in the Bronx, is off all drugs and medications and, in addition to performing a dozen or more hours a week of volunteer outreach work for Pathways to Housing, an organization that serves homeless people with mental illness in New York City, also works a regular forty-hour week as a full-time security guard for Prestige Management in the Bronx.

I think of first-person accounts I have been reading in professional journals—*Psychiatric Services, Schizophrenia Bulletin, THE JOURNAL of the California Alliance for the Mentally Ill, Psychiatric Rehabilitation Journal*, and others—and how these journals now include in each issue personal narratives written by individuals who have recovered from serious mental illness.

I think of others I have met within the past year: the seventeen workers at CRREL, and the thirteen graduates of the B.U. program, and the dozens of graduates of the Odyssey House program, and the dozens of people I have met at various clubhouses (including the Starpoint Clubhouse in my hometown of Northampton, and the Mosaic Clubhouse in London), all of whom have had serious mental illnesses and who are out here in our world, working at part- and full-time jobs that range from dishwashing and fast-food service to computer engineering and graphic design. I think of friends, colleagues, and acquaintances who have, since the appearance of *Imagining Robert*, told me of their hospitalizations, and of their months and years of shame and anguish, and of how they, too, are out here in the world with jobs and careers that are not in any significant or outward way compromised by their histories of mental illness.

I think of my own family—cousins, aunts, uncles, and the children of cousins, aunts, and uncles—who have had breakdowns, been hospitalized, and who, dispersed to cities and suburbs around this country and the world, seem no different, outwardly, from *their* friends and neighbors, and I wonder: Is there *anyone* out there who has *not* been hospitalized for mental illness at some point in his or her life, or who doesn't have a close family member who has?

When you're in love, the whole world is Jewish. . . . I smile, recalling the old saying, and I think: Maybe it's true that when you're in love—*madly* in love?—the whole world is schizophrenic too. For not only are the mad, like the poor, with us always, but it seems that the *formerly* mad are also with us, and in abundance, and that they are often with us in invisible ways because most of the time, unless they choose to tell us so, we have no way of knowing that they were once where my brother is still.

"Where to begin?" Paula writes. "Well, I was born in Kalamazoo, Michigan, on December 1, 1948, the first of four girls. It seems like my childhood was similar to everyone else's in my neighborhood—fathers went off to work, our mothers stayed home and took care of us, we had an empty lot for kickball games, a sledding hill and a corner drugstore where we could wander off on our own to get ice cream cones.

"My high school years were filled with cheerleading, long talks with my girlfriends about the boys in and out of our lives, and the highlight of being crowned homecoming queen."

Paula attended Michigan State University, and "seemed to be thriving," she writes. She made friends easily, dated, joined a sorority, and then her life "began to unravel."

"I was just depressed all the time, and it wouldn't go away, and I just felt so *humiliated*," she writes, "that I couldn't ever imagine asking *anybody* for help.

"The strongest memories I have are of the shame I experienced at knowing something was terribly wrong with me and being afraid to tell anyone," she continues. "I remember an essay exam where I couldn't make sense of the questions. I rambled on, doodled designs over the paper and then wrote an apology to the instructor. With friends I tried to be upbeat and hide my growing insecurities and fear of the change going on inside of me. It is clear to me now that I was depressed: But back then no one talked about depression. One day I collapsed on the floor in my dorm and my roommate had me taken to the health clinic."

Paula writes that she was scared, numb, anxious, profoundly embarrassed, and that she had constant suicidal thoughts—she recalls "praying to God that [she] might die in her sleep"—but that she "could not cry out for help and tell someone what was really going on" inside her.

She saw specialists in Chicago, spent time at Chicago's Wesley Memorial Hospital, dropped out of school, lived at home, slept a lot, gained weight, and continued to feel extremely depressed and suicidal. Three months after her return home, she was hospitalized again, and this time she was placed in a locked psychiatric ward.

When she and her mother were told that she had been put on the psychiatric ward because she was depressed—"Finally, someone had said the word I couldn't say," Paula writes—her mother "adamantly spoke up saying that I *never* got depressed."

"It was years later that I realized my mother could never see my depressed state," Paula explains. "When my mother was nine years old she and her three younger sisters and father had been out running errands. On their return home they walked into the kitchen to find their own young mother slumped over on the floor. She had committed suicide by sticking her head in the oven."

For thirty years nobody spoke about the grandmother's suicide, and Paula believes that "one or two of my sisters and

I took on our mother's unspoken grief and loss. Three of us have suffered from clinical depression."

Paula was discharged from the psychiatric ward after a month; she returned to Michigan State the following September, but began to fall apart again. "It was as if I had become a new and improved version of my former cheerleader, homecoming queen self. By November my mind was racing so fast that I recognized I needed some help."

Paula decided she would drive to Chicago to see her psychiatrist at Thanksgiving, and "secretly" believed her mother would be proud of her for no longer being depressed.

"I had no idea my creative energy, sleepless nights, and million and one ideas were simply manic behavior. My roommate and parents were concerned about me also, and without telling me what they were planning and why, showed up early one morning to put me in the car, lock the doors and drive me from East Lansing down to Chicago. I was hospitalized on November 18th and remained there until the following May.

"I took on the life of a mental patient," Paula continues. "The way I was hospitalized, without being told what was going on and why they thought the hospital would help me, made me very angry. Soon I was on Thorazine, feeling drymouthed, slowed down, and numb. By December I was told I would go off the Thorazine (hurrah!) and be treated with insulin shock treatment. There was no discussing this as an option—it was simply what the doctor ordered."

Paula recalls that she never talked with her parents about her treatments, though she does recall being told that the insulin shock comas would "slow her down."

"As if," she writes, "the Thorazine hadn't slowed me down enough already!"

(In *Imagining Robert*, I describe insulin comas, their rationales and effects, and quote from an entry in the 1975 edition of *The Comprehensive Textbook of Psychiatry* that reads in part: "Patients who never hallucinated before may develop hallucinations during the state of hypoglycemia. The speech becomes dysarthric. Aphasia and apraxia may be noticed. The motor phenomena during the second hour consist of automatic movements, forced grasping, myoclonic twitchings, and various dystonic manifestations. . . . The deepest coma is reached when the patient no longer responds to painful stimuli with a needle or to supraorbital pressure. At this stage, spasms similar to those of decerebrate rigidity may occur, the pupils do not react to light, and the deepest or so-called midbrain stage is characterized by a change of the pupils from dilation to miosis, absence of the corneal reflex, and disappearance of tendon reflexes. . . .")

Paula received ninety insulin coma treatments.

Before dawn each morning, a nurse would administer an injection of insulin into her and her roommate, after which, she writes, "the two of us would amble down the hall to the coma room, get back into bed, and fall asleep. When we awoke from our 'comas,' [the nurse] would give us orange juice to raise our blood sugar level and then we would go back to the dayroom where lunch was being served. . . .

"We were told to eat regularly to prevent an unscheduled coma from happening, and to let someone know if we felt weak. During one patient floor meeting, I began to tremble and feel detached from what was going on. One of the nurses noticed and brought me a glass of orange juice mixed with Karo syrup. I was already losing consciousness and couldn't drink it. Later I was told that I had fought against the nurses as they tried to stabilize me — that I was yelling and thrashing about. It only occurs to me now that my anger was likely justified."

Paula writes that the treatments made her feel tired, nauseated, and "truly insane," and that she never understood how they were helping her. Fortunately, she says, someone on her ward told her that since she was over eighteen, she was legally of age to refuse treatment, and, after several sessions with her doctor in which she protested the treatments, they were stopped.

"Looking back," Paula writes, "I think this was one of the first steps I took in regaining my sanity. Before this, I never believed I could effect change or that someone would listen and take me seriously. Being a mental patient is not, after all, empowering."

In later years, when Paula was again overcome by depression, she still felt so traumatized by her earlier experience that she chose not to go to medical doctors or psychiatrists, fearing they would treat her with drugs and hospitalization. Despite recurrent bouts of depression throughout her life, however, and several manic sprees, after her first three hospitalizations she has never again had episodes troubling enough to warrant hospitalization.

What made the difference? she asks. "Three things," she answers, and enumerates: "Family, work, and therapy."

Paula talks about how being married and having children — having a home and a job and everything that came with family life, neighbors, and a work situation — made her feel that she "was normal somehow — like everybody else."

And psychotherapy, which she has worked at for varying lengths of time during the past two decades, was crucial, she says. Now fifty years old, Paula is once again seeing a therapist; this time she is working several times a week in a more analytic therapy than those that helped her in the past. Paula believes it is the psychotherapy itself — the slow and steady working through of her problems, history, fears, and feelings — that has enabled her to avoid hospitalizations, to have survived in our world, beyond madness and outside hospitals, and to have gained the life and the strengths that are now hers.

"There are still things that come up — all the old fears, and some buried stuff, and real depression — and I know it's a luxury I vote for myself, to be able to talk with somebody whose only interest is in helping me — but why not some selfishness?" she asks. "It enables me to keep going, and to do for others, but most of all, because of the therapy, I feel that I have so much more *knowledge* — more real understanding of what happened and why, and it's this knowledge that has become my safeguard, and that lets me believe that what happened once won't happen again."

"I thought the city was under attack and only I could save it," Lynne Douglas writes, concerning her third major breakdown, which occurred when she was twenty-three years old, and a student in her second year of medical school. "Even normal traffic sounds or hospital sounds were construed by me to be sounds of an invasion. Two friends I worked with took me to the Emergency Room. They went along with me in my story so as not to alarm me, I guess, because it was all still making perfect sense to me. I babbled to anyone who would listen—the intake doctor, a med student, nurses, anyone. I didn't sleep for more than forty-eight hours and they finally had to sedate me. I just kept talking to people. I sat up all night with the night aide, the two of us smoking cigarettes together. It seemed so *real*.

"My room made sense—I was, of course, a soldier, and had to be mobilized. Of course they would segregate the men from the women—we were in training. It wasn't scary. I kept rationalizing everything to fit my story. When the drugs kicked in, I caught up on my sleep. The story went away, and I was bewildered, but then reality set in. Whose reality? Mine. I had messed up."

After three weeks in the hospital, and "chomping at the bit to get out," Lynne left, still not understanding why things had gone wrong again.

"I had been in therapy," she writes, "I had taken my antidepressants, no drugs, some alcohol, but not excessive, and I had felt good. Too good, I guess."

Since it was Christmas, she decided to go home to visit her mother.

"Big mistake," she writes. "I really needed to get back into my own routine and not someone else's. I became real agitated again, despite or because of the meds, saw yet another psychiatrist, tried some other drugs, and wound up becoming catatonic.

"I couldn't move. Not to eat, move off the bed, or bathe. My mother had to do all those things for me. God knows where *I* was. I remember feeling like a big log. And not able to emote, or think, or anything. I thought this was how it was to die. My world had shrunk to one room and one part of one bed. My hope for the future had gone, I couldn't visualize anything beyond the room — heck, I couldn't even move my arms.

"After another week of more drug changes, I became psychotic again, thinking voices were talking to me. I started on lithium, thank goodness, but had to be hospitalized because I was so active my mother couldn't manage me."

To her relief, the lithium "worked," and after her fourth hospitalization, she writes, "I knew I was back to 'normal' because I'd get good and mad. At myself, usually. Not in a self-deprecating way, but in a useful way. Like, 'OK, Lynne, get your butt in gear, you're burning daylight. Lost days, things to tend to.'

"Those hospitalizations did serve as deterrents in the coming years," Lynne believes, but these years proved difficult in the extreme. Much as she welcomed the lithium, "I was kind of pissed," she writes, "that this medication, which turned me around so fast, hadn't been used before.

"And I was awfully dulled by it too," she adds. "For the next four years I felt blurry, and unexcitable, but afraid enough of another hospitalization that I took the medicine that kept me out. It was the loss. The loss of independence, of personality, of sense of self.

"Why do any of us wake up each day and do the things we do?" Lynne now asks. "And when you physically or mentally can't do those things which you do *to be you*, what happens to you?"

Lynne avoided her family, took her medications, and, not long after her fourth hospitalization, she began taking courses again. Keeping distant from her family seemed as essential as it was difficult. Starting with her first hospitalization "and in subsequent admissions," she writes, "my father would visit me every day—every single day he would travel over sixty miles, after work." She regards his devotion and constancy as having been central to her recovery. Her breakdowns were hard on her mother too, she adds, since only "a few weeks before she had been using a spoon to feed me. I was so far gone—so paralyzed and catatonic—that I would obsess about whether to wash my face or turn the pillow over."

Lynne began to put her life back together, she now believes, by hard work and by building on a series of "small successes."

She also, at this time, she writes, "opened my life and heart to a guy I would be hooked up with for the next three years. Real different, previous druggie, had lived with a transvestite before, real earthy, gentle, and fun-loving. My folks flipped when they found out we were living together, not even knowing any of his background, but when they met Donald and saw what I saw, they were OK. I wasn't seeing him to spite them or because of them. It was for me.

"And again," Lynne says, repeating a sentence that occurs frequently in her letters, "what could be worse than being mentally ill?"

During the free hours of her remaining years in medical school, Lynne worked nights as an extern, doing admissions and assisting in obstetrics, and she also took out more school loans. "It was so important to me not to be beholden financially to anyone, so I could make my own decisions. Money is power when used that way. I made some good decisions and some bad ones. But they were *mine*."

She is not sure what enabled her to survive her last two years of medical school. "I must have a lot of endurance," she writes. "I just kept on. I'm one of those who curses things while they are going on, but they do go on. I chop onions with a knife. It hurts my eyes, stings my eyes, but I finish chopping."

"I also," she notes, "spent a lot of time by myself to learn how to be comfortable with being myself."

When Lynne graduated from medical school, she matched her internship to a hospital near her mother, and they lived together in what was, she says, "a truly great year."

"I had broken off things earlier with Donald—he'd gone to Florida to work with his family for a while, and so I dated around. I really thought we'd always have a friendship. It was grand to know we'd had a good relationship. A small success."

Like Paula—and like Gaston, Moe, and others, including Robert—Lynne's early years were filled with worldly ambitions and successes, but without outward signs or warnings that were predictive of the troubles to come—or, when the troubles did come, of outward signs predictive of the recovery that would come after the troubles. "I'm not so sure I can accurately recount the episodes of craziness I encountered in my life in the last thirteen to sixteen years," she writes.

Even now, when she is the director of radiation oncology at the Washington State University Health Sciences Center, the married mother of two daughters, ages four and six—and notwithstanding her desire to set down her story, and her ability to do so at great length and in vivid detail—she remains somewhat tormented by her past, and sometimes fearful for her future.

"The people in my family who helped me pick up the pieces time and again would probably have the facts more precisely," she says. "I try not to think about the particulars too often or in great detail because I start getting those creepy feelings and begin to worry that I'm headed that way again."

Lynne was born the fifth of seven children—four boys and three girls—in Ratner, Kentucky. Her father was a career

U.S. Army man, and Lynne's early years were like those of other typical Army brats, she says.

"Growing up, we moved to a new community—sometimes Army, sometimes civilian, every one to three years," she writes. "It was a game my mother would play—clean out the closets, give stuff away, start anew. Us kids were so used to taking on new personas, we adapted every time, even trying new sports and band instruments, and we rarely fit or needed to fit into any cliques (groups of friends) already in existence at the schools."

When she was an undergraduate, her parents divorced, and the years that began with the news of the divorce, she writes, "were the most tumultuous and changed me with the most velocity I'll ever know.

"I felt lost. My whole foundation crumbled. I've had major losses since then—a second-trimester miscarriage, loss of my freedom and sanity in lockup wards, and loss of my stepson in an automobile accident at age sixteen—but this felt like *falling*. Nothing to hold on to, nothing and no one to catch you—you can't *ever* end it—and it's just like this bad dream that goes on and on forever."

Despite, or because of, the divorce and its effect on her, Lynne worked harder than ever, and graduated from college with a 3.9 average, receiving only two grades below A in her four years as an undergraduate. (In high school she had had a perfect 4.0 average.) Then, during her first year in medical school, her anxiety attacks began.

"I'd get prickly on my arms and breathe fast and I couldn't get my mind to slow down," she says, and she recalls that in high school she had had similar anxieties, along with hormonal imbalances that led to rashes and to the loss of large amounts of hair.

Now, in medical school, she started seeing a psychologist. She spent Christmas at home—"in tears"—and, witnessing with horror the ways in which her family, in the aftershock of divorce, was "all split," she became persistently and inconsolably sad.

When she returned to medical school after Christmas, she developed neurogenic dermatitis—rashes and huge welts on her skin—and an ongoing, disturbing siege of insomnia. She also began drinking heavily. She continued to work with her psychologist, and she recalls him suggesting to her that what she needed were "some small successes."

Shortly before her twenty-third birthday, however, she "went from being somewhat stressed to being led away in handcuffs to a mental health center and subsequently to an inpatient mental health wing in a downtown hospital."

More episodes, breakdowns, and hospitalizations followed. She often felt lost and frightened, and would stop sleeping and eating for days at a time. "It was all so unreal—like I was living in a screenplay, or worse, in a sci-fi movie," she writes.

She recalls leaving her adviser's office one day, having reassured him that she was all right—"I became pretty good at putting on a good face"—and then not remembering how to get back to her apartment.

"I was more mad than frightened," she says. "I could not remember what direction to go in. Everything familiar was just not there. Like being in a foreign city, with no map and no idea how to speak the language well enough to ask the way back. This began what I later found out was one of my psychotic episodes. I envisioned that every car that passed me had someone covertly in the know, who knew what I needed to know. How to get home. I started flagging down cars. Then I started running. And flagging down cars. No one stopped. (Thank God. A crazy person, no ID, babbling about being ready—I'd of ended up in jail or at the state hospital on Thorazine for sure. Maybe.) Years went by, it felt like anyway, before I made it home that day."

Lynne tried several apartments that looked like hers, or might have looked like hers, but they were all locked. When she finally got to her apartment, she tried to calm down by running a bath, but her skin began to crawl, and because she had put plastic over her windows during the winter, she became very hot.

"I decided RIGHT THEN I had to take the plastic down. While the bath was running, I started on that. Forgot about the bath, remembered, it ran over, then didn't want to do anymore and thought I would take a nap. No go. It was like a circus, all the clowns running around. Except, I was all of them."

When her roommates came home, they managed to get her to the mental health center, where she was "handcuffed by the police again, and taken to the hospital."

After this episode, feeling painfully embarrassed and ashamed, Lynne withdrew from medical school.

"I've looked back and tried to figure out what and why and how things happened," she now writes. "I've decided that I couldn't handle the change in structure and routine which I had come to rely on in the years prior to my first episode. Gosh, I felt like my world had crashed down, and I guess by all standards it had. I figure, too, that I had to 'break' in order to establish my own identity.

"Partly because I was raised a good Catholic, I guess, I'm usually charitable and forgiving when I think on this. Charitable to myself, and being the Pollyanna type, I think that there's good in everything that happens—even being diagnosed with mental illness. It's taken years for me to feel good enough about myself to forgive myself and move on. I was pretty afraid to take risks again. For a long while. Then and sometimes since then, I will have a revolution going on inside me—parts wanting to get out, parts wanting to get together, get apart, and get in. It would take years before I would get peace and feel settled."

When in mid-July 1998, Lynne comes east for a family reunion, we meet and have breakfast at a Sheraton hotel in Springfield, Massachusetts, the city where her husband was born and grew up. Lynne's mother, who has a master's degree and a doctorate in nursing, joins us.

Like her letters, Lynne is animated, forthcoming, and uncommonly candid. She has shoulder-length, straw-blond hair pulled back behind her ears; she wears black slacks, a sleeveless blouse, and a Western-style silver-embroidered vest over the blouse. She does not lack for energy, intelligence, intensity, or warmth, and while we talk I feel a bit as if a character from one of my novels has suddenly materialized and is sitting across from me.

Lynne has been corresponding with me for a year, and we have talked by phone occasionally. She has sent me several dozen single-spaced typed pages in which she has set down the story of her childhood, breakdowns, recovery, and family life. Now she introduces me to her husband, their two daughters, and her stepson—they arrive when we are about halfway through breakfast, and they sit at the table next to ours.

"Family got me through too," Lynne offers, and when she tells me about how she *always* knew that her parents "would be there" for her, she says these things as if she is stating salient clinical facts.

"I always knew I was loved," Lynne says, "and that was important. I was always taught that I was *a good person*, no matter what troubles I had."

We talk about what life might be like for individuals who have had breakdowns and hospitalizations similar to Lynne's, but had not received from their families what she received from hers in her early years and in the years since, and we agree that the life-giving value of this—of unconditional love and support in a life of whatever degree of difficulty—cannot be overestimated.

"But the hard times still come, you know," Lynne says. "They never go away fully."

One of Lynne's daughters comes to our table, snuggles against her mother, asks when they are going to go swimming. Lynne is easy and affectionate with her daughter, tells her we are having a talk, that they will go swimming in a little while, but that she and her sister can go with their father and get changed and started if they want.

"I probably should have been on meds some of the time,"

she says. "I haven't been on any meds for, what is it now? more than a dozen years—but two summers ago I was really stressed out and fearful. I thought the old stuff was coming back, and that I might have to—I don't know—maybe cut down on my work, or stop dong the clinical part entirely. It was really bad. So I went to a psychiatrist and checked myself out, and he said he thought the kind of anxiety I was having—and the rest—was 'situational.' I saw a psychologist for a while and that helped. Therapy always helps. I've been in therapy a lot through the years, and it's been crucial to getting me through."

Lynne laughs, and talks about how, when her depressions hit, she starts to feel as if she is bad at everything—"I'm a bad doctor, a bad mother, a bad lover, a bad daughter—it's awful the way I feel—and I'm always under a lot of pressure at work, and then there are the children, and my husband, and the house—and all the ordinary stuff of life. . . ."

Lynne leans back, smiles. "The ordinary stuff of life," she says again. And then: "I remember thinking that if I was ever unable to continue with my clinical duties—with seeing patients, and handling that, along with the administrative stuff—that I might become a writer. A medical writer. I've always liked to write, and there's a huge need for good medical writers."

Lynne talks about her work with cancer patients—how difficult and heartbreaking it often is—and she speculates on why it is that, with the same presenting symptoms and conditions, some patients have a swift and terrible last few months of life, while others go on for years, in remission.

She makes a parallel between those afflicted with cancer and those afflicted with mental illness—about how little we truly know about what causes these illnesses, and about how little we know about what, for those of us who recover and survive, makes the difference.

She says she is doing a lot of research on survival—on people who survive their cancers—and I smile and talk about the time, when I was nineteen, that I had cancer. Lynne recalls, from having read *Imagining Robert,* that I had Hodgkins' disease — that I was operated on and received cobalt radiation treatments. In the forty-one years since, I have never had a recurrence.

Lynne's mother informs me that she and Lynne are participating in a Johns Hopkins Medical School research project concerning mental illness and possible genetic linkages between mothers and daughters. They have been interviewed, have provided family histories, and have given blood. They believe that Kay Jamison or her husband, Richard Jed Wyatt, is involved in the research project. We talk about Kay Jamison's book, *An Unquiet Mind,* for a while, about its depictions of manic sprees. Lynne's mother shakes her head, and returns to our conversation about Lynne's breakdowns, to the times Lynne was catatonic, and how frightened she was that Lynne might never come out of it.

Lynne asks if her mother recalls the name of the drug she was on then, because in her memory the medication for the catatonia was worse than being catatonic. She was terrified, and thought she would never come out alive. She says she needs to remember to send for her medical records from those times.

"But what saved me one time," Lynne says, "was this nurse who said to me, 'You know — if you don't pull out of this, you're going to wind up in the state hospital down the road, and you might stay there for the rest of your life.' " Lynne rolls her eyes. "That scared me — and it got me angry too: I said to myself, 'OK, Lynne — you've got to do whatever you have to to get the hell out of here.' "

I tell Lynne and her mother about Shery Mead, and about others I've been talking with — and about myself, and my history of rages, and of how the therapy helped me work them through. I say that it seems to me the will to get well is frequently accompanied by anger — by ordinary, literal madness — and how it is my sense that often the difference between those who do and don't recover has to do with the ability, at key junctures of life, to make your rage work *for* you instead of *against* you. But how and why and when this happens, we agree, remain a mystery—a vague theory without practical application or issue.

Lynne and her mother talk about several of Lynne's siblings who have had histories of severe mental illness—about a brother and a sister who still become very angry periodically, and of how the anger only seems to produce more troubles, and how it is the anger itself, in fact, that seems at times to *be* the trouble, and to be limitless.

"Writing to you—setting it all down—that's been a help," Lynne says to me shortly before I leave. "It was very cathartic for me to go back, and to work at putting things together. I'd never really done it before." She pauses. "It never leaves, you know. The condition is always there, just under the surface, and sometimes not so far *below* the surface, and it comes bubbling up, but you learn to live with it—I mean, what's the choice?—and to manage it, and not to be so terrified of it. I've been very blessed, very lucky."

We agree that much of what happens, for good and for ill, seems a mystery—that medications help, that families help, that friends help, that therapy helps, that knowledgeable, dedicated doctors help, and that timing helps. Lynne's mother talks enthusiastically about a psychiatrist she works with, and how, even though she was educated on and believes in a physiological biomedical model, in her opinion it is *compassion* and not medications that seems to play the major role in their successes—in how the elderly citizens she and the psychiatrist work with respond.

Lynne agrees that the doctors who just prescribe pills and don't pay attention to their patients are not doing their jobs, but she also says that she thinks for her and for others, it's also *luck*—simple, mysterious, unpredictable luck—that often makes the difference.

"I got lucky," she says. "I got real lucky. We shouldn't ever underestimate luck."

Lynne and her two daughters walk me downstairs to the hotel's lobby, and Lynne tells me she is excited because she's going to be able to get in some kickboxing at the hotel—that this shows just how lucky she can get sometimes.

"You're into *kickboxing?*" I ask.

"Oh yes," she answers. "And I love it. You get hurt sometimes—I have some bruises—but I love it."

She shrugs, as if to say, "Who can tell how our lives turn out, how we become the people we become? but here I am!"—and then she and her daughters say good-bye to me, and I head north, for home, feeling both very exhilarated and very humbled by the hour and a half we have spent together.

Where oh where, I wonder, in people like Lynne does such extraordinary strength—this amazing human quality we call resilience—come from, and how is it that, despite all she has been through, and despite the fears and doubts she still lives with, she is able to move on, hour by hour and day by day and year by year, with such energy and such determination, and with such love and such hope: raising her children, attending to her family and to her friends, working with her patients and helping them through their painful last journeys, or through difficult times that, as in her own life, open into years that are also filled with all those other ordinary and extraordinary events, feelings, and moments that she refers to, always with a half-smile, as the ordinary stuff of life?

Like Lynne Douglas, Kate Fontaine attributes a large measure of her recovery from mental illness to having found the right medications at the right time.

"For years, I'd been in and out of places, in and out of trouble, and one day I just, you know, I just had enough of it," she says. "I didn't know what to do and I didn't even go up to the DMH because I'd been *drinking.* It was the first time, in fact, that I went up there when I *hadn't* been drinking. I said to myself I'm not gonna do that.

"It was around Christmastime, and I was waiting there about six hours and I thought of leaving. But I says to myself,

'What the hell am I going back out to?' I would've been going back out to the same old stuff, and I just, you know, I felt that this was the last time for me. This doctor had gone on vacation when I first went into the hospital for three weeks, and I'd OD'd while she was gone, and when she got back she wasn't even surprised. Not even shocked.

"So she took me off my meds and really started working with me. And that's when every day she'd come in in the morning, first thing, and talk with me. She walked with me and she talked with me every single morning. And she was always one step ahead. Plus, she told me about the medications, and it sounded like it would take care of *everything* that was bothering me. That's how she described it for me. It was like the anxiety, the depression, the binges—whatever—the self-consciousness—all of it—it would *all* be taken away. That's what she told me.

"And it took three weeks for the medication to start working but once it did—oh my God, it was *incredible*! When I think of the most incredible experience I've had in my life, that was it. Oh yeah. And then I stayed away from my family for a while too. I stayed away for a year, and—I mean, things got crazy there also. It wasn't all good stuff. I mean, things got *really* crazy, but it's like I had to change how I acted with my mother, and how we got on together—it changed because I no longer—"

Kate laughs, shrugs. "It was weird. It's hard to explain," she says. "But things had changed—were just *different,* you know?—with my mother and father and stuff."

Kate and I are sitting in a second-floor office at Genesis, a clubhouse in Worcester, Massachusetts, where ten years before, when it first opened, Kate was one of the original members. Kate is trim and athletic-looking, with long brown hair and a spontaneous, animated way of talking that reminds me of the direct manner of some of the girls I grew up with in Brooklyn: tough and savvy and seemingly uninhibited, as if to say: "Hey—I been through hell, and I got nothing to hide, and I'm gonna tell you all about it, okay?"

She is so forthcoming that I am surprised to hear her say that when she first came to Genesis, she would walk around with her eyes on the ground *all* the time.

"I can't believe I'm actually doing this now—sitting down and talking to you," she says, about halfway through our conversation, "because when I first started here I couldn't look at people and stuff. I was like that. Oh yeah. I could never look at anyone. I kept my bangs a lot longer than they are, to cover my eyes, and my head was always down, and I kept headphones on all the time. But my doctor helped with that too—with learning to talk with people, and not to feel so ashamed, like I had to hide myself all the time."

Kate tells me about her job at Memorial Hospital, where she has worked for the past six years. At Memorial Hospital, she is a production assistant in food service, working with computerized menus and recipes, and having responsibility for special supplements and desserts, and she talks about how happy she is because she is "just so busy" all day long.

She earns $8.57 an hour now, and is due, within the month, for a 4 percent raise. Her short-term goal is to be earning $10 an hour. Kate has been off Social Security disability income for more than two years, and she says that coming off it was *very* hard for her, and that she still owes Social Security about $5,000 due to past hospitalizations, but that she is paying them back $50 a month.

"I don't mind that," she says. "It was hard. But I made up my mind to do it."

She sees a psychotherapist intermittently—when she has hard times, or feels a need to talk—and a psychiatrist about once every three months, to review her medications. She complains because her health insurance only covers her for a half-hour appointment once a month.

"I still have a hard time on slow days, see," she says, "and with the other jobs, even though they were good jobs, like at the Worcester Art Museum, but when it was slow I didn't know what to do with myself. I'd try sweeping the floor, or anything, just to keep busy. And everybody would tell me to bring a book and read and stuff, but it was the same when I was in charge of credit at Atlantic Food, and I didn't have enough to do."

Kate talks about her childhood, and about how, looking back, she can see that her emotional problems started when she was very young.

"Oh it had been going on for a very long time," she says. "I don't know if this counts or not, but when I was about three I thought I was Batman and I jumped out a third-floor window, and I was just always in trouble from the beginning. I could never control my impulses and stuff. By the time I was fifteen, I quit school, and even when I was younger than that I was into different things. I went out with my friends, I drank, I smoked, I did a whole bunch of stuff. Then, by the time I was eighteen, it got really bad and my father, who I was living with — he and my mom had been divorced a long time — my father said, 'That's it — I've had it. She's outta here.' So he called his lawyer, and his lawyer got on the phone with me, I remember, and he told me I either had to go to Worcester State voluntarily or get committed.

"But I was in hospitals before that, like for alcohol and drugs and stuff from when I was fifteen. And after a while it just got bad, you know? I just had a lot of problems and by the time I was eighteen I was in my first program, and, you know, ever since then.

"When I was in Worcester State the stay was usually about six months. My last time was six months — that's eight-nine years ago — and whenever I went in, even if I was going to counseling and taking my meds, I just wouldn't be able to take it anymore. I would get just so sick of everything. And I had agoraphobia, and panic attacks, and depression. Really bad. It's kind of hard to explain."

Kate talks about the difference that the Genesis Clubhouse, and its director, Kevin Bradley, have made in her life.

"You've got other programs around — I been in some of them — but they're not like this place. I mean, the people and the place — what they offer here — it's not just how you're treated, but with the philosophy of it all. Like I can never explain it and I'd say to Kevin, because I picked him as my adviser and stuff a long time ago, but like they talk to you like they talk to the other staff, if you know what I'm saying.

"In the other programs it's like you're not a *member* — they don't even call you members, they call you 'clients' and stuff. But you can feel it, the difference — how they kind of look down on you. But here you just come in and they say, 'Hi Kate,' if it's Margaret or Kevin or any of the staff, and 'Hi — how're you doing today?' Like you're a human being like anyone else, and like I used to be here a lot, you know, when I first started working. They got me my first TE jobs — I only had three TE jobs before I got to work full time. Then after a while, because of my hours and stuff, I couldn't spend as much time here, and now I just drop in to say 'Hi' because I don't need the place anymore."

We talk about Genesis, and about how Kevin and others helped her to get jobs and keep jobs. The TE — Transitional Employment — jobs that clubhouse members obtain through the Genesis employment office are varied: jobs in fast food, radiology, sales, telemarketing, custodial services, libraries, etc. There are more than 350 clubhouses worldwide, over 250 of them in the United States, and 25 new ones are being established each year, and like the other clubhouses, Genesis works and succeeds at creating sustained relationships with employers. (Fountain House, in New York City, has maintained partnerships with some employers — TV stations, Wall Street firms, advertising firms — for more than twenty years.) Genesis guarantees to the employers the number of hours per week a member will work at a TE position (two members will usually split a forty-hour week between them) and will contract for a specified length of time, usually six months.

Genesis has its staff learn all aspects of the jobs, and then has its staff train members for the jobs before they begin work. Genesis assists members through the personnel and interview process (having to explain a major hiatus in job history, or having no work history at all, can be terrifying for members), and, when necessary, it works with its members directly on their job sites. It also makes a key commitment to the employer: If a clubhouse member cannot show up for work, whether for a day or a week or a month, Genesis will send another trained person to work in the employee's place. In most instances, the replacement worker will be a staff member.

Kate was paid the prevailing wage at the jobs she held, and also like many clubhouse members she moved up the "ladder of success," graduating from Transitional Employment, to Supported Employment, to Independent Employment. Genesis emphasizes member choice: Members choose jobs, from those available, that they think will be meaningful to *them*.

Genesis has also begun moving beyond these traditional forms of assisted employment to what it calls "Career Employment," where members will have fully independent careers in the workplace that are no different from the careers of men and women who have never had psychiatric disabilities.

In 1998, 190 Genesis members were gainfully employed, earning a total of nearly $700,000: 63 through Transitional Employment, 46 through Group Placement, 34 through Supported Employment, and 47 in Independent and Career Employment. Genesis also provides a wide range of other services: it provides educational services and supports as well as housing services and supports; it has an outreach team that works at staying in touch with members who cannot, for reasons of physical or mental health, come to Genesis; it operates a full-time "Warm Line"; it has an active social unit that, like a peer support center, offers a variety of leisure activities; and it also serves as an international training center for clubhouse staff from around the world.

While Kate and I talk, I find myself thinking of Jeff Geller—an original Genesis board member who was instrumental in setting up the Genesis Clubhouse—and of his pride in what the clubhouse has accomplished in less than a decade. Genesis is housed in downtown Worcester, in a gorgeously restored three-story Victorian house that was formerly a funeral home; it has recently purchased the house next door, to be used for recreational and educational services, and to provide guest facilities for international visitors; and it also owns a separate guesthouse, a few blocks away, that it uses for visitors.

Beginning with a dozen individuals who felt there were no resources in the Worcester area capable of helping family members return to the community—to work, school, independent living, friendships, and family life—Genesis has grown and has become an organization of more than four hundred members, with an average daily attendance of seventy-four. When Genesis started a decade ago, Kevin Bradley tells me, there were only two or three clubhouses in all of Massachusetts; now there are twenty-six—yet another indication, he suggests, of how much progress has been made in programs for people with mental illness. In that decade, Kevin proudly says, showing me newsletters, data printouts, and framed photos that chronicle the lives of Genesis members, Genesis has helped several hundred individuals like Kate regain lost and broken lives.

Meeting with Kate and with others in my visits to Worcester—as I have done in visits to clubhouses in Boston, Northampton, New York, London, and elsewhere—I also find myself thinking of Jeff Geller's theory of discordancy. Perhaps Kate is doing so well in the world, as Jeff hypothesizes, because she started out with fewer worldly ambitions and expectations—from her family, or from her peers, or from herself—than individuals like my brother Robert did. Thus, when she broke and fell, and when she recovered, the distances covered, in both directions, though often harrowing, were not as great or as difficult as the distances traveled by people like Robert.

Well into his fifties, for example, Robert, both when he is in hospitals and when he is out, still tortures himself with the fact that he never finished college, and still wonders, as he did while at Park Manor, if he can get back the scholarship he won thirty years before. He still talks — fantasizes? — about becoming a film director or a museum curator, and about owning a combination bookstore and tobacco shop. Until Alzheimer's disease did away with our mother's memory a few years ago, when she was in her early eighties, she continued to reinforce Robert's frustrations by asking him when he thought he would be going back to college, or when he thought he might be getting a job, and getting married, and raising a family.

Although individuals like Shery Mead, Lynne Douglas, Gaston Cloutier, and Moe Armstrong have recovered and gone on to lives of exceptional worldly achievement, and although we sometimes hear and read about famous people who have overcome their emotional disabilities — entertainers and writers like Patty Duke, William Styron, Joanne Greenberg, and Mike Wallace — the majority of people who suffer from mental illness, and most of the millions of people who recover from it (like the several hundred graduates of Genesis) are like Kate Fontaine: men and women who are out here in the workaday world at workaday jobs — neighbors, coworkers, and colleagues who most of the time are neither eager to talk or write about their past histories, nor particularly practiced at doing so.

"I don't take my meds during the day," Kate tells me, "because I don't want them interfering with my job, and that's fine with my doctor. I don't let anybody at work know about me. See, that's the thing. When I first went into my job at Memorial, people knew I came from some program, and in the beginning they would say, 'Aren't you from that place?' And they couldn't even pronounce the name right. And then after a while, I just came into my job and now nobody says a thing. Now it's 'How ya doin'? You working double shift today?' Now it's just like I'm like everybody and that's why I don't wanna mess it up. If something came up where I had to take time off, I mean . . ."

Kate breaks off, looks away from me for the first time.

"You see—that's what prevents me from a lot," she says. "I don't want people up there knowing anything. I'm usually quiet at work. I don't say too much and they leave me alone. But I wouldn't want a lot of people knowing my business. I mean, even my family—if I'm having a financial problem, my father wants to know right away. That's something he can help me with. But if I'm having a hard time emotionally, or whatever—if something comes up the way it does—I don't even . . ."

Kate's voice trails off again. I ask if she has much free time—much of a social life.

"That's what I mean," she says. "That's one problem where I just—I don't know. It used to be really bad, but now I just go to Bingo and to different places. Otherwise I stay home. That's okay with me. I don't go into bars. I don't go to—you know—whatever. And a lot of times, that's a burden too—just laying on the couch, watching TV.

"But—oh yeah—I call one of the girls at work just to talk and say 'Hi' sometimes. But I don't get together with anybody much. We did once a while ago—we went out to one of the clubs, and that was OK."

Suddenly Kate becomes more cheerful. "And I have a dog!" she exclaims. "A little poodle. Her name is Brandy and she's my baby—I got her from one of the girls at work—and she's three, and she's just *adorable*! I've got pictures of her—"

Kate shows me pictures, and talks about the times she spends with her family, and how she spends weekends, often with one of her sisters and her sister's children, and of how she and her sister have great times together at the Foxwoods gambling casino. I tell her about the times Robert and I went to the casinos in Atlantic City together and about how Robert loves to play the slot machines, and Kate says that she and her sister have been to Atlantic City too.

Kate has served as a faculty member of Clubhouse's International Center, and has flown around the country—to Virginia, Washington, Wisconsin, and elsewhere—to give talks, including keynote addresses, and to help in the accreditation of other clubhouses. She has enjoyed this work immensely, and believes it makes a real difference in people's lives.

It would make a difference too, she offers, if people like her could go into state hospitals and talk to the people there.

"I always stick with a goal in mind," she says, "and I had this idea that if we could set up like meetings and stuff there, and try to get through to some people, and say, 'Hey—I been where you are, and worse'—and show that we've already moved on, that might help. Even if you only get to one person. I volunteered to do it, and got started, but the red tape and everything with the state got to be too much."

She talks again about the difference the doctor who walked and talked with her made in her life.

"What I'd *really* like is to be able to talk to her sometime, even if it's just by phone," she says. "I mean, she was a resident, I guess, and she moved away somewhere—Boston, I think—but what I'd really like is for her to know how well I'm doing now. I'd like that a lot."

I tell Kate that if she gives me the name of the doctor I will try to locate her.

When I return home that night, I call several people, get a phone number for Kate's doctor, and telephone Kate with the information.

"Oh my God!" she exclaims. "Oh my God, and thank you, but—I mean, you don't know how happy I am—how important it is for me to let her know."

Afterward, it occurs to me that the key moment in Kate's story is nothing if not paradigmatic. What was it that helped Kate get through—and what was the key element, or elements, that informed those moments when her life, instead of deteriorating and becoming chronic, started to shift in the directions it did, toward the life she has now?

Was it the *medications*? Or was it the *relationship* with this doctor who decided to talk with her and to walk with her "every single day"?

Or was it some combination of the two—some great good luck that simultaneously brought an effective medication and an effective relationship into her life at a particularly fortuitous time? If the doctor had not, for a sustained period of time, talked and walked with Kate, and had not enlisted her trust, and had not told her the ways the medications were going to work so that Kate believed her, would the medications have worked as well? And, if the doctor had prescribed different medications, would *they* have worked as well?

And: Will we ever know?

And isn't the "placebo effect," I speculate—where sugar pills are as effective for some individuals as medications—proof itself that the brain has a mind of its own, and that it often changes, and changes itself, its mappings, its structures, its ways of functioning, its chemical and electrical processes, and acts upon us and in us—our consciousness, thus, forever *evolving*—in ways that make the relation of mind to body ever more complex, more mysterious, and more wondrous?

I think of Kate, and of others I've been meeting, and of the personal narratives of recovery I've been reading, and I hear Kate's voice again—bright and ebullient—and I try to imagine what she might be feeling at the prospect of talking with a doctor who, by doing her job, seems to have made all the difference in Kate's life—and when I do, I find myself recalling another old saying: *The rabbis tells us,* I remember being taught, *that a person who does not believe in miracles is not a realist.*

NINE

APPROACHES TO THE MIND

*Sorrow comes in great waves—no one can know that bet-
ter than you—but it rolls over us, and though it may almost smother us it leaves us on the spot and we know that
if it is strong we are stronger, inasmuch as it passes and
we remain. It wears us, but we wear it and use it in
return; and it is blind, whereas we after a manner see.*

—HENRY JAMES
in a letter to Grace Norton
at the time of his
fortieth birthday, 1883

Between 1896 and 1899, Emil Kraepelin, a German psychiatrist, formulated the first systematic classification (nosology)
of what we now call mental illnesses, and his work became
the basis for virtually all subsequent diagnostic systems, including the Diagnostic and Statistical Manuals of the American Psychiatric Association *(DSM-I, -II, -III, -IIIR, and -IV)*.
His separation of different forms of madness, based upon
voluminously researched and described cases, into two major
categories—what he called *dementia praecox* and "psychotic

manic depression" — is largely responsible for everything we have come to know as descriptive clinical psychiatry. (*Dementia praecox* means, literally, "being prematurely out of one's mind" — i.e., being insane in a way that is progressive, extreme, and irreversible, and that leads inevitably to deterioration and chronicity. And manic depression, as Kraepelin defined it, included *all* forms of serious and recurrent affective illness, including clinical depression.)

Like other clinicians of his time, Kraepelin subscribed to the then-new scientific system for classification of diseases, a system predicated on an unfolding sequence, linear in character, of cause, onset, course, and outcome. This way of understanding illness reflected the belief that disorders were natural and organic in cause, and had histories (courses) that were inflexible and predictable. Mental deterioration, Kraepelin argued, was not, as was previously hypothesized, the occasional outcome of depression, mania, or hypochondriasis — or, most important, the result of *external* causes — but was present in an individual from the start as an inborn, distinct clinical entity.

Until Kraepelin put forth his views, the overwhelming tradition of psychiatric diagnosis was based upon what were termed "symptoms of first prominence," whether understanding of these symptoms was arrived at clinically, or from psychological or neurological presuppositions. Kraepelin's new classification — his bold new hypothesis — was predicated instead on *etiology* — upon knowledge of *cause* — and his assumption that physical processes alone underlay the outward signs and symptoms of madness has been with us ever since.

Thus, the concept of disease that, in the late nineteenth century, had become the basis of Western medicine generally — to place any bodily or mental disturbance in a single, linear sequence made up of incidence and distribution, anatomy, pathogenesis, etiology, symptoms and signs, differential diagnosis, course and outcome, prognosis, treatment, and prevention — now also became the principal basis for psychiatry.

Kraepelin combined case after case of *dementia praecox* —
what we today call schizophrenia, or what Eugen Bleuler, a
dozen years after Kraepelin published his initial findings,
called "the schizophrenias" (a pluralism often forgotten) —
into a singular disease entity because of its relentless, downward, deteriorating course, and uniformly poor outcome. (It
was Bleuler who in 1911, first introduced the term "schizophrenia," from the Greek for "split mind," as a replacement
for *dementia praecox*, though by "split mind" he meant dissociation between thoughts and affects and not, as is popu-
larly believed, between separate selves or identities coexisting
or warring *within* the mind and bringing about what is commonly called "split personality.")

Although Kraepelin initially reported that 13 percent of
cases of *dementia praecox* resulted in *lasting* recovery (and this
was at a time when the only treatments for madness, other
than physical restraints, were opium, morphine, scopola-
mine, and hashish, and the only sedatives were chloral hydrate, ether, alcohol, chloroform, and bromides), he later
revised his estimates downward to between 2 and 4 percent,
and in 1899 he definitively differentiated *dementia praecox*
from other forms of madness, especially manic depression,
which he believed was marked by a favorable longitudinal
course and outcome. Prognosis, thus, as often remains the
case a hundred years later, confirmed diagnosis. If a person
who had all the symptoms of *dementia praecox* improved,
then Kraepelin routinely considered that the patient had
been misdiagnosed.

This way of understanding mental illness (the once-a-
schizophrenic-always-a-schizophrenic postulate), though it
has not always been in the ascendancy (cf. the strength of
the mental hygiene movement in the early part of this century, or the rise of social psychiatry, and of psychodynamic
and psychoanalytically oriented psychiatry after World War
II), has persisted and gained influence in our times due
largely to a renewal of interest in the biological and physiological mechanisms that lead to mental disorders. Recent

DSM manuals of the American Psychiatric Association, for example—the manuals physicians use as the bases for classification and diagnosis (and insurance payments)—state with reference to the course and outcome of schizophrenia: "The most common course is one of acute exacerbations with increasing residual impairments between episodes." And, as recently as 1987, the revised version of the 1980 *DSM-III* manual concludes that "a complete return to pre-morbid functioning is unusual—so rare, in fact, that some clinicians would question the diagnosis."

If schizophrenia is an endogenous psychosis with, as Kraepelin believed and others have believed since, a profound genetic and hereditary basis, then the content of a patient's communication and behavior becomes less significant than its form—it becomes, that is, a mere manifestation of disease, and it is to the disease and not to the host of the disease that attention is directed, thereby putting the clinician in the position of seeing his or her primary function as that of evaluating signs of disease. And these signs, when charted, come much closer to what we think of as *objective* medical facts than more private, personal, cognitive, perceptual, or emotional experiences.

The advantages of this in more recent times, especially when it has involved the funding of psychiatric research that has biological and physiological bases, seem clear. An emphasis on somatic mechanisms allies psychiatry with the biomedical sciences (whose prestige and funding have risen enormously), and it also, as Gerald Grob has noted, "[seems] to eliminate the gap between psychiatry and other medical specialties."

And because both scientists and nonscientists often tend to believe that medical "facts" represent a higher-than-ordinary truth (a *scientific* truth), and rarely think that in seeing madness this way we are being *merely* objective, this model of understanding psychosis is often persuasive in convincing us that biology and biochemistry quite literally and predictably *do* determine destiny. Chance and free will, and everything that, in our thinking, feeling, and living, might derive from chance and free will, are deemed absent in those designated as mad, and thus character, preordained by one's genetic inheritance, inescapably becomes fate.

Still, as Leston Havens, professor of psychiatry at Harvard Medical School, explains in his book *Approaches to the Mind,* Kraepelin's clinical methods were based on individual case material that Kraepelin considered to be "preeminently objective." Kraepelin was "more interested in signs that all observers can share in," Havens writes, "than in symptoms, which depend on the patient's description of his inner state." Havens continues:

> The patient was himself treated as an object, observed, talked about, in his very presence and perhaps at the sacrifice of some finer feelings. This is the common practice in medicine; concern is with disease, which the patient "gets" or "has." The disease is not his "fault," remains separate from the personality, and therefore comments about it should not be taken "personally." Such a psychiatry or medicine favors traits or signs of sufficient obviousness to cross the barriers between patient and physician, and, as [Harry Stack] Sullivan was to emphasize, subject to distortions by that passage. Obviousness tends to be equated with importance, as in politics or advertising.

"We must ask," Havens submits, "whether this impression of the isolation of dementia praecox patients from environmental events was a facet of the overwhelming power of an endogenous disease process or whether it was a manifestation of *withdrawal* from life and *uncommunicativeness* about what has been happening to the person involved. In short, was the classic poverty of historic detail in the stories of these patients clinical fact or artifact?"

And, we might add, how many of us truly believe that the complexities of human character, and the ways in which any individual lives out his or her life—the infinite series of experiences, reactions, interactions, choices, terrors, joys, thoughts, losses, achievements, failures, triumphs, accidents, friendships, struggles, and the rest—can ever be reduced, in the sane or the insane, to anything resembling *objective* facts, medical or otherwise—to some pure or imagined set of biological and chemical processes, inborn or not, that is capable of accounting not only for all relations between mind and body, but for these relations as they change and evolve through the course of time?

The notion of madness as being innate also carried with it for Kraepelin and others, in his time as in ours, the belief that those men and women who are mad are not merely afflicted with a particular disease, but that the disease transforms these men and women into human beings who are so *different* in their essence from the rest of us that they are somehow less than human, and certainly less human—less worthy, valuable, or godly—than those of us who are not considered mad.

This concept of madness carried with it, that is, the belief that while madness can transform us, we cannot transform madness.

According to the government's Epidemiological Catchment Area (ECA) study, as we noted earlier, 22.1 percent of the U.S. population will have at least one diagnosable psychiatric disorder in the course of any one year, and between 28.8 percent and 38 percent of the population will have at least one serious psychiatric disorder in the course of a lifetime. The study also estimates that 3.5 percent of all children (more than two million boys and girls) will experience a *severe* mental illness in any six-month period. (In a more recent 1996 study of lifetime prevalence, Dr. Ronald Kessler and his colleagues at the University of Michigan estimated that 48 percent of us will have "a diagnosable mental illness" at some point in our lives.)

Since, that is, more than one out of every four of us will go mad for a time, and since most of us may often sense, in a "There-but-for-the-grace-of-God-go-I" way of thinking, that we are not all that different from friends and relatives

who *have* gone mad, small wonder that the fear of madness —
of being afflicted and punished by seemingly causeless,
unpredictable, episodic, chronic, and often unbearable emotional and behavioral difficulties—is so pervasive, and that
the fear so often brings with it a terrible hostility toward
those designated *as* mad.

The notion that those we call mad are different, alien, and
"other" easily leads, then, as critics of orthodox psychiatry
have pointed out, to policies and attitudes that ultimately
generate, reinforce, and sanction not only harsh and inhu-
mane treatment of those called mad, but to organized and
pervasive *neglect* of these individuals. (Kraepelin's case notes,
one critic suggests, indicate that it was perhaps *he* who was
failing to communicate, and that his patients' muteness could
and should have been read by anyone who was attuned to
truly listen, especially to silences, as a quite eloquent response to these individuals' experiences, feelings, thoughts,
and inner worlds, as well as to the outer world that had stigmatized them, ostracized them, and condemned them to their
grim and circumscribed lives.)

Contrary to Kraepelin, however, and to his followers in our
time—to those who believe that individuals diagnosed with
schizophrenia, or any other form of mental illness that is severe, persistent, and long-term, can never be "cured" and
will always remain essentially mad and disabled, or at best
lead marginal lives in which they will have to be monitored
and cared for as if they were dependent children—the evidence now strongly demonstrates that the majority of these
people *do* improve and recover, and in substantial ways and
in surprising numbers.

In many longitudinal studies that have followed sizable
groups of individuals hospitalized for schizophrenia—historically and medically the most intractable of all the psychoses—and have followed them for periods of twenty, thirty,
and forty or more years, and no matter what system is used
to establish diagnosis or to evaluate outcome, the overwhelming weight of evidence is that most of these individuals

do, in fact, improve and get better, and join us in ordinary and imperfect ways in our ordinary and imperfect world.

In numerous studies and meta-analyses that make use of new and exacting methodologies, and that have also, over several decades, taken scrupulous account of all criticisms of their own data and methodologies, Dr. Courtenay Harding, professor of psychiatry at the University of Colorado School of Medicine, and others, including (as major coinvestigators) Dr. John S. Strauss, professor of psychiatry at the Yale University School of Medicine, and the late Dr. Joseph Zubin, professor of psychiatry of the Veterans Administration Medical Center in Pittsburgh, conclude that fully one half to two thirds of more than 1,300 subjects from 5 separate, long-term longitudinal studies, all of whom were initially diagnosed with schizophrenia, and all of whom were studied for more than 20 years, achieved "recovery or significant improvement."

Although some researchers dispute minor details of these findings, all long-term follow-up studies of outcome in schizophrenia, no matter the differences in their design, have produced astonishingly similar results, and confirm Dr. Harding's conclusions.

Until recent decades, and the advent of new antipsychotic medications (Thorazine, Stelazine, Haldol, lithium, et al.), most individuals hospitalized for psychotic episodes were diagnosed as being schizophrenic. The term "schizophrenia," until the early fifties, was used generally as if it were synonymous with psychosis, especially in first episodes requiring hospitalization. In their researches, Dr. Harding and her colleagues take account of this, and attempt, based upon material available, to make tentative suggestions as to how, given the current narrower definitions of schizophrenia, and the broadening of the categories of major affective disorders (a heterogeneous group of depressive disorders that includes unipolar *and* bipolar depression), the individuals under study would, by current standards, be diagnosed.

But as David Mechanic, René Dubos Professor of Behavioral Sciences, and director of the Institute for Health, Health Care Policy, and Aging Research at Rutgers University, has pointed out, "even prior to 1955," and the advent of medications and policies that led to the policy of depopulating public mental hospitals, "most inpatients in public mental hospitals returned to the community." (Dr. Mechanic also points out that basic data on admissions, releases, and deaths "indicate that the [recent] deinstitutionalized population is a heterogeneous collection of varying cohorts." Nor is it clear who among deinstitutionalized patients of the last few decades would have been the long-stay patients of earlier eras. In fact, Mechanic writes, "the populations that alarm the community are later cohorts most of whom have never been long-stay inpatients and some who have never had a psychiatric admission at all.")

Even in the nineteenth century, Gerald Grob reports in his study of the history of madness, considerable numbers of individuals were discharged from asylums in better condition than when they entered. "One late nineteenth century study that followed about 1,000 patients discharged as recovered until they died," he writes, "found that about fifty-eight percent were never again hospitalized." An analysis by Morton Kramer of fifteen thousand patient cohorts admitted to Warren State Hospital in Pennsylvania in the first half of this century (1916–1950) found that "the probability of release of first admissions of functional psychotics within twelve months increased from forty-two to sixty-two percent between 1919/ 1925 and 1946/1950." It is, in part, the high proportion of chronic and aged individuals placed in state mental hospitals, when factored into such findings, Grob suggests, that has "led many to overlook the reality that substantial numbers of patients were admitted, treated, and discharged in less than a year."

Like David Mechanic, Gerald Grob, and others, Courtenay Harding also shows an acute awareness of the multitude of factors that influenced and continue to influence the favoring of one diagnosis over another, and the ways in which this affects the design and conclusions of outcome studies: economic considerations (e.g., what to call a condition so that the state or the insurance company will reimburse for expenses), the availability of new and more effective medications, the changing of *DSM* criteria, true increases in the prevalence of some disorders, etc. Thus, in a 1993 *American Journal of Psychiatry* study, "Shifts in Diagnostic Frequencies of Schizophrenia and Major Affective Disorders at Six North American Hospitals, 1972–1988," the investigators conclude that there was, in the six hospitals during these years, a threefold decrease in the diagnosis of schizophrenia and a fourfold increase in the diagnosis of major affective disorders.

In presenting her findings, Harding, along with others who have in recent years come to similar conclusions, draws attention to the old notion, familiar to most doctors—and still current (over the past few years psychiatrists have quoted it to me as if it were an indisputable fact upon which to base diagnosis, prognosis, and treatment)—that when it comes to schizophrenia, "one third get better, one third stay the same, and one third get worse."

To counteract such myths, Dr. Harding and her coinvestigators point out that when they did follow-up studies over several decades on 269 back ward patients released from Vermont State Hospital "over one-half of these once profoundly ill, long-stay patients had achieved a much higher level of functioning than had been predicted by our own research team during the early days of the patients' community tenure," and that "their achievement is even more remarkable given their original levels of chronicity."

In a 1994 article in the *American Journal of Psychiatry*, "One Hundred Years of Schizophrenia: a Meta-Analysis of the Outcome Literature," another team of researchers (Drs. James Hegarty, Ross Baldessarini, et al.) note "the difficulty of accurately and consistently defining clinical outcome in schizophrenia," and go on to posit principles, from hundreds of studies, nearly identical to those used by Dr. Harding.

"By consensus," these authors write, "we translated each study's outcome data to ratio measures of improvement (the number of patients considered improved divided by the total number per cohort), using criteria that suggested attainment of substantial levels of functioning and freedom from psychotic symptoms. Thus, patients considered as 'improved' in follow-up had to have been described as recovered in remission, well without residual symptoms, minimally or mildly symptomatic, improved without significant deficit, socially recovered, or working or living independently."

Yet even when studies such as this one attempt to define the concepts of recovery and improvement in the narrowest manner and to limit its follow-up to under six years (while acknowledging that outcomes *do* tend to improve when looked at for longer periods of time); and even when a study such as this is skeptical about results and claims slightly more sanguine than its own, it still reaches the conclusion that, during the thirty-year period 1956 to 1985, "the proportion of patients who improved increased significantly," to "48.5 percent."

Such studies, along with others that advance even more optimistic conclusions (*all* studies conclude that *most* individuals recover from first episodes of schizophrenia), also note additional factors that should be taken into account when looking at long-term outcome for schizophrenia: that outcome results may often reflect "a more Kraepelian emphasis on duration and course"; that most studies "include a high proportion of [other] studies with imprecise and potentially unreliable diagnostic or outcome criteria or clinically heterogeneous samples"; that, according to all studies, outcome is *vastly* improved when there is early and consistent treatment with (the newer) antipsychotic medications; and—perhaps most important—that "modern treatment may tend to remove persons with favorable responses to treatment from the pool of subjects followed."

To put this another way, as a 1984 *Archives of General*

Psychiatry article, "The Clinician's Illusion," does, the longer the duration of an illness, the greater the chance that the subportion of the patient population with the *severest* form of the illness will show up in clinical caseloads and the greater the chance that those who do recover (like Lynne Douglas, Paula Kline, or Carl Pickus) may often slip back into our world in ways that remove them, not only from madness and debilitating fears of madness, but from the consciousness and researches of those who study the course, history, and outcome—the human sequelae—of madness.

Dr. Kessler's team also noted another finding consistent with the ECA study: that only one out of every four individuals reporting a mental illness has sought treatment. As the American Psychiatric Association (APA) argues in its 1996 Guide, *Let's Talk About Mental Illness*, "This is an indication that many illnesses do not impair function, and that many people recover on their own or with the help of family and friends, *just as do many with other medical illnesses*," and that it is often "fear and stigma, coupled with the lack of adequate insurance [that] discourages many from seeking treatment."

Most individuals who have had severe breakdowns that have led to hospitalizations do not go around, generally—as they might if they had recovered from, say, a heart attack, cancer, or (even) AIDS—telling friends, colleagues, and acquaintances, "Oh yes, I was once diagnosed with schizophrenia, and spent a considerable amount of time in state mental hospitals, but I'm all better now."

Since a group under treatment, or study, at any one time may represent only a fraction of persons who have had episodes of serious mental illness, Harding submits, further doubts arise as to whether chronicity is a necessary or inherent outcome of acute psychotic disorders.

At the time of their selection for the Vermont long-term study in the mid-1950s, the 269 patients chosen from the state mental hospital had been ill for an average of 16 years, totally disabled for 10 years, and hospitalized continuously for 6 years. They were considered to be the most hopeless and deteriorated patients—in the bottom 19 percent—of all those confined to the back wards of Vermont's state mental hospital. These 269 men and women, whose average age was forty, were released between the years 1955 and 1960 in a program of planned deinstitutionalization, and—revolutionary for the times—were encouraged to participate in a pioneering psychosocial rehabilitation program that provided basic community supports.

(Another ongoing study has tried to match these individuals by age, gender, diagnosis, and length of chronicity to several hundred patients from the Augusta, Maine, state mental hospital, where the only significant difference between the cohorts was that the patients released from the Maine hospital did *not* participate in a rehabilitation program. Begun in the 1950s, the Maine study has followed individuals for an average of thirty-seven years, and the initial results, still under review, indicate that without the rudimentary forms of psychosocial rehabilitation the Vermont patients were offered—the only quantifiable variable—the Maine patients did not, overall, recover or improve to the degree the Vermont patients did. Still, nearly half of the Maine cohort— 48 percent—did recover or improve significantly.)

When the 269 men and women from the Vermont State Hospital were followed up thirty years later, in the 1980s (they had also been followed up at earlier intervals, in 1965 and 1975), one half to two thirds, whether alive or deceased, and whether diagnosed by *DSM-I* or *DSM-III* guidelines, were determined to have achieved significant recovery or improvement, as rated by the Global Assessment Scale, the Strauss-Carpenter Levels of Functioning Scale, as well as in individual interviews and by thirteen other classic scales and schedules.

For the *living* individuals diagnosed according to *DSM-III*, 34 percent had achieved "full recovery" in both psychiatric status and social functioning, while an additional 34 percent had "significantly" improved in both areas. For those critics who were skeptical of this study because the 269 backward individuals came from a mental hospital in a rural area of a state with low population density—and thus, the critics suggested, from a more peaceful, less turbulent social, economic, and geographic setting than a mental hospital with a population drawn from poor urban sections of cities such as New York or Chicago—Harding pointed out that understanding and quantifying the impact of rural life on the course of mental illness is an enormously complex enterprise. Thus, although most epidemiological studies show a clear relation between poverty and acute mental illness—poor people *are* more vulnerable ("One of the most consistent findings in the epidemiology of mental disorders," the article on "Psychiatric Epidemiology," from the most recent *Handbook on Mental Health Policy in the United States*, states, "is that the lower class has higher rates of psychiatric disorders than higher social classes")—there is no clear relation between setting, rural, urban, or suburban, and severity or chronicity of illness.

"Despite its ecological niches and visual beauty," Harding noted, Vermont has been among the nation's leaders, in several categories, in rates of suicide, alcoholism, incest, domestic violence, child abuse, unemployment, and poverty. And if Vermont did not have some of the problems particular to urban areas, such as those that come from overcrowding, crime, and drugs, it did have long, difficult winters, along with the hardships that result from living in isolated areas where the inaccessibility of ordinary health care and/or the unavailability of mental health programs created their own unique problems.

The other four long-term studies reviewed in detail by Dr. Harding yielded results similar to those of the Vermont study. During the years 1942 and 1943, for example, Manfred Bleuler—Eugen Bleuler's son—began following 208 patients who were either first admissions or readmissions to Burghölzli Hospital in Switzerland. He followed this cohort for a period of twenty-three years, and reported that 53 percent of the group "significantly improved or recovered." When the first admissions were separated out, 68 percent were found to have recovered or improved.

Bleuler also noted something else, a puzzling statistic that seemed to indicate how dubious was the notion that schizophrenia, in particular, was an exclusively endogenous and/ or hereditary condition. Since marital and fertility rates of people with schizophrenia were far below general rates, worldwide (and since, in addition, the mortality rates were higher)—since, that is, the genetic pool from which individuals diagnosed with schizophrenia came diminished steadily and globally, and no family research had ever been able to demonstrate that the occurrence of schizophrenia followed anything like Mendelian laws—how did it happen that all studies, no matter the time period, or the nation, or the culture, or the subculture, continued to put forth incontrovertible data showing that the percentage of the population with schizophrenia, despite the dimishing genetic pool, remained constant, worldwide, at 1 percent? ("If we assert that mutation of a gene is the main background of schizophrenia, we must conclude that the mutation rate is very high," Bleuler remarks. "As a matter of fact," he adds, "it would have to be much higher than any known mutation rate.")

A Bonn study that examined 502 individuals at an average of more than twenty-two years after admission found 57 percent recovered or significantly improved, and concluded: "Schizophrenia does not seem to be a disease of slow progressive deterioration. Even in the second and third decades of illness, there is still potential for full or partial recovery."

Rating outcomes on the basis of four categories—residential, employment, symptoms, and marital status—a thirty-seven-year study of 186 patients from the Iowa State Hospital concluded that 46 percent of these patients had recovered completely or improved significantly. And a twenty-four-year Japanese study of 140 patients diagnosed with schizophrenia concluded that "57% achieved a favorable social outcome which included return to premorbid level of social functioning and independent social life without clinical interventions, as well as maintenance of a normal family life."

What Harding, Strauss, and Zubin also conclude, in a 1992 follow-up—citing additional studies (from the World Health Organization, The International Pilot Study of Schizophrenia, Boston State Hospital, etc.) that, though shorter in term, all confirm the conclusions of the five longitudinal studies Harding's group has considered—is that when looking at why people who suffer long-term from mental illness do or do not recover, it is the very *concept* of chronicity that needs to be reevaluated.

When I read this, I think of those environmental conditions and external forces that have affected my brother, Robert, including physical and emotional abuse, excessive use of medications, debilitating side effects of medications, lack of decent programming or rehabilitation services, incompetent and ever-changing and often uncaring staff, abysmal residential situations, chronic unemployment, loss of property and of money and of friends and of self-esteem and of dignity and of rights and of hope. Wherever and whenever, during the past four decades, these conditions and forces, separately or collectively, acted upon Robert—whether in emergency wards, mental hospitals, halfway houses, welfare hotels, or the streets—it seems clear that, at the least, they compounded and intensified, and in infinite and cruel ways, whatever of madness may have risen up within him on its own.

In attempting to understand chronicity, Harding writes, *many* characteristics need to be taken into account, and she lists some of them: the residual effects of the disorder itself (such as negative symptoms), the effects due to institutionalization (including "learned helplessness"), the lack of rehabilitation and/or therapy, reduced economic opportunities, chronic unemployment, reduced social status, side effects of medications, the lack of staff expectations, self-fulfilling prophecies, and the loss of hope.

When these elements are factored in, Harding's study proposes, the form of the diagnosis itself will be seen to be in need of revision in order that it might more accurately reflect not only the heterogeneity of the condition, but the heterogeneity of the outcome, and—a crucial distinction—"the probability that schizophrenia is primarily a prolonged illness rather than a chronic one."

In another recent (1997) review of follow-up studies, "The Varied Outcomes of Schizophrenia," two Yale Medical School professors, Thomas H. McGlashan, a psychiatrist, and Larry Davidson, a psychologist, consider follow-up studies of schizophrenia that include examinations of both long-term conditions and of early (or first) episodes.

McGlashan and Davidson review hundreds of outcome studies, including the Harding studies, the Maine studies, and all available meta-analyses, and, even taking into account follow-up studies of first-episode cases, they conclude that there is a "broad heterogeneity in long-term outcome of schizophrenia, with 21% to 57% of subjects achieving a good outcome ranging from mild impairment to recovery," and they note what Harding has observed about long-term course: "These studies," they write, "provide further evidence that deterioration occurs within the first few months of onset, followed by a plateau in functioning which then may or may not be followed by gradual improvements later in the course of disorder."

They also confirm what most studies do: that "assertive rehabilitation efforts appear to improve long-term outcome, while responsiveness to biological treatments early in the course of illness may be strongly predictive of long-term outcome." They conclude by emphasizing the heterogeneity and variations inherent in schizophrenia, and they offer, too, their belief that, despite the complexity of the condition and our imperfect understanding of it, we have "gained a few important insights about the course and outcome of schizophrenia over the last few years."

"First," they say, "it appears that the broad prognostic heterogeneity that was initially discovered through long-term follow-up studies may already be present at the time of the first episode. It also appears that the most significant amount of deterioration in functioning that will occur for many individuals with schizophrenia has already occurred by the time of the first episode, if not by the prodromal [premonitory] phase."

This knowledge, along with knowledge of the individual, cultural, and historical variations in outcome, lead them to conclude that in addition "to applying these findings to improvement of clinical and rehabilitative efforts," we need to understand that *prevention* of schizophrenia is now very much within our means, so that "an equally important challenge will be to focus intensively on the prodromal and early phases of the course of disorder in a concerted effort to prevent disability and chronicity.

"Progressing from recognition of heterogeneity in outcome to efforts to prevent the worst outcomes from occurring represents a logical next step in the evolution of schizophrenia research and treatment," they state, and submit that "this is a new conceptualization of a disorder once assumed to have a progressive course leading inevitably to premature dementia."

Long-term outcome studies of individuals diagnosed with bipolar disorder (manic depression) and unipolar disorder (major, or clinical depression) yield results that are even more positive than outcome studies of individuals diagnosed with schizophrenia.

Virtually all outcome studies of individuals diagnosed with unipolar disorder (approximately 5 percent of the U.S. population in any one year) are unanimous in stating that, when treated — with medications, psychotherapy, or both — individuals diagnosed with unipolar disorder recover fully or improve significantly about 80 percent of the time. "Devastating as this disease may be," a NAMI brochure, *Understanding Major Depression*, states, "it is treatable. Between 80 percent and

90 percent of those suffering from depression can be effectively treated."

"In any one year period," the APA Guide *Let's Talk About Mental Illness,* states, "9.6 million adults suffer from this disease. One in four women and one in 10 men can expect to develop it during their lifetime. Eighty to 90% of those who suffer from depression can be effectively treated, and nearly all who receive treatment benefit."

When individuals with unipolar depression remain untreated, however, studies tell us that as many as 15 percent will commit suicide. And, too, the NAMI brochure cautions, "we now think that 80 to 90 percent of the people who have one episode of depression will have a second, and without treatment, after two episodes the chances of having a third episode are even greater. After three episodes, the chances of having a fourth are greater than 90 percent."

As a result of methodological differences that arise from varying diagnostic, treatment, and hospital practices, as well as from differences and inconsistencies in research designs, the epidemiology of bipolar illness (approximately 1.2 percent of the U.S. population will suffer from bipolar disorder in any one year) is more complicated than that of unipolar depression. Still, the basic outlines of what we know about the course of illness and the outcome for individuals diagnosed with bipolar disorder are clear and, as with outcome studies of schizophrenia and unipolar disorder, they are cause for optimism.

"Until the middle of this century, manic-depressive [bipolar] illness had remained intractable, frustrating the best efforts of clinical practitioners and their forbears," Drs. Kay Jamison and Frederick K. Goodwin tell us in *Manic-Depressive Illness.* "This long history ended abruptly with the discovery of lithium's therapeutic benefits. In an ironic turn of events, the pharmacological revolution then mobilized a renaissance in the psychotherapy of manic-depressive patients. Substantially freed of the severe disruptions of mania and the profound withdrawal of depression, patients and therapists could sustain their focus on the many psychological issues related to the illness and also confront basic developmental tasks.

"To be sure," Jamison and Goodwin continue, "even the combination of drugs and psychotherapy cannot yield a completely satisfactory outcome for every patient. *But the treatment approaches now available do allow most manic-depressive patients to lead relatively normal lives* — lives that are less painfully interrupted by illness and less often prematurely ended by suicide" (italics added).

All epidemiological studies bear out this optimistic conclusion. "In a report of a 35-year follow-up of the original 100 patients initially admitted for mania [bipolar I] in the Iowa-500 study," Jamison and Goodwin report, "Tsuang and colleagues (1979) found that, when marital, residential, occupational, and psychiatric (symptomatic) status were combined, outcome was good in approximately 64 percent of patients, fair in 14 percent, and poor (i.e., chronic) in 22 percent."

More recent studies cited by Goodwin and Jamison, in which remission is defined as being relatively symptom-free for two years or longer, posit chronicity figures for bipolar illness as low as 18 percent and 6 percent. And a 1989 NIMH study found the rate of chronicity of bipolar patients who were treated mainly for depression to be 11 percent.

Taking into account differing results due to varying methodologies and data (patients initially diagnosed as bipolar are often rediagnosed as schizophrenic, and vice versa), Goodwin and Jamison estimate that, with optimum treatment — medications *and* psychotherapy — the incidence of chronicity "would certainly be substantially below one third." And all available outcome studies confirm their thesis: that *most* individuals with bipolar disorder do recover into "relatively normal lives."

When I meet with Dr. Harding and others who have been working on outcome studies, including government researchers at the Center for Mental Health Services (CMHS) and the Substance Abuse and Mental Health Services Administration (SAMHSA) of the U.S. Department of Health and Human Services, as well as private researchers associated with NAMI, the Mental Health Association, McLean Hospital, the Institute for Health Care Policy at Rutgers University, the Boston University Psychiatric Rehabilitation Center, Harvard University Medical School, the National Empowerment Center, and the Human Services Research Institute of Cambridge, and no matter the large and small disagreements between researchers, their differing assumptions and methodologies, or the differing results of their studies, they all tell me essentially the same thing: that, in trying to understand and treat a condition that, classically, has been the most refractory of all illnesses, there is, at last, cause for real optimism and that, yes — for individuals with serious and persistent mental illness:

- there are more and better forms of care, treatment, rehabilitation, and therapy;
- there are more and better programs, and they are increasingly available for increasing numbers of individuals;
- there is more tolerance and less stigma, and more organizations effectively advocating *for* people with mental illness, and *against* stigma and discrimination, whether in housing, employment, education, or in insurance coverage;
- there is more and better understanding of the disease processes themselves, and of the interactions of both medications and experience with what we think of as disease processes;
- there is more and better understanding by those afflicted with serious mental illness of the nature of their own conditions, lives, and choices, and more active and effective involvement of these individuals in their own care and treatment; and
- there are, quite simply and without doubt, more and better

outcomes for increasing numbers of individuals who have experienced and continue to experience severe and persistent mental illness.

Although large areas of concern remain as mysterious as ever—we are, for example, still in the dark when it comes to understanding the *causes* of the major mental illnesses, and still pretty much in the dark when it comes to understanding why, when, and how certain medications work, and why and when and how they work for some individuals and not for others—we are beginning to gain a few important insights. We are able, for example, to create outcome studies that give us specific and useful information, that tell us which programs and medications, and which combinations of programs and medications, work, and to what degree.

In order to accelerate and monitor our understanding of what works under varying conditions, the government has mandated that 15 percent of mental health and substance-abuse budgets for the National Institute of Health be devoted to health *services* research. The government also requires that a percentage of funds awarded for research on mental illness go specifically to outcome studies, and that all research proposals—whether they are concerned with housing or medications, education or psychotherapy, employment or rehabilitation—contain a component that is capable, in a rigorous manner, of evaluating outcome. In this way, even when we dispute one another's findings about best (and worst) practices, we will, with regard to research, begin to bring mental illness into parity with other illnesses by finding methods and methodologies that more accurately tell us what certain forms of care and treatment actually do and do not do, how they work and for whom, and at what cost, both human and economic.

We are, that is, beginning to understand in more precise ways, what, in those things that constitute care and treatment, can and does make a difference in the lives of men and women who suffer from serious mental illnesses.

Numerous studies, for example, demonstrate conclusively the value of ACT programs; of programs informed by the principle of continuity of care; of the superior efficacy, in almost all instances, of treatment that relies on both medications *and* psychotherapy, as opposed to treatment that relies exclusively on one or the other; of the superior efficacy, in the treatment of individuals who have dual diagnoses — mental illness plus substance-abuse problems — of *integrated* models of care and treatment; of the importance of early intervention and treatment; of the importance of comprehensive service programs that eliminate fragmentation; and of the importance of programs that are committed to long-term treatment that sees the therapeutic alliance as crucial to recovery.

What researchers, administrators, and individuals I talk with also insist upon is that the medications themselves are better — enormously so — and their side effects less debilitating.

This is confirmed not only by outcome studies, by my visits to programs, and by my conversations with hundreds of individuals who tell me what Eleanor, Paula, Kate, Gaston, Rose, Ed, and Moe have been telling me — that new medications have changed their lives for the better, and sometimes miraculously so — but by Robert's experience at Bronx Psychiatric Center after his transfer there, and after he begins taking Clozaril, the one medication *everyone* contends is the first new medication in decades that has made a real difference for individuals with long-term mental illness.

"My phone's been ringing off the hook," Larry Kohn tells me, "with family members and residential treatment centers wanting us to do rehabilitation and recovery workshops, and you know why? It's because those men and women who used to stay in back rooms, or wards, zonked out on drugs, and watching TV or smoking away or sleeping all day — they're on the new meds, and they're suddenly *alive* again, and they're restless and active and want to do something with their lives for the first time in ages, and the people who care for them just don't know how to cope."

Other mental health workers reiterate what Larry tells me, and confirm the paradoxical effect of the new medications: that precisely because they are effective, they create a need for more rather than for fewer services. Formerly docile and sedated patients who experience awakenings from their conditions now need *more* labor-intensive assistance to help them in their reentry to our world: more psychotherapy, more psychosocial rehabilitation, more supports for education, housing, and employment, more help with basic social skills, and with feelings, needs, and desires long forsworn.

The literature I read about Clozaril and other new medications (and about newer ones now in preparation) corroborates what I am hearing. In a typical example, the 1997 *Handbook of Clinical Psychopharmacology for Therapists* (authored by a clinical psychologist, a pharmacist, and a psychiatrist) declares that newer "antipsychotic medications have truly revolutionized the treatment of psychotic disorders. Their effectiveness is so vastly superior to previous treatments that they have ushered in a new era in the treatment of severe mental illnesses."

Given Robert's long history of institutionalization and the dreadful effects, and side effects, medications have had on him, along with what has often been an exclusive reliance upon and an excessive use of medications that have had a more custodial than medical purpose, I have, through the years, become resistant, and sometimes antagonistic, both to the use of antipsychotic medications and to claims about their allegedly miraculous powers.

In my experience, and that of others who have led lives like Robert's, exaggerated claims and false hopes (for example, *Time* magazine's assertions about wonder drugs, or E. Fuller Torrey's prophecy about the imminence of a "cure" for schizophrenia within the next five to ten years) have often added cruel burdens of disappointment to lives already overburdened with sorrow.

My talks with people who have been medicated, over-medicated, medicated against their will, and medicated on the basis of a misdiagnosis or diagnoses geared more to institutional than to human needs, and my talks with their friends and families, along with everything I have seen and read since Robert's first breakdown in 1962, when he was nineteen years old—when I witnessed the effects on him of large doses of Thorazine, Stelazine, and Prolixin and of other treatments, such as straitjackets and insulin shock therapy, and when I, along with Robert and our parents, suffered promises from doctors about various new medications and their imagined magical properties—all this has made me skeptical in the extreme.

The possibility of creating systems that can deliver complex care and treatment, long-term, to complex individuals who have lengthy histories marked by illness, failure, and despair, presents, to say the least, daunting and humbling challenges. And for individuals who have lost substantial portions of their lives to the ravages and misery of mental illness, and who are beginning to recover—and no matter the efficacy of medications, it has seemed to me—skilled, caring, and long-term *human* attention to their needs and desires, especially as they begin to make their way back into our world, remains essential. Without this kind of labor-intensive and sometimes costly attention, recovery, in my experience, simply does not occur.

In recent years, however, the accounts I hear and the literature I read about the new range of what are called "atypical" antipsychotics ("atypical" because they do not cause the typical, and terrible, side effects of conventional antipsychotic medications—i.e., they are typical in their efficacy but atypical in their side effects) make me not only less resistant to the possibility that new medications might make a difference for many individuals with mental illness, but that they might do so, despite the years gone by, for my brother Robert.

And so, while Robert is still at South Beach Psychiatric Center, and before his transfer to the Bronx, I find myself advocating on his behalf for a trial of one of these new medications. When, at my insistence, Robert is given a thoroughgoing medical review, and is, for the first time in his life, put on an atypical antipsychotic, Risperdal, he makes swift and exceptional gains.

Even Mark Kaplan expresses surprise at how well Robert does and tells me that Robert is "the best he has seen him in years." The staff agrees with Mark, Robert is moved to the top of the list for discharge, and he is given passes so that he can leave South Beach (and Staten Island) during the day.

But when there are delays in his transfer to the "one and only" place the staff deems suitable for Robert, and Robert's life alternates between sleeping on a locked psychiatric ward at night with people far more ill than he is, and being left to wander the city during the day, without guidance, structure, or therapy—without anyone to talk to about his days or his feelings or the imminent changes in his life—Robert inevitably, as in the past, begins to deteriorate, and whatever gains he has made rapidly fade.

When we arrive at Bronx Psychiatric Center, however—twenty-eight months after the Risperdal trial (and failure), and sixteen months after his brief (and disastrous) release to Park Manor—and when the intake psychiatrist asks Robert if he would be willing to try Clozaril, and Robert answers with an unequivocally affirmative response—"*Yes!* And I'll take the blood tests too!"—I find that I am silently elated.

How, given his experiences—given his life!—he can still welcome new medications with enthusiasm is a wonder, and shows not only that he has not given up hope in things worldly, but, more heartening still, that he has not given up hope in and for himself.

Although Robert's first weeks, and months, at Bronx Psychiatric Center are tumultuous and labile in the extreme—he is both calmer and angrier than he has been for a while, more reasonable and less reasonable, happier and more depressed—the Clozaril, from the start, makes a clear and welcome difference.

Those who have taken Clozaril, and those who have prescribed it, and those who have witnessed its effects, give glowing accounts of its wonders—of the kinds of "awakenings" they have experienced or have witnessed. Studies indicate that as many as 40 percent of individuals suffering from *chronic* mental illness who have failed to respond to any treatments, or to any of the typical antipsychotics such as Thorazine, Stelazine, Trilafon, Prolixin, Mellaril, Haldol, or Navane (all of which Robert has taken), respond, and respond well, to Clozaril.

The only reservations I hear about Clozaril have to do with its side effects (it causes heavy drooling, is *extremely* sedating—cf. Gaston Cloutier's reaction—and can also inflict a host of other adverse effects, including constipation, rapid heartbeat, weight gain, headaches, nausea, and fatigue), and with the fact that the drug does not work for everybody, and that when it does work, it does so to different and unpredictable degrees for different individuals, and nobody knows why.

Because Clozaril may cause a bone-marrow toxicity known as agranulocytosis, a rare and fatal blood disease in which white blood cells are destroyed, and because this disease can prove fatal for approximately 1 to 2 percent of those who take the drug, mandatory once-a-week blood tests are required. There are, however, according to some psychiatrists, beneficial side effects of this requirement. Dr. Samuel Rofman, a practicing clinical psychiatrist and medical director of the Massachusetts Behavioral Health Partnership—he was chief of psychiatry at the Edith Nourse Rogers Memorial Veterans Hospital in Bedford, Massachusetts, when that hospital was involved in the first clinical trials of Clozaril in this country— suggests that because the obligatory blood tests require that the individual in treatment see somebody about his or her condition at least once a week, these weekly appointments come to represent a kind of constancy and continuity, thereby providing a multitude of nonquantifiable but positive benefits, especially for individuals who are recovering from long-term mental illness, and whose recovery will usually be prolonged.

"Simply having your blood pressure and pulse taken—a literal laying on of hands—can be incredibly important to an individual whose feelings and condition require a medication such as Clozaril," Dr. Rofman says. "And because of the weekly visits we are able to pick up relapses and the possibility of relapse—noncompliance—much more quickly, and so can work to prevent them."

Dr. Rofman, like other mental health professionals I talk with, issues an additional caution: The sudden awakening experienced by someone who responds well to Clozaril is often so extreme and intense that one has to be especially vigilant if and when this awakening occurs, since an individual who has been living with severe mental illness for an extended period of time, and feels alive and well for the first time in years, may now look around at his or her current situation and possibilities, or may look back upon his or her life, with a clarity that is both terrifying and shocking. When they see their lives clear and whole for the first time since prepsychotic times, these people often experience a new and quite different feeling: a startling and acute sense of loss, both of time and of self, that can itself bring on new and unbearable feelings of despair.

"When the individual begins getting *well*—" Dr. Rofman explains, "that's when you have to be most attentive, most careful."

What I notice the first time I visit Robert after he has begun taking Clozaril is that despite his shoutings, tantrums, and demands—which are considerable—his eyes are the clearest they have been in years, and his speech, even when at high volume, is lucid, focused, and intelligible. He is *alert* in ways he has not seemed in a long time, and he is also—still—funny, warm, affectionate, eccentric, and antic.

In the first few months following his transfer to the Bronx, his screaming—sudden volcanic spasms of rage—become so intense and alarming that frequently, after telling him it doesn't feel good to be screamed at, I add that if he continues to do so, I will have to leave; when I say this, he is usually able to gain control of himself.

But even his tirades, I notice, are more coherent than they have been in the past. "You put me here," he rails at me over the phone one night, in a high-pitched bill-of-particulars, "and you said it would be closer and you would see me more often, and you only see me every four weeks; and you said you would bring more visitors, and you only brought your sons once; and the only reason you come is so I can give you twenty dollars for your children, and because you want my money!" He takes a breath and continues, his voice rising higher: *"And the fifth thing is, I love you!"*

Dr. Guptan, Robert's medical doctor, talks with me frequently and at length. He tells me that "we have a lucky break" because "Robert is one of the fifty percent of long-term patients who respond positively to Clozaril." Although Robert yells and complains a lot, and causes some upset on the ward, he also "takes redirection quite well." His violent and aggressive acts seem "purely verbal," and the staff is devoted to him, and enjoys him immensely. He is, Dr. Guptan declares, a most delightful and fascinating man.

And he is also, I think, still the entertainer and clown he was in childhood, forever trying to amuse and give pleasure to others.

When I telephone the ward, the staff — aides and nurses — always talk with me instead of ordering me to call back on the pay phone. "I bet you're wanting to know how your brother is doing" is the way they will usually begin a conversation — and when I visit, they tell me what Dr. Guptan and Alan Epstein, Robert's social worker, have been telling me: that though Robert shouts a lot and loses his temper frequently, he is improving — they can see it! — and that they truly enjoy having him around, that they appreciate his humor, his intelligence, and his kindness, and that they don't mind indulging him.

"We really spoil him," one nurse tells me, after which she

humors Robert out of a tantrum that at South Beach would have earned him room restrictions, loss of privileges, and isolation.

When I hear and see the ways in which Robert is difficult—unlike most patients on his ward, he is manic, loud, and verbally aggressive rather than docile and quiet—I am not surprised. It is as if, to the hospital's statement "We like you, Robert, and we think we can help you to get better," he is responding, *"Oh yeah?! You really think so? Well, just watch my smoke, folks—and see just how difficult a veteran madman like me can be . . . !"*

During Robert's first months on the ward, he drinks his own urine (not a medical problem, since one's own urine is sterile), gets into fights with and tries to hit, sexually, on other (male) patients (the staff worries that he may pick the wrong man—many men on the ward have criminal records; a few have killed people), and carries on loudly and inconsolably when he does not immediately get his way. When I call and visit, he is sometimes wonderfully calm, warm, and civil—introducing me to other patients and to staff, looking through photos with me, talking with me about what he wants to do when he gets out of the hospital, giving me articles and advertisements he has clipped from magazines—and sometimes he is enraged and frustrated in ways that do cause me to cut my visits short.

He is, by turns, affectionate and distant, realistic and unrealistic, elated and depressed. He is also, by turns, happy to be in a new ward, and angry at me for—his word—*putting* him there. He is eager to go to the open ward, and resistant to going there (during community meetings on the open ward, to which he is invited, he acts out in outrageous and disruptive ways); he is sad, and speaks to me of his great fear: that he has no future other than to remain where he is forever ("Please get me out of here, Jay. Please, please . . .").

"Oh Jay, we had a really good visit until I started shouting at you, didn't we?" he says first thing one evening, when I telephone him a few hours after an afternoon visit.

However, when a few months into his stay, both Dr. Guptan and Alan Epstein remark on the fact that Clozaril continues to have a positive and sustained effect and that Robert is making "slow and steady gains"—he is learning to control his rages, he is interacting more easily with others, he is not starting fights, he is being "realistic" and "appropriate" about most things, and that he has begun kibitzing playfully with everyone—I find myself smiling and doing something I had not previously imagined possible: praising the powers of an antipsychotic medication's ability to make a difference in my brother's life.

When I check in at the security desk one time at the start of a visit, and the security guard hands me a pass, I ask him if he knows my brother Robert. The guard smiles broadly. "Who *doesn't* know your brother!" he replies.

"And oh yes," Dr. Guptan tells me in his lilting Indian accent at the end of one of our talks, "I meant to tell you—your brother has taken to calling me 'Rabbi.'" He pauses. "But I think this is a respectable term for me," he adds.

I assure him that it is.

Al Pam calls one morning to tell me that *everyone* has been talking about what Robert did the previous day: Asked to provide a urine sample, Robert went into the bathroom, filled the flask, returned to the nurse's station and, handing over the sample, asked for a receipt.

Al and I laugh together, and I say to him that in many ways the rising and falling of Robert's sense of humor provides the most reliable way of measuring his mental and emotional state. He agrees.

Al and I talk regularly, and he tells me that he too thinks Robert is making genuine progress, and that the staff remains optimistic. He stops by to see Robert periodically, and has begun to think of who, when Robert comes to his ward

(Ward 12, the open ward), might be the best person to assign as Robert's psychotherapist.

Being more clear-eyed and clearheaded, Robert is now able—often through humor, but also through his work with Alan—to gain perspective on himself and his situation. The fading of his total self-absorption brings with it, too, an increase in his generous impulses: He shares food, cigarettes, and money with others on the ward; he is solicitous about my health, and seems genuinely proud when I bring him a newly published collection of my short stories, *Don't Worry About the Kids*, which he shows around; and he asks me to buy gifts for his niece and nephews, using money from his *Imagining Robert* bank account: candlesticks for Miriam, when she moves into a new home in Arlington, Virginia; art supplies for Eli, when he has a one-man show at a New York City gallery; an inscribed Zippo lighter for Aaron—who smokes as much as Robert—when he graduates from college.

On separate visits, Eli and Aaron come with me to Bronx Psychiatric Center, and they confirm my sense of things: that Robert is doing better than he has in years. Robert talks with his nephews about wanting a job—working in a library—and about going to the open ward, and about things the boys should make sure to do in New York City. They shouldn't, he says, repeating an old family line, forget to have a good time.

"You know," Eli, now twenty-three years old, says to me on our walk to the subway after our visit, "this is the first time in years I can remember feeling that I was visiting my *uncle*."

Dr. Guptan and Alan begin to prepare Robert for his transfer to the open ward, but then, a week or two before the move is to take place—will some things never change?—Alan himself, without warning and on two days' notice, is abruptly transferred.

"Alan's not my social worker anymore," Robert snaps when I call one evening and ask about how how he and Alan are getting along. "Mr. Matthews is my social worker now. Alan was promoted or something."

When I start to respond, Robert cuts me off angrily, demands to know what I am going to bring him the next time I visit, and when I don't immediately promise I am going to do exactly what he has commanded, he hangs up on me. "This is my home, Jay," he says, a few days later. "This is where I'll always be. Why should I go anywhere else?"

Robert remains incredibly distraught for several weeks ("He is in mourning," Dr. Guptan says), and, as if to confirm the obvious and necessary connections in his life between medications and human relationships—which of us, no matter our strengths, frailties, or histories, does not need and desire others upon whom we can rely, especially during hard times?—he deteriorates swiftly.

He becomes enraged, manic, uncooperative—he hangs up on me frequently after screaming at me ("You put me here, so you get me out of here, you goddamned son-of-a-bitch cocksucking bastard!"), and even when he is not enraged, his talk often degenerates into streams of childlike associations that are sometimes random, and sometimes pointed.

When I visit and bring him the food he has requested, he refuses to eat it. "You eat it, Jay," he yells. "I don't want it. *You* eat it. Mother made it! Can't you tell? Mother made it!"

Al Pam apologizes on behalf of the hospital for the sudden staff changes, and he tells me that a new administration is swiftly downsizing so that from now on there will be only one social worker assigned to each ward instead of two.

"What you wrote about in your book is coming true here," he says. "I thought we were better than that, but it seems we're not anymore."

Things are changing so fast in fact, Al says, that he wants to get Robert to the open ward before there are *more* changes. Alas, though, when a bed becomes available on the open ward, Robert refuses to go there, declaring that he wants to remain where he is forever.

When I ask about doing something to protest Alan's abrupt departure—writing letters, making calls, asking for a conference—Al says he doesn't think anything will make a difference, that he feels truly helpless in the face of the new policies. Still, the violation of what everyone who has ever studied the care and treatment of those called chronically mentally ill is in agreement about—that continuity of care is the basis on which all care and treatment must rest—finds me writing a letter to the hospital's medical director, as much out of my need to vent my frustrations as in the hopes that my words will have effect.

In the letter, I say pretty much what I have said to Al Pam and to Dr. Guptan: that while Alan Epstein's "transfer may have satisfied institutional needs, it surely did not satisfy my brother Robert's very human needs."

> Robert had, since his arrival at Bronx State, come to rely on and trust Alan—they got along really well, on a daily basis, and Alan himself had said, only a week or two before his transfer, that "Robert was like a new person!" and that he thought Robert would be going to the open ward (Ward 12) within a week or so.
>
> So I write to express my dismay, and to ask if there is anything I might do—anyone I might write to—to see that such seemingly thoughtless transfers do not happen again, and do not adversely affect my brother, and patients like my brother. In a vulnerable and fragile life, when one comes to confide in somebody—to work with that person regularly—it is incredibly destructive and painful, it seems to me, when that person is suddenly taken away.
>
> What I kept thinking and wanting to say to the administrator responsible for the transfer, was: How would you feel if you arrived home one day and were told, "We're transferring your wife (or husband)—but don't worry,

we're going to get you a new wife in a week or so. She's coming from Wyoming." In Robert's life, a person like Alan plays at least as intimate and crucial a role as somebody's trusted spouse; moreover, given Robert's history, the fact that things are, once again, proving inconstant, and that he is helpless to control those things that control his life, can only exacerbate the situation. In addition, Robert now knows that if he is to graduate to Ward 12, and eventually to leave BPC, he must begin all over again the process of learning to trust—which also means having to let somebody new—a stranger—know the most personal (and often, in his mind, shameful) things about him: something most of us would have a hard time with, especially given the kinds of intimate matters, worldly and emotional, that a social worker would want to know in order to be of help to Robert.

I write the letter on a day after a visit with Robert—March 18, 1998—and in it I note that I was not surprised "to find Robert beginning to decompensate somewhat: His anger returned, his lack of concentration and focus returned, and his general calm and optimism—that had been building so wonderfully and sweetly—suddenly began to disappear."

I register my unhappiness with what seems "administrative thoughtlessness," and conclude with questions that, after nearly forty years of dealings with state institutions, still seem to need asking: "Do the people who make these decisions ever stop to think of the impact such transfers have on individuals like Robert—and of the difference the presence of someone like Alan in Robert's life—as a steady, constant presence—can make? And of the difference the *lack* of constancy and continuity can make in such a life?"

For anyone who doubts that conditions are sometimes as bad now as they have ever been for many patients institutionalized in city and state facilities—the horror stories as maddening as they were in previous decades, when books such as Mary Jane Ward's *The Snake Pit* (1946), Albert Deutsch's *The Shame of the States (1948)*, and Susan Sheehan's *Is There No Place on Earth for Me?* (1982) alerted us to the scandalous conditions in state mental hospitals—a 1998 essay by Kevin Heldman, "7½ Days," will serve as a sobering corrective.

Heldman, winner of the 1998 National Mental Health Association award for excellence in mental health reporting, checked himself into Woodhull, a New York City hospital, saying that he needed help, that he was depressed and was thinking of killing himself.

General hospitals like Woodhull, as Heldman reminds us, "have become the primary providers of inpatient care in the United States in recent years because of the profound reduction in the number of beds in state psychiatric hospitals." While deinstitutionalization has emptied out or closed state hospitals nationwide, the rate of psychiatric admissions to general hospitals continues to rise—in New York City, for example, from 40,477 in 1990 to 55,281 in 1996.

What Heldman discovers, alas, is that for men and women with acute psychiatric problems—especially if they are counted among the uninsured poor—matters are at least as dreadful as they ever were. Despite the improved means of care and treatment at our disposal, Heldman's experience suggests that for those most in need—especially those who do not have friends or families to care for them and advocate for them—there has been little if any progress in the past quarter-century.

Heldman's experience at Woodhull convinces him that "despite years of public awareness, many of the problems that fueled the deinstitutionalization movement have yet to be resolved," and that "the current inpatient model is remarkably similar to what psychologist David Rosenhan described in his classic study, 'On Being Sane in Insane Places,' published 25 years ago."

Heldman summarizes Rosenhan's project and conclusions:

Based on an experiment in which participants entered psychiatric hospitals undercover, Rosenhan described an environment where staff members were casually indifferent to patients, abused them verbally and segregated themselves. Patients experienced an almost traumatic sense of depersonalization: admission, discharge and diagnosis criteria were arbitrary; and patients' natural reactions to staff mistreatment and to the hospital setting were misattributed to their psychiatric disorders. The overall environment was custodial rather than therapeutic.

Heldman's description of his 1998 experience is at least as alarming and disturbing as Rosenhan's, more so when one considers the twenty-five years that have passed. Heldman is given medications without their being identified, and without explanation. The admitting psychiatrist (who sees Heldman eleven hours after Heldman is locked up) interviews him briefly and, despite Heldman's protests, with the door to the interview room wide open. Staff members are, at best, indifferent and, at worst, lazy and abusive. Heldman does not take a shower for an entire week and no staff member seems to notice. Heldman sees a social worker once in his seven and a half days—when the social worker gives him his discharge date and paperwork. Heldman is provided with neither his "Notice of Status and Rights," nor the name and phone number of the Mental Hygiene Legal Service, both of which the staff is required by law to give to all patients. Nor is the legal status of his admission, his right to request a court hearing (for release), or the amount of time he can be detained ever explained to him.

When Heldman describes his life on the ward, he could be describing the worst wards I visited twenty-five and thirty-five years ago and wards not very different from some Robert has lived in more recently. "In the middle of the ward is a large nursing station, a Plexiglas cage with a small opening near the bottom of one window similar to a subway clerk's booth," he writes. "Patients sleep, pace the floors, go in and out of their rooms aimlessly. They spend their days being stuffed with television, snacks, medication and cigarettes, begging one another for pay phone quarters.

"All told," Heldman writes, "I stayed in the hospital for seven-and-a-half days. I was locked up, never told when I would get out or how I could get out and never informed of my rights. Hospital staff made almost no attempt to get to know me or my problems. I spoke with a psychiatrist for approximately six minutes over the course of six days on the ward. I was provided with virtually no counselling or other substantive treatment. I refused Medicaid coverage, and was informed that I would be billed $1,400 dollars a day."

Given the change in policies at Bronx Psychiatric Center, Al Pam decides on a change in strategy. He is afraid that Robert's frustration, anger, and melancholy—along with habits bred by years of institutionalization—may cause him to regress to old ways and prevent him from being accepted on the open ward, which Al sees as the only long-term hope for him at Bronx Psychiatric Center. Therefore, Al decides to accelerate things, and to assign one of his therapists (an intern in psychology) from Ward 12 to Robert while he is still on Ward 15, so that she can begin working with Robert and preparing him for the transfer to Ward 12, after which she will continue to be his therapist.

The therapist, Carol Ornstein, completing her doctorate in clinical psychology, was a corporate lawyer for ten years. Carol telephones me, sometimes from her home at night, to talk about Robert and she urges me to call her anytime, at home or at work. She tells me she has begun working with Robert in twice-a-week regular therapy sessions. In addition, she checks in on him every day, and works with him in other ongoing ways: She preps him for Ward 12 community meetings—talking with him beforehand and discussing his fears, anxieties, and concerns—along with his behavior: what would and would not be appropriate—and then talking with him afterward, about how things went, and—always—about his feelings.

She does the same thing with Robert before and after my visits, and when my son Aaron, newly moved to New York City, tells me he has decided—a first in his life—to visit Robert on his own, I give him Carol's phone number. He arranges a visit, and before and after, Carol talks with both Aaron and Robert about the visit.

Within six weeks, Robert's progress is so marked—and his own desire to get well, and to leave the hospital, so much stronger—that, when the next bed becomes available on Ward 12 and is offered to him, he accepts eagerly.

Carol is marvelous with Robert—firm, warm, thoughtful, direct—and Robert thrives on the individual attention. Carol loves working with him ("He is such a good listener," she says to me at one point. "He really *wants* to be heard. And yes—he is very funny too—but we already knew that"), and when I visit Robert, she spends time with the two of us. She is aware of how bright Robert is and, consequently, of how inadequate the general activities offered to patients—what passes for art therapy (filling in pages of coloring books), or music therapy (singing in a small room with an Asian graduate student whose English is minimal), or make-work (putting plastic eating utensils in plastic bags in a sheltered workshop)—are for somebody of his intelligence and imagination. She is trying to come up with activities that can, in her words, challenge and stimulate him, and she tells me she is looking into a computer program.

Although Robert does not fit the profile for the research project ("The Rehabilitation of Cognitive Deficits in Schizophrenia") that is providing the computers because his cognitive skills are too advanced, Carol persuades the project's chief investigator to let him be part of the project so he can use a computer, acquire computer skills, and—more important—so that he does not languish in boredom.

Robert loves working with the computer, and with Nadine,

the woman in charge of the project. He talks to me in virtually every conversation about how much he is enjoying it, about what he is learning, and about what he might want to do when he leaves the hospital.

When Aaron and Eli decide to visit Robert together, Robert is delighted, and when I say to him jokingly, a day before their visit, that I hope he won't forget to give his nephews their father's regards, he answers, without missing a beat, "Oh, Jay—don't worry about the kids, all right?"

The second time I visit Robert after Carol has begun working with him, the three of us go out to City Island together for lunch, and on this warm summer day—looking across Pelham Bay at people bathing and sunbathing on Orchard Beach, watching the sailboats come and go, eating outdoors on the restaurant's veranda, feeding the gulls and swans— Robert seems like someone who, for a few hours, he actually is: a most happy middle-aged man doing what anyone his age might be doing on a pleasant summer afternoon.

He is a bit nervous—how not on this, his first true day out in nearly a year?—but he is also calm and centered in ways he has not been for a very long time.

"Is it true you're going to be leaving soon?" he asks Carol, and when she says that it *is* true—she will be leaving in about a month, but that before her departure she hopes to talk with the intern who will become his new therapist—Robert nods, then says that this makes him very sad and that he will miss her.

I watch Carol swallow hard, but even this moment—and the silent knowledge we share of how difficult the separation is going to be, for both Robert and Carol—does not take away from the unexpressed pleasure we take, simply, from being here together, and from feeling the satisfaction that comes with being able to be here.

Carol says that if Aaron and Eli want to go out with Robert for a meal, or on any kind of outing, that can be arranged now too—they should call her and she will take care of the bureaucratic stuff—and, sitting across from my fifty-five-year-old brother and watching him become, by turns, sad and animated, quiet and talkative, pensive and exuberant— he eats a whole lobster for the first time in his life; he tells funny stories about his times in California, when he was a waiter at a restaurant in Monterey, and served the actress Kim Novak; he reminisces with me about old friends from Brooklyn; he talks about where he might want to live when he leaves Bronx Psychiatric Center—I find myself at least as happy and optimistic as he seems.

TEN

PATHWAYS TO RECOVERY

When the broken window was repaired and the stove began to spread its heat, something seemed to relax in everyone, and at that moment one prisoner proposed to the others that each of them offer a slice of bread to us three who had been working. And so it was agreed. Only a day before a similar event would have been inconceivable. The law of the camp said: "Eat your own bread, and if you can, that of your neighbor," and left no room for gratitude. It really meant the camp was dead. It was the first human gesture that occurred among us. I believe that that moment can be dated as the beginning of the change by which we who had not died slowly changed from prisoners to men again.

—PRIMO LEVI,
Survival in Auschwitz

Virtually all the new antipsychotic medications, especially the atypical medications such as Clozaril, Risperdal, Seroquil, and Zyprexa (known also by their generic names, clozapine, risperidone, quetiapine, and olanzapine), trace their efficacy to a theory that psychopharmacologists call the dopamine hypothesis. For more than twenty years now, this theory has provided the primary working hypothesis concerning the biological causes of psychosis, and, thus, the primary working theory that underlies most research and development of antipsychotic medications.

The dopamine hypothesis is based on the assumption that the psychotic symptoms of severe mental illness, and of the schizophrenias in particular, are caused by increases in dopaminergic activity in the brain. Dopamine, a chemical produced and stored in neurons, and transmitted from one neuron to another, performs a multitude of functions, many of which we have barely begun to understand. We are fairly certain, however, that dopamine located in the basal ganglia, for example, helps to regulate motor functioning, while dopamine located in areas of the limbic and reticular systems appears to be significant in the regulation of emotional control, and in the screening of stimuli.

Dopamine itself, indigenous to and created in the neurons, is a neurotransmitter—it carries messages across synapses from specialized sites on one neuron to specialized sites on another, and is received by receptors—dopamine receptors—and designated as D1, D2, D3, etc. (Studies so far indicate that Clozaril interacts with at least nine known receptors, though we do not yet know which of these receptors, or which combinations of them, mediate its special clinical efficacy, and therefore cannot predict for any individual which if any symptoms it will or will not affect.)

According to the dopamine hypothesis, it is excessive dopaminergic activity that leads to symptoms such as agitation, a failure to screen stimuli adequately, and disorganization of perception and thought. Dopaminergic activity, that is, can lead to what we classify as the symptoms of psychosis: to mania, hallucinations, delusions, catatonic behavior, distortions or exaggerations in thought, language, and speech, and disorganized or "floridly bizarre" behaviors.

Researchers further hypothesize that medications that decrease dopamine will decrease or arrest these so-called *positive* psychotic symptoms. (Most diagnostic nosologies divide severe mental illnesses into positive and negative symptoms — the negative symptoms include, principally, combinations of the following: blunted affect, apathy, extreme passivity, emotional withdrawal, social withdrawal, difficulty in abstract thinking, inability to experience or desire pleasure, marked restriction in range and intensity of emotional expression, marked inability in fluency and productivity of thought and speech, and — see also Bleuler's original concept — avolition: a marked "inability to initiate and persist in goal-directed activity" — an inability, that is, to have one's actions follow intentionally from one's thoughts and desires.)

"Modern psychopharmacology," Dr. Steven Stahl, clinical research director and professor of psychiatry at the University of California at San Diego Medical School, states in the opening sentence of his book, *Essential Psychopharmacology*, "is largely the story of chemical neurotransmission."

Although *within* neurons, communication between one part of a cell and another takes place via electrical impulses, communication *between* neurons takes place chemically. Once the transmission has taken place — a neurotransmitter chemically binding to a receptor — the interaction is reconverted into an electrical impulse within the receiving neuron.

There are already several dozen known and named neurotransmitters, the most notable being the biogenic amines: dopamine, serotonin (5-HT and 5-HT2A), acetylcholine (ACH), epinephrine, and norepinephrine; the amino acids: GABA, glycine, aspartate, and glutamate; and the neuropeptides.

"Based upon theoretical considerations of the amount of genetic material in neurons," Stahl writes, "there may indeed ultimately prove to be several hundred to several thousand unique brain chemicals. Originally, about half a dozen 'classical' neurotransmitters were known. In recent years, an ever-increasing number of neurotransmitters are being discovered as new members. That is, the classical neurotransmitters were relatively small-molecule-weight amines or amino acids. Now we know that strings of amino acids called peptides can also have neurotransmitter actions, and many of the newly discovered neurotransmitters are peptides."

The study of neurotransmission, still in its infancy, is not unlike what the study of the atom was in its infancy: Each new discovery—the opening of the atom to electrons, neutrons, protons, hadrons, quarks, pi-mesons, et al.—revealed yet more complex and wondrous worlds—new elements, new questions, new quandaries, new discoveries, new mysteries.

For example, although each neuron in the brain was originally believed to make use of only one neurotransmitter, we now know that many neurons have more than one neurotransmitter, and this knowledge has given rise to the concept of cotransmission and cotransmitters.

We are also learning more about ways in which the neuron itself, within the brain, changes and evolves. It is, as Stahl and others believe, "quite 'plastic,' changeable, and malleable," and the process of change (the neuronal plasticity) that begins *in utero*, we now know, continues throughout the life of the neuron. ("Information is indeed 'processed,' as the brain 'solves' its various perceptual, emotional, motor, and conceptual 'problems,' " Edward Hundert writes. "But evolution, in selecting for the best 'problem solver,' has presumably selected for maximum *plasticity*, not for innate ideas which 'fit' a given environment only.")

Contrary, too, to much that has been believed about brain cells dying and not being reproduced during our adult lives, recent studies concerning new neurons found in the hippocampus (discovered by researchers at the Salk Institute in California and the Sahlgrenska University Hospital in Goteborg, Sweden) conclude that neurons do replicate throughout our lives, and, as is the case with most cells, new neurons do come into being when others die.

The dopamine hypothesis, arising from the theory of chemical neurotransmission, is given credibility not by theory alone, but by many specific observations, including, most significantly, observations of the ways medications and other drugs affect dopaminergic activity.

We know, for example, that the effects of antipsychotic drugs correlate closely with their ability to bind to and block what are called postsynaptic dopamine (D2) receptors in the mesolimbic pathway, one of the four major known pathways in the brain through which dopamine neurotransmitters travel, and are (or are not) received by dopamine receptors.

We know, too, that stimulant drugs such as cocaine and the amphetamines also cause the release of dopamine and, when given repetitively, bring about extreme behavioral reactions—paranoid psychoses, manic flights—that are virtually indistinguishable from the symptoms of severe psychosis. When amphetamines are given to patients diagnosed with schizophrenia, for example, the amphetamines exacerbate these psychotic symptoms in extreme ways that closely mimic the symptoms of paranoid schizophrenia.

While it is generally agreed that the new atypical antipsychotics such as Clozaril have become the most effective medications we have for treating psychosis (psychiatrists and psychopharmacologists frequently tell me Clozaril is "the gold standard" by which all other antipsychotic medications must be measured), especially for treating long-term or so-called chronic schizophrenia, it turns out that the atypical antipsychotics block *less* dopamine than the earlier generation of antipsychotic medications such as Thorazine and Haldol did.

Clorazil is, in fact, a *weak* blocker of the D2 receptor—the receptor that most antipsychotic medications are thought to act upon, and the one now considered central to our understanding of the presence or absence (rising or falling)—the etiology—of psychotic symptoms.

At the same time, Clozaril turns out to be a fairly strong antagonist (blocker) of another group of neurotransmitters, largely composed of serotonin (5-HT and 5-HT2A). And the ability to block serotonin appears to allow these new atypical antipsychotic medications to alleviate the negative symptoms of psychosis too.

Less, that is, becomes more. Clozaril and other atypical antipsychotics seem to restrict their effect largely to a single dopaminic pathway in the brain, the mesolimbic, at the same time that they do *not* block as much dopamine in the three other major known pathways: the mesocortical, the tuberinfundibular and, most important, the nigrostriatal.

The nigrostriatal pathway (which projects from the substantia nigra to the basal ganglia) is believed to control our bodily movements, and when dopamine is heavily blocked in this pathway, as it is by drugs such as Stelazine and Haldol, the results are not merely the slowing down of physical movements but, if dopamine is blocked for extended periods of time, neuroleptic-induced parkinsonism (effects that mimic the symptoms of Parkinson's disease — tremors, muscle stiffness, and slowness of motion), and irreversible conditions such as tardive dyskinesia — involuntary and irregular movements of mouth, tongue, lips, hands, arms, and limbs (e.g., the writhing and/or zombielike movements of patients when treated with heavy doses of earlier generations of antipsychotic medications).

Numerous studies confirm what researchers note as this key and welcome finding: that Clozaril, and to a lesser degree the other atypical antipsychotics, are greatly more selective than typical antipsychotics for the mesolimbic dopamine pathway than they are for the nigrostriatal pathway. In addition, although earlier antipsychotic medications blocked more dopamine (Haldol, for example, blocks more than 80 percent of D2 receptors), they blocked fewer serotonin receptors (Haldol blocked virtually none). Clozaril, on the other hand, as we have learned from PET scans, blocks only between 30 and 60 percent of D2 receptors, but 85 to 90 percent of 5-HT2 (serotonin) receptors.

Psychopharmacologists conclude that it is overactivity specifically occurring *in* the mesolimbic pathway that mediates the positive symptoms of most psychoses, and that it is, therefore, the blocking of the postsynaptic receptors specific to this pathway that mediates the effectiveness of antipsychotic drugs, and that accounts for their ability to greatly diminish or arrest psychotic symptoms.

The atypical antipsychotics, then (when they work), appear to reduce both positive and negative psychotic symptoms more effectively because they restrict their effect largely to the mesolimbic pathway, thereby reducing symptoms without creating the most troublesome extrapyramidal side effects. (Clozaril actually seems to be helpful, at times, in *arresting* the symptoms of tardive dyskinesia, and, according to Dr. Samuel Rofman, was originally used in V.A. hospital clinical trials in the late seventies in the hopes it would prove helpful to veterans who had developed tardive dyskinesia.)

Not all researchers agree concerning the validity of the dopamine hypothesis. In a 1997 article ("Schizophrenia, Psychosis, and Cerebral Spinal Fluid [CSF] Homovanillic Acid [HVA] Concentrations"), in *Schizophrenia Bulletin*, researchers from the University of Texas Health Science Center state that "the evidence from studies of HVA levels in CSF strongly negates the hypothesis that dopamine turnover in the brain is increased in patients with schizophrenia, as a group." They conclude that "a substantial number of studies, including the current one, have found levels of HVA in CSF and the severity of psychosis to be significantly correlated. The evidence from nonschizophrenia patient populations is, if anything, stronger than that in schizophrenia patients," and that "it is possible that in the schizophrenia group the effects of long-term treatment with dopamine-receptor-blocking agents and changes in CNS [central nervous system] dopaminergic function over the course of chronic schizophrenia tend to obscure the relationship between CSF levels of HVA and psychosis in this illness."

"With cerebrospinal fluid (CSF) studies producing weak or negative findings," Drs. S. E. Chua and P. J. McKenna write in a 1995 article ("Schizophrenia—a Brain Disease?

A Critical Review of Structural and Functional Cerebral Abnormality in the Disorder") in the *British Journal of Psychiatry*,

and after it became clear that post-mortem studies would always be confounded by the effects of neuroleptic treatment in life, hopes of a definitive answer to the question of a functional dopamine excess in schizophrenia came to rest on studies using functional imaging to quantify D2 receptor densities in drug-naive [medication-free] patients. Unfortunately two studies using positron emission tomography (PET) and sophisticated methods of analysis have produced completely contradictory results, and five further studies have found evidence of at most minor alterations in D2 receptor numbers.

"With a genetic theory facing limitations and with the dopamine hypothesis showing little prospect of resolution," they continue, "biological approaches to the etiology of schizophrenia have come to rely increasingly heavily on attempts to identify a structural or functional brain abnormality in the disorder—the lesion of schizophrenia. Opinion on the status of this work is divided, even polarized."

Chua and McKenna, having reviewed the research, claim that contrary to assertions about brain lesions and changes in brain size providing the evidence for designating schizophrenia as a brain *disease*, "methodologically rigorous studies," reveal "no convincing evidence," from either postmortem studies and/or neuropathological findings relating to questions of reduced overall brain size in schizophrenia, or of size reduction of basal ganglia, limbic subcortical nuclei, or of the hippocampus.

In place of the dopamine hypothesis and of brain disease theories, Chua and McKenna favor an approach that sees schizophrenia as a disorder that is both clinically and etiologically heterogeneous—one in which brain pathology will prove to be subtle rather than gross, and in which brain pathology will take "the form of quantitative differences that must be isolated against a background of often wide normal variation."

They suggest further — a preliminary hypothesis — that the functional imaging abnormalities we see may themselves be associated "not with schizophrenia but with certain schizophrenic symptoms," and further (based on evidence from MRIs and other similar tests) that schizophrenia may be "associated with a subtle form of hypofrontality that only becomes apparent when the prefrontal cortex is challenged with a cognitive task" — i.e., that what is termed a neurological "vulnerablity" or "predisposition" to schizophrenia in an individual results in a diagnosis of schizophrenia only when the neurological predisposition is activated by particular *experiences*, and by the complexity of experience as it makes itself felt in the brain, and, in particular, as it alters and is altered by "normal reciprocal patterns of activation between anatomically related areas of the cerebral cortex."

Intriguing, too, to those who study the brain and its relation to psychosis is the fact that, as far as we know, most antipsychotic medications — both typical and atypical — act upon the parts of our brain located in the subcortical areas, the limbic system, basal ganglia, reticular system, and brainstem, and *not* in the cerebral cortex.

Yet it is the cerebral cortex that we posit as being responsible for most of what we think of as being uniquely human: perception, complex cognitive processes, reality testing, initiation of behavior, judgment, imagination, language, and all those acts, thoughts, and feelings we believe create and derive from consciousness — and, thus, as being responsible for most of the behaviors and symptoms that lead us to decide that an individual is more or less mad.

To this point in time, however — another indication of how rudimentary and provisional our inquiries into and understanding of the brain are — virtually all major psychopharmacological research is devoted *not* to what happens in the cerebral cortex, but to biological dysfunctions taking place in the *other* two major regions of the brain: the brainstem (and its attendant structures) and the central core (which includes the limbic system and basal ganglia).

What we do know, however, and with a fair degree of certainty, is that whenever there is increased dopaminergic activity in the mesolimbic pathway that accompanies positive psychotic symptoms, there is frequently a parallel decrease of activity in the prefrontal cortex, and this decrease correlates with a decrease in negative psychotic symptoms.

"The exact relationship between these phenomena is not fully understood at this time," the *Handbook of Clinical Psychopharmacology for Therapists* states, and continues, in a passage indicative of the complexity of current research: "It has been suggested (Bachus et al. 1996) that hypofunction of the glutamate neurons, which interconnect the four main areas shown to be abnormal in schizophrenia (prefrontal cortex, mesolimbic, striatum/nucleus acumbens, and medial temporal lobe), may be the underlying pathophysiology. The different neurochemical basis dictates alternative treatment approaches. . . ."

Until recent decades we made our suppositions about how the brain worked based largely upon observed behavior, from postmortems performed on individuals who had suffered brain injuries, or from the study of brain diseases. But in the last quarter-century, and for the first time in recorded history, through newly developed and developing neuroimaging techniques—PET scans, CAT scans, SPECT scans, and MRIs—we are beginning to be able to actually look into the *living* brain while it is functioning. This allows researchers— as in the study of the actions of atypical antipsychotics (where one can observe radiolabeled medications binding with known receptors)—to view actual metabolic activity in the working brains of living human beings.

Although the brain is hardly, as *Time* would have it, "finally giving up its secrets," new technologies are allowing us to see into parts of it, to isolate localized areas, and to perform experiments that provide us with data about sites of drug action or binding, and about changes between pre- and posttreatment status of particular brain structures.

At the same time, new laboratory procedures allow neuroscientists to analyze neurochemical by-products found in blood, urine, and spinal fluid, and thereby to help us gain additional knowledge about the underlying pathophysiology of the brain.

Along with new technologies and knowledge have come new theories, and while the dopamine hypothesis is currently in the ascendancy, even those who believe most devoutly in its general correctness know that scientific hypotheses are put forth in order, as in the article by Chua and McKenna, to be modified, disproven, rejected, and supplanted.

Research that tests old hypotheses and suggests new ones, then, is ongoing, expanding, and expansive. Researchers who work in genetics, for example, are trying to identify "abnormal" genes, and the consequences such genes might have on the molecular regulation of neurons in individuals diagnosed with schizophrenia, hoping to discover if there is some degenerative process that somehow "turns on" a gene genetically, and if there might be some pharmacological agent that could "turn off" such unwelcome and destructive processes within genes.

However, as Dr. Kenneth Kendler, director of the Psychiatric Genetics Research Progam at Virginia Commonwealth University, reminds us, "DNA contains the recipe for making human organisms in the form of 3.3 billion base pairs, any one of which might have a mutation that causes schizophrenia. The base pairs make up 80,000 to 120,000 individual genes. Mutations can occur in individual base pairs, or whole pieces of chromosomes may split off or be arranged."

We are making some progress concerning psychiatric disorders, especially in drug development, Dr. Kendler believes. Still, he notes, "we do not understand on a fundamental, biological level what causes these disorders."

Some researchers favor neurodevelopmental approaches, and hypothesize that the disease process in mental illnesses may be the result of abnormal brain development that begins early in life, and that such illnesses may be amenable—our new understanding of neural plasticity making this a possibility—to selective therapeutic applications, even in adults, by using genetic therapies capable of "instructing" the genes of the developmentally abnormal neurons.

Because the precise neurochemical dysfunction in individuals diagnosed with bipolar disorder has not been established with anything like that of the schizophrenias (where we still work, largely, in the dark), theorizing about its biochemical and neurological etiology has been more speculative, and the precision of our diagnoses and prognoses, along with what, based on diagnosis and prognosis, we prescribe, remains tentative, changeable, and fallible. Thus, for example, while Robert's principal diagnosis for more than twenty years has been bipolar disorder, he has responded well to Clozaril—better, in fact, than more than 50 percent of those diagnosed with schizophrenia.

The "kindling model" of mood (or affective) disorders, which include bipolar disorder along with depression, for example, hypothesizes that the symptoms of bipolar disorder are the result of cumulative subclinical biochemical changes in the limbic system, and that a progressive buildup of these changes causes neurons to become more and more excitable, until the point at which they issue forth in observable symptoms. This model often attempts to explain treatment resistance by showing how acute events in one's environment have long-lasting effects on brain chemistry and microstructure. Based upon what we know about neural plasticity, researchers theorize that acute psychosocial stresses such as separations and losses affect gene expression. While first episodes of bipolar disorders, for example, may be provoked by life events, the theory hypothesizes that bipolar episodes subsequently take on a life of their own, with one episode seeming to kindle another, even in the absence of psychological stress.

About thirty years ago, researchers observed that a hormone of the adrenal gland, cortisol, was hypersecreted in depressed patients. We already knew that the secretion of cortisol from the adrenal gland was controlled by the secretion of another hormone, called ACTH (adrenocorticotropic), and this hormone, too, was elevated in blood levels of depressed individuals. Further research revealed that a peptide hormone, corticoropin (CRF), caused the secretion of ACTH, and that CRF was *also* hypersecreted in drug-free depressed patients. Utilizing this knowledge, researchers are now trying to develop a CRF receptor antagonist as a new treatment for severe depression. In addition, experiments with nonhuman primates (and rodents) show that severe abuse in early life can cause a permanent increase in the gene expression for CRF; so researchers are following this trail also to see if a causal connection can be made between severe childhood abuse and adult depression (if such a connection applies to humans), and if, then, a medication can be created that will "turn off" the CRF gene.

Another theory, the "chaotic attractor" theory, is predicated on a presumed biochemical defect that leads to dysregulation of neurotransmitter synthesis. Relying on chaos theory and on the knowledge that the dysregulation itself is consistent, researchers hypothesize that the varying symptoms of bipolar disorder—either mania or depression—may depend on physiological or environmental conditions of the given (and random) moment.

Some studies have been attempting to identify genetic transmission of bipolar disorder through a specific gene on the X chromosome, while some twin studies are attempting to elucidate the importance of shared environmental factors. And, as with schizophrenia, there is in the study of mood disorders a good deal of ongoing research that focuses on excitatory and inhibitory neurotransmitters, neuroendocrines, and neuropeptides—along with the study of subtypes of central and peripheral GABA receptors, and dopamine receptory subtypes—in the hopes that, as with the dopamine hypothesis and the atypical antipsychotics, a viable neuro-biological hypothesis might lead to the creation of effective psychopharmacological interventions.

Before the discovery of antipsychotic drugs in the early fifties — Thorazine and lithium, together with the first antidepressants and minor tranquilizers (iproniazid, Tofranil, Librium)—the study of the possible biological origins of psychosis was lim-ited to investigations of psychological dynamics, and/or to simple descriptive nosologies; the specialty of psychophar-macology was virtually nonexistent.

None of the early medications for the treatment of psycho-sis, in fact, were developed specifically for mental illnesses, or were developed or discovered as a result of a particular theory of neurochemical dysfunction. Nor were their mech-anisms of action at all known. It was only accidentally that we discovered their utility for reducing psychotic symptoms. Thorazine, for example, was developed originally for the treatment of traumatic and surgical shock, and lithium as a salt substitute in the treatment of heart disease (cf., also, the use of the anticonvulsants Tegretol and Depakote, usually prescribed for epilepsy, as mood stabilizers for my brother Robert and others).

The discovery that drugs like lithium, Thorazine, Haldol, and Tegretol could alleviate symptoms of mental illness, however, seemed to provide the first firm evidence that psy-chosis had some kind of *physical* basis (cf. the theories of Kraepelin and of the early Freud), and that physiological modes of interventions could be successful in treating psy-chosis.

In a special 1998 issue of *Schizophrenia Bulletin* devoted to the newest research on the pathophysiology of schizophre-nia, the editors review the history of the ways we have, until now, understood the workings of the brain and of disease processes, and they point out that it was only during the 1960s and 1970s that our understanding of the pathophysiology of psychosis began to be based upon our knowledge of neurotransmitter dysfunction.

Hopes for cures for mental illness at that time rested in part on the successes in our researches concerning the causes for, and treatment of, Parkinson's disease. As was the case with Parkinson's disease, so it was believed with schizophrenia: Dysfunctions characteristic of psychosis were assumed to be occurring in brains where so-called normal neuroanatomical structures were intact; from such hypotheses came the notions that "chemical imbalances" were responsible *for* schizophrenia.

Since then our study of and understanding of the brain's neuroanatomy has increased enormously, and with this new knowledge has come a new respect for the brain's extraordinary complexity, along with, one hopes, the elimination of simplistic neurological, genetic, or biomedical theories that, often, are only the old "bad seed" theories gussied up in pseudoscientific jargon. For to permanently eliminate or engineer away genetic material we hypothesize as being the cause of an illness, or symptom, may be to eliminate an entity that, in itself and in its interactions with other genetic and neuronal elements, may serve humankind well in other settings (e.g., sensory gating "deficits," which in a hunter-gatherer society might make sensitivity to all incoming stimuli an asset), and may, also, unknown to us, be responsible, in its neurological and biochemical interactions, for processes we currently regard as beneficial.

Postmortem studies — ongoing and increasing in number (there are now several well-endowed "brain banks" in the United States) — and *in vivo* neuroimaging studies of the brain, for example, have begun to reveal not merely chemical imbalances in the brains of those diagnosed as schizophrenic, but a variety of hitherto unknown and unexpected neuroanatomical abnormalities.

"Models of neurochemical imbalance have begun to give way to models of disturbed neural circuitry," the editors of *Schizophrenia Bulletin* explain. "These new models have be-

gun to take into account the interplay among different neurotransmitter systems and the complexity of different modes
of neurotransmitter release and receptor responses. In addition, concepts of neurodevelopment, including the *genesis*
and programmed death of individual neurons throughout the
life cycle are now being integrated into these new pathophy-
siological formulations" (italics added).

Even as we embark on these new journeys of discovery,
however, journeys that greatly increase our understanding of
the brain and of disease processes, and that thereby increase
the possibility we will find better ways of ameliorating many
of the symptoms (and perhaps the causes) of madness — what
seems clearest is not merely that this journey is itself new,
and is scientifically, humanly, and intellectually exhilarating —
we *can* at last begin to see into the living brain just as we
have previously been able to see, for example, into living
muscles and organs such as the heart, kidneys, and lungs —
but that we have barely begun our journey and have no real
idea of what discoveries lie ahead, or of what uses we may
be able to put them to.

"Our knowledge of brain neurocircuitry and physiology,"
the editors of *Schizophrenia Bulletin* say in a noteworthy un-
derstatement, "is still grossly incomplete in many areas."

But how could this not be, given the complexity of *any*
single human brain, a living and endlessly changing and
evolving wonder in which there are more potential synaptic
connections than there are particles in the entire known uni-
verse?

As an indication of just how complex the study of what we
call mind is, consider that researchers estimate there are at
least one hundred billion neurons in any individual brain,
that each of these neurons is capable of making connections
with at least ten thousand other neurons, and that each neuron can itself send out up to a hundred messages per second.
And as an indication of how complex the study of mind and
brain is in relation to madness — and of how little we know,

and how early our explorations — consider the following "Abstract" from this special issue of *Schizophrenia Bulletin* for the concluding essay, "A Candidate Molecule Approach to Defining Developmental Pathology in Schizophrenia":

The evidence that schizophrenia may have its origins from early in life, possibly during prenatal brain development, is based primarily on a constellation of nonspecific anatomical findings and on the results of surveys of obstetrical complications and of childhood neurological and psycholgical adjustment. The developmental processes implicated by this evidence are uncertain, but speculation has centered around abnormalities of neuronal proliferation, migration, and connection formation. These developmental milestones are the results of complicated cellular processes involving molecular interactions between cells and between the extracellular and intracellular milieus. To understand how these abnormalities could relate to schizophrenia, it is necessary to characterize the molecular events that define the processes. In this article, we discuss the potential impact of a number of molecules that are important in the sequence of cellular events implicated in schizophrenia. In particular, we focus on molecular mechanisms related to cell proliferation, axonal outgrowth, cell migration, cell survival, synaptic regression, myelination, and developmental aspects of early life. These various candidate molecules regulate different aspects of cell growth and cell-cell interactions and are involved in the regulation of deoxyribonucleic acid (DNA) expression.

"Very few of these molecules," the "Abstract" concludes, "have been studied in the schizophrenic brain."

Then, too, as Oliver Sacks, Israel Rosenfield, Edward Hundert, and other students of neurobiology have emphasized, whatever the causes of those conditions we call mental illness, and however the conditions are brought into being, they are probably best understood as diseases or conditions of *consciousness* and, therefore, given the changing and evolving nature of consciousness itself, not likely to be amenable, ever, to mechanistic understandings or treatments.

"To reduce a theory of an individual's behavior to a theory of molecular interactions is simply silly," Gerald Edelman writes, "a point made clear when one considers how many different levels of physical, biological, and social interactions must be put into place before higher order consciousness emerges. The brain is made up of 10^{11} cells with at least 10^{15} connections. Each cell has a fantastically intricate regulatory biochemistry constrained by particular sets of genes.

"These cells," he continues, in a summary of the complex processes we call consciousness, "come together during morphogenesis and exchange signals in a place-dependent fashion to make a body and a brain with enormous numbers of control loops, all obeying the homeostatic mechanisms that govern survival.

> Selection on neuronal repertoires leads to changes in myriad synapses as cells die or differentiate. An animal's survival and motion in the world allow perceptual and conceptual categorization to occur continually in global mappings. Memory dynamically interacts with perceptual categorization by reentry. Learning involving the connection of categorization to value (in its most subtle form within a speech community) links symbolic and semantic abilities to conceptual centers that already provide embodied structures for the buidling of meaning.

"A calculation of the significant molecular combinations of such a sequence of events, even in identical twins, is almost impossible," Edelman concludes, "and in any case, useless."

But even if research into the brain, and into new and improved medications that can more specifically target hypothesized disease sites, or combinations of sites, gives us reliable information about which sites are responsible for this or that symptom of this or that set of behaviors, or this or that state of being we call mental illness, what do we do when the illness itself, often from its onset, whether observable or not, is compounded not merely by ordinary experience, but by experiences that are themselves beyond what we ordinarily believe most human beings can bear? What if mental illnesses are compounded by lives that are themselves overladen and overwhelmed by experiences that are severe, traumatic, disabling, and persistent?

Since we now know that our experiences, thoughts, and feelings influence the very matter (and plasticity) of our brains — that the brain, and the infinite ways neurons are capable of interacting within it, can change and evolve throughout our lives *as a result of* our experiences, thoughts, and feelings — what do we do for individuals whose mental illnesses are caused and/or exacerbated by deadly, insidious ills that are, alas, all too common to many lives?

What do we do for men, women, and children whose mental illnesses are caused and/or exacerbated by poverty, by alcoholism, by drug abuse, by acts of violence, by illiteracy, by incarceration in prisons, by institutionalization in mental hospitals, by homelessness, and by other serious and/or chronic medical problems?

What do we do when mental illness, to whatever degree, is caused or exacerbated, or both, by early childhood experiences marked by abandonment, malnutrition, terror, violence, emotional abuse, physical abuse, sexual abuse, and by the absence of those things — love and kindness not least among them — most of us believe are the birthrights of all children, and are essential to all those developmental processes that ordinarily accompany the adjectives "healthy" and "normal"?

How, at any moment of life, knowing biologically what we have always known humanly — that traumatic, loveless, terror-filled childhoods severely and malignantly — biologically, psychologically, *and* developmentally — determine who we are in our minds and in our bodies and in our feelings — how, knowing this, do we hope to enable individuals afflicted not merely with mental illness, but with childhoods and adult lives wounded in the extreme by worldly conditions and by gross misfortune—misfortune that is itself miserably complicated by individual acts, choices, and judgments that often are or seem to be irreversibly destructive to self and to others—how do we even begin to aid such men, women, and children and to help them to find and journey along paths of recovery?

When I ask one prominent psychopharmacologist what his hope for the future is—what, in his opinion, would make the greatest difference in the next half-century for individuals with mental illness—his answer, echoing what I hear from others, is swift and unequivocal: "Clozaril without side effects."

But if there are no systems in the world that are organized so as to allow an individual taking Clozaril to make use of its beneficial effects in a sustained way, what then? If, like my brother, individuals with long-term histories of madness and of institutionalization—along with homelessness, poverty, drug abuse, prostitution, incarcerations, and violent acts perpetrated and/or endured—suddenly, through the agency of medication, come back literally and clearly to their senses, what do they do then? If medications suddenly and miraculously alleviate symptoms—and even their *causes*—what do these individuals do in the next hour, day, month, or year of their lives? What do they do, for starters, with regard to the basics of life—food, clothing, shelter, education, finances, and employment? What do they do with their desires for friendship and love? What do they do with their fears and their sorrows?

Beginning in the late summer of 1997—two weeks before Robert's transfer from Staten Island to the Bronx—when I am in New York City to visit with him, I also begin spending time at Pathways to Housing, a not-for-profit organization that has its main offices on West Twenty-third Street in Manhattan. Pathways to Housing was founded in 1992, and its mission, according to its one-page Mission Statement, is to "end homelessness" for individuals who are both "homeless and have histories of psychiatric disabilities."

"While there are many organizations in New York City that provide housing for people with psychiatric disabilities and/ or substance-abuse problems," the Mission Statement says, "Pathways is unique in that it provides housing to people who do not meet the traditional restrictions of housing providers. Pathways provides outreach, case management, rehabilitation, and acceptable housing options to people who fall outside traditional prerequisites for housing and have been labeled 'unmanageable,' 'treatment resistant,' or 'not ready for housing.' They have therefore been unable to navigate the social service system to find the help they need, and have thus remained on the streets, in the parks, in transportation terminals, subway stations, and in public spaces of New York City."

What differentiates Pathways from other organizations that attempt to serve individuals and families who have co-occurring conditions of mental illness, homelessness, and substance abuse is, simply, that Pathways is dedicated to working with those people whom others reject, and whom others believe have passed beyond the possibility of treatment or recovery.

What also separates Pathways from other such organizations is its remarkable record of very real successes.

Beginning in 1993, Pathways personnel went out in the streets, alleys, shelters, parks, and subway tunnels of the city, and actually *gave* housing to homeless people with psychiatric disabilities, after which the organization provided them with a full range of mental health services.

Pathways organized its own ACT teams (case managers, nurses, psychiatrists, psychologists, vocational and educational rehabilitation specialists, and peer support specialists), and these teams worked with clients to enable them to find apartments; to find medical, psychiatric, and psychotherapeutic services; to find food, jobs, substance-abuse programs, day care, and schools.

At the end of Pathways' first five years, its clients had a housing retention rate, for all 248 clients served since 1993, of 85 percent, this rate based upon clients being stably housed for two years or more without relapse into homelessness; i.e., Pathways' total dropout rate, for all 248 clients over this five-year period, was 15 percent.

For a comparable period, and for a similar population (and using methodologically identical criteria to evaluate outcome), the city of New York reported that its housing retention rate was 60 percent. The city's rate, however, was based upon a homeless population in which the very clients Pathways was serving—because such clients were deemed "not housing ready"—had been selected out.

"For most housing providers," Pathways' Mission Statement explains, " 'housing ready' means to have been 'clean and sober' for a period of months, to have agreed to participate in 12 step and other programs, to be taking psychiatric medications if needed, and to have had no history of violent behavior."

In other programs that serve homeless men and women who have coexisting psychiatric and substance-abuse problems, clients move along a linear continuum where they must constantly earn their freedom and privileges, and can "graduate" to independent, supported housing based upon their demonstrations, to staff, of an increasing adherence to fixed sets of rules, expectations, and behaviors. In other programs, clients are rejected *for* housing and removed *from* housing for violating rules: for not taking their medications, or for taking and selling drugs, or for being charged with a criminal offense. In the Pathways program, clients lose their housing only by losing it in ways any citizen or tenant loses housing: by not paying their bills, by having the police discover they are running a drug den, by acts of violence, by creating disturbances intolerable to neighbors, etc.

What Pathways did, that is, was to separate homelessness from treatment. What Pathways did was to treat homelessness by giving people homes, and then to treat mental illness by intensive and individualized programs that sought out clients, and actively worked with clients—and with a commitment to work with them for however long things might take—in order to address their emotional, psychiatric, medical, and human needs, and on a twenty-four-hour, seven-day-a-week basis.

Pathways, which was the first agency in New York State to employ ACT teams, became the first program in the United States to offer homeless street-dwelling men and women with dual (and triple, and quadruple, and quintuple) diagnoses immediate access to independent apartments of their own. Pathways did not put people in group homes, or in proprietary homes. Pathways did not require that individuals be off drugs, or be taking their medications regularly (though case managers encouraged them to do these things), or be obeying curfews. Pathways did not require that individuals not have criminal records, or not wear jewelry, or not have facial hair.

"Street life," the Pathways Mission Statement explains, "renders people incapable of managing the most basic daily routines, and affords people little room to contemplate matters such as treatment or recovery. For these reasons, Pathways provides people with housing *first*, so that they may find a reprieve from the war zone that is homelessness.

"Assistance is then provided to access services and begin the long journey through the rehabilitation process," the statement continues, and it lists some of the many kinds of assistance Pathways teams of experienced and reasonably well-paid ACT teams provide for Pathways clients, actively and persistently. (Case managers, called service coordinators at Pathways, earn $30,000 to $35,000 per year; ACT team leaders earn $40,000 to $45,000; and the director of programs, promoted in 1998 from his position as a team leader, earns $65,000.)

When I visit the West Twenty-third Street offices, I rarely find service coordinators there, since they are out of the office at least 75 percent of the time, working with clients—in their apartments, in the courts, in stores (shopping), on job sites, at schools, at medical centers, in doctors' offices. Approximately 49 percent of the ACT team members are fully salaried peer specialists, and these peer specialists have all experienced either mental illness, homelessness, or major substance-abuse problems, thereby, Pathways believes, providing "models of recovery for tenants and staff."

After I have spent some time with one service coordinator, Hugh Murphy, a six-foot-seven middle-aged Irishman (and divorced father of a teenage daughter) with a dramatic handlebar mustache, he tells me he was in Creedmoor for five years when he was a young man, between the ages of sixteen and twenty-one, that he had many insulin coma treatments, and that, when he was on the insulin coma ward in Creedmoor, he used to play chess regularly with my brother Robert.

Pathways staff, the Mission Statement says—and at a cost for each client ($15,000 in 1997–1998) well below what it costs the city of New York to provide a cot in a municipal shelter, and nothing else: no case manager, no apartment or room of one's own—"helps every tenant develop a rehabilitation plan that is tailored to individual needs, and to learn the skills required to maintain an apartment. Each tenant also receives assistance in planning for long-term goals such as continued education, job training, and reconnecting with family and friends." Moreover, as Pathways notes in a 1998 paper prepared for SAMHSA, the Pathways ACT teams "differ from other ACT teams for the dually diagnosed in that the tenant is an active participant in formulating the service plan and in determining the frequency and intensity of services."

"Providing housing first," the Mission Statement asserts in its concluding paragraph, "gives people a tremendous incentive to obtain treatment so as to keep the housing and maintain it."

In addition to having a major psychiatric disability and having been homeless, most clients served by Pathways since 1993 suffer from many of the other ills that have troubled our inner cities in recent decades: poverty, malnutrition, sexual abuse, substance abuse, child abuse, crime, alcoholism, lack of education, lack of decent medical care, and lack of hope. Doubtless, too, as critics might charge, and as all Pathways clients and staff I talk with agree, these individuals have often collaborated with the world, and in large, terrible, cruel, stupid, lazy, and ingenious ways, in their own suffering and undoing.

All Pathways clients have been diagnosed as having major psychiatric disorders, and virtually all have spent considerable amounts of time in city and state psychiatric wards. Fifty-eight percent of Pathways' clients have had major substance-abuse problems, and a majority of these clients have spent time in detoxification and drug rehabilitation centers. All Pathways clients have been homeless for extended periods of time, all have been frequent victims of crime and violence, and nearly 60 percent have criminal records.

Pathways is, then, an organization dedicated to providing care and treatment for a population as difficult, intractable, desperate, miserable, and needy as any in America. Yet not a single one of the dozens of Pathways clients I spoke with, no matter their lives or the extent of their psychiatric disability, told me that the criminal justice system or the mental health system or their families or society or plain bad luck, genetic or otherwise, was the cause of their ills. They all, and in their own ways—no common language here—refused to consider themselves victims, and eagerly talked about taking and wanting to take responsibility for their own lives, past, present, and future.

"We are all mirrors of one another," Louise Carr tells me,

"and that's why when I work for Pathways, with the clients, I never forget where I came from. I never forget that once upon a time I felt helpless and hopeless and lost, had a low self-esteem, and didn't believe nobody cared. So I know that I'm not the only one that's like that. So I reach out now. I don't look back, but I remember, because we should never forget where we come from and we should never boast or brag or be too proud or put a person down because we could be right back where we were any minute."

Louise, a forty-year-old African-American woman who works forty hours a week as a security guard for Prestige Management, in the Bronx, and part time as a volunteer for Pathways, was first hospitalized for mental illness when she was twelve or thirteen. Louise was born in Queens—in Jamaica Hospital (the hospital where my mother received her nurse's training)—and grew up on Long Island. After her early hospitalizations, Louise lived in various children's shelters and foster homes. At the age of about seventeen, she became a street person and spent the next dozen or so years homeless and on drugs, moving in and out of hospitals, jails, and makeshift dwellings in subways, alleys, storefronts, and abandoned buildings. One of Louise's sisters died at twenty years of age, of a drug overdose.

"I used to dream that one day I was gonna grow up and have this big house and help everybody," Louise tells me. "I didn't know who I was going to be helping, but I remember that dream—this was when I was going in and out of foster homes and psych wards, detox centers too sometimes—and I dreamed I was gonna grow up and be married and have kids like my mother and father and be living in a house."

Louise laughs. "I was kind of a daredevil when I was a kid. Like remember those old light poles, the wooden ones? I used to climb to the top of them," she says. "Now I got a place of my own—one bedroom with a living room a little bigger than this room [about ten by eighteen], and a kitchen as long as this room, and I got my kitty cat—that's her name, Kitty Kat—and if I see somebody out there, even if I know they doing drugs or something, I still give them a quarter or try to at least give them some advice, tell them about Pathways. Because charity consists of giving people things the way you be picking up a stone up off the road so nobody trips or hurts themselves. And I don't forget that. I remember when I thought nobody cared, and I try to show people that people care because they might not see it yet the way I didn't see it. Oh I didn't see it for a long time, and I was at the point where I gave up even trying to see it."

Louise talks about the times when, homeless, she would try to talk other homeless people out of living in abandoned cars, and of how she lived in the subways, washing up at fire hydrants, changing clothes in subway tunnels, and of how it was love, she believes, that helped her through.

"Love is so strong," she tells me several times. "Love is so strong that even if people don't always come back the way we like them to be at, if you just show them love—enough love—that would give them enough to go on and get to the next day, because even if people lose all hope, at least they know in their heart and soul that there is somebody that loves them, and people need that.

"Look at me," Louise says then. "I didn't believe nobody cared until Pathways. That's why I say we are all mirrors of one another. That's why I say even if you only show your love to a poor, hungry dog, that's love too."

Dolores Keane, an African-American woman in her early forties, tells me that she is about to go into a detoxification center for twenty-one days. This will be the third or fourth time she has gone into a detoxification center since, five years before, she started working with Pathways. Despite having given up two of her six children to foster care—she became pregnant with three of them against her will, she says—and despite recurring drug and psychiatric problems, Dolores has remained stably housed for five consecutive years. This, she and her service coordinator believe, reduces the risks to her, to her children, and to others, and gives her "a step up" toward recovery.

"I was living under the Brooklyn Bridge," Dolores tells me, "in this big pothole—and I slept in other places you wouldn't believe. Sometimes I went ten-twelve days without sleeping, and then I'd be in these psych wards, where it was even more scary—you wouldn't believe, getting raped and stuff there too—and then I got hooked up with Pathways.

"So I'm not sleeping on the street no more. I got a place of my own and that's good because I never was good room-mate material. Because there's nothing like, you know, just having your own place. And you don't have to worry if somebody else don't like you to stay up late, and you can open your refrigerator however many times you want to, and you can invite people over when you want, and nobody telling you what to do all the time."

Dolores makes no excuses for her life and is heartbroken about having given up her children, but says she knows she wouldn't have been able to give her children a healthy home. She is optimistic about the future—at group meetings I attend she is outspoken and militant about people taking responsibility for their lives and their actions—and she takes a long view of what is needed for her life to change.

"I don't give up, though," she says. "Once I set a goal, that's it, and I meet that goal—whether it's relationships or stopping smoking or whatever, only I just don't seem to take regular inventory of my shit sometimes, see. I mean, I'm not perfect. I'm not dressing up my shit. But I stay focused mostly, as far as what I have to do and not be a failure, and it's like a miracle I'm still here."

Like Louise and Dolores, Jean Baba Gogard tells me the main thing that makes Pathways different from other organizations and places he has known is that "Pathways doesn't give up on you."

Jean works out regularly, weight lifting and doing pushups daily (he sometimes does two hundred pushups in the Pathways office while waiting to meet with his service coordinator), and riding his ten-speed bicycle—his pride and joy—everywhere; he has a broad, cocoa-colored face, with short, light curly hair and, though he is in his mid-forties, the trim, muscular body of a well-conditioned man ten years younger. Jean came to the United States from Haiti, with his sister, when he was fourteen years old.

He has spent time in many emergency wards and psychiatric hospitals, including Bellevue, Manhattan Psychiatric Center (five years), and Mid-Hudson, a forensic mental hospital (where Robert lived for a while). He has also served several years in prison, once for nearly killing a man. Although he takes his antipsychotic medications regularly, he tells me that he continues to hear voices all the time. He works part time at odd jobs: moving and hauling, mostly, and he has also worked, for long stretches, as a waiter (at Lundy's, in Brooklyn), and as a bellhop.

For nearly four years now he has been working with Pathways, and he meets with his service coordinator every day. If he doesn't seek out his service coordinator, the service coordinator comes to him.

"I like having my own place," he tells me. "I have a bedroom and a living room, and it's more comfortable—people don't tell you what to do, you know what I mean? Nobody messing with your mind the way they do in prison, or in the shelters. I used to sleep in the subways, and I talk to myself sometimes and sometimes I lose my temper bad.

"That's why my case manager is important. I got a good job now, with a moving company, and I want to keep it, and my case manager he work with me every day—I'm trying to get my sense, to keep it, you know—and he sit down with me and see how my job is going or help me to get work. Stuff like that. You know—'How you doing today, Jean?' and 'Are you taking your medicine?'—and sometimes when I start working I get sick again, so what happens is I know he get me through and started after, like when I did this roofing job but I got sick and started talking to myself again."

I talk with Eve Sorella, an African-American woman in her early thirties. Eve is well dressed, and very direct and articulate. She works as a nurse's assistant, approximately thirty hours a week, but intends, with support from Pathways, to go back to college and get a degree in business. She rolls her tongue around a lot while we talk, and her lips tremble; she apologizes, telling me these are side effects from medications she is taking. Eve has been homeless since the age of twenty-one, has had major drug addiction problems, has been a prostitute, and was hospitalized for nearly five years for schizophrenia.

"I grew up on fast food," she tells me, laughing. "And I've been trying to get out of fast food ever since. I've been in fast food from when I was seventeen, but it's time to change and I plan to go back to school no later than December or January. I've tried college two times, once when I was working as a nurse's assistant, but it was too hard for me because the medications make me suck my tongue and get my lips to shaking all the time the way you see, only worse, and I had cramps in my neck and *everything* would shake—my feet and legs too—but I was afraid to lower the doses because I was afraid I'd start hearing the voices again.

"Sometimes I still hear them. I don't know what they're saying but I know they're talking to me—and sometimes I get very paranoid and think *everybody* is staring at me, and that something really terrible is suddenly going to go wrong. This happens when I go into stores, or just riding the subway sometimes.

"When I was growing up I thought I was going to have an easy life—work as a nurse, and get a good job, and get a boyfriend and have kids, and raise a family—I thought it was going to be a piece of cake—but I got involved with some girls and they were users and I starting being a user too. Cocaine.

"But with schizophrenia—I always heard the voices but I thought *everybody* was hearing them—it becomes very hard to concentrate, because sometimes you can be thinking about one thing and your mind is on another." She laughs. "Sometimes that works for me, you see—and sometimes it works against me."

Eve tells me that she is a member of a clubhouse in the city, and that they refer her to social groups. She wants to be able to "socialize on a higher level," she says, and with people who have been *successful*. Although her apartment is in a run-down neighborhood in the Bronx, she loves it and wants to keep it until Pathways can help her find a better one.

Three years ago, she also tells me, when she went back on cocaine, she became pregnant, but she lost the child.

"I guess God said it wasn't time for me to have it," she says.

"I lived in South Carolina, in a small town called Hemenway, about sixty-five miles from Myrtle Beach, until the age of thirteen," Thayer Gamble says. "I was a runaway. I was, as they said back then, a very bad kid. I started drinking at a very young age, you know—when I was ten years old—but never got into the heavy drug scene until later in my life."

Thayer Gamble pauses, looks down at his wrists—they are both heavily scarred, from suicide attempts—then looks straight at me, his eyes unwavering.

"I don't read or write," he says.

Thayer Gamble is forty-one years old. He is a neatly dressed and well-spoken African American who talks slowly, measuring his words thoughtfully. He wears a New York Yankees baseball cap, and has a close-cropped beard. Thayer has an eight-year-old son he has not seen since the boy was four months old. Thayer has been in psychiatric hospitals, diagnosed as having paranoid schizophrenia (his present psychiatrist thinks that borderline personality disorder, with impulse control disorder, is a more accurate diagnosis). He has spent time in detoxification centers and in prison (for armed robbery, domestic violence, dealing and using drugs). He has worked as a house painter, a roofer, and construction worker. He has also been a male prostitute.

"I've done everything that there is that you can name, you know," he says. "I'm not proud of it. I feel sometimes that if I would have stayed home and been a child, maybe then all this excess baggage that I have carried around for years and years—maybe I might have gotten rid of it."

When he was a child, Thayer's father beat him frequently, and also beat his mother.

"One time he tied me to a tree and beat me," Thayer says. "He's still alive and I try to have communication with him, but it's very difficult. When I went to visit him to help him put a new roof on the house last year, he started in on me again, and my sisters told me to leave because he was going to get the gun. When I was a child he always told me, 'You better run from me because I'm going to kill you.' At least once a month now I try to mend things, but there's a lot of hatred there, I think, from both parties."

Thayer tells me he has been very abusive toward women, and that he believes he inherited some of this from his father.

"In my self-conscious mind," he explains, "the seed was planted, and I lived out my life exactly like my father told me I would when I was a boy. As a child I said that *I* could never do that—what he did—but sometimes you try to control somebody else because you feel bad about yourself. Before I ever see my son again, I want to be certain I would never do to him what my father did to me. He'd be better off without me if that was the way.

"There was always this void in my life, you know. When I was a child, in school, they just passed me along from one grade to the next even though I couldn't read or write, and I would spend my time lost in these dreams. I can't remember the dreams, except they were there all the time. But I got married eventually, and I started beating my wife, accusing her of things that she wasn't doing, imagining what was not there.

"I spent eight hundred dollars on cocaine some nights, and if you had the cocaine you had the women, and having the cocaine—I liked it—made me feel that all my insecurities were gone. I was the life of the party, and could talk to anyone, but I could never pinpoint these other feelings that made me want to kill myself and I would never consider myself as a person with a psychiatric problem.

"But then I cut my wrists. I cut all the arteries and my tendons and nerves and everything. I almost lost my left hand. I had talked with psychologists before this, for help, but they said the only reason I was acting out was because I was using drugs. I used to tell them no, I'm using the drugs because the drugs make me feel good, make the void go way. They told me it was the drugs, but in reality I was trying to kill myself all the while, you see."

Thayer talks openly about his marriage, his hospitalizations, his drug addiction, and his prison experiences. He tells me about a woman he lived with, with whom he fought constantly, and how the woman had him arrested.

"I felt at the time that I could not live without her, and I didn't want to ever live without her, you know," he says. "Actually, I think that what I was doing was using her as my medication. I wasn't using drugs at this time. I think I used her as my medication since I didn't go back on the drugs, you see. Because my entire focus was on satisfying her and proving to her that I was a good man and that I was really trying to prove that to myself, you know, now that I look back on it. But I thought I could keep her from leaving me, and be the perfect person, but it didn't work. No matter how much I did for her it seemed all I really did was push her away, further and further from me." He nods. "Eventually I ended up going to jail for domestic violence. I did a year at Riker's Island for domestic violence."

Thayer has been in the Pathways program for nearly five years. In the weeks before he found out about Pathways, he was living in a shelter, and one of Pathways' service coordinators, Ben Tallerson, came there and told Thayer about Pathways. Thayer began going to Ben's office, talking with him, telling Ben about how depressed he was, and about how every time he walked across the bridge to Ward's Island, he would think of jumping into the river.

"I tried to be a very consistent person then," Thayer says. "And I kept telling doctors about all the crazy feelings going through my head, and eventually, with Ben's help, I changed hospitals and started seeing the doctors at St. Vincent's. I tried to be very consistent and to talk with them. And I found that those doctors were listening to what the patients were saying. And the doctors at Metropolitan, where I had been, were listening to what they wanted to hear. And this made a big difference to me."

Thayer tells me about how, before he met Ben Tallerson, he was sleeping in shelters, or in Central Park, eating out of garbage cans, and that he realizes he had *chosen* the life he had.

"I didn't care if I lived or died," he says.

After he started working with Pathways, he continued to have major problems. "But," he says, "they keep an eye on you even when you don't realize it. Sometimes when Ben would try to talk with me I would give him holy hell, and he called the cops on me three or four times because I was threatening to stab people. But they didn't give up. That was the key. They didn't give up."

They believed him, Thayer tells me, and they believed in him. "They stuck with me right from the start, and now I live in the building they picked for me." Thayer smiles. "It's a gorgeous building—with, you know, locked doors, and laundry in the basement, and police officers on the premises, and since this past November, although I'm still a member of Pathways, my apartment is no longer in Pathways' name. My apartment is in my name.

"I'm still in Pathways because I choose to be a member, and I don't want Pathways out of my life because I'd be scared without them. I need the support system. But my apartment is in my name. I pay my own rent. I pay all my bills myself. I have a banking account. I have a savings account. I have a checking account. I do practically everything for myself now. I have no desire to do drugs. I look forward to waking up in the morning, taking care of business, you know. And I just thank God. And I am no longer on medications either."

Thayer works part time — often off the books — doing plastering, Sheetrock work, masonry, scaffold work. He also does jobs for some of Pathways' offices and apartments. He tells me that Ben Tallerson knows everything about him — his entire life — and that there are no secrets between them. Even when Ben is not getting paid, Thayer says, he is there for him. When he has had hard times, Pathways staff have come to his apartment and sat with him, talked with him, gone to the doctor with him, and waited all day long with him in medical centers.

"I wouldn't have made it without them," he says. "I wouldn't have gone to the doctor and waited all day long. I probably would have been out there doing drugs again and hurting people and losing everything I had."

Now that he has an apartment, work, and friends, and now that he is also stable medically, Thayer has set himself several other long-term goals.

"I want to go back to school," he says. "I want to learn how to read. I think I can learn to read, you know. They keep telling me that I can — I was tested. Sometimes, like when I meet a woman, I am very embarrassed. I'm illiterate. I don't know how to read or write.

"But before I do that," he adds, "I want to see my son. If I can't be a father to my son, I would at least like to be a friend and to let him know that I can take my responsibility now. And let him know he has a family, and a father who still loves him even though I didn't before — even though I wasn't there for him when I should have been."

"I was running Project HELP for the city of New York," Dr. Sam Tsemberis, executive director of Pathways to Housing, tells me, "which was like a psychiatric emergency room on the streets. We'd find people who were mentally ill on the streets and bring them to Bellevue with or without their consent, but my feeling, increasingly, was that most people didn't need to go to Bellevue. They needed something else, and the only something else I knew in the system at that time were these drop-in centers that were like Christian Science Reading Rooms for the homeless and mentally ill, where they could at least get some meals and some rest from wandering around.

"Then I started working with Bill Anthony—this was in 1991—and we got a grant to open a drop-in center on West Forty-eighth Street, and we got pretty good at getting people who were very disturbed to come off the streets into these centers. And you know Bill Anthony, right? Well, with Bill, the whole approach is: Whatever you want, we'll get it for you. So you want spiritual—we'll get it. You want emotional, you want psychiatric, you want food? But not housing.

"These people were actively delusional, and suicidal, and they were actively using. And it was impossible to get them into the housing system because they needed to be clean and sober, and drug free, and on the *right* medication, and off the *wrong* medication, and a hundred other things. The whole system, you see, is set up on the premise that housing and treatment are the same thing. But what the housing providers had done was simply to create smaller, hospital-like institutions in the community—which is an incredibly confounded way of thinking about mental illness and housing. I approach housing from a homelessness pespective, so that the solution for homelessness for the mentally ill is the same as the solution for homelessness for the nonmentally ill."

Sam and I are sitting in his twelfth-floor office on West Twenty-third Street. It is late afternoon, and after talking with me, Sam will still have more work to do—he is trying to meet a deadline for a grant proposal—before he takes the subway home to Brooklyn. Sam recently moved to Brooklyn and lives near Grand Army Plaza, a few minutes from the brownstone my son Eli is living in. Sam's building is about a twenty-minute walk from the apartment building, across

the street from Prospect Park, in which my parents were living when I was born, and about a half-hour walk from the
apartment Robert and I grew up in.

Sam is forty-nine years old. He is a strikingly good-looking
man—six feet tall, well built, with a swarthy complexion, a
healthy shock of salt-and-pepper hair, and a close-trimmed
salt-and-pepper beard that accentuates his large, brown eyes.
His features are broad and strong, but when he smiles,
spider-web wrinkles fan out from his eyes, and everything
about him softens.

Sam married for the first time three years ago, and he and
his wife, Cherie, an M.D. who is medical director for the New
York City Department of Mental Health's Crisis Intervention
Center, have a two-year-old daughter, Elena. Sam plays tennis regularly and competitively, and were he not sitting at a
desk piled high with psychology books and papers, and were
people not coming into his office regularly to talk about grant
proposals and landlord problems, I might feel as if I were
sitting in the office of a middle-aged Greek-American movie
star who had recently become the CEO of a major motion
picture company. Sam is enthusiastic, warm, direct, and very
focused.

He was born in Skoura, Greece, and when he emigrated
to Montreal at the age of seven, he spoke only Greek. He
grew up in one of Montreal's immigrant communities until
he was ten, and then in a mostly Jewish neighborhood near
Montreal's Jewish Public Library. He attended public elementary and high schools, and Concordia University. After
he graduated from Concordia, he worked as an elementary
school math and art teacher in Montreal, and in New York
City, where for a year he taught at a Greek-American school
on the West Side.

His father, who started out in Canada as a driver of
eighteen-wheel vehicles, eventually went into and succeeded
in the restaurant business; he wanted Sam to join him in the
business, but when Sam returned to Montreal from New
York City, he continued to work as a teacher, teaching drama

and special education. Because he believed he could be better at helping children with special needs if he knew more psychology, he returned to New York and earned a master's degree from The New School, and then a doctorate in clinical psychology from N.Y.U.

"The history of housing and treatment," Sam says, "goes back to the institutions, in my opinion. Listen: Have you seen the photos of what happened when they went to empty out a lot of the large state hospitals? Well, there are photos of many of these people—elderly people, for the most part—and they were all holding these new suits, on hangers. Do you know why?"

I say that I don't.

"They were burial suits. When these men and women were put in mental hospitals, you see, they brought the suits with them—it was understood they would be there from beginning to end. A life sentence. A death sentence, really, I guess. And they were ready. But that's where a lot of the idea comes from, about people being housed *and* living in treatment. Only it turns out that people with mental illness are not necessarily dysfunctional as far as their ADLs—their activities for daily living—go.

"When your brother is denied housing, they don't say, 'Robert, do you like having a place of your own with a key and privacy and your own toilet, where you can take a shower when you want, watch TV when you want, have people over when you want, have a beer if you want?' They're not assessing that. They're assessing: Will this guy take his medication? Will he go to group? Will he meet our curfews, or whatever their requirements are.

"So we separated housing and treatment. If you fuck up as a tenant, there are consequences the way there are for anyone else. And we try to help you to avoid screwing up. But if you relapse or have a crisis, or if your psychiatric disability acts up, the criteria are different. It takes a lot to survive on the street, you know, and the skills transfer: You learn who to trust, and how to get a meal, and how to budget your money, and how to shop and how to bargain and how to use public transport and how to keep warm and how to get your laundry done.

"But it's hardly an enviable life, and I guess I would argue, finally, that housing should be a basic human right. That's what we say in our literature and proposals and the rest. If you don't have a place to live, who *are* you, and how can you do anything and even begin to make a life?"

In Brooklyn, Sam and his family live across the street from the library where I spent many hours when I was a boy. I talk about still being close friends with men and women with whom I grew up in the neighborhood where he and Eli now live. When Sam reminisces about his early years in Montreal, I ask him what, given this childhood, he thinks might have led him to the kind of work he does.

"It's really simple," Sam says, smiling. "I discovered when I was doing my internship at Bellevue that I was good at it. I did good work. I could make a difference. And I felt for these people.

"I didn't have the easiest childhood myself, or the kindest environment—my father was a very abusive guy—abusive and unpredictable: a deadly combination. He was mood driven, and went from tyrannical to very loving. Being a Greek immigrant in Montreal marginalized me for sure, if you want to see things in terms of the psychology of childhood — not speaking English and being ostracized and the rest—and even as a kid I can remember closing my eyes and going to sleep and wishing that when I opened my eyes I would be back in Greece.

"But this is only a *personal* way of explaining things. I think that I do what I do also because it is an incredibly rewarding job. Being able to actually impact somebody's life, and for the good. In most of the mental health business you're working as a cog in the wheel. Individual-based solutions can be rewarding. Sure. But for the first time I was getting a taste of *systems*.

"I always studied systems. My specialty as a clinical psychologist was family systems, and for the first time I found myself in a position to actually have an effect *on* systems — family and community — and to create programs, and to make a difference that would outlast me. Because if I leave here tomorrow, there are six or seven people in Pathways who can do my job and do it well, and Pathways would keep going. I mean, I never ran an agency like this before and I'm doing a lot of work I don't want to be doing. Personnel and administration — man, I hate that stuff. But suddenly, you know, you see people — lots of them — who were psychotic and homeless and worse, and they're doing *well*. They have new lives, and at the end of a day — yes — I can feel I helped make a difference."

When Sam talks about homelessness and mental illness, he talks with great intensity, and with passion. He does not believe that Pathways creates or can create miracles, and he does not believe its way of doing things is either the best or the only way to provide housing and treatment for people who have psychiatric disabilities and are homeless — there are, in his words, *lots* of things that work — but he does believe that having a place of your own significantly improves the chances of your mental health improving.

"There's always a line," he says. "Every organization and program has a line, and if you cross over the line they don't serve you. That's how you define a program. We do *this* — but we don't do *that*. And the minute you take that kind of approach with people who have lived with lifelong rejection and failure, you know they will fail again, and are going to find that threshold — that line of yours — and cross it and then end up out on the streets again, thereby confirming their own sense of worthlessess, pain, stigma, and whatever else.

"What *we* do is we take away their money. We become the representative payee, and that's the line we draw. So that their rent and utilities are paid by us. And we require that tenants meet with their service coordinator a minimum of twice a month, and to consider participating in our program's money management plan."

Sam shrugs. "The demands are consistent for all our people, but we apply them flexibly. For instance, if a person coming off the streets after years there feels distrustful about agreeing to money management, we don't deny them housing services. But—and this happens with most of our people after a while—we work with them so that they take increasing responsibility for their own finances. That's the aim. But until then we'll keep cutting checks, smaller or larger, and having the service coordinator stay on the case so that we do the best we can to keep them housed, to keep them on their meds, and to keep them off drugs."

I suggest that what Pathways seems to be trying to do is to systematically build in, as a programmatic element, the equivalent of unconditional love. No matter what their clients do, it seems, Pathways never gives up on them.

"We're working on a manual now," Sam says, "and the manual will spell out what we do—the core values, the basic components—asking people what they want, separating housing from treatment, using ACT teams and peer support, making the system tenant driven, and the rest. But unconditional love?" Sam smiles. "I'll buy that. It *is* a love thing. Call it what you will, but I think that love is at the heart of it. Otherwise, why are we here? What's it all for? I'm not embarrassed to talk about love. Love is a component. Love is real. Love is good. It doesn't conquer all, but if you listen, people will tell you what they need, you know, and what they need—especially if nobody has ever cared for them or about them—is love.

"So we build that in—we try to—and we let the tenants tell us what they want and what they need, and we write grant proposals and we get money from the feds and the city and the state, and we go out and argue with landlords who put locks on the doors of our clients because they can get higher rents now that the city's in good economic shape than they were able to get when our clients first moved in. We're just out there twenty-four hours a day, seven days a week."

Sam picks up a stack of paper, glances at it, then shakes

his head sideways, eyes closed, in anticipation of work he would rather not have to do.

"This grant's about writing a manual so that what we do here is replicable elsewhere. We can export this," he says, referring to the paper in his hand. "We can tell you that a viable case load is ten clients, and that if you're a case manager you can't come back to the office and tell your supervisor the person wasn't home. You wait. You search. You find. You make sure things happen. And you make sure you hire people—peer specialists—who have been there themselves, and who know, and who have recovered. You can build in accountability—that's the *good* part of managed care—parameters and indicators that ensure you're practicing the program the right way."

Sam looks at the sheaf of paper in his hand, as if surprised to still find it there. He puts the papers down on his desk, and shrugs.

"We're not doing anything fancy," he says.

EPILOGUE

INTIMATIONS OF POSSIBILITY

In some ideal village of my imagination, when my brother Robert leaves his apartment in the morning and walks to the local library—he has worked there as a staff assistant, in charge of the art and music division, for the past six years—he stops first at the newsstand near his home, buys a copy of *The New York Times,* and exchanges morning greetings in elegant Sign with Arnie, the deaf newsdealer, a man who has known him since Robert was a child. Then Robert walks to the local bakery for the cup of coffee and bagel he gets each morning on his way to work. Usually he will sit in the bakery's coffee shop for a half hour or so, reading his paper, and talking and kibitzing with others who regularly frequent the bakery at this hour of the day.

But if, on any given morning, as happens several times a year, instead of waiting patiently in line with others, or reading his paper, Robert becomes impatient and begins demanding immediate service—if he begins harassing people who come into the bakery, or who work there, and if nothing anyone says or does calms him, what I imagine is that the store's owner—a baker, like our grandfather—will come out from behind the counter, put his arm around Robert, and talk with him.

The baker has known Robert for many years—*his* father worked as a baker with our grandfather—and he also knows me. The baker invites Robert into his apartment in the back of the shop as he has before. Would Robert like to call me? Would he like the baker to call me? Maybe Robert would like to have his coffee and bagel by himself, or to be left alone for a while.

If Robert says, "Yes, please call my brother," but if I am not at home, and if Robert becomes increasingly agitated and difficult—if he goes back into the store and starts accusing people of taking his place in line, say, or stealing his newspaper—the baker will telephone somebody else: a friend, a coworker from the library, Robert's niece or nephews, one of our cousins. Or perhaps the baker's son, home from college, offers to walk Robert home, or to the library. Perhaps somebody else jokes with Robert, or comforts him by word or by touch in a way that enables Robert to gain control of himself. Perhaps Robert suddenly closes his eyes, shakes his head, and says he feels fine now—really—that he was just having a difficult morning. Mornings, he might say, joking with the baker, can sometimes turn out to be like bagels— very hard, right?

But if Robert's behavior becomes more alarming—if he becomes manic and enraged, or if he begins to weep uncontrollably, or if he threatens to harm himself or others, or if he talks rapidly in ways that make no apparent sense, I see that somebody else, not the baker, has gone and fetched the local policeman.

In the ideal village of my imagination, the policeman knows Robert. He has been with Robert when Robert experienced some of his worst breakdowns, and he has known Robert in the life Robert led before and after these breakdowns. Several times, in fact, it is this policeman who has driven Robert to the state mental hospital a few miles away. The policeman might have gone to high school with Robert.

Why not? Perhaps they were on the tennis team together, or on the literary magazine, or in the chess club. Perhaps on Sunday afternoons, now, they play chess together in the nearby park.

In the ideal village of my imagination, I watch Robert leave the bakery with the policeman, and I listen to the policeman talk with Robert and find common ground with him—safe places, far from Robert's anguish and confusion—by discussing the weather, or the planned addition to the local library. I watch the policeman and Robert drive through town in the patrol car—Robert does not resist getting into the car—and I am comforted because I know that Robert trusts the policeman, and with good reason, since the policeman is a kind and thoughtful man who is experienced in dealing with Robert at times like this.

I watch Robert and the policeman pull up in front of our local medical center. I enter the building with them, wait with them in the waiting room, and then watch as Robert goes into the doctor's office to talk with the doctor—or no, not with the doctor but, better still, with a psychiatric nurse who has known Robert for many years and who, in fact, three years before, married our cousin Gabriel at a wedding both Robert and I attended.

In the meantime, the policeman, or the baker, or somebody else who was in the bakery has telephoned the library. Or perhaps—given how grim, until recent years, so much of my brother's adult life has been, why not let these imaginings be rich with the possibility of hopeful beginnings, satisfying middles, happy ends?—an elderly neighbor, a retired teacher from our high school who spends many hours in the library these days, researching a history of our village, and who has known Robert since he was a boy, when Robert was as delightful and mischievous as any child in the village—perhaps this neighbor, arriving at the library about now, will explain to the head librarian that Robert seemed to be having a hard time this morning, and has gone to see his doctor.

What this neighbor knows, having himself spent seventeen

months in the state mental hospital when he was in his mid-twenties, at a time when the only treatments for mental illness were electroshock (and lots of it), insulin shock, wet sheet packs, seclusion, restraints, chloral hydrate, and some nasty barbiturates, is that times like these are the hardest of all—harder in many ways than the days and months that come after incarceration, because they are more purely frightening. These are the moments when you fear the return of all previous terrors, and fear that with the old terrors will come new ones so awful that you will *never* regain your sense, and never again return to ordinary life.

These are times when the darkness seems so vast that you see no reason to go on living—times when the rage rising up in you is so powerful that you are afraid it will make you, and everything around you, explode and decay. For others, the elderly neighbor thinks, a bad morning, or a bad day, or a bad week, is usually just that—a bad morning, or a bad day, or a bad week: times that are, perhaps, informed by sadness, or anxiety, or feelings of frustration, anger, or gloom. But if you have not been where he and Robert have been, you are usually fairly confident that, as before, the bad times will eventually pass, and that life will go on pretty much the way it had been going before the hard times came.

If you have been where this man and Robert have been, however, a morning like this may carry with it the weight of all the terrifying and desperate mornings of your life, mornings that have turned into days and nights in which all sense and all human kindness—all faith in those people, things, and feelings that even on a good day give you a most fragile purchase on this world—will seem gone forever, and in their place only immeasurable sorrow, confusion, despair, or fear. If you have been there, this man thinks, then you know.

I watch the nurse talk with Robert. She does not ask him how he is feeling, or if he feels safe, or if he stopped taking his meds, or what precipitated his difficulties this morning. Instead, like the policeman, she talks with Robert about ordinary things: about the day care center in which she has put her two-year-old child, or about the U.S. Open, which began the week before. She tells Robert she likes the bowtie he is wearing, and that she wishes her husband, our cousin Gabriel, would wear bowties, and would take pride in his appearance the way Robert does.

That evening—I have been out of town researching a novel set in New York City at the turn of the century, and that has to do, I suspect, with a Polish immigrant who works underground as a laborer in the construction of the new IRT subway line—I return home to find several messages on my answering machine, about Robert and from Robert. Robert says he has had a rough day, and asks if I can stop by—there's no rush, no need to call—but if I get back early enough, before, say, ten-thirty, he would appreciate a visit. I should just come over.

It is a fifteen-minute walk to Robert's house, and I take my usual shortcut, past our elementary school, along the river, and through the town's old cemetery. When I arrive at Robert's apartment, he offers me a glass of wine—he does not drink wine himself, since it interacts badly with his medications, but he knows I like wine, and so he always has some on hand for me—and he asks me how my work went, how my children are doing.

And how come, he asks, does it happen that every time *I* go out of town, *he* seems to go out of his mind?

He smiles then, and talks with me about his day, and about how he is still a little shaken up by it. He tells me that he and the nurse decided to make a slight adjustment in his medications, and that he has also scheduled an extra session with the psychotherapist he sees once a week. He'll see her tomorrow morning, he says, and after he tells me this, his eyes suddenly grow large with delight, and he says that the *main* thing he wanted to tell me is that he spent his afternoon break at the library—he was able to put in a half-day—researching the trip we've been talking about taking, and using a new computer program to try to locate the summer camp we went to as children.

"Listen, Jay," he says. "I found out that it's still there. It's still *there*, Jay, and I spoke with my boss at work, and we arranged it so I can take a week off in August, any week I choose, so what I was thinking was that the two of us could go there together. And maybe we could go up to Saratoga also, and play the horses the way we used to. Or go to the ballet. The New York City Ballet is there now. So what do you think, Jay? What do you think?"

I tell him I think it's a great idea, and then we look at a calendar together, and at a map, and we talk about hotels, and who we might see on the way there, or on the way back—friends, cousins—and the next morning, after Robert has seen his therapist, he telephones me from work, and tells me that . . .

Although many of us, especially in dark and lonely times, like to imagine that when troubles come there will be help available for us within a community not unlike the help we often conjure up in the villages, families, and neighborhoods of our imaginations, most of us, these days, live in what Steve Leff, director of the Human Services Research Institute in Cambridge, Massachusetts, calls "prosthetic communities."

Many of us live far from the places where we were born—far from the families, nuclear and extended, we grew up with, and far from the communities in which we were raised. Many of us, like the men and women Pathways serves, don't even know where our families are. If services for severe mental illness—emergency or ongoing—exist at all, they usually exist in places set apart from the larger community in which we reside, and the services are usually provided by people who have not known us during our previous hard times (or good times), and who may not know us at all until the moment of our great, desperate, and terrifying need.

Instead of living in places where we know and are known by others—where we have long-term relationships not only with friends, neighbors, colleagues, priests, rabbis, ministers, teachers, storekeepers, townspeople, cousins, aunts, uncles, nieces, nephews, and grandparents; or long-term working relationships with medical and mental health professionals we have come to know, and to rely on—most of us are dependent on ever-changing, underfunded, fragmented, and inadequately constructed systems of service. Most of us who need care and treatment for acute psychiatric disorders receive our care and treatment in shelters, behavioral care residences, emergency wards, halfway houses, adult care facilities, day care centers, nursing homes, and state hospitals—and from human service organizations, support groups, social workers, case managers, respite workers, mental health aides, peer support centers, residential counselors, telephone hot lines, clubhouses, and ACT teams.

Sometimes, in the relationships we create in a clubhouse, or a peer support center, or a hospital—or those that we create over time with a psychiatrist, friend, social worker, case manager, or therapist—we get lucky. Sometimes, as with Kate Fontaine when she was in Worcester State Hospital, or Robert, after he moved to the Bronx, we benefit from happy circumstances, coincidences, and convergences. Sometimes—as happens in lives that are *not* afflicted by major psychiatric disorders—we may happen to find what we consider the right relationship, the right place, the right person, the right professional, the right medication, or the right program at what seems like the right time—people and programs that not only help us survive, but that enable us to work, play, and love in ways that get us through, and *enhance* our lives and the lives of others. Whether we have experienced mental illness or not, when we think about what has made large differences in our lives—for good or for ill—luck and timing rarely prove to be insignificant.

When people call or write me, telling me that their child—or spouse, or brother, or sister, parent, or friend—has had a breakdown and is living at home, or has been hospitalized, or that they or their loved one have had a life not so different from Robert's, that the burdens have finally become intolerable, and that they wonder if I have any suggestions, what I have found myself saying often is that there are no maps.

Sometimes, if the person calling lives in a place where I know somebody, or know of people who might be helpful, I will suggest calling these people. If I don't know of anybody living near where they live, I will usually suggest locating a local Alliance for the Mentally Ill chapter, or calling NAMI's national office to find out where the nearest chapter is, in order to talk with others who have been where they are now, and who have needed assistance, and who have probably spent many days or years despairing of assistance. I may recommend calling the local DMH, or looking in the yellow pages for a local human service agency. If the need and situation are specific enough, I can sometimes give names and telephone numbers for organizations that have expertise in dealing with depression, or with depression *and* substance abuse, or with situations that might benefit from a particular medication or form of psychotherapy, or a particular type of psychosocial, vocational, or educational rehabilitation.

I may suggest talking with their primary care physician, or with someone from the local or regional school system, or with their priest, rabbi, or minister. I sometimes mention books and articles, and I usually say I will ask around, and that I will call people I know who live near them or who might be helpful. Have they heard of Gould Farm? Are they aware of the Pathways program, or of Odyssey House, or the clubhouse programs, or the National Empowerment Center?

I urge them to call me again and let me know how things are going, and I usually tell them that they are not overreacting—how could they be?—that living with somebody who has a mental illness, or *being* somebody who has one, is more than most of us can ordinarily bear, and I usually add a few general comments: about thinking in terms of care instead of cure; about thinking long-term instead of short-term; about trying to find another person—a case manager, a therapist, a social worker—who can put together a program of services and monitor it—someone who can be a locus of responsibility, authority, and accountability so that the family members can get some relief, and can attend to their loved one as sibling, parent, or spouse while somebody else attends to logistical details.

I may suggest that they think in terms of continuity of care—of trying to get a person or system in place that will stay in place *long-term,* since serious mental illness usually needs long-term management, often across a lifetime. If they can find such a person, I may recommend that, when the present crisis is over and things are calmer, they all work out a crisis plan together, for the future. I may encourage them to try not to have unduly high expectations, and to try to accept the fact that having a mental illness doesn't mean that anyone is to blame, and that going through a crisis, or a series of crises, doesn't mean that all possibilities for happiness or what passes for ordinary life are gone forever.

What interesting life is without conflict and struggle? I may ask. Do they know that recovery rates for individuals with heart disease and lung disease are way below those for people with mental illness? Are they letting unrealistic expectations and hopes disable them from enjoying and loving the person they know and care about? Are they feeling ashamed of, or humiliated by, a person—or a situation—when there is no reason for shame? Are they—understandably, given the views and attitudes of others—confusing difference with deviance, or illness with failure?

I will encourage them to try to enjoy and love their friend or family member not for who they wish that person to be, but for who he or she truly is, in all the wonder of his or her being, complexity, and mystery, and I will also urge them to make sure they take care of *themselves* while they are trying to take care of someone they love.

Alas, though, I will usually repeat, there are generally no maps—no clear pathways to recovery—because each situation is unique and will require a unique set of solutions; because services are often expensive, hard to find, and hard to come by; and because the only services we can usually find or afford are often provided by bureaucracies that are rarely human in scale, and have all the liabilities inherent in bureaucracies, and so are lacking in those very qualities essential to what we need: kindness, flexibility, imagination, and the ability to think and act in terms of complicated *individual* situations.

Alas, too, unless we can find a program nearby that works, and works for our particular situation, we often have to create our own systems: find the doctor, the funds, the therapist, the psychopharmacologist, the housing, the educational consultant, the respite worker, the emergency shelter, and, while still coping with the person in crisis, to coordinate this impossibly wide array of hard-to-find services.

There are no cures, miracles, or quick fixes, I might say, but these are, of course, only my opinions and suggestions. I am not a psychiatrist, psychologist, social worker, neurobiologist, or someone who has himself experienced mental illness. I speak only as a brother who knows some of what others with family members suffering from mental illness know.

But I will add that difficult as things are, and fragmented and inadequate as services may be, and as awful, unpredictable, and debilitating as it can be to live with this kind of chronic condition or with somebody who suffers from it, people *do* recover, and people *do* get well, and — after decades of the worst symptoms, the most hopeless lives, the absence of anything resembling decent care and treatment — people *do* come back to us.

And the really good news is that this is happening for more and more individuals, and in more and more places, and in more and more ways. There *is* an abundance of good programs and good people out there that are dedicated to working with individuals with severe and persistent mental illness, and that have real records of real successes.

I can tell you the stories, I say, and more often than not I do. I will talk about Moe and Larry and Shery, or Lynne and

Gaston and Rose—about Al Pam or Larry Kohn or Sam Tsemberis or Thayer Gamble or Louise Carr. I will talk about programs that have enabled ex-patients to own and run their own businesses—movie theaters, construction companies, photocopy centers; having moved beyond disability, I might add, they have also moved beyond thrift shops.

I may talk, also, about residential programs I have seen, like the one administered by the Veterans Hospital in Bedford, Massachusetts, where hundreds of veterans diagnosed with chronic mental illness live not at the hospital but in private homes in nearby towns, where they partake of ordinary life, where they have ongoing friendships with other veterans and with neighbors, and where the hospital staff ensures continuity of care by having the same doctors, nurses, and social workers who treated the veterans in the hospital go out to their homes to work with them, instead of making them return to the hospital.

There are, I will say, new medications and newer combinations of medications, and new programs, and new therapies, and newer combinations of programs and therapies and medications, and new systems of providing care and treatment that can make use of our new knowledge, and that all these programs, therapies, medications, and systems have made enormous differences for enormous numbers of people who have suffered for years from severe and persistent mental illness.

Researchers and administrators continue to find new ways that make differences, and new methods of evaluating those medications, programs, therapies, and processes that can make differences. There is real and good reason not to despair.

Still, even if we now know that 50 or 60 or 70 or 80 percent of individuals with a particular psychiatric condition or in a particular program do, with treatment, improve and recover, we are talking about statistics, and not about individual human beings. For these same statistics that give us cause for hope are telling us that twenty or thirty or forty or fifty men and women out of every hundred afflicted with serious mental illness do *not* improve or recover. And if one of those who does not recover is you, or your child, or your spouse—or your brother or sister or mother or father or dear friend—then all these statistics, studies, and stories will seem meaningless, or worse than meaningless: They may only intensify your sense of just how hopeless and impossible your life is.

In the late summer and early fall of 1998, I spend time with Moe and Shery, Thayer and Jean, Sam Tsemberis, Rose Tompkins, and Gaston Cloutier, and talk by phone, letter, and e-mail with many of the other people I have been writing about.

Slightly more than a year before, in the late spring of 1997, Moe began suffering from severe back spasms and other symptoms that required him to stop taking Risperdal. A few days after Moe had gone off his medication, I drove to Boston to spend some time with him, and I found him uncharacteristically subdued. He told me he had been having night sweats and night terrors, and that they were worse than anything he had *ever* experienced—worse than what had happened to him when he had come down cold turkey off hard drugs and alcohol. He was very worried, he said, that he wasn't going to make it and was going to end up as a real mental patient again.

"All I could do the first few days was to lie in bed and tremble like a frightened little rabbit," he told me then. "I feel a little better now, and sometimes I feel okay by the afternoon—I have a few clear hours—but I'm really flipped out and terrified the rest of the time the way I might be again tonight."

Moe told me things got so bad one night that he went into the bathroom, held a bottle of a hundred pills in his hand, got down on his knees, and for forty-five minutes he just wept and prayed that it would stop—that the awful stuff overwhelming him would just stop. He had never in his life been this close to willing himself to leave this world.

" 'Please God, please,' I kept praying," Moe said. " 'Just let it stop.' "

Now, in September 1998, Moe tells me what I know from our talks and visits since: that he is doing better than he ever has, and without medications. He has lost more than fifty pounds, he is meditating every morning, he is swimming regularly, he is riding his bike daily, he is taking enormous amounts of GABA (amino acids) and vitamin B-6 (which he says helps him to calm down), and he feels that his turnaround has been totally amazing.

"I'm running on herbs," he says, and laughs. He says that he has had his first night of complete sleep in fourteen months. We talk about his recent appearance on the *Larry King Live* show, in the aftermath of a sensationalized killing by a former mental patient, and Moe repeats what he said on the show, when King came on to him ("You're a schizophrenic, Moe, so why don't *you* tell us what families can do to keep these people from violence. . . ."). Families, Moe had said, as he says now, are already burdened enough by having a family member with a psychiatric condition. What we need are systems that help the families. We need lots of one-on-one help for families and for people with psychiatric conditions. We need an army of foot soldiers—consumers helping patients, consumers calling other consumers, outreach workers—anything that cuts the isolation, the stigma, the fear, and the burden.

Moe has just returned from Washington, D.C., where NAMI, at its annual national convention, awarded him the Lionel Aldridge Award for "personal courage, leadership, and advocacy on behalf of others living with serious mental illness."

He tells me that he is scheduled to visit various mental health programs in this country, as well as in Cuba and China, to give talks and to find out how things work elsewhere. He is still working forty, fifty, and sixty hours a week for Vinfen. He says that he, Naomi, and Sano are doing well together, and that it was Naomi who really got him through during his dark night of the soul. He says he doesn't believe in miracles, but that his comeback during the last fourteen months is as close to a miracle as he has ever come in this life. He feels as if he died and came back to life.

"Things are still hard, though," he says. "I miss the Risperdal—it's a really great med—it gave me tremendous clarity and stopped me from hearing and seeing things that weren't there. But I'm up early these days, doing my Moe Armstrong thing, and I've never felt better. It's a new life, Jay."

Moe is glad to hear that Robert is doing better. He tells me he has just sent me about three hundred poems he wrote during the past year, that he has sent Robert a batch of these poems too, that he hopes the two of us can go down to New York and visit Robert again soon, and that he is getting ready to fly to Las Vegas for a reunion—the first in about eight years—of the 3rd Reconnaissance Battalion. He laughs about me not only updating his life, but about the possibility of up*grading* it. "I could use an upgrade." He laughs, and then he signs off the way he always does: "See ya later, Jay!"

During the previous half-year, I have visited Shery Mead and the crisis respite center in Claremont, New Hampshire, several times. In its first ten months, the respite center has served more than fifty guests—I've met and talked with some of them—and in exit interviews all guests, without exception, have said that being able to go to the respite center (and at a cost to the state, Shery reminds me, of only about $130 a day) was what enabled them to avoid hospitalization.

More important, though, guests say that utilizing the center has helped normalize things for them during a crisis, has enabled them to sustain old relationships (with people, places, family, employers), and also, with the help of the support center, has enabled them to establish new relationships that give them the promise of gaining some constancy and continuity in their lives—some ongoing friendship, support, and services from and with people who understand them.

Guests keep emphasizing the fact that, when compared to their previous experiences in hospitals, the respite center was of enormous benefit because it *humanized* the experience for them: because it gave them freedom of choice by letting them come and go when they wanted; because it gave them a sense of responsibility by letting them be in charge of their medications, visitors, and daily schedules; because it gave them somebody to talk with and be with when they wanted—which they never had in hospitals, where mostly they were left alone; and, most important, because it gave them a chance to reevaluate, with others who had been where they were, what their illness meant to them and what they might be able to do about it, and thereby helped them to believe they *did* have control over their own lives, and thus more genuine hope than they had previously imagined possible.

In the meantime, Shery's life, like Moe's, has not been without struggle. She has been dealing with excruciating physical pain resulting from cartilage problems in her hips, along with the frustration of not being able to be active physically. And several times in the past year things have become so difficult for her emotionally that she feared she would have to be hospitalized again. But she and her therapist—the same therapist she has been working with for eight years now—got her through.

"What I decided, though," Shery tells me, "is that it's OK to have a million feelings—some of them pretty scary—and it's also OK to work them through with the people you trust, and that life is probably just always going to be like this for me."

"I'm continuously grateful," she writes me during her most difficult period, when she fears the voices in her head may destroy not only her sleep, but her life, "that at least my kids are doing well and making their ways in the world. It would really put me over the edge if something happened with them."

In August 1998, Shery has surgery on both hips and, when we talk on the night before her three children return to school, the week before Labor Day, she is in good spirits and full of news about how the respite center is thriving; about how they are receiving communications from organizations all over the country that want to model their respite programs after it; about a crisis respite manual Stepping Stone is preparing in order to get the word out; about the research she is doing at Dartmouth Medical School with Kim Mueser and others; and about the consulting and teaching she has been asked to do. As always, we talk about our children for a while—about the frustrations, joys, and everyday madness that come with being single parents—and we agree that after school starts, I will drive up to New Hampshire again to see how the respite center is going, and so that Shery and I can spend some time together.

When I get off the phone I find that I am shaking my head in amazement and admiration at the ways Shery keeps moving ahead—raising her three children by herself; working a full-time job that is more than a full-time job; having a rich life with her friends, her music, her children, her skiing, her jogging, and her other passions—and at the ways she remains, in a life shadowed perpetually by memory and fear, so boundlessly optimistic.

Gaston Cloutier and his wife Christine have moved from Framingham to Marlboro, he tells me when he calls in late August. He is still working full time at CAUSE; he has a caseload of thirty clients, fifteen in college and fifteen preparing to go to college. He has also won a graduate fellowship, and is beginning part-time work toward a master's degree in religious studies so that he can become a pastoral counselor. He says he still has his ups and downs, and has had to leave work early a few times when stress and anxiety became too much for him. He also tells me that to celebrate their third wedding anniversary he and Christine went to see a production of *Beauty and the Beast* at the Wang Center in Boston.

"Only I forgot that the archvillain was named Gaston," he says, and he laughs. "So the first few times somebody on-stage called out, *'Gaston!'* I kept jumping up out of my seat."

Rose Tompkins is now a student in the master's degree program in rehabilitation counseling at Boston University, and is also working part time for the Psychiatric Rehabilitation Center, running recovery workshops. When in mid-summer, we spend time together at a conference in western Massachusetts, in the offices of Windhorse, she tells me proudly, and with her typical exuberance, about the fact that she has had no relapses in the longest time she can remember, and that—can I tell?—she has lost fifty-eight pounds.

Lynne Douglas, after being offered a better-paying job as director of radiation oncology at a medical center in Portland, Oregon, has decided to stay in Seattle. She is enthralled by the new equipment her medical center has recently acquired, and she talks to me of how this equipment enables her to see different cuts of the body in three dimensions, and in ways she hadn't imagined possible, and of how helpful this has been in her work with cancer patients.

She also tells me the story of a resident who was working in her program. This younger woman was on the verge of an emotional breakdown, and Lynne advised her to take a week off. They talked, and after a while Lynne found herself telling this younger woman her own story. The resident, Lynne says, was astonished, and said that she never would have guessed that Lynne—her *mentor* all these years—could ever have experienced what she herself was frightened to death was about to happen to her.

"On occasion," Lynne writes me, "I'm in a meeting or giving a talk, and I'll think for a nanosecond about the contrast between me in one of those episodes, and me talking in front of colleagues and professionals. And I laugh at myself. I think if ever the opportunity presents itself, I'll 'come out' and divulge that part of me—but the need for it may not be there yet."

Dave Hilton, Shery calls to tell me, is back at work full-time as director of consumer affairs for the state of New Hampshire after experiencing a crisis that kept him in hospitals and rehabilitation for four months.

Kate Fontaine tells me she is working weekend shifts so that she can take a more extended vacation this year, and that she and her sister are making plans to go to Foxwoods gambling casino again. She, too, has had some hard days, and she and her doctor have decided to increase her medications slightly, but this hasn't affected her work—she got the raise she was hoping for—or being able to get along with her father in their house, or her social life, or—she laughs—her dog Brandy, who is now three and a half years old.

Paula Kline and I talk during the last week in August, a few days after her oldest son's wedding. Her two other sons are now living together in Denver, and her daughter is attending Kansas University. Paula has recently spent three peaceful weeks in a cottage on Lake Michigan; she is thinking of taking a trip to Italy; she is still working at The Tattered Cover and finding the work there enjoyable and challenging; and she finds that it is—her word—*exciting* to be wondering what, now that her four children are gone from home, her life is going to be like. She finds it exciting to be wondering what, as in any good story, is going to happen next.

When I am in New York City to visit my sons (Aaron, like Eli, is now also living in Brooklyn) and Robert, I stop by Pathways regularly. Sam Tsemberis has completed his manual, and has received a $700,000 two-year HUD grant to do a longitudinal study of the effectiveness of Pathways' program when compared to traditional programs.

Hugh Murphy is working full time, and, as ever, overtime, and he has talked with Robert by phone. Hugh is pleasantly surprised that Robert remembers that Hugh was president of what passed for patient government on their ward at Creedmoor thirty years ago. He will be visiting Robert and renewing their friendship in person, he says, during the last week of September. He asks me about the kind of housing I think might work for Robert, and says he plans to talk with him about what the best situation for him might be when he is discharged.

Dolores is back in her apartment, and Eve is still working at her job as a nurse's assistant, and, like Dolores, living independently.

Louise Carr continues to work full time as a security guard for Prestige Management in the Bronx, and part time as a volunteer for Pathways. In early August, she and Walter Harrison, a man she has known for two and a half years—Walter works for the New York City Transit Authority—were married.

Jean Baba Gogard is working regularly—moving and hauling, housecleaning—and he sees his doctor twice a week. He has had a good summer, he tells me—lots of outings: boat parties, trips to Bear Mountain, swimming, biking—and, best of all, no hospitalizations. In fact, Jean has not had a relapse since he began working with Pathways four years before.

Thayer Gamble has just returned from Florida, where he attended the funeral of his oldest brother. It is the first time he has been to Florida in twenty-two years. His brother was forty-eight years old, had had open-heart surgery, and was, at the time of his death, still using hard drugs.

"He didn't take care of himself," Thayer says. "He just wouldn't take care of himself. When they took me to his apartment, I couldn't go into that place, it was so awful. But I looked into where he was living, and I said to myself, 'That could have been me if somebody had not come forward to help me.'"

Thayer talks about the times he tried to get his brother into treatment. "You've got to *want* something in life," Thayer says, "and I guess he never did. And what I think is that you wind up hurting other people who really care about you because you don't care about yourself. When I saw him the way he was at the end, I thought of how lucky I got, how with me, it's like I was born back from the dead."

Thayer tells me about Marie, a woman he has been seeing

for three years, and when he does, and when he talks about the woman's youngest daughter Anna, who is five years old, he grins broadly.

"My friend is the single parent of four children," Thayer explains. "The oldest girl is eighteen, and the others are sixteen and fourteen — plus Anna — and I said to Marie, that 'I can't be with you and deal with you and *not* include your children.'" He laughs. "And those children, they bring joy into my life, Jay. That little girl Anna — she's so *bad*, but she is just so *cute*, and she wakes up with a smile every morning, no matter what. Every single morning. This is one very happy child."

Thayer is making arrangements with Sam Tsemberis for getting one-on-one help, so that he can learn to read. "It's frustrating, though," Thayer says. "I just get so frustrated. But when that little girl comes home from school and wants me to help her with her ABCs — well — when she comes home, I want to be able to do that with her."

Carol Ornstein left Bronx Psychiatric Center in mid-August, and when she did, Robert reacted with rage — complaining loudly and often about the hospital, being confrontational with staff and others on his ward, hanging up on me or ordering me around. The good news, however, Carol notes when we talk in early September, is that he *is* feeling the loss of a relationship that worked for *both* of them. It is, clearly, she says, easier for him to express his anger than it is to express his sorrow, his pain, or his fear.

Who will care for him now? he must be wondering, Carol says, and she adds — I agree — that if she had had another six months to work with him, she is confident he would have been able to leave the hospital, and to begin to make a better life for himself on the outside. The good news, Carol says, is that he *is* able to care about someone, and to let someone care about him, and if he can do it with her, he will be able to do it again with someone else.

"I found leaving him heartbreaking," she says then, and

states that her feelings, and his, "are testimony to the fact that he *can* form relationships that have value."

It is also, we agree, an indication that for all the good the medications do, as Clozaril has for Robert, when there is no ongoing relationship—or if a relationship ends—the medications can do little to help someone like Robert through his anger, sorrow, and fear, or to rebuild the life that has fallen apart yet again and that he still seems determined to have.

In *A Safe Place: Laying the Groundwork of Psychotherapy*, Leston Havens writes about the unwillingness, often, of mental health professionals—medical students, in particular—to recognize their own importance. "It may seem strange to say this of a profession regularly accused of vanity and self-importance," he states, in a passage that speaks to the relapses Robert and other patients experience when they lose the presence in their lives of a professional they had come to depend upon. But the fact is, Havens continues, "that many professional people allow themselves to come and go among patients as if their knowledge and skills were all that counted, their persons not at all. One sees this most vividly with medical students, who cannot believe in their importance to the people they take care of. Yet we are the great placebos of our pharmacopeia, and the power of the placebo can be measured by the results of its withdrawal."

Al Pam, Carol, and others on the staff at Bronx Psychiatric Center are very attentive to Robert and to his needs before, during, and after Carol's departure (the week before Robert's new therapist is assigned, Carol returns to the hospital, and she and Al take Robert to lunch on City Island), and this makes a clear and large difference.

Less than a week after Carol's departure, Robert begins to form a new relationship—with a therapist assigned on an interim basis, until the assignment of a new intern in psychology after Labor Day—and his tantrums and complaints diminish rapidly. This is, I tell Al and Carol, his quickest recovery from an experience of separation and loss—and from a period of mania and rage—that I can remember. His resilience, as ever, astonishes me.

When I visit with Robert, the second week of September, his new therapist, Stephanie Schacher, joins us. Robert is given a pass, and the three of us sit out on the lawn, geese all around us (Robert feeding them), and spend some time together. Robert tells me he likes Stephanie, and he talks about enjoying the freedom to come and go from his ward when he wants. He also talks about where he might live and what he might do when he leaves the hospital.

When I show him recent photos of my children, he asks me to give each of the boys $20, and to tell Miriam that she should buy a pair of earrings that will be a gift from him. Miriam and her friend Seth are coming to the city the next day, driving up from Washington, D.C., where they live and work. I show Robert a picture of the two of them, and tell him that it looks as if they will be getting engaged.

Robert smiles broadly, and I see that his eyes go moist. "I'm happy, Jay," he says. "I'm very happy for them."

When it's time for me to leave—we have returned to his ward—Robert says he doesn't want to walk me to the door because it will make him cry. But after we embrace and say our good-byes, he does walk with me to the door, and we embrace again, and kiss, and say our good-byes again, and while I walk to the subway I think of how *uneventful* the visit was: We passed the time talking about ordinary things—life on the ward, friends and family, religion and politics (the upcoming Jewish New Year; the prospects for the elections, given the Clinton-Lewinsky scandal), and about Robert's prospects.

On the subway, heading to Manhattan to have dinner with my two sons, I think of how much happier—calmer, more hopeful—Robert is than he was a year ago, and how wonderful it is to spend some ordinary time together—no crises, no tantrums, no long lists of complaints and demands, no especially memorable incidents, no noteworthy exchanges

—some time in which we talk together easily about times past and the time and the life to come.

I am reminded, too, of the fact that some individuals, no matter their desires or ours, and no matter how good their care and treatment, simply are happier and better served in institutional settings than in communities outside institutional settings, and that it is often criminal to try to force these people into community residences and programs when they cannot make it on their own in our world and require the kind of sanctuary—the literal asylum—a secure, stable, and well-run institutional setting can provide. As awful as state mental hospitals have frequently been, group homes, shelters, and halfway houses have been and can be just as bad, while not providing the essentials many individuals are incapable of providing for themselves: food, clothing, shelter, medical care, and all those things, tangible and intangible, that can alleviate and minimize shame, fear, and despair.

What matters most is not *where* an individual who suffers from the most debilitating ravages of mental illness receives care and treatment, but the quality of that care and treatment, and the quality of life experienced by and made possible for that individual. Couldn't there be, I muse, facilities for people with serious mental illnesses that would be located not in isolated areas but within cities and towns—facilities that might be modeled, for example, on the kinds of well-conceived and -administered assisted-living facilities in which many elderly people live? These could be places where, depending upon an individual's desires, needs, and levels of functioning, he or she might receive total care and treatment, as in a well-run state hospital; or they could be places where people might come and go from their homes or apartments freely, taking care of their needs and desires in the ways most of us do, with only minimal assistance and supervision, as in good community residential programs. Perhaps, too, a facility could be designed for maximum flexibility and diversity, so that one did not have to relocate every time one's condition or needs changed, and so that one was not living *only* with others who suffered from serious mental illnesses. Nor, in such places, would individuals needing maximum care and treatment be denied the kinds of excellent rehabilitation services and continuity of care provided for individuals living outside locked or custodial facilities. In this way, the possibility for moving from a hospital back to our world would be maintained and maximized, so that if and when someone did move from a community within an institution to a community outside an institution, the only major change in that person's life would be location.

During my visit to Bronx Psychiatric Center this time, I also have lunch with Al Pam and Stephanie Schacher, and while we eat and talk, I find myself remarking on the wonder of the work they do: how people like Al, Stephanie, and Carol, who have chosen to work with those whom the world designates as mad, are doing what doctors have always hoped to do: they are treating a whole person from a wide range of perspectives — biological, neurological, psychological, and sociological — by trying to understand the relations in that person, not only between feelings and behavior, and between that person's biology and his or her environment, but the infinite and mysterious relations between mind and body, between past and present, between illness and health, and between what we call sanity and what we call madness.

We talk too about the many ways in which doctors and therapists are frequently able to help individuals draw on their strengths, and how one of the most obvious things about madness is that it does contain great strengths. Think, I say in passing, of how playwrights and novelists have frequently seen madness as ennobling, as the source and means — whether in Oedipus or Hamlet, Lear or Don Quixote — of those powers that enable us to heal ourselves and those around us (and the state itself, in many of Shakespeare's plays), and that enable us, ultimately, to know ourselves more truly than we did before we became mad, and to accept and know ourselves in unexpected and large ways. Just as Gloucester gains insight only after he goes blind, so Lear, like other tragic figures, gains wisdom only after he loses his reason. By transforming madness into self-knowledge and understanding, we can often come to ways of being and acting that are life-changing and life-giving.

Take away shame, I say, quoting Moe Armstrong, and anything's possible. Look at what happens after nearly forty years of madness and misery, of locked wards, straitjackets, and neglect, when Robert receives ordinary human attention to his ordinary human needs and his very human condition. Biochemically and emotionally — are they different? — hope and kindness sometimes really do keep us alive.

I tell Al and Stephanie about some of the people I have been meeting, of how they have helped transform my view of what Al and Stephanie do — of their profession — and I say that things really *are* much better that they used to be, that it seems we *do* have the means and knowledge to do what we have rarely been able to do in the past: to transform that condition we call madness, and often to do so by transforming our sense of what madness is, and what it is not. In this way, we are able to deprive it of a large measure of its destructive power, and so are free to draw on sources of strength and energy previously unavailable to us, and, thereby, to restore ourselves to who we are and who we may yet become.

We don't, of course, have to look only at individuals like Robert or Lynne, or Moe or Shery or Kate or Thayer, to understand just how resilient human beings can be, but we can, by knowing them, take real hope from the particularity of their lives and of their stories. We can take real hope — and gain courage — from seeing people we know transform those elements, experiences, and conditions that have previously transformed them, and thereby move from states of illness and despair to states of well-being and recovery. We can take real hope from seeing people we know move beyond disability, beyond survival, and beyond recovery. We can take real hope from seeing people we know and love make lives for themselves that, while remaining rich with conflict, struggle, and fear, also become rich beyond our imaginings with intimations of possibility.

ACKNOWLEDGMENTS

In the writing of this book, I have benefited from the extreme generosity of many people, and it is a pleasure to be able to thank them here. I only hope I have forgotten no one. As I trust the book makes clear, my appreciation for the mystery and complexity of mind and feeling—of everything that results from and issues in behavior, choice, and act; of everything, in short, that comes with being alive, and being a sentient and conscious being—has been transformed considerably during the past few years. My understanding of mental illness—of what we do and do not know about it, and of what it is like to live with it long-term—has been transformed and enriched, above all, by the presence in my life of those individuals who, for purposes of this book, agreed to talk with me about their lives openly and directly and at length. By serving their lives and their stories fairly and accurately, I hope I have begun to give back to them the trust they have so freely given me.

My profound gratitude, first of all, to my dear friends and faithful guides Moe Armstrong and Shery Mead. Their courage and good humor—their immense love of life—has been a comfort and an inspiration. I consider myself lucky that they count me among their friends. My debt to them, as well as to my other subjects, is one that I discharge with happy gratitude. My heartfelt thanks, then, to Gaston Cloutier, Rose Tompkins, Paula Kline, Lynne Douglas, Ed Roy, Kate Fontaine, Dori Fagerson, Carl Pickus, Dolores Keane, Sarah Reiss and her parents, Eve Sorella, Jean Baba Gogard, Louise Carr, and Thayer Gamble. My debt to them is as infinite as is my admiration for them.

I am most grateful to those mental health professionals who talked with me about their work and their lives, and who, like those who agreed to let me use their words and tell their stories, did so without preconditions. My thanks for irreplaceable expertise, for exhilarating discussions, for gracious hospitality, and for a multitude of pleasant and stimulating hours and days, to Bill Anthony, Lisa Bellafato, Judi Chamberlin, Marianne Farkas, Cheryl Gagne, Larry Kohn, Robert Salafia, and LeRoy Spaniol of the Boston University Center for Psychiatric Rehabilitation; to Tony Zipple of Vinfen; to Kevin Bradley and the members of Genesis Club; to Peggy Collins and the Starpoint Club of Northampton; to Donna Williams and the Mosaic Clubhouse of London; to the staff and members of Webster House (I and II) in Boston; to staff and members of the Stepping Stone Peer Support Center in Claremont, New Hampshire, and the Next Step Peer Support Center in West Lebanon, New Hampshire; to Naomi Pinson and the residents of Market Street Apartments; to Carol Ornstein, Alvin Pam, Stephanie Schacher, and the staff at Bronx Psychiatric Center; to Steve Leff and the Human Services Research Institute; to Jeff Fortuna and my friends and neighbors at Windhorse Associates; to David Hilton and Charlene Webber of the New Hampshire Department of Mental Health; to Arnold Unterbach and members of the Odyssey Behavioral Health Care Residence and of the Odyssey Family Center; to Phil Wyzik and the staff of West Central Services; to Sam Tsemberis and everyone at Pathways to Housing; to Elsa Ekblaw and the staff at CAUSE; to Lauri Cole and the Association for Community

Living Agencies in Mental Health; to Gerald Landsberg, Deborah Padgett, and the NYU School of Social Work; to Ethan S. Rofman and Richard Sheola of the Massachusetts Behavioral Health Partnership; to Patricia Deegan, Dan Fisher, and the National Empowerment Center; to Robert Freedman, Courtenay Harding, and others at the University of Colorado School of Medicine; to Alexander Blount and Jeffrey Geller of the University of Massachusetts Medical Center; to Bernard Arons, Thomas Bornemann, Neal Brown, Michael English, Ron Manderscheid, and others at the U.S. Department of Health and Human Services, and the Substance Abuse and Mental Health Services Administration; to Ken Dudak and Peter Yee of Fountain House; and to Albert Gaw and staff at the Edith Nourse Rogers Memorial Veterans Hospital in Bedford, Massachusetts.

The patience and graciousness these individuals and their organizations have shown in welcoming me into their programs and into their lives, and in explaining why and how and when and where they do what they do, is itself, in the midst of their difficult and often overwhelming obligations, a small indication of the commitment, patience, and loving-kindness they give so knowledgeably to the people for whose care and treatment they are responsible. The skill, imagination, and energy they devote to their work and to their clients, along with the excellence of the programs themselves, is more than heartening; their modesty and humility about their own achievements is, happily, equaled by the passion they sustain for the good work they do.

I am particularly grateful to friends, old and new, who talked with me early on, when I was most doubtful and at sea—as writer and as man—and who continued to talk with me, and to argue with me, and to educate me throughout my work on this project. Whatever errors of style, fact, and judgment exist in this book are mine; much of what I hope will be useful and engaging is due to the exceeding kindness of these friends.

For encouragement and enlightenment early on and continuing—and for the pleasure of their company and the gift of their friendship—my warm thanks to Kristin Bumiller, Elissa Ely, Leston Havens, Leon Eisenberg, Peter Rossi, Patricia Deegan, Robert Brick, Janet Sheppard, Robert Goodman, LeRoy Spaniol, Joanne Greenberg, Gerald Friedland, Sam Rofman, Jeffrey Geller, Tom Bornemann, Al Pam, Holly Robinson, Jerome Charyn, Steve Kellman, Catherine Coursaget, Lee Edwards, Gail Hornstein, Norbert Goldfield, Michael Robbins, Richard Tessler, Courtenay Harding, Sam Tsemberis, and Phil Yarnell.

In the course of writing this book I have called upon many individuals for suggestions, for advice, for information, for answers to questions specific and general, for introductions to people and programs, and for guidance; it is a pleasure to be able to thank them here for their help and for the easy, thoughtful, imaginative, and cheerful ways in which they have responded to my repeated queries, confusions, doubts, and needs.

Warmest thanks, then, to Gerald Grob, David Mechanic, Alan Horowitz, Peter Kramer, William Glazer, Richard Restak, Carl Salzman, Ken Minkoff, Jennifer Gamblin, Linda Zebley, Susan Stubbs, Karen Unger, Jill Bolte Taylor, Carolyn Perla, Bernard Neugeboren, Richard Weingarten, Scott Masters, Philip Graubart, Richard Evans, Carol Owen, Michael Posner, Milton Klein, Mary Auslander, Sue Estroff, R. Walter Heinrichs, Stuart Mitchner, Robert Goldstein, Douglas Whynott, Madeline Blais, George Cuomo, Larry Hott, Diane Marsh, Rex Dickens, Elmer Struening, the late Peter Wyden, and Alexander Vukovic.

Elise Feeley, reference librarian at the Forbes Library in Northampton, has provided me with much information and encouragement, and her cheerfulness and amazing resourcefulness have brightened many a dark moment. I owe similar debts to the reference staffs of the Forbes Library, the University of Massachusetts library, and the medical library at the Veterans Administration Hospital in Leeds, Massachusetts. Jane Rosenberg's spirited and eager assistance in finding articles and data, and in debating central concerns and challenging my often inchoate thoughts, were invaluable. I am indebted also to Colleen Sackheim for transcribing tapes, to Greg Tulonen and Patricia Matthew for bibliographical assistance, and to the English Department at the University of Massachusetts—especially its chair, Stephen Clingman—for indispensable support.

I have talked often with my children, Miriam, Aaron, and Eli, about this book, and their love and enthusiasm has been the sweetest and most heartening of gifts. Their suggestions, along with their affectionate tolerance for their father's many moods, have been a constant source of practical and indispensable sustenance. Their own ongoing lives—and the quite wonderful, generous, and idiosyncratic adults they are in these lives—make me a most happy, proud, and blessed man.

I am blessed, too, in my agent and friend, Richard Parks, whose great good sense has sustained me in more ways than I can here enumerate.

My editor, Paul Bresnick, has been a good friend to both author and book, and I am ever grateful to him, and also to the staff of William Morrow and Company, especially to Katherine Beitner and Ben Schafer, for providing me with everything I needed—not least of all, timely and helpful responses to my wants—to sustain me.

My brother Robert's courage and resiliency remain central to my life and work, and I remain everlastingly grateful to him for the vast optimism of his spirit.

Working on this book has been the most surprising and inspiring of experiences. I have been surprised again and again by the remarkable generosity of others in giving so freely of their time, of their expertise, and especially of themselves. The freedom I have been granted due to such generosity to witness the infinite, mysterious, complex, and wonderful ways in which courage and resiliency regularly show themselves forth in lives being lived all around us has been the most precious of gifts. Before I began work on this book, I could not have imagined the lives and people I have come to know, or that they would have graced my life in such extraordinary ways. Surely I could not have imagined the very real and often happy ways in which their struggles and stories have provided me with unexpected and wondrous intimations of possibility, and with immense stores of astonishment, renewal, and inspiration.

A NOTE ON SOURCES

I am pleased to acknowledge my immense debt to those whose researches and writings have been useful to me in the preparation of this book. What follows is a most incomplete sampling of much that I have read, and I trust it will prove helpful to readers. I suggest that readers wanting more extensive and/or intensive information about particular subjects consult the bibliographies and the bibliographical essays in books listed below.

The categories I have used to organize materials are arbitrary in the extreme and are intended to serve as brief guides for further reading. I hope they will make it easier for readers to find information, articles, and books on specific subjects. Mostly, this commentary allows me to express my gratitude to those whose writings have influenced me significantly and have thereby enhanced my understanding of mental illness and of what we do and do not know about it.

GENERAL BACKGROUND AND REFERENCE

In the making of this book, as in the making of *Imagining Robert*, my principal source for general information about mental illness has been the wonderfully encyclopedic *Comprehensive Textbook of Psychiatry*. I have made frequent use of both the 1975 and 1990 editions, edited by Alfred M. Freedman, Harold I. Kaplan, and Benjamin J. Sadock (Baltimore: Williams and Wilkins, 1975, 1990). Both editions contain an abundance of knowledgeable, useful, and fair-minded essays on virtually all subjects and individuals having to do with mental illness. They also, generally, provide judicious perspectives by placing information and technical data within historical contexts.

These textbooks have provided me with my introductory and primary sources of information concerning the etiology, diagnosis, prognosis, care, and treatment for the specific (and major) categories by which mental illnesses are usually described: schizophrenia, depression (unipolar disorder), and manic depression (bipolar disorder).

The American Psychiatric Association's *DSM-IV: Diagnostic & Statistical Manual of Mental Disorders,* fourth edition (Washington, DC: American Psychiatric Press, 1994) is valuable in that it reflects current practices and standard ways of describing and understanding the many heterogeneous conditions we call by various clinical names.

For basic information about bipolar disorder, and its care and treatment, I have relied heavily on Frederick K. Goodwin and Kay Redfield Jamison's marvelously comprehensive *Manic-Depressive Illness* (New York: Oxford University Press, 1990). Diane and Lisa Berger's *We Heard the Angels of Madness: A Family Guide to Coping with Manic Depression* (New York: William Morrow, 1991) is what its subtitle says it is, and it offers an adequate introduction to the subject.

Readers looking for information about schizophrenia might begin with the revised edition of E. Fuller Torrey's *Surviving Schizophrenia: A Family Manual* (New York: Harper & Row, 1983, 1988) and the more newly revised third edition, *Surviving Schizophrenia: A Manual for Families, Consumers, & Providers* (New York: HarperCollins, 1995). Although Torrey's book often favors a narrow, neo-Kraepelinian view of what schizophrenia may or may not be, it contains a good deal of basic information and many practical suggestions, especially for individuals and families experiencing first episodes of the illness. *Troubled Journey: Coming to Terms with the Mental Illness of a Sibling or Parent* by Diane T. Marsh and Rex M. Dickens (New York: Tarcher/Putnam, 1997) is a well-informed and refreshingly realistic guide for families.

For detailed information and guidance concerning depression, readers might consult two books: John H. Greist and James W. Jefferson's *Depression and Its Treatment,* second edition (Washington, DC: American Psychiatric Press, 1992), and Leon Grunhaus and John F. Greden's *Severe Depressive Disorders* (Washington, DC: American Psychiatric Press, 1994).

Schizophrenia and Manic-Depressive Disorder: The Biological Roots of Mental Illness as Revealed by the Landmark Study of Identical Twins by E. Fuller Torrey in collaboration with Ann E. Bowler, Edward H. Taylor, and Irving I. Gottesman (New York: Basic Books, 1994) is a representative example of those writings that set forth the case for a biomedical basis for understanding mental illness, while Alvin Pam and Colin Ross's *Pseudoscience in Biological Psychiatry: Blaming the Body* (New York: John Wiley, 1994) provides a persuasive review of the literature critical of more purely biomedical views.

The debate between those who favor more or less biomedical views and those who favor more or less psychological views is extensive. Readers interested in reviewing the arguments central to this debate might look first at Irving Gottesman's *Schizophrenia Genesis: The Origins of Madness* (New York: W. H. Freeman, 1995); "Psychotherapy Versus Medication for Depression: Challenging the Conventional Wisdom with Data" by David O. Antonuccio, William C. Danton, and Garland Y. De Nelsky, in *Professional Psychology: Research and Practice,* Vol. 26, No. 6 (December 1995); and R. Walter Heinrichs, "Schizophrenia and the Brain: Conditions for a Neuropsychology of Madness," in *American Psychologist,* Vol. 48, No. 39 (March 1993). For a critique of treatment that relies excessively or exclusively on medications, see Peter R. Breggin's two books *Toxic Psychiatry*, Vol. 1: *Psychiatry's Assault on the Brain with Drugs & Electroshock* (New York: St. Martin's Press, 1991) and *Toxic Psychiatry: Why Therapy, Empathy & Love Must Replace the Drugs, Electroshock Therapy & Biochemical Theories of the "New Psychiatry"* (New York: St. Martin's Press, 1994).

Two books by Michael Robbins, *Experiences of Schizophrenia: An Integration of the Personal, Scientific, and Therapeutic* (New York: Guilford Publications, 1993) and *Conceiving of Personality* (New Haven: Yale University Press, 1996), offer densely textured and insightful studies of schizophrenia and its relation to psychoanalysis, philosophy, anthropology, and neuroscience. *Experiences of Schizophrenia* also offers case studies that detail psychoanalytically based treatment of individuals with long-term mental illness. Robbins's review of the psychological, psychiatric, and neurobiological literature is extensive and impressive.

I am indebted to Ronald W. Manderscheid, chief of the Survey and Analysis Branch, U.S. Center for Mental Health Services, for guidance in searching out much of the data contained in this book, especially statistics on epidemiology, costs of treatment, and outcome measures and findings.

I will not list here the many sources consulted for various statistics, but I suggest that those interested in data concerning epidemiology, costs, and outcome begin with the annual volumes of *Mental Health, United States*, published by the U.S. Center for Mental Health Services. Through most of the writing of this book I made use of the 1996 edition: *Mental Health, United States, 1996*, edited by R. W. Manderscheid and M. A. Sonnenschein, DHHS Pub. No. (SMA) 96-3098 (Washington, DC: Superintendent of Documents, U.S. Government Printing Office, 1996). For more specific information, I have frequently relied on listings from the the U.S. Bureau of the Census, *Statistical Abstract of the United States* (e.g., "Hospital Facilities—Summary," "Mental Health Facilities—Summary by Type of Facility," "Population in Institutions and Other Group Quarters, by Type of Group Quarters and State," etc.). In addition, the annual *Mental Illness Awareness Guide* published by the American Psychiatric Association Division of Public Affairs (1400 K Street N.W., Washington, DC 20005) contains a good deal of reliable data.

Readers will find "Spending for Mental Health and Substance Abuse Treatment, 1996," by David McCusick, Tami L. Mark, et al., in *Health Affairs,* September–October 1998, a carefully conceived survey of spending trends in this decade.

I am profoundly indebted to the writings of Oliver Sacks and Sherwin Nuland. Their many books are a continuing source of inspiration. In particular, Sherwin Nuland's *How We Die: Reflections on Life's Final Chapter* (New York: Alfred A. Knopf, 1994) and Oliver Sacks's *An Anthropologist on Mars: Seven Paradoxical Tales* (New York: Alfred A. Knopf, 1995) encouraged me to believe that it was possible to explore that wondrous and strange country we call mind and to render our explorations and discoveries humanly, accurately, and movingly. Without losing sight of the relations of mind and body to mortality, or those of biology and history to the joys and struggles of daily life, they remind us repeatedly of the ordinary and extraordinary ways in which human beings affected by the most curious conditions and fates manage to live out their lives in our world.

Oliver Sacks's essay "Neurology and the Soul" in *The New York Review of Books,* Vol. 37, No. 18 (November 22, 1990) was instrumental in changing my ways of thinking about mind, brain, memory, madness, consciousness, and human nature. In a similar manner, Leon Eisenberg's essays, by their good sense, their wealth of information, and their refreshing way of placing psychiatry and mental illness within the larger context of medicine and health, and of public health in general, have informed much of my thinking during the writing of this book. See especially "The Future of Psychiatry," in *The Lancet,* December 15, 1973; "Development as a Unifying Concept in Psychiatry," in *British Journal of Psychiatry,* Vol. 131 (1977); "What Makes Persons 'Patients' and Patients 'Well'?" in *The American Journal of*

Medicine, Vol. 69 (August 1980); and "Mindlessness and Brainlessness in Psychiatry," in *British Journal of Psychiatry,* Vol. 148 (1986).

Readers interested in informing themselves about the care and treatment of individuals diagnosed as having dual diagnoses might begin with essays by Ken Minkoff and others in Norman S. Miller's two books *Treating Coexisting Psychiatric and Addictive Disorders* (Center City, MN: Hazelden Educational Materials, 1994) and *The Principles and Practice of Addictions in Psychiatry* (Philadelphia: W. B. Saunders, 1997).

For information on post-traumatic stress disorder and its relation to severe mental illness, I have relied on *Tramautic Stress: The Effects of Overwhelming Experience on Mind, Body and Society,* edited by Bessel A. Van der Kolk, Alexander C. McFarlane, and Lars Weisaeth (New York: Guilford Publications, 1996), and on other essays by Bessel Van der Kolk, especially "The Psychobiology of Posttramatic Stress Disorder," in *The Journal of Clinical Psychiatry,* Vol. 58 (1997). Other informative works on this subject are Judith Herman's *Trauma and Recovery* (New York: Basic Books, 1992, 1997), Colin Ross's *Dissociative Identity Disorder: Diagnosis, Clinical Features & Treatment of Multiple Personality* (New York: John Wiley, 1996), and articles by Robert Drake, Kim Mueser, and others in M. Harris and C. L. Landis's *Sexual Abuse in the Lives of Women Diagnosed with Serious Mental Illness* (Amsterdam: Harwood Academic Publishers, 1997).

In a quite different and altogether remarkable way, Pat Barker's trilogy of novels about World War I—*Regeneration* (New York: E. P. Dutton, 1991), *The Eye in the Door* (New York: E. P. Dutton, 1994), and *The Ghost Road* (New York: E. P. Dutton, 1995)—provides, among a multitude of pleasures, an exceptional and original rendering of possible causes, effects, care, and treatment of trauma.

Leon Eisenberg's essay "The Social Construction of the Human Brain" (*American Journal of Psychiatry*, Vol. 152 [November 1995]) offers an excellent introduction to an understanding of what we call neural plasticity and of the many ways our brains, interacting with experience, reconfigure themselves throughout our lifetimes. Readers interested in learning more about what we have been discovering in recent years about ways in which brain, mind, experience, emotion, memory, madness, and consciousness are (and may be) related will, I expect, find the following books as informative, suggestive, and enchanting as I did: Merlin Donald, *Origins of the Modern Mind: Three Stages in the Evolution of Culture and Cognition* (Cambridge: Harvard University Press, 1991); Edward M. Hundert, *Philosophy, Psychiatry, and Neuroscience: Three Approaches to the Mind: A Synthetic Analysis of the Varieties of Human Experience* (Oxford: Oxford University Press, 1989); Gerald M. Edelman, *Bright Air, Brilliant Fire: On the Matter of the Mind* (New York: Basic Books, 1992); and Israel Rosenfield, *The Strange, Familiar, and Forgotten: An Anatomy of Consciousness* (New York: Alfred A. Knopf, 1992). Two other excellent and fascinating introductions to the world of neurobiology are J. Allan Hobson's *The Chemistry of Conscious States: How the Brain Changes Its Mind* (Boston: Little, Brown, 1994) and V. S. Ramachandran and Sandra Blakeslee's *Phantoms in the Brain: Probing the Mysteries of the Human Mind*, with a foreword by Oliver Sacks (New York: William Morrow, 1998).

Equally fascinating (if less contemporary with respect to recent research, technology, and theory) are A. R. Luria's marvelous *The Mind of a Mnemonist*, with a foreword by Jerome S. Bruner (Cambridge: Harvard University Press, 1968, 1987) and *The Man with a Shattered World*, with a foreword by Oliver Sacks (Cambridge: Harvard University Press, 1972, 1987). Luria's *The Working Brain: An Introduction to Neuropsychology* (New York: Basic Books, 1973) continues to provide basic and stimulating insight and information concerning the relations of mind to brain.

Richard M. Restak's handsomely illustrated companion books to the PBS television series on brain (*The Brain* [New York: Bantam Books, 1984]) and mind (*The Mind* [New York: Bantam Books, 1988]) offer detailed, reliable, and accessible introductions to these fields. His collection of essays *The Brain Has a Mind of Its Own: Insights from a Practicing Neurologist* (New York: Harmony, 1991) — like the essays of Oliver Sacks (*The Man Who Mistook His Wife for a Hat: And Other Clinical Tales* [New York: Summit Books, 1985]), Harold Klawans (*Toscanini's Fumble: And Other Tales of Clinical Neurology* [Chicago: Contemporary Books, 1988]), and John R. Searle (*Mystery of Consciousness* [New York: New York Review of Books, 1997]) — offers illuminating theories, insights, and case studies in delightful ways. Russell Martin's *Matters Gray and White: A Neurologist, His Patients, and the Mysteries of the Brain* (New York: Ballantine Books, 1986) is an engaging introduction to the working life of a clinical neurologist.

For a brief survey of our current understanding of the relations between mind, brain, neurology, and mental illness, see Nancy C. Andreasan's excellent and clearheaded article "Linking Mind and Brain in the Study of Mental Illnesses: A Project for a Scientific Psychopathology," in *Science*, Vol. 275 (March 14, 1997).

PSYCHOPHARMACOLOGY

Stephen M. Stahl's *Essential Psychopharmacology: Neuroscientific Basis and Practical Applications* (Cambridge: Cambridge University Press, 1996) is a model of clarity and comprehensiveness. Stahl's advice, "that novices first approach this text by going through it from beginning to end and reviewing only the color graphics and the legends for these graphics," is well taken (especially for one, like me, whose weakest subject in high school was chemistry). The graphics and legends are original, effective, and affecting.

I have also depended greatly on John D. Preston, John H. O'Neal, and Mary C. Talaga's *Handbook of Clinical Psychopharmacology for Therapists,* second edition (Oakland, CA: New Harbinger Publications, 1997), which explains complicated matters in comprehensible ways, and without diminishing the complexity of the subject. Donald W. Goodwin and Samuel B. Guze's *Psychiatric Diagnosis*, fifth edition (New York: Oxford University Press, 1996) offers an excellent introduction to the relation of diagnosis to psychopharmacology.

Peter Kramer's *Listening to Prozac* (New York: Viking Press, 1993) is helpful in understanding ways in which clinicians balance the claims of experience against the claims of biology and treatment. Sherwin Nuland's review of this book (*The New York Review of Books,* Vol. 41, No. 11 [June 9, 1994]) provides a concise description of scientific method as well as a splendid antidote to excessive psychopharmacological optimism.

The December 1996 issue of *The Journal: A Quarterly Publication of the California Alliance for the Mentally Ill*—"Discovery: NARSAD Research" (Vol. 7, No. 4)—has an abundance of essays that update psychopharmacological and neurological research. I have also relied upon regular issues of the *NARSAD Research Newsletter* and *Schizophrenia Bulletin* (see in particular Vol. 23, No. 4 [1997], an issue devoted to "Clinical Challenges in the Psychopharmacology of Schizophrenia") for information concerning new and current research developments.

A good introduction to ongoing research on the relation of nicotine to mental illness can be found in "Schizophrenia, Sensory Gating, and Nicotinic Receptors," by Lawrence E. Adler, Ann Olincy, et al., in *Schizophrenia Bulletin,* Vol. 24, No. 2 (1998).

Donald Drake and Marian Uhlman's *Making Medicine, Making Money* (Kansas City: Andrews and McMeel, 1993) and Greg Critser's "Oh, How Happy We Will Be: Pills, Paradise, and the Profits of the Drug Companies" (*Harper's Magazine,* June 1996) provide basic introductions to the economic relations of the drug industry to medical practice. *The Wall Street Journal* has run several excellent investigative series on the drug industry, especially a three-part series by Ellen Joan Pollock and Carol Hymowitz (July 13, December 1, and December 21, 1995). Other information on this subject has come from articles, journals, and investigations too numerous to list, including *Drug Topics* (May 6 and July 8, 1996), *The Congressional Record* (see especially records of the 1990 congressional hearings on drug company promotional practices), and *Consumer Reports* (February and March 1992; August 1996). The article on young professionals and Prozac appeared in *The New York Times* on December 13, 1993. Eli Lilly's promotion of Prozac to high school students was reported in *The Washington Post* on January 22, 1995. "7½ Days" by Kevin Heldman appeared in the June–July 1998 issue of *City Limits Magazine*.

History and Social Policy

Gerald N. Grob's writings on mental illness and its care and treatment in the United States are a great gift to anyone wishing to learn about the changing ways we have understood and treated individuals who suffer from psychiatric disorders. His first study, *The State and the Mentally Ill: A History of Worcester State Hospital in Massachusetts, 1830–1920* (Chapel Hill, NC: University of North Carolina Press, 1966), is particular to one institution. The three-volume history of American mental health that followed this study is scrupulously researched, marvelously insightful, and written with great insight, fair-mindedness, and grace. I found *From Asylum to Community: Mental Health Policy in Modern America* (Princeton: Princeton University Press, 1991) particularly stimulating and useful during the writing of this book. The other two volumes in Grob's trilogy are *Mental Institutions in America: Social Policy to 1875* (New York: The Free Press, 1973) and *Mental Illness and American Society, 1875–1940* (Princeton: Princeton University Press, 1973).

In *The Mad Among Us: A History of the Care of America's*

Mentally Ill (Cambridge: Harvard University Press, 1994), Grob draws upon and summarizes much of his earlier work. *The Mad Among Us* is, however, as Grob states in the preface, an independent work that incorporates his more recent thoughts; its "focus is less on the mentally disordered themselves (although they are not ignored), and more on the ways in which Americans have responded to the presence of such individuals in their midst."

Grob's concluding and cautionary paragraph from a recent essay, "Psychiatry's Holy Grail: The Search for the Mechanisms of Mental Diseases," in *Bulletin of the History of Medicine*, Vol. 72 (1998), is especially instructive:

> The history of psychiatry and mental health policy also holds important insights for those concerned with health policy. Unlike the general health-care system, the mental health system has traditionally dealt with a population whose chronic illnesses created dependency. By definition, chronic diseases do not lend themselves to cure; they require a blend of care, management, and therapy. As the general health-care system increasingly confronts chronic illnesses (as compared with the earlier preoccupation with acute infectious diseases), those involved in its reshaping may well benefit from the experiences of their psychiatric colleagues. It would be ironic if psychiatry — recently regarded as an anachronistic medical specialty — were to become a model for the future reconstruction of America's health-care system. It would be an even greater irony if psychiatry, in its thrust to identify with pure neuroscience and genetics, were in effect to abandon a clinical foundation that traditionally began with the human needs of severely and persistently mentally ill persons.

Leston L. Havens's writings, like those of Gerald Grob, have influenced me profoundly. *Approaches to the Mind: Movement of the Psychiatric Schools from Sects Toward Science* (Boston: Little, Brown, 1973), first published in 1972 and reissued in 1987 (Cambridge: Harvard University Press, 1987), is, like

Grob's work, a deeply conceived and gorgeously written contribution to intellectual history. Among its many virtues, it provides readers with a detailed, shrewd, and wonderfully informed narrative of the ways in which our understanding and treatment of psychiatric disorders have developed during the past one hundred years. Havens's *A Safe Place: Laying the Groundwork of Psychotherapy* (Cambridge: Harvard University Press, 1989) is an elegant and eloquently sane and humane essay on the nature of the therapeutic process. The final chapter, "The Future of Healing," opens with a passage that, like Gerald Grob's, quoted above, is sound, sensible, and instructive:

> The future belongs to psychiatry because finding a safe place for the psyche, the individual life, is its central concern. The concern is biological, neurological, psychological, and sociological: psychiatry is the only systematic study that addresses human life from all these perspectives. This is more than an academic advantage—threats to human existence come from lesions of brain and body, unconscious conflict, and the isolation, domination, and submission found everywhere in social life. The protectors of human existence must confront all these dangers.

Roy Porter's *A Social History of Madness: The World Through the Eyes of the Insane* (New York: E. P. Dutton, 1989), a historical study of the ways we have responded to those we call mad, is rich in reference, allusion, and detail, and wonderfully suggestive, as are Erving Goffman's two books *Stigma: Notes on the Management of Spoiled Identity* (Englewood Cliffs, NJ: Prentice-Hall, 1963) and *Asylums: Essays on the Social Situation of Mental Patients & Other Inmates* (New York: Doubleday, 1961). Readers will also find David M. Rothman's studies of the development of American mental health policies and practices useful—*The Discovery of the Asylum: Social Order and Disorder in the New Republic* (Boston: Little, Brown, 1971) and *Conscience and Convenience: The Asylum and Its Alternatives in Progressive America* (Boston: Little, Brown, 1980). Although the factual bases for Michel Foucault's theorizing in *Madness and Civilization: A History of Insanity in the Age of Reason* (New York: Random House, 1965) have been called into question by scholars, his book remains marvelously provocative and stimulating.

David Mechanic, Gerald Grob's colleague at the Rutgers University Institute for Health, Health Care Policy, and Aging Research, has written extensively on mental health and social policy, and his numerous books and essays have informed my book in ways that are, I trust, faithful to his meticulous attention to fact and detail. His newly revised *Mental Health and Social Policy: The Emergence of Managed Care*, fourth edition (Boston: Allyn & Bacon, 1999) is indispensable. For a preliminary introduction to Mechanic's researches and writing on mental health policy, see his earlier essays "Toward the Year 2000 in U.S. Mental Health Policymaking and Administration," in *Handbook on Mental Health Policy in the United States*, edited by David A. Rochefort (Westport, CT: Greenwood Press, 1989), and "Integrating Mental Health into a General Health Care System," in *Hospital and Community Psychiatry*, Vol. 45, No. 9 (September 1994). Mechanic is particularly good, as in his studies of deinstitutionalization, at revealing and correcting myths and misconceptions by looking closely at what has actually happened—at data, research, and relevant reports and findings—and then moving on to compassionate considerations of the hows and whys of what we may actually be able to accomplish.

Rochefort's *Handbook,* cited above, provides many thoughtful and informative essays on mental health policy, as does the previously mentioned *Mental Health, United States, 1996.* Books in the series *New Directions for Mental Health Services,* published quarterly as paperback sourcebooks in *The Jossey-Bass Social and Behavioral Sciences Series* (San Francisco: Jossey-Bass), provide a wealth of information and perspectives on mental health programs and policy. I found the essays of John A. Talbott particularly sensible and stimulating (*The Perspective of John Talbott*, 1988).

Stand and Deliver: Action Call to a Failing Industry—The NAMI Managed Care Report Card by Laura Lee Hall, Elizabeth R. Edgar, and Laurie M. Flynn (Arlington, VA: NAMI, 1997) offers a fair and thoroughgoing evaluation of the complicated and endlessly changing developments and policies that fall under the heading of managed care. Just as there are good and bad—and less good and less bad—state institutions and community mental health programs, so there are good and bad—and less good and less bad—managed-care plans.

In my own state of Massachusetts, for example, the managed-care company responsible for most mental health services stands to make three times the profit on state-mandated performance standards than it does on cost savings, thus providing more incentive for care than for profit. The result: better and more efficiently delivered treatment. In addition, in Massachusetts, as in other states with well-conceived, well-monitored, and well-administered managed-care programs, short- and long-term therapy (individual and group), psychosocial rehabilitation, and consumer participation in decision making are central to services rendered.

David Mechanic's newly revised *Mental Health and Social Policy,* cited above, provides a good starting point for an understanding of managed care, and of the changing and evolving relations of care and economics to policies and outcomes, as does Eric Gopelrud's 1995 paper, available from SAMHSA (Managed Care Initiative, Room 12-C-10, 5600 Fishers Lane, Rockville, MD 20857), "Managed Care for Mental Health and Substance Abuse Services."

Bernard Neugeboren's books—*Organization, Policy, and Practice in the Human Services* (Binghamton, NY: The Haworth Press, 1991) and *Environmental Practice in the Human Services: Integration of Micro and Macro Roles, Skills, and Contexts* (Binghamton, NY: The Haworth Press, 1996)—offer generous overviews concerning the interrelations of policies and practices in the human services generally, and in mental health in particular.

Peter Wyden's *Conquering Schizophrenia: A Father, His Son, & a Medical Breakthrough* (New York: Alfred A. Knopf, 1998) is a well-researched and optimistic survey of new and promising developments, especially in psychopharmacology.

Courtenay Harding's most recent update of her studies of the relation of outcome to social functioning, and to policies that enhance or restrict recovery for individuals with long-term histories of psychiatric disorders, "Long-Term Outcome of Social Functioning," coauthored with Andrew B. Keller, appears in *Handbook of Social Functioning in Schizophrenia* (Boston: Allyn & Bacon, 1998). See also her essay "Chronicity in Schizophrenia Revisited," with Joseph Zubin and John S. Strauss, in *British Journal of Psychiatry*, Vol. 161 (1992), and, with James H. Zahniser, "Empirical Correction of Seven Myths About Schizophrenia with Implications for Treatment," in *Acta Psychiatrica Scandinavia*, Vol. 90 (1994).

Another recent and important study concerning outcomes is "Pattern of Usual Care for Schizophrenia: Initial Results from the Schizophrenia Patient Outcomes Research Team (PORT) Client Survey" by Anthony F. Lehman, Donald M. Steinwachs, et al., in *Schizophrenia Bulletin*, Vol. 24, No. 1 (1998).

Keith Doubt's *Towards a Sociology of Schizophrenia: Humanistic Reflections* (Toronto: University of Toronto Press, 1996) — one of Moe Armstrong's favorite books — is thoughtful and stimulating.

PROGRAMS AND PRACTICES

The variety and abundance of new and evolving programs and practices for individuals with serious mental illness is vast and heartening, and I will make note here mainly of where I have obtained valuable information for many of the programs and modes of treatment mentioned in this book, and of where readers might obtain further information, guidance, and resources.

Diane T. Marsh's *Serious Mental Illness and the Family: The Practitioner's Guide* (New York: John Wiley, 1998) offers an excellent and comprehensive introduction to current practices. It is wide-ranging, richly informed, and wonderfully sensible.

Psychological and Social Aspects of Psychiatric Disability, edited by LeRoy Spaniol, Cheryl Gagne, and Martin Koehler (Boston: Boston University Center for Psychiatric Rehabilitation, 1997) contains a generous variety of essays on psychosocial rehabilitation, recovery, family, advocacy, and empowerment. *Psychiatric Rehabilitation* by William A. Anthony, M. R. Cohen, and Marianne Farkas (Boston: Boston University Center for Psychiatric Rehabilitation, 1990) is fundamental to an understanding of psychosocial rehabilitation. A new edition, taking into account developments in the last decade — managed care, new medications, and so on — will appear in 1999. *The Recovery Workbook: Practical Coping and Empowerment Strategies for People with Psychiatric Disability* (Boston: Boston University Center for Psychiatric Rehabilitation, 1994) by LeRoy Spaniol, Martin Koehler, and Dori Hutchinson illustrates the practicalities of psychosocial techniques and strategies.

Readers interested in reviewing full texts of expert consensus guidelines for the treatment of various psychiatric disorders should contact the American Psychiatric Association (1400 K Street N.W., Washington, DC 20016) or *The Journal of Clinical Psychiatry* (Physicians Postgraduate Press, Inc., P.O. Box 752870, Memphis, TN 38175-2870). Those interested in PORT (Patient Outcomes Research Team) findings and recommendations should contact the Agency for Health Care Policy and Research at the National Institute of Mental Health (5600 Fishers Lane, Rockville, MD 20857). The World Health Organization (WHO) also provides a wide variety of books and materials; see especially two volumes edited by Christopher J. L. Murray and Alan D. Lopez: *The Global Burden of Disease*

(Cambridge: Harvard University Press, 1996) and *Global Health Statistics* (Cambridge: Harvard University Press, 1996).

Much has been written about the Assertive Community Treatment Programs (PACT and ACT) developed by Leonard I. Stein and Mary Ann Test. David Mechanic's "Therapeutic Intervention: Issues in the Care of the Mentally Ill," in *American Journal of Orthopsychiatry*, Vol. XXXVII, No. 4 (July 1967), is probably the earliest articulation of the basic principles that have informed these programs. Stein and Test's "Alternative to Mental Hospital Treatment," in *Archives of General Psychiatry*, Vol. 37 (April 1980), along with *The Training in Community Living Model: A Decade of Experience* (*New Directions for Mental Health Series*, No. 26, June 1985), offers overviews of the progam's tenets, policies, and outcomes. For more recent studies and evaluations of these programs, readers might consult the "Special Section on Assertive Community Treatment: An Introduction" by Robert E. Drake and Barbara J. Burns, in *Psychiatric Services*, Vol. 46, No. 7 (July 1995), and "Models of Community Care for Severe Mental Illness: A Review of Research on Case Management" by Kim T. Mueser, Gary R. Bond, et al., in *Schizophrenia Bulletin*, Vol. 24, No. 1 (1998).

For information, practical and historical, on supported education, see Karen V. Unger's *Handbook on Supported Education: Providing Services for Students with Psychiatric Disabilities* (Baltimore: Paul H. Brookes, 1998) and a special issue of *The Journal of the California Alliance for the Mentally Ill*, "Supported Education," Vol. 8, No. 2 (June 19, 1997).

For information on alternatives to hospital care, see *Alternatives to the Hospital for Acute Psychiatric Treatment*, edited by Richard Warner (Washington, DC: American Psychiatric Press, 1995). Leonard I. Stein and Mary Ann Test's *Alternatives to Mental Hospital Treatment* (New York: Plenum Press, 1978), though two decades old, also remains valuable.

Edward M. Podvoll's *The Seduction of Madness: Revolutionary Insights into the World of Psychosis and a Compassionate Approach to Recovery at Home* (New York: HarperCollins, 1990), a book central to the Windhorse program, is in addition, as Oliver Sacks has written, "an eloquent, and phenomenologically fascinating, meditation on the structure of the mind."

Fountain House: Portraits of Lives Reclaimed from Mental Illness, edited by Mary Flannery and Mark Glickman, with a foreword by E. Fuller Torrey (Center City, MN: Hazelden, 1996), provides many first-person accounts by clubhouse members, as well as a directory of U.S. and international clubhouse programs, and the "Standards for Clubhouse Programs" utilized by these programs worldwide.

Michael Winerip's *9 Highland Road: Sane Living for the Mentally Ill* (New York: Pantheon, 1994) has much to say about mental illness and its relation in recent years to homelessness, institutionalization, and community residences. Its portraits of individuals with mental illness—their friends, families, and the professionals they rely on, and the ways they interact with one another and with their communities—are excellent and compelling.

For detailed and diverse renderings of the lives of individuals suffering from various forms of mental illness, and of their interactions with others—families, friends, and mental health professionals—I can recommend the following books to readers: Susan Sheehan's *Is There No Place on Earth for Me?* (New York: Houghton Mifflin, 1982), Frieda Fromm-Reichmann's *Principles of Intensive Psychotherapy* (Chicago: University of Chicago Press, 1950), Judi Chamberlin's *On Our Own* (London: Mind, 1977), Susan Baur's *Dinosaur Man: Tales of Madness & Enchantment from the Back Ward* (New York: HarperCollins, 1991), Joanne Greenberg's *I Never Promised You a Rose Garden* (New York: Holt, Rinehart & Winston, 1964), Jules Henry's *Pathways to Madness* (New York: Random House, 1972), and the essays in *The Experience of Recovery*, edited by LeRoy Spaniol and Martin Koehler (Boston: Boston University Center for Psychiatric Rehabilitation, 1994).

There has been an abundance of books published in recent years wherein men and women recount their own experiences of mental illness, and many of those books may already be familiar to readers—e.g., William Styron's *Darkness Visible* (New York: Random House, 1990), Kay Redfield Jamison's *An Unquiet Mind* (New York: Alfred A. Knopf, 1995), Susan Kaysen's *Girl, Interrupted* (New York: Random House, 1993), Patty Duke's *A Brilliant Madness* (New York: Bantam Books, 1992), Lori Schiller's *The Quiet Room: A Journey out of the Torment of Madness* (New York: Warner Books, 1994), Kathy Cronkite's *On the Edge of Darkness: Conversations about Depression* (New York: Doubleday, 1994), and Elizabeth Swados's *The Four of Us: The Story of a Family* (New York: Farrar, Straus & Giroux, 1991). Readers interested in searching out other personal narratives, historical and/or contemporary, that describe the experience of mental illness from the point of view of the person experiencing it might begin by consulting the bibliographical essay "Reading Suggestions" in Roy Porter's *A Social History of Madness,* or the listings in either the NAMI or the NDMDA book catalog. See also *A Mad People's History of Madness,* edited by Dale Peterson (Pittsburgh: University of Pittsburgh Press, 1982) and *Women of the Asylum: Voices from Behind the Walls, 1840–1945*, edited by Jeffrey L. Geller and Maxine Harris (New York: Anchor/Doubleday, 1994).

Otto Wahl's *Media Madness: Public Images of Mental Illness* (New Brunswick: Rutgers University Press, 1995) is rich in detail and anecdote, and especially good at showing the many ways in which false views of mental illness, purveyed in the media, shape the ways even the most enlightened of us view the world around us. Wahl has written a more recent study for NAMI, *Consumer Experience of Stigma: Results of a National Survey* (Arlington, VA: National Alliance for the Mentally Ill, 1997).

The literature on homelessness and its relation to mental illness and to public policies that deal with both these conditions is vast. Peter Rossi's *Down and Out in America: The Origins of Homelessness* (Chicago: University of Chicago Press, 1994) is an excellent introduction to the subject. Other thoughtful and reliable books are Christopher Jencks, *The*

Homeless (Cambridge: Harvard University Press, 1994) and Martha R. Burt's *Over the Edge: The Growth of Homelessness in the 1980s* (New York: Russell Sage Foundation, 1993). *The Homeless Mentally Ill: A Task Force Report of the American Psychiatric Association,* edited by H. Richard Lamb (Washington, DC: American Psychiatric Press, 1984) contains excellent essays on matters relating to mental illness, homelessness, and social policy. Jennifer Toth's *The Mole People: Life in the Tunnels Beneath New York City* (Chicago: Chicago Review Press, 1993) gives an informative account of homelessness in New York City. Readers interested in more information concerning the Pathways to Housing program should see "From Streets to Homes: An Innovative Approach to Supported Housing for Homeless Adults with Psychiatric Disabilities" by Sam Tsemberis (*The Journal of Community Psychiatry,* forthcoming in 1999) or write directly to Pathways at 155 W. 23rd Street, New York, NY 10011.

RESOURCES

I have relied on the following periodicals to keep me regularly informed about a wide range of new and ongoing developments relating to mental illness:

Advances: The Robert Wood Johnson Foundation Quarterly Newsletter
College Road East
P.O. Box 2316
Princeton, NJ 08543-2316

The Harvard Medical School Mental Health Letter
74 Fenwood Road
Boston, MA 02115

The Journal
California Alliance for the Mentally Ill
1111 Howe Avenue, Suite 475
Sacramento, CA 95825

NAMI Advocate
200 North Glebe Road, Suite 1015
Arlington, VA 22203-3754

NARSAD Research Newsletter
60 Cutter Mill Road, Suite 404
Great Neck, NY 11021

National DMDA News
National Depressive and Manic-Depressive Association
730 N. Franklin, Suite 501
Chicago, IL 60610

National Empowerment Center Newsletter
599 Canal Street
Lawrence, MA 01840

OMH Quarterly
New York State Office of Mental Health
44 Holland Avenue
Albany, NY 12229-0001

Psychiatric Rehabilitation Journal
Boston University
940 Commonwealth Avenue W.
Boston, MA 02215

Schizophrenia Bulletin
Government Printing Office
Washington, DC 20402

Many of the mental health organizations listed below regularly publish brochures, informational pamphlets, guides, individual papers on particular subjects, and books, and all of these organizations have trained staff members who will respond knowledgeably to requests for information and help.

American Psychiatric Association
1400 K Street, N.W.
Washington, DC 20005

Phone: (202) 682-6220
Fax: (202) 682-6850
E-mail: apa@psych.org
Website: http://www.psych.org

American Psychological Association
750 1st Street, N.E.
Washington, DC 20002-4242

Phone: (202) 336-5500
E-mail: centralprograms@apa.org
Website: http://www.apa.org

Association on Higher Education and Disability (AHEAD)
P.O. Box 21192
Columbus, OH 43221

Phone: (614) 488-4972
Fax: (614) 488-1174
Website: http://www.ahead.org

Center for Psychiatric Rehabilitation
Boston University
940 Commonwealth Avenue W.
Boston, MA 02215

Phone: (617) 353-3549
Fax: (617) 353-7700
Website: http://www.bu.edu.sarpsych

**International Association of Psychosocial Rehabilitation
Services (IAPSRS)**
10025 Governor Warfield Parkway
Columbia, MD 21044

Phone: (410) 730-7190
Fax: (410) 730-5965

National Alliance for the Mentally Ill (NAMI)
200 North Glebe Road, Suite 1015
Arlington, VA 22203-3754

Phone: (703) 524-7600
Fax: (703) 524-9094
E-mail: frieda@nami.org
Website: http://www.nami.org

NAMI Helpline: (800) 950-NAMI (6264)

National Alliance for Research on Schizophrenia and Depression (NARSAD)
60 Cutter Mill Road, Suite 404
Great Neck, NY 11021

Phone: (516) 829-0091
Fax: (516) 487-6930
Website: http://www.mhsource.com/narsad.html

National Association of Psychiatric Treatment Centers for Children
1025 Connecticut Avenue, NW, Suite 1012
Washington, DC 20036

Phone: (202) 857-9735
Fax: (202) 362-5145
E-mail: naptcc@aol.com
Website: http://www.air-dc.org/cecp/teams/stratpart/
naptcc.htm

National Coalition for the Homeless
1012 Fourteenth Street, NW, #600
Washington, DC 20005-3410

Phone: (202) 737-6444
Fax: (202) 737-6445
E-mail: nch@ari.net
Website: http://nch.ari.net

National Depressive and Manic-Depressive Association (NDMDA)
730 N. Franklin, Suite 501
Chicago, IL 60610

Phone: (312) 642-0049
(800) 82-NDMDA (826-3632)
Website: http://www.ndmda.org

National Empowerment Center
599 Canal Street
Lawrence, MA 01840

Phone: (978) 685-1518
(800) POWER2U (769-3728)
Fax: (978) 681-6426
Website: http://www.power2u.org

National Institute of Mental Health (NIMH)
5600 Fishers Lane
Rockville, MD 20857

Phone: (301) 443-4513
E-mail: nimhinfo@nih.gov
Website: http://www.nimh.nih.gov

National Mental Health Association (NMHA)
1021 Prince Street
Alexandria, VA 22314-2971

Phone: (703) 684-7722
(800) 969-NMHA
Fax: (703) 684-5968
E-mail: nmhainfo@aol.com
Website: http://www.nmha.org

National Mental Health Consumers' Self-help Clearing-house
1211 Chestnut Street, Suite 1000
Philadelphia, PA 19107

Phone: (800) 553-4KEY (4539)
Fax: (215) 636-6310
Website: http://www.mhselfhelp.org

The Robert Wood Johnson Foundation
College Road East
P.O. Box 2316
Princeton, NJ 08543-2316

Phone: (609) 452-8701
E-mail: mail@rwjf.org
E-mail: publications@rwjf.org (for publications)
Website: http://www.rwjf.org

U.S. Department of Health and Human Services
Substance Abuse and Mental Health Services
   Administration
Center for Mental Health Services
5600 Fishers Lane
Rockville, MD 20857

Knowledge Exchange Network (KEN)
(800) 789-2647 (voice)
(301) 443-9006 (TDD)
(800) 790-2647 (Bulletin Board)
Fax: (301) 984-8796
E-mail: ken@mentalhealth.org
Website: http://www.mentalhealth.org

INDEX

Achebe, Chinua, 89
adrenocorticotropic hormone (ACTH), 297
affective (mood) disorders:
  defined, 250
  kindling model of cause of, 296
  see also depression, clinical; manic-depressive illness
African Americans, 61–64, 72, 126, 150–151
agranulocytosis, 269
Alcoholics Anonymous, 157
Alliance for the Mentally Ill, 78
  see also National Alliance for the Mentally Ill
American Journal of Psychiatry, 125, 252–253
American Psychiatric Association (APA), 121, 125, 243, 246, 254, 261
Amichai, Yehuda, 57
amphetamines, 289
anger, 13, 229–230
Anthony, Bill, 25–26, 320
antidepressant medications, 118, 298
anxiety attacks, 224
Approaches to the Mind (Havens), 247
Armstrong, Moe, 31, 32–58, 64, 213, 223, 351
  background of, 32–34, 45–47, 93–94
  on hospital care, 81, 95, 97, 98–99, 101–102
  on improvement of mental health system, 38–43, 50–53, 85, 86, 94, 150

mental illness of, 32, 38, 39–40, 45–47, 49, 338–340
professional career of, 31, 32, 57, 72, 150, 171, 339
on residential facilities, 81–82, 83, 84
Robert Neugeboren's visits with, 87–88, 91–97, 99–103, 340
writings by, 35–37, 39, 45, 51, 54–56, 87, 102–103, 340
Arrow of God (Achebe), 89
Asperger's syndrome, 86
Assertive Community Treatment (ACT), 124, 155–157, 170, 207, 305, 307–308
Association of Medical Superintendents of American Institutions for the Insane, 53–54
autism, 86
avolition, 287

Baldessarini, Ross, 252–253
Baldwin, James, 151
Beacon of Hope, 192, 197–198
Bellafato, Lisa, 23–24
Berlin, Isaiah, 111
bipolar disorder, *see* manic-depressive illness
blacks, 126, 150–151
  as mental health workers, 72
  residential discrimination against, 61–62, 63–64
Blake, William, 213
Bleuler, Eugen, 245, 256, 287
Bleuler, Manfred, 256–257

Borstin, Robert O., 142
Boston University Center for
    Psychiatric Rehabilitation, 14–16,
    21–25, 27, 32, 78–79, 214, 263,
    343
Bradley, Kevin, 234, 235, 237
brain function:
    of cerebral cortex vs. subcortical
        areas, 293
    complexity of, 299–304
    neural plasticity and, 17–20, 288,
        295–296
    neurotransmission in, 286, 287–291,
        297–300
    new technologies for study of, 294–
        295
    psychobiological effect of traumatic
        experiences on, 47–48
brain scans, 185–186
Bright Air, Brilliant Fire (Edelman), 17–
    18
Bristol-Myers Squibb, 138
British Journal of Psychiatry, 292
Bronx Psychiatric Center, 102–104,
    106–109, 132, 175, 195–197, 199–
    201, 265, 268, 270–277, 280–283,
    346–347, 350
Buddhist philosophy, 191–192
Bumiller, Kristin, 86–87, 170–171
Burch House, 190

cancer patients, survivals of, 228–229
Canterbury House, 66
Carling, Paul, 206
Carr, Louise, 214, 309–311, 312,
    345
Cassady, Neal, 33
Cather, Willa, 29
Catholic Charities U.S.A., 192
CAUSE, 72–73, 76, 77, 161, 342
Cavett, Dick, 213
cerebral cortex, 293
chaotic attractor theory, 297
Chapin, Eric, 195
children:
    adolescent, 187–188, 210
    independence cultivated in, 108
    mental illness of, 30, 248
    of mentally ill parents, 187, 188–
        189, 216–217, 312, 319
    of parents with substance-abuse
        problems, 130–131
Chua, S. E., 291–293, 295
civil rights movement, 150–151
Cloutier, Christine Duffie, 76, 77, 79,
    342
Cloutier, Gaston, 72–79, 80, 81, 161,
    212–213, 223, 269, 338, 342–343
Clozaril (clozapine), 11, 76, 77, 78, 199–
    200, 265, 266, 268–271, 273, 285–
    286, 289–291, 296, 304, 347
clubhouse programs, 83, 157, 166, 234–
    237, 239–240

Cold Regions Research and
    Engineering Laboratory (CRREL),
    159–161, 165–166, 168, 169, 170,
    171, 214
Cole, Jonathan, 75
college education, 72–73, 206
Comprehensive Textbook of Psychiatry,
    The (Freedman, Kaplan and
    Sadock, eds.), 217–218
computer training programs, 14, 23–
    24, 281–282
consumer movement, 40, 95, 99
Consumer Reports, 118, 119, 137
Continuing Medical Education (CME),
    credits, 139
continuity of care, 265, 274–277, 335,
    337
corticoropin (CRF), 297
cortisol, 297
cotransmission, 288
Creedmoor Hospital, 83, 109, 209,
    308, 344
crime, 38, 59, 309
crisis respite program, 165, 186, 190
    individual crisis plans in, 181–183
    residential model for, 190–191
    success of, 340–341, 342
    training session on, 173–184
crisis stabilization unit (CSU), 83–84
Crossing Place, 190
Cruz, Henry, 24

D'Agostino, Carl, 211
Dartmouth–New Hampshire
    Psychiatric Research Center, 153
Davidson, Larry, 259–260
day centers, 83
    see also clubhouse programs
deaf people, neural plasticity in, 20
Deegan, Pat, 167, 213
deinstitutionalization, 51–52, 97–98,
    112, 157, 251, 278
dementia praecox, 243–244, 245
Depakote, 298
depression, clinical (unipolar disorder):
    biochemical aspect of, 65
    long-range outcomes of, 260–261
    neurobiological theories of, 296–298
    see also manic-depressive illness
Deutsch, Albert, 278
Dimock Community Health Center,
    51
discordancy, degree of, 161–162, 237
diseases, scientific classification of,
    244
divorce, 224
Don't Worry About the Kids
    (Neugeboren), 274
dopamine hypothesis, 286–292, 294,
    295
Douglas, Lynne, 141–142, 212–231,
    254, 343
Douglass, Frederick, 173

Duffie, Christine, 76, 77, 79, 342
Duke, Patty, 213, 238

Edelman, Gerald, 17–18, 302
education, 70–73, 206
Eisenberg, Leon, 17
Ekblaw, Elsa, 77
electroconvulsive therapy (ECT), 10,
    11, 76, 105, 135
Eli Lilly, 136, 137, 146
employment:
    clubhouse-model programs for
        return to, 83, 157, 235–236
    community care support on, 157–
        158, 159–162
    in custodial positions, 160–162, 166,
        168
    flexible schedules of, 77, 160
    healing influence of, 195, 233–234
    training programs for, 14–16, 23–24,
        27, 157–158
Epidemiologic Catchment Area Study of
    Prevalence Rates of Mental
    Disorders, 29–31, 248, 254
Epstein, Alan, 201, 271, 273, 274–277
Essential Psychopharmacology (Stahl),
    287–288

Fagerson, Dori, 212
Fair Housing Amendments Act (1988),
    59
Farini, Nick, 98–99, 100, 198–199
Fields, Steven, 113–114
Fisher, Dan, 16–17, 21–22, 167, 171,
    213
Fontaine, Kate, 213–214, 231–241, 333,
    344
Fortuna, Jeff, 186, 190–195
Fortuna, Molly, 194
Fountain House, 83, 124, 157, 235
Four Guys and a Big Truck, 195
Freedman, Robert, 114–116, 208
Freud, Sigmund, 298
Fuller Mental Health Center, 83

Gamble, Thayer, 315–319, 338, 345–
    346
Geller, Jeffrey, 161–162, 236, 237
general hospitals, psychiatric
    admissions to, 278–280
Genesis Clubhouse, 232, 233, 234–237
genetic theory, mental illness linked
    to, 295, 297
glutamate, 287, 294
Goethe, Johann Wolfgang von, ix
Gogard, Jean Baba, 312–313, 338, 345
Goldwater, Barry, 61–62
Goodwin, Frederick K., 261–262
Gracie Square, 197
Greenberg, Joanne, 238
Grinker, Lori, 97, 99–101
Grob, Gerald N., 51, 52, 53, 54, 246,
    251

group homes, community resistance
    toward, 58–61
Guptan, Dr., 271, 273, 274, 275, 276
Gurdjieff, G., 79

Haas, Lyn, 186, 190, 193
Haldol, 250, 289, 290, 298
Halloween, mental patients exhibited
    on, 64
Handbook of Clinical Psycho-
    pharmacology for Therapists
    (Bachus), 266, 294
Harding, Courtenay, 250, 251–252,
    256, 258–259, 262
Hargreaves, William A., 135
Harrison, Walter, 345
Havens, Leston, 247, 347
Hayes, Richard, 213
Hegarty, James, 252–253
Heldman, Kevin, 278–280
Hillel, 39
Hilton, David, 150, 159, 175–176, 183–
    184, 202, 206, 207, 213, 344
Himes, Chester, 133
Hogan, Michael, 134, 135
homeless people, mental illness
    among, 29–30, 97–98, 214, 305–
    309, 320
hope, 16, 21, 134–135
hospital care:
    change of population in, 97–98, 197,
        251
    community care models vs., 154,
        155, 177–178
    comprehensive care received
        through, 51, 349–350
    cost issues of, 27, 98, 177, 275, 280
    crisis respite vs. 177–178, 341
    criterion of eligibility for, 98
    deinstitutionalization process and,
        51–52, 97, 98, 112, 157, 251, 278
    funding tied to, 52
    of general hospital psychiatric
        admissions, 278–280
    history of, 53–54
    legal rights of those in, 279
    maximum asylum population and,
        53–54
    for mental illness coupled with
        substance abuse, 97–98, 197
    outpatient care after, 156
    patient activities in, 281–282
    physical abuse during, 70, 73
    physical conditions of, 95, 106, 197,
        200–201, 279–280
    staff attitudes in, 91–95, 98–109, 196–
        199, 200–201, 271–272, 279, 280
Hott, Larry, 197, 198–199
Housing and Urban Development
    Department (HUD), U.S., 58, 59,
    344
housing program, 304–309, 322–326
Hu, John, 1

Hubel, David, 17
Hundert, Edward, 17, 288, 301–302

Imagining Robert (Neugeboren), 2, 4,
    12, 39, 41, 80, 84, 90, 91–92, 96,
    201, 208, 214, 217, 229, 274
innovations, time lag between
    conception and realization of, 205
insulin coma treatments, 209, 217–
    218, 267, 308
isolation, 22, 39

James, Henry, 243
Jamison, Kay Redfield, 169, 229, 261–
    262
job interviews, 15–16
Johns Hopkins Medical School, 229
Journal of Clinical Psychiatry Guidelines,
    121, 123

Kaplan, Mark, 10–11, 89–97, 100, 102,
    103–106, 198, 268
Katz, Ben, 89–90
Keane, Dolores, 311–312, 345
Kendler, Kenneth, 295
Kessler, Ronald, 248, 254
kindness, 53, 194, 230
King, Larry, 339
Kline, Paula, 208–211, 212, 215–220,
    223, 254, 344
Kohn, Larry, 15–16, 66, 68, 71, 79–81,
    171, 265–266
Kraepelin, Emil, 121, 243–245, 247,
    248, 249, 253, 298
Kramer, Morton, 251
Kramer, Peter, 149

language, sensory capacities attuned
    to, 19–20
learned helplessness, 167
Lee, Nathaniel, 120
Leff, Steve, 332
Leonardo da Vinci, 213
Levi, Primo, 285
Lewontin, R. C., 20
Lidz, Charles, 62–63
lithium, 75, 78, 105, 221, 250, 298
loneliness, 114
Lowell, Robert, 213

McGlashan, Thomas H., 259–260
McKenna, P. J., 291–293, 295
McLean Hospital, 75, 212, 263
managed care, 144–145
manic-depressive illness (bipolar
    disorder):
    as early diagnostic classification,
        244, 245
    long-term outcome studies of, 260,
        261–262
    medication for, 75, 77–78
    neurobiological causation of, 296–
        298

Manic-Depressive Illness (Jamison and
    Goodwin), 261–262
Massachusetts, University of, Medical
    School of, 161
mastectomy, sensory remapping of
    brain after, 19
Mead, Shery, 162–172, 174, 175–190,
    193, 212, 213, 338, 344
    background of, 162–165, 184–190,
        341–342
    crisis respite program developed by,
        165, 171–172, 175–184, 340–341,
        342
    peer support centers run by, 162,
        163, 169
    on recovery strategies, 166–167, 168,
        202–203, 206
Mechanic, David, 250–251
Medicaid, 133
medical alert bracelets, 38
medications, psychiatric:
    blood tests required for, 269–270
    compliance concerns and, 125–126,
        154
    dopamine hypothesis and, 285–292
    economic factors of, 122, 135–139
    effectiveness of, 231, 232, 240–241,
        265–266, 273, 347
    improper use of, 266–267
    industry marketing efforts for, 122,
        135
    maintenance dosages of, 49
    for manic-depressive illness, 75
    psychotherapy vs., 116–119, 121,
        124, 135, 240–241, 262, 265
    as quick fix, 146–147
    recovery process after use of, 49–50,
        304
    side effects of, 39–40, 77, 114–115,
        125–126, 221, 238, 265, 267, 269,
        291, 304
    widespread use of, 149
Mental Health Association, 116, 263
mental health system:
    community care models in, 152–170,
        304–309
    consumer input in, 50–51, 179, 207
    continuity of care needed in, 265,
        274–277, 335, 337
    cost concerns of, 27, 31, 38, 52, 123–
        124, 133–134, 178, 308
    decentralization of, 169
    deinstitutionalization process in, 51–
        52, 97, 98, 112, 157, 278
    history of, 52–54
    in home environments, 186, 190–
        195
    moral treatment model in, 53–54
    in New York vs. Massachusetts, 81
    pay levels in, 124, 307
    systemic improvement of, 85, 86–87
    treatment guidelines developed by,
        120–127, 134

mental illness:
  brain function abnormalities and, 289–301
  complex causality of, 300–304
  daily living priorities and, 112–114
  early classifications and prognoses of, 243–250
  family impact of, 140–144, 149–150, 222, 229, 334–335, 339
  general hospital admissions for, 278–280
  genetic linkages and, 229
  health care discriminatory limits on, 144–145
  homelessness and, 29, 30, 97–98, 305–309, 320
  isolation induced by, 22, 39, 112
  lack of treatment in, 29, 50, 143–145
  physical disabilities vs., 25–26, 116–117, 139–140, 228–229, 335
  police policies on, 38
  positive symptoms vs. negative symptoms of, 287
  prevalence of, 29, 30, 31, 148, 149, 248
  in prison population, 30, 313
  psychotherapy vs. medication for, 116–119, 121, 124, 135, 240–241, 262, 265
  recovery potential from, 4, 14–15, 22, 41–43, 249–267, 335, 336–338
  simplistic biomedical models of, 146–147, 302
  social attitudes toward, 50, 52–54, 58–64, 113, 140–142, 145–151, 208, 249, 263
  social factors as influence on chronicity of, 26, 303–304
  substance abuse combined with, 30, 33–34, 44, 97–98, 197, 265, 306–307, 309, 316–317
  violent behavior and, 38, 59, 62–63
  in youth population, 30, 248
mesolimbic pathway, 290–291
Miller, Rose, 24
Mills, Sally, 196–197
mood (affective) disorders, see affective disorders; depression, clinical; manic-depressive illness
moral treatment, 53–54
Mosaic Clubhouse, 214
Mueller, Lisa, 160–161, 170
Mueser, Kim, 178–179, 342
multiple personality disorder (MPD), 65, 67–68, 69, 71
multiple sclerosis, 116
Murphy, Hugh, 308, 344–345

National Alliance for Research on Schizophrenia and Depression (NARSAD), 136
National Alliance for the Mentally Ill (NAMI), 64, 112–113, 116, 117, 118, 126, 150, 155, 260–261, 263, 334, 339
National Depression Awareness Day, 137, 138
National Depressive and Manic-Depressive Association (NDMDA), 116
National Empowerment Center (NEC), 17, 167–168, 263
National Institute of Mental Health, 30, 117, 118, 135–136, 262
National Mental Health Advisory Council, 29, 30
Neugeboren, Aaron, 201, 274, 281, 282, 344
Neugeboren, Eli, 201, 274, 282, 320, 323, 344
Neugeboren, Miriam, 274, 348
Neugeboren, Robert:
  author's visits with, 1–12, 89–91, 95–97, 99–100, 102–103, 106, 115, 270–271, 272–273, 282–283, 340, 344, 347–348
  diagnosis of, 296
  family relationships with, 7, 141, 202, 274, 281, 282, 348
  in hospital care, 2, 3, 4–5, 9–13, 20–21, 28, 39, 40, 84, 90–95, 97, 98, 99–106, 109, 132, 195–196, 198, 199–201, 209, 258, 271–277, 280–283, 308, 313
  humor of, 10–11, 41, 271, 273, 281
  improvements in care for, 81, 85, 87, 96, 97, 101–104, 109, 152, 153, 175, 333, 347–349, 351
  long-term outlook for, 81, 327–332, 344–345
  medications received by, 11, 32, 77–78, 105, 196, 199–200, 258, 265–271, 296, 298, 347
  poetry written by, 21, 39
  in residential facilities, 1–10, 192, 197–198
  therapy relationships of, 10–11, 21, 89–93, 96, 102, 103–106, 196–197, 274–277, 280–282, 346–348
  youth of, 2, 3, 237–238, 267
neural plasticity, 17–20, 288, 296
neurotransmitters, 286, 287–291, 297–300
Newman, Marvin, 7–8
New York Times, 149
Next Step Peer Support Center, 162
nicotine, medication side effects ameliorated with, 114–115, 208
nigrostriatal pathway, 290
9 Highland Road (Winerip), 60
Northampton, Mass., residence for mentally ill opposed in, 58–61, 64

Odyssey Behavioral Health Care Residence, 127–131, 133, 214
olanzapine (Zyprexa), 105, 285–286

"On Being Sane in Insane Places" (Rosenhan), 278–279
On the Road (Kerouac), 33, 75
Ornstein, Carol, 280–282, 346–347, 350

Pam, Alvin, 106, 107, 108–109, 195, 201, 273–276, 280, 347, 350, 351
Parkinson's disease, 290, 299
Park Manor Adult Care Facility, 1–2, 5–6, 7–8, 9
Partners for Change Conference on Recovery, 205–208
Pathways to Housing, 214, 304–326, 332, 344, 345
Patient Outcomes Research Team (PORT), 121, 125–126, 134, 135
peer support, 22, 162, 165, 166
    consumer empowerment through, 179
    in crisis respite center, 173–184
    meeting rules in, 174–175
peptides, 288
pharmaceutical industry, 122, 135–140, 146
Pickus, Carl, 211–212, 254
Piersall, Jimmy, 213
Pinel, Philippe, 53
placebo effect, 241
"Pluralism" (Berlin), 111
Podvoll, Edward, 191
post-traumatic stress disorder (PTSD), 47–48
prison population, mental disorders in, 30, 313
Progress Foundation, 113–114, 149
Project HELP, 319–320
Prolixin, 267
Prozac, 137–138, 146
psychiatry, severe mental illness as focus of, 54
psychosocial rehabilitation, lack of support for, 121, 123–124, 125, 135
psychotherapy:
    cognitive behavioral therapy, 192
    for inpatients, 280–281
    medication vs., 116–119, 121, 124, 135, 240–241, 262, 265
    in residential programs, 192, 193
    responsibility issues in, 189–190
    support received in, 186–187, 219–220, 228, 280–281
Putting Knowledge to Use (Glaser, Abelson, and Garrison), 205

Question of Hu, The (Spence), 1
quetiapine (Seroquil), 285–286

racism, 150–151
recovery process:
    belief in potential of, 22, 167, 194, 202–203, 206, 207, 240, 241
    beyond disability status, 202–203, 206–215
    early expectations as deterrent in, 161–162, 237–238
    hope in, 16, 21, 134–135
    individual needs accommodated in, 43, 52
    learned helplessness vs., 166–167
    long-range community care in, 157, 158
    maintenance vs. cure as goal in, 52
    personal responsibility developed in, 107–108, 158–159, 171, 182, 189–190, 207, 229
    physical disability model of, 25–27
    social rehabilitation in, 49–50, 304
    supportive relationships in, 21–24, 71, 72, 79–80, 84–87, 107, 222, 227, 232, 240–241, 311, 313, 319
Reich, Wilhelm, 198
religious faith, 76, 77, 78, 80
residential programs, 1–10, 81–83
    availability of, 83
    behavior-based rule structures in, 128–129
    community integration with, 337
    costs of, 27, 82
    family center linked to, 129–131
    neighborhood resistance toward, 58–61, 64, 83
    physical condition of, 5–6, 82, 127–128, 191, 193
    staff care in, 190, 192–195
    of Windhorse, 190–195
responsibility, 81, 108, 128, 158–159, 171, 182, 189–190, 207, 222, 309
Retreat, The, 212
Riesman, David, 138
Risperdal (risperidone), 32, 39–40, 49, 122, 268, 285–286, 338, 340
Rofman, Samuel, 269–270, 291
Rosenfield, Israel, 17, 301–302
Rosenhan, David, 278–279
Ross, Bud, 158, 159, 163, 170
Roy, Ed, 213

Sacks, Oliver, 20, 301–302
Safe Place, A (Havens), 347
Salafia, Rob, 27
Sarzynski, Julie, 158–159, 176, 202
Schacher, Stephanie, 348, 350, 351
schizophrenia:
    brain function abnormalities and, 289–294, 298–301
    chain smoking and, 115
    cure promised for, 147, 266
    defined, 245, 250
    early prognoses on, 245–246
    genetic linkage to, 246, 257, 295
    heterogeneity of, 135
    long-range studies on outcomes of, 249–260

schizophrenia (*continued*)
  treatment guidelines on, 125–126, 135
  violent behavior and, 63
Schizophrenia Bulletin, 156, 291, 298–301
Schizophrenia Research Center, 114
Schumann, Robert, 213
Seduction of Madness, The (Podvoll), 191
segregation, community support of, 61–62
self-help, 22, 81, 152, 158–159
Seligman, Martin, 167
Semrad, Elvin, 189
Seroquil (quetiapine), 285–286
serotonin, 47, 287, 289–290
ServiceNet, 58, 59
"7½ Days" (Heldman), 278–280
sexual abuse, 47, 65–66, 68–69
Shah, Agha, 100
Sheehan, Susan, 278
smoking, medication side effects ameliorated by, 114–115
Social Security disability income (SSDI), 213, 233
Song of the Lark, The (Cather), 29
Sorella, Eve, 314–315, 345
Soteria projects, 190
South Beach Psychiatric Center, 2, 4–5, 7, 9–12, 89–97, 99–106, 109, 197, 198–199, 267–268, 272
Spaniol, LeRoy, 32, 33, 34, 36, 81
Spence, Jonathan, 1
Stahl, Steven, 287–288
Starpoint Clubhouse, 214
Stein, Leonard I., 155
Stelazine, 250, 267, 290
Stepping Stone Peer Support Center, 162, 165, 173–184, 186, 189, 342
Strauss, John S., 250, 258
Stubbs, Susan, 59, 60–61
Styron, William, 213, 238
Substance Abuse and Mental Health Service Administration (SAMHSA), 97, 136, 263
substance abuse disorders, 30, 97–98, 127, 128, 130–131, 197, 306–307, 309, 316–317
suicidal thoughts, 186
Sullivan, Harry Stack, 247
Survey Research Associates, 112–113
Survival in Auschwitz (Levi), 285

Tallerson, Ben, 317–318, 319
tardive dyskinesia, 290, 291
Tegretol, 298
television, violent portrayals of mental illness on, 63
Test, Mary Ann, 155

Thorazine, 217, 250, 267, 289, 298
Time, 139–140, 146, 266, 294
Tompkins, Rose, 64–72, 85, 213, 338, 343
topobiology, 18
Torrey, E. Fuller, 62, 147, 266
tranquilizers, 298
Transitional Employment (TE), 235, 236
treatment guidelines, 120–127
Tsemberis, Cherie, 321
Tsemberis, Elena, 321
Tsemberis, Sam, 319–326, 338, 344, 346
Tunefoolery, 41, 96
Tymoczko, Maria, 58

unipolar disorder, *see* depression, clinical
Unquiet Mind, An (Jamison), 169, 229
Unterbach, Arnold, 129–131, 132, 133
Unterbach, Kenneth, 129, 132

van der Kolk, Bessell A., 47
"Varied Outcomes of Schizophrenia, The" (McGlashan and Davidson), 259–260
Venture program, 190
Veterans Hospital, 337
Vietnam War, 33, 45–46
Vinfen Corporation, 31–32, 35, 43, 44, 50, 81–83, 339
violent behavior, 38, 59, 62–63

Wallace, Mike, 238
Ward, Mary Jane, 278
Waskey, Laura, 140
Webster House, 83
Westboro State Hospital, 72, 73, 75–76
West Central Services, Inc., 152–161, 164, 165–166, 168, 169, 170, 171, 177
Wiesel, Torsten, 17
Williams, Kelly, 145
Windhorse Associates, 186, 190–195
Winerip, Michael, 60
Woodhull Hospital, 278–280
Woolf, Virginia, 213
World Health Organization, 148–149
Wyatt, Richard Jed, 229
Wyzik, Phil, 153–154, 157, 158, 159, 163, 164, 170

"Yehuda Ha-Levi" (Amichai), 57

Zipple, Tony, 81
Zubin, Joseph, 250, 258
Zyprexa (olanzapine), 105, 285–286